D0872388

'This landmark book takes us on an unforgettable journey across disciplines, countries, spiritualities, and techniques to teach us twenty-first century psychologies of liberation. Authors Watkins and Shulman transform the discipline of psychology, showing us its connections to all disciplines concerned with liberating the imagination. Across international fields of difference, these authors never give up the prize: social and psychic emancipation. In doing so, they define what "decoloniality" means for the twenty-first century.'

Chela Sandoval, Associate Professor of Liberation Philosophy,
Chair, Department of Chicana and Chicano Studies,
University of California, USA.

Also by Mary Watkins

INVISIBLE GUESTS: The Development of Imaginal Dialogues

TALKING WITH YOUNG CHILDREN ABOUT ADOPTION (*with Susan Fisher*)

WAKING DREAMS

Also by Helene Shulman

LIVING AT THE EDGE OF CHAOS: Complex Systems in Culture and Psyche

Critical Theory and Practice in Psychology and the Human Sciences

Series Editor: Professor Tod Sloan

Titles include:

Mary Watkins and Helene Shulman
TOWARD PSYCHOLOGIES OF LIBERATION

Derek Hook
FOUCAULT, PSYCHOLOGY AND THE ANALYTICS OF POWER

Critical Theory and Practice in Psychology and the Human Sciences
Series Standing Order ISBN 978-0-230-52113-1 (hardback) and 978-0-230-52114-8
(paperback)
(outside North America only)

You can receive future titles in this series as they are published by placing a standing order. Please contact your bookseller or, in case of difficulty, write to us at the address below with your name and address, the title of the series and the ISBN quoted above.

Customer Services Department, Macmillan Distribution Ltd, Houndmills, Basingstoke, Hampshire RG21 6XS, England

Toward Psychologies
of Liberation

Mary Watkins

and

Helene Shulman

First published 2008 by
PALGRAVE MACMILLAN
Houndmills, Basingstoke, Hampshire RG21 6XS and
175 Fifth Avenue, New York, N.Y. 10010
Companies and representatives throughout the world

PALGRAVE MACMILLAN is the global academic imprint of the Palgrave Macmillan division of St. Martin's Press, LLC and of Palgrave Macmillan Ltd. Macmillan® is a registered trademark in the United States, United Kingdom and other countries. Palgrave is a registered trademark in the European Union and other countries.

ISBN-13: 978-0-230-53768-2   hardback
ISBN-10: 0-230-53768-5   hardback

This book is printed on paper suitable for recycling and made from fully managed and sustained forest sources. Logging, pulping and manufacturing processes are expected to conform to the environmental regulations of the country of origin.

A catalogue record for this book is available from the British Library.

A catalog record for this book is available from the Library of Congress.

10   9   8   7   6   5   4   3   2   1
17   16   15   14   13   12   11   10   09   08

Transferred to digital printing in 2008.

Contents

Preface   xi

Introduction   1

Part I Compass Points   9

1. Beyond Universals: Local Regeneration   13
   Inadequacy of current psychological models   13
   Redrawing disciplinary boundaries   14
   Practices of assisted regeneration   15
     Association of Maya Ixil Women, Guatemala   16
     The Green Belt Movement, Kenya   17
     Dynamics of liberatory work   19
   Symbolic interruptions   20

2. Beyond Ideology: Dialogue   23
   Martín-Baró's critique of Eurocentric psychologies   24
   Martín-Baró's radical proposals   25
   The call to liberation psychologies   27
   Marginalization and liberation   28
   Colonialism as institution and structural metaphor   30

3. Beyond Development: Liberation   32
   Development as a preconception   32
   Underdevelopment   33
   Liberation theology's critique of development   34
   Engaged Buddhist critiques of development   37
   Participatory communication and
       post-development   40
   Counter-development   43
   Psychological counter-development   45
   From development to liberation   46
   Contested history of the term "liberation"   46
   Liberation as jailbreak   47
   Liberation and the new commons   48

**Part II   Psychic Wounds of Colonialism and
            Globalization**   49

4. Symptoms and Psychologies in Cultural Context   53
   Symptoms as memorials in depth psychologies   53
   Early psychoanalysis and social justice   55
   The whitening of psychoanalysis and the loss
       of "night vision"   56
   Ignoring and misreading of symptoms   59

5. From Bystanding toward Engaged Witness   64
   Bystanding   64
   Psychic wounds of bystanding   66
       The severing of the self   66
       Preoccupation with personal survival and success 67
       Comparative neurosis   67
       Loneliness   68
       Narcissism   68
       The degrading of others   68
       Fear of oneself, of the abject   69
       The empty self   70
       The replacement of being with having   71
       Greed and false feelings of entitlement   72
       Psychic numbing   73
       The obsessive-compulsive rehearsal of violence 73
   Dissociation   74
   Mending dissociation   75
   Symptom as a tunnel that connects the outside
       to the inside   79

6. Pathologies of Perpetration   81
   Breaking with silences about the past   83
   Doubling, derealization, and disavowal   84
   Effects of psychic splitting on families   86
   The work of cultural anamnesis   88
   Killing one's own humanity   89
   Isolation and burnout in perpetrators   91
   The normalization of violence   93
   Diminished subjectivity in the absence of collective
       memory   94
   Awakening from violence   96
   Exposing our own histories   99
   The refusal of violence   101

7. Mourning and Witness after Collective Trauma 105
  Collective trauma 106
  Effects of collective trauma 108
    Fatalism 111
    Internal colonization 113
    Resistance to Westernization 114
    Belated memories 115
  Witness as a powerful defense against collective trauma 116
  The work of mourning 119
    Isolation of memory in buried crypts 121
    Non-redemptive mourning 122
    Mourning without understanding 123
    Post-memory and non-redemptive mourning 124
  Constructing spaces of recollection 126
    Clearing away frozen identities 128
    An aesthetics of interruption 129
    Re-thinking multicultural encounters 130

Part III   Springs for Creative Restoration 131

8. Rupture and Hospitality 133
  Habitual thinking 133
  Unexpected rupture 134
  Liminal spaces 135
  Loss of liminal spaces 137
  Renormalization 138
  Narrative framing 140
    Narratives of dissociation 142
    Narratives of fatalism 144
    Narratives of messianic transformation 145
    Narratives of participation 147
  Centrifugal and centripetal energies 149
  An ethics of hospitality 150
  Communities of revelation 151
  Relatedness and interdependence 152
  Undermining exiled consciousness 154
  Cultivation of liminal spaces 155

9. Non-Subjects and Nomadic Consciousness 158
  An ethics of subjectivity 158
  From fixed and stable to fluid and reflexive identities 162
  From the singular center to the multiple peripheries 165
  Wounded cosmopolitanism 166
  Without predetermined destinations 167

Interrogating whiteness   169
Beyond national identities   170
Imagining ourselves differently   171
Playing with subjectivity: Chosen and practiced exile   173
Non-subjects and turning toward history   174

10. Dialogue   176
The development of dialogical capacities   176
Differentiating and coordinating the
    perspectives of self and other   178
Sustaining one's voice among others   184
Witness and dialogue   187
Council and circle: Practicing self-expression
    and deep listening   190
From cultures of silence to liberatory dialogue:
    The work of Paulo Freire   192
Utopic imagining   196
Appreciative inquiry   199
Bohmian dialogue   200
The art of questions: Dialogue amid divisive conflict   202
Coda   205

**Part IV   Participatory Practices of Liberation
             Psychologies**   **207**

11. Communities of Resistance: Public Homeplaces and Supportive
    Sites of Reconciliation   209
Communities of resistance   209
Community homeplaces   210
Re-building public homeplaces   213
The "Loving Third"   216
Communal dreaming   219
Earth democracy: Place and resistance   220
Grassroots postmodern regeneration   222
Los caracoles/Snail shells   223
Interstitial spaces for reconciliation   225

12. Liberation Arts: Amnesia, Counter-Memory, Counter-Memorial   232
Erasure, amnesia, and contested memory   234
Silence, suffering, and violence   236
Counter-memory and counter-memorial   238
Living memory and kinesthetic imagination   242
A survey of liberation arts methodologies   243
    Music and dance   243
    Radio   247

Altars and memorials   248
Storytelling circles   250
Theater practices   252
Photovoice and other visual arts   254
Video   256
Performances, happenings, conceptual arts   258
Qualities of liberation arts   262
Conclusion   264

13. Critical Participatory Action Research   266
Re-orienting psychological research: Principles of critical
   participatory action research   266
From center to margin   272
From colonizing research to indigenous research   275
From claims of universality to appreciation of
   social location   278
From pure knowledge to the synthesis of critical
   reflection and action   281
From expert to vulnerable co-participant and advocate   284
From manifest to latent: Listening for gaps, silences,
   and polyvocality   287
From speaking "for" to speaking "with" to
   testimonial practices   293
Toward contextual, interpretive, catalytic, and psychopolitical
   validity   295

14. Placing Dialogical Ethics at the Center of Psychological
Research   299
Early stages of formulating research   302
Invitation to work with community participants   303
Gathering of co-participants   304
Transparency and informed consent   305
Confidentiality   306
Selection of interviewers   306
Collection of data   307
Analysis of data   308
Discussion and communication of findings   310
Implementation of findings   310
Conflicts of interest   311
Social responsibility   311

15. Dreams of Reconciliation and Restoration   313
Prerequisites for reconciliation   315
Government projects of reconciliation   317
Retributive versus restorative justice   321

Restoration through civil society   323
Remorse, apology, and forgiveness   331

Afterword—*Tikkun Olam*: The Restoration and
Repair of the World   334

Acknowledgments   338

References   341

Author Index   358

Subject Index   364

Preface

Why not review the horrific list one more time? Civil war, genocide, violent crime, political corruption, state-sponsored violence and torture, extreme poverty and malnutrition, destruction of cultures and languages, forced migration, sex trafficking, rampant substance abuse and addiction, child labor, outrageous salaries for corporate executives, racial discrimination, environmental degradation ...

We tend to be overwhelmed with sadness and rage as we peruse lists such as this one. Or we intellectualize. I find myself thinking, for example, that perhaps a similar array of societal dysfunction and horror would characterize any era of human history. But I am still disturbed by the fact that humanity's recent progress in establishing general material comfort in broad regions has not been paralleled by efforts to promote widespread social well-being around the globe.

Most professors, practitioners, and students in psychology and related service professions are aware of these forms of suffering. Their work often directly addresses the emotional and practical consequences of trauma and social disruption. Sometimes their coursework or training introduced them to these realities. In general, however, the professions informed by psychology and other social sciences do very little in response to their awareness of massive social problems such as extreme poverty and genocidal violence. In part, this inaction is due to distance. Affluent societies that can afford to fund behavioral science faculties and extensive social services are usually far away from, or insulated from, the societies where millions live a hand-to-mouth existence or suffer daily violence. It is difficult to organize and connect across distances. But the limited response is also due to professional roles that are defined within individualist ideology. Problems are identified and located at the level of the individual. The system's contribution is obscured. Thus, understanding and helping one person or one family at a time is the predominant mode within the psy-complex (the industry surrounding the assessment and treatment of troubling emotions and deviant behaviors). In classes, system transformation is suggested as a secondary activity, but it is rarely listed in job descriptions of counselors, social workers, and psychologists. Basically, the psy-complex would not be thriving if it did not sustain the social system as presently constituted.

Meanwhile, political, economic, and military machines grind away, uprooting communities, destroying local economies, killing the leaders of resistance movements, turning infants into addictive adolescent and adult consumers, replacing meaning with sensation, fueling racism, sowing fear, anxiety, depression, and narcissism, and fabricating the case for the next war.

Faced with these threats to the core of human existence, one must ask: Where are the forms of psychological, cultural, and social practice that would stand up to the forces of oppression and exploitation? Where are sustainable and creative modes of reflective living finding roots and thriving? Where are the psychological insights and practices that would accompany and sustain the social movements for peace, environmentally sustainable economies, and social justice?

In this book, Mary Watkins and Helene Shulman embrace these questions with courage and wisdom. They energetically introduce readers to the psychological dimensions of the emerging counter-empire, a vast lifeworld in which the needs of humans, other-than-human animals, and life in general are deeply felt and articulated in everyday practice. They invite you to join them in their passionate exploration of the possibilities for wise psychological and cultural practices that would contribute to the flourishing of the social movements that will reverse the destruction of life and meaning on earth. These liberation psychologies are a critical element of the global uprising. I urge you to accept the authors' warm invitation as if your life depended upon it, to dialogue with their insights, and then do your part to usher in a new world of compassion and solidarity.

Tod Sloan
Editor, Palgrave series on Critical Theory
and Practice in Psychology and the Human Sciences

Introduction

This book re-thinks the goals and practices of psychology in an age of disruptive globalization. At the beginning of this new millennium, after hundreds of years of colonialism and neocolonialism, we cannot escape the disturbing fact that we live in a world where more than a billion people lack sufficient shelter, food, and clean water; where lakes, rivers, and top soils are dying; and where cultures clash and war, genocide, and acts of terrorism seem ordinary. Transnational corporations with vast reach and power control land, media, economies, and elections. Their policies are decided away from public view, in national and international arenas where the super-rich and super-armed preside. Economic globalization undermines much that is local and personal, affecting possibilities for housing, jobs, cultural expression, and self-governance. Such globalization has created a tidal wave of displacement, undermining families, neighborhoods, and cultures. Many who fear these changes blame newcomers and outsiders, reverting to xenophobic and nostalgic narratives, imagining a simpler and "purer" prior history.

The psychological effects of deepening divides between the rich and the poor, unprecedented migrations, and worsening environmental degradation mark this era as one requiring extraordinary critical and reconstructive approaches. As the margins of many cities in the world swell with refugees, immigrants, and the homeless, and the countryside with the hungry and the unemployed, new practices and theories are emerging for addressing psychological suffering and rebuilding communities. Practitioners of these innovative projects are sometimes trained psychologists working under the rubrics of critical, peace, community, or liberation psychologies, but just as often they are artists and cultural workers, women's movement activists, youth and environmental justice advocates, public health professionals, liberation theologians, or community organizers. Although they aspire to improve the miserable living conditions of the most marginalized, part of their emerging vision is the need for creating solidarities and dialogues with more privileged people whose environments and psychological well-being

1

are also undermined by the fragmentation of community, the widening of social divides, and the often insidious self-doubt that accompanies crises of personal and cultural meaning. Sandoval (2000) argues that now "the emotional ground tone of the once centered, modernist, first world citizen-subject [is] shot through with intensities so that it resembles the emotional territory of subordinated peoples" (p. 33).

Institutional arrangements and ways of thinking that grow out of centuries of colonialism need to be questioned by those on both sides of the divides that have been created. Colonialism structured economic and social institutions through culturally constructed racialist hierarchies that were presented as though given in nature. Strategies of power and control that depended on violence were developed in colonial wars abroad, and then repeated as part of the democracy practiced at home. Viewing some people as less than human allowed slavery, genocide, brutal policing, and the systematic economic deprivation of marginalized populations. The current military strategy of preemptive war has drawn on these well-rehearsed ways of thinking and acting to designate the Middle East as a site of the less than human other to be brought under American surveillance and control. The outcome of a history embedded in colonial thought has been a psychology of forgetting and denial in private and public spheres—a forgetting that has yielded a traumatic lack of witness of individual and community wounds caused by the larger social context (Shulman-Lorenz & Watkins, 2002b). The only choice is to grow numb with amnesia, or to find and engage models for critically exploring the past and creating alternative futures. All over the earth, innovative liberation psychologies are asking what kinds of psychological approaches might enhance capacities for critical thinking, collective memory, peacemaking, and the creative transformation of individuals, groups, and neighborhoods.

One of the most profound problems of the current era is that many people do not have any viable visions of what could be different in their lives or communities. This is a psychological problem sometimes referred to as fatalism, anomie, or symbolic loss: a despairing sense that social networks, valued customs, and shared memories are irretrievably weakened, lost, or forgotten. Attempts to imagine new and vibrant social arrangements with others seem hopeless. Symbolic loss (Homans, 2000) is a catastrophic decay of the fabric of meanings and rituals that link individuals in a common culture. Sometimes symbolic loss involves complete cultural disintegrations that render rituals and customs seemingly pointless, and histories forgotten. Such symbolic loss affects hearts and minds, physical health, and abilities to build community. It is a psychological issue that profoundly impacts possibilities for democratic processes. Passive, disengaged, and divided populations can be more easily manipulated and controlled. In such environments, psychologies of regeneration are needed, ways to imagine rebuilding psychological spaces where one can develop a critical analysis of one's situation, improvise new practices for the healing of individuals and communities, and recover or create a sense of common purpose and vision.

Imagination is a psychological phenomenon that occurs at the level of the local in individuals and communities. It gives those in isolating, asphyxiating, and exhausted social structures new possibilities. To create cultural alternatives, people have to break with taken for granted ways of thinking that prevent them psychologically from interrupting the status quo. They need to do work that "renews the past, refiguring it as a contingent in-between space, that innovates and interrupts the performance of the present" (Bhabha, 1994, p. 7). Learning to create conditions for social and personal regeneration, for an awakening of hope and imagination, is one of the central psychological tasks of our era.

We have been tracking compass points or orientations in the form of ideas, practices, and projects that nurture an imagination of alternative ways of thinking and acting together that can transform participation in social, economic, and ecological change and address psychological sufferings. We call these orientations "psychologies of liberation," imagining them as potentially a great river fed by many streams emerging from underground springs and from mountain runoffs in numerous local settings. We see liberation psychology as a river with a definite direction and longing, reaching for a distant sea.

When we perceive and think in terms of liberation psychologies, we witness a new sensibility struggling to be born in the world in varied locations. For many, there is a conviction that contemporary scripts have worn thin, and that neighbors must be more creative in the ways they live together in the world. In this book, we want to help connect the streams of current conversations we hear going on in separate locations, helping to draw them together to form a variegated field with a provisional name. There are already existing traditions with many elders and ancestors, as well as networks, but further links need to be articulated so that their coalescence can feed a sense of possibility. We need to understand the intersection of unifying themes within these traditions in order to strengthen them.

We name this coalescence "psychologies of liberation," taking heed of Belenky, Bond, and Weinstock's (1997) advice that the naming of a tradition is critical in order for it to thrive:

When a tradition has no name people will not have a rich shared language for articulating and reflecting on their experiences with the tradition. Poorly articulated traditions are likely to be fragile. Without a common language the tradition will not become part of a well-established, ongoing dialogue in the larger society. Institutional supports to develop and refine the tradition's philosophy and practices will not be developed. Leaders' efforts to pass the tradition on to the next generation will be poorly supported. Existing educational institutions will not hire faculty who are experts in the tradition; appropriate curriculum and apprentice-ships will not be developed. This situation is increasingly problematic as more and more of society's caring work is now being carried out by pro-fessionals who receive all of their professional training within the formal education system.

(pp. 293–4)

For the most part, academic psychology in the United States has not been sufficiently helpful in recognizing or supporting emerging liberation psychologies. The mainstream academic marketplace in psychology in America continues to favor cognitive behaviorism, neuroscientific approaches, and quantitative methods. These emphases position the discipline of psy-chology within the powerful natural sciences, a move that has characterized the dominant core of the discipline since its conception. This is a move that has been contested since that early moment as well. These dominant approaches within psychology are exported throughout the world. International graduate students studying in American departments of psy-chology disseminate them when returning to their home countries—with questionable consequences. It would not be difficult to find an American mental health expert in a refugee camp in the Sudan teaching Euro-American definitions of "trauma," and then following this up with the provision of inappropriate trainings and short-term funded services to individuals that often undermine long-term community resources and connections. In general, approaches to treatment that are supported in clin-ical psychology programs tend to focus on individuals in isolation from their communities, and very often do not take into account local cultural differences.

Because of its positivist scientific orientation, much of mainstream psy-chology has emerged as a search for universals, for norms of emotional life and behavior, and for modes of treatment for individuals who deviate from these norms. This orientation decontextualizes the individuals under its scrutiny. Obscuring the impact of collective trauma on mental health has led to treatments for single individuals while leaving intact the social environments that mitigate against psychological well-being. In order to address social issues, a critical psychological approach to symptoms is called for, an approach that is careful to understand the dynamic interrelation between psychological suffering and cultural and historical context (Prilleltensky & Nelson, 2005). A new picture emerges when individual thought and behavior are seen in wider context, and when psychology is placed in the service of addressing the healing of individuals within this larger frame. When conservative and heteronormative gender roles were challenged in the United States, for example, symptoms that were once seen as deviant were reinterpreted as signs of protest against restrictive social roles. In other arenas, when massive immigration, economic development, state terror, or war interrupt previously stable customs, those who hold on to older norms may come to be seen as rigid, unrelated, and repetitive, while those who evolve outside of them might be interpreted as resilient and resourceful.

Rather than searching for stereotypical norms, liberation psychologies place stress on identifying, supporting, and nurturing the psychological attempts of individuals and groups alike to re-author their own sense of identity. This requires a critical analysis of oppressive power relations, including those within psychology itself. Psychologies of liberation gather together resources to help people understand possibilities for multiple layers of interpretation through which the world that has been imposed on them can be understood and reorganized. With embodied practices, people are able to evolve ways to resymbolize their worlds through creative conversation and activity in the arts. They are able to commit to transformative efforts through social and political action. Liberation psychologies develop the research and practices that lead to understanding and supporting such directions.

Contrary to a universalizing approach, we have set about learning practices of psychological liberation that are like wellsprings erupting out of the ground in many places throughout the world, each marked by its own culture and location. We recognize these practices when they focus on the well-being and self-organization of people and their communities, when they promote critical reflection and transformation in local arenas, and when their goal is not the imposition of a prescribed yardstick of development but an opening toward greater freedom in imaging the goals of life. This opening is based on the interrelatedness of individuals, communities, cultures, histories, and environments. For many of the projects we have studied, the recollection of a repressed or denied history is a key element in reclaiming vitality. Most of these projects involve learning the skills of dialogue and reconciliation across different points of view in order to build new solidarities. Such work tends to proceed slowly over months or years as people learn to let go of fixed ideas and to allow new symbols, emotions, and relationships to enter their lives. Often it begins in small groups that develop ways of speaking about and symbolizing elements of the local environment that slowly seep out into the larger culture and begin to affect community discourses.

Our focus on psychologies of liberation has emerged from prolonged wrestling with psychotherapeutic and research paradigms, critiquing mainstream approaches to psychology, and researching liberatory psychological practices in different parts of the world. We are both trained in depth psychology, that is, the psychologies of the unconconscious set out by Freud, Jung, Klein, Horney, Hillman, Lacan, Kristeva, and others, and we draw from these approaches in our understandings of possibilities for individual transformation. Our working understandings have led us to place psychodynamic clinical theories and individual treatment within historical and cultural context. We have increasingly understood the needed healing potentials of family, small group, and community-based dialogical approaches to psychological well-being. We have moved increasingly toward participatory research and the importance of the arts for both individual and community expression and visioning.

We have collaborated in developing a graduate program in psychology that respects the interdependence of psyche, family, social and economic arrangements, culture, and environment. Students spend two years planning and carrying out experimental community and ecological fieldwork and research while studying the compass points of liberation psychology (Community/Ecological Fieldwork and Research, n.d.). Our students convene groups or apprentice themselves to pre-existing settings such as hospices, schools, prisons, juvenile halls, theaters, centers for community arts, environmental projects, and centers for creative aging. They learn and practice the dialogical and collaborative approaches to group and community restorative work that we will be presenting in this book: liberation arts, council, dialogue, appreciative inquiry, participatory research, imaginal work, Theater of the Oppressed, and public conversation. Learning as much from failures as from successes, we use a participatory research model through which we collaboratively study the dark sides of our hopes, the limitations of our vision, and the impasses in truly listening. Each year we have reorganized the curriculum and rewritten research guidelines based on what we have experienced. This book presents a summation of this process of collaborative learning.

Each of us has arrived at this book slowly over decades, coming from differing directions. For one of us, Mary Watkins, this work has involved a deconstruction of and divestiture from much of her formal training in psychotherapy and psychological research. Her early education as a Quaker attuned her to issues of social justice and to respectful, nonhierarchical, collaborative relational practices that honor the sacred in each person. Coming to understand the broad historical, cultural, political, and economic contexts of the psychological theories and practices in which she was schooled allowed her to take a critical distance from psychiatric diagnosis, individualistic understandings of human suffering, normative ideas of family and child development, and hierarchical and disempowering clinical and research relations. Her earlier work was rooted in depth psychology's emphasis on the vital role of imagination in interrupting internalized norms and in suggesting alternative ways of being. Discovering the community and cultural work of Freire and Martín-Baró, and the feminist developmental work of Gilligan and Belenky provided paths to understanding psychological suffering in historical and cultural context. For her, psychological healing has become indelibly linked with community and ecological restoration. The abiding connecting thread between these domains is the development of dialogical relations.

Helene Shulman was educated in a conservative Jewish community deeply affected by the Holocaust and profoundly aware of the wounds and dangers of social exclusion. She began to develop new ideas about community dialogue and transformation as a graduate student studying philosophy and phenomenology while participating simultaneously in the Civil Rights Movement in Louisiana. In the 1970s and 1980s, she enjoyed an inspiring period of work in community building, solidarity efforts, and cultural arts in collaboration with Latin American and Native American organizations in California and Latin America. Eventually, hard lessons in the difficulties of effecting social change that were being learned by political movements all over the Americas drove her to study depth psychology formally as well as critically, searching for new ways to understand psychological and cultural factors in individual and social transformation.

Our authorship is fully shared. Each of us wrote a draft of half of the chapters. A process of multiple revisions allowed us to interlace our words and thoughts, a process we have enjoyed for ten years of writing and teaching together. For both of us, a re-thinking of our academic disciplines has required years of sifting through psychological and cultural work and imagining both anew. In our efforts to re-orient depth psychological theory and practice toward liberatory ends, we hold a common vision of what it might be like if students of psychology and cultural workers could collaborate at the convergence of these several paths—a place where what is needed from psychology has been winnowed out and wed to creative efforts of individual and community regeneration.

During the decade of our work together, culture wars have been raging in the academic world. Debates within the field of psychology have arisen over whose point of view and whose culture will be represented and voiced within the curriculum. We found it necessary to re-orient psychological theory so that universalism, Eurocentrism, sexism, and racism can be challenged and disrupted in order to realign psychology's work in this century with pressing needs for individual, community, ecological, and cultural liberation. We have experienced directly the forces of resistance to such goals.

Thus this book is not a naïve offering; neither is it meek in its ambitions. We are aware of the price that is paid for challenging paradigms and for transgressing disciplinary boundaries. As a result, we have been heartened by, and devoted to, work happening throughout the world that understands interdependence, and that turns its efforts toward nourishing needed critical insight, and toward developing capacities for dialogue, imagination, and creative action. Is it possible for more of psychology to align itself with and support these efforts to contribute to a peaceful and just society? Just how would it need to re-orient? How might those working psychologically with individuals and those working with groups and communities explore where the other's work is crucial to their own, creating improvisations of healing at multiple sites in addition to and beyond psychotherapy on the one hand and social action groups on the other? This is the task to which we turn, encouraging sharing of the springs of community regeneration and individual restoration that have surfaced. Our hope is to contribute to their sustenance and vitality.

* * * *

This book is organized into four parts: Part I: Compass Points; Part II: Psychic Wounds of Colonialism and Globalization; Part III: Springs for Creative Restoration; and Part IV: Participatory Practices of Liberation Psychologies. They address the following unfolding questions. Part I: What are the goals of liberation psychologies? What does one need to "unthink" from mainstream psychology and developmental theory in order to re-orient toward liberatory work? Part II: What are the psychological frameworks that have allowed people to adapt to and identify with dysfunctional cultural arrangements? How does social location affect experience and from what do people suffer psychologically as a result—as bystanders, perpetrators, victims, and witnesses? Part III: How are people able to change their points of view? How does one learn to host the liminal spaces that are created through rupture and trauma? How can one nurture capacities for dialogue that will assist in the restoration of communities, cultures, environments, and individuals? Part IV: Finally, in communities, and between communities, in research and in healing work, what are the participatory practices one can create that flow from new understandings of social pathologies?

The idea of liberation psychology evolved in Latin America as a critique of the tendency of mainstream psychologies to shore up the status quo. Like liberation theology, it asked "Whom does this work serve?" Deeply indebted to Latin American models for psychologies of liberation (Hollander, 1997; Martín-Baró, 1994; Montero, 1996), we have also sought out kindred models in Africa, Asia, the Pacific Islands, Europe, and the United States. We speak of "liberation psychologies" in the plural because our hope is that the work will be seen as dynamic, ongoing, never to be finally achieved, and never capable of being taught from above. To work in the pluralism of liberation psychologies is to state our sense that we must always be involved in the seeing through of psychological theory, putting it into conversation with other disciplines, working interculturally, learning from resonant practices, and deepening our reflections on where we are standing and placing our advocacies. In their diverse locations and cultures of origin, the streams of thought we consider to be thematically linked are called by many different names. They need not share a common name, but we hope that they can more often come together in dialogue that contributes to their long-term sustenance and catalytic vitality.

Part I Compass Points

At the heart of every major approach to psychological theory, research, and practice, we encounter a description of what we suffer from psychologically, an analysis of the causes of this suffering, and a proposal for practices of healing. These are oriented by values—announced or unannounced—about the preferred goals and hopes for human development, such as capacities for work and love, individuation, psychic differentiation and integration, and interdependent relations (Kaplan, 1983a, 1983b). They are also oriented by the level of explanation the approach favors: community, familial, intrapsychic, or biochemical. Our efforts at understanding and addressing human suffering embody favored focal points and explanatory narratives arising from our milieus of origin. They also encompass our milieus' blind spots and patterns of avoidance. Over time, the suffering that is avoided and not seen, and the suffering that is misunderstood and reduced to inadequate formulations, accumulates in the shadows and begins to demand to be seen, named, understood, and addressed. The dominant explanatory narratives start to break down under the weight of the problems they did not see or assumed they could avoid. Such is the situation today as the savage income inequalities of a globally triumphant capitalism make impossible for most persons on earth the personal healing and wholeness sought by present-day Euro-American psychotherapies. This has long been true for those largely left out of mainstream psychology's focus: the economically marginalized in the global South and in the postindustrialized North as well. Mainstream psychologies have failed to account for the widespread psychological distress being endured even in fairly privileged communities: drug and alcohol dependence, social isolation, depression, and experiences of meaninglessness and futility. We are confronted on our own doorstep with the need for liberation psychologies that include within their circle of concerns the social, economic, and environmental circumstances of their subjects.

Like other psychologies, psychologies of liberation also describe what is being suffered psychologically, analyze the causes of this suffering, and propose healing practices. Yet liberation psychologies emphasize that these descriptions, analyses, and practices reflect the local conditions under which they are forged, while at the same time responding to the ongoing crisis of corporate globalization that envelops all of our lives in different ways. Like other psychologies, liberation psychologies are guided by a vision of the telos of human existence. But their distinctive vision is of individuals-in-community working toward justice and peace, through which the contemporary Euro-American emphasis on an isolated self cedes place to a full inclusion of others.

While working to understand the interdependent relations between the intrapsychic, interpersonal, community, economic, and environmental contributions to the structure of experience, liberation psychologies turn to the larger frames of culture and history in which these are embedded. Here the psychological legacy of 500 years of colonialism and its evolution into transnational capitalism, and then twenty-first-century globalization weighs heavily in the analysis. Such psychologies turn as well to the particular social and ecological location of individuals and their communities. Resolutely working from an interdependent paradigm, they seek to ground us both in the global waves of history during the last 500 years and in the specific location where the legacies of this history are experienced in the present. The strands of individual, community, cultural, and ecological well-being are held tightly together, and are seen to be necessary to one another. Psychological health is understood to emerge as capacities to create meaning are reignited, hopes are rekindled, and actions forged for achieving peace and economic and social justice. As the chains of racism and economic oppression are cast off, it will be possible to more deeply reclaim cultural histories, traditions, and languages. The hope for peaceful, just, and ecologically vibrant communities that support psychological well-being inspires a set of practices that seek to nourish capacities for dialogue, complex and multifaceted identity formation, critical analysis and action.

For psychology to be part of the efforts of confronting and healing the traumatic effects of colonialism and transnational globalization, there has to be an explicit re-orientation in its values, and in the ways it approaches psychological suffering and healing. In Part I, we will articulate the compass points that orient the necessarily interdisciplinary approach to psychology that we have embarked on describing and that we feel is needed at this time. Much of this approach involves rethinking fundamentals, reworking basic assumptions and starting points. In Chapter 1, we show how a search for universal psychological truths can be replaced by evolving local, situated understandings. We discuss sample projects that illustrate the compass points of liberation psychologies, articulating the ways that they draw out possibilities for re-subjectification and resymbolization on the path to developing the sense of agency needed to transform human communities. In Chapter 2, we focus on the work of Martín-Baró, the social psychologist in El Salvador, who first coined the term "liberation psychology." We will consider ways in which psychology has supported the status quo, and ask what would have to be given up in order to think about psychology differently. In Chapter 3, we critique an approach to development that has reflected and further induced myopia regarding the effects of economic and ecological degradation on psychological well-being. We show how post-development and counter-development theorizing yield an understanding of the interdependence of psychological suffering and well-being with community, economic, and ecological well-being (Prilleltensky & Fox, 1997). To make this shift to an interdependent model of understanding requires a critique of the way development has ordinarily been understood within conventional psychological and economic theories. In this chapter, we demonstrate a convergence between new ideas about the effectiveness of participatory communication in development projects and ideas of participatory process in liberation psychologies.

1
Beyond Universals: Local Regeneration

> By revolution of the mind, I mean not merely a refusal of victim status. I am talking about an unleashing of the mind's most creative capacities, catalyzed by participation in struggles for change.
>
> (Robin Kelley, 2002a, p. 191)

To talk of psychology in the singular has always been inaccurate. From its beginnings the proper focus for psychology has been contested, resulting in multiple approaches to theories and practices, or to what we are calling "psychologies" in the plural. While certain approaches undoubtedly have prevailed in creating what could be called a mainstream, holding the bulk of institutional funding and positions, many alternate approaches to psychology have thrived in small pockets. Those psychologically minded people who have been schooled in the mainstream, and have been later able to improvise and join the kinds of cultural work needed to transform colonial and (post)colonial legacies, have undergone a re-orientation in how they approach psychological suffering and healing. Of what does this re-orientation consist?

In this chapter, we will discuss some of the inadequacies of the current models of mainstream psychology, and propose an alternative approach. We will give several examples of successful liberation psychology projects and discern what they accomplished and what they have in common.

Inadequacy of current psychological models

Though we have been trained as psychologists, we have each found it necessary to defect from professional interpretations focused entirely on individuals and families, and on mental constructs separated from the cultural, social, and economic worlds in which they are embedded. We do not want to assume that the role of psychology is to help individuals and families adapt to the status quo when this present order contributes so massively to

13

human misery, psychological and otherwise. Our psychology should not exist in a vacuum of disconnected theory where classrooms, research, and clinical encounters are considered apart from conflicts and suffering in society, where personal history is severed from the historical context and social institutions one has inherited.

Individual psychology began in the early twentieth century and flourished in the United States within a medical model that framed the professional psychologist as a quasi-medical expert who could work with issues too problematic, repetitive, or taboo to discuss casually with friends. For those who could afford individual treatment on an ongoing basis, and who lived in cultural contexts where various sorts of silencing made visits to a psychotherapist a healing strategy, the process could be extremely helpful. Many still benefit from individual therapy. However, the situation surrounding therapy and its original foci has changed dramatically. Incest, child abuse, domestic violence, sexuality, and drug and alcohol abuse are more widely discussed. Many see such issues not only as individual matters, but also as linked to issues of normalized power structures, gender relations, and ongoing cultural trauma. Further, the incidence of issues of collective trauma, where the victim is not a sole individual but a whole group, has grown astronomically. Here, sheer numbers make individual work impractical. Psychological scars and post-traumatic stress from war, violence, terror, genocide, sudden toxic pollution, natural disaster, and resultant displacement and forced migration have led to a need for psychological practices that can repair the bonds among people as well as the narrative threads of an individual life history. Lost rituals, social networks, beliefs, and trust are not only individual but collective issues, and cannot be rebuilt in private spaces alone. Other forms of ongoing group trauma, such as racism, sexism, and homophobia, affecting vast numbers of people who no longer need to be silent about their suffering, can perhaps best be dealt with in public rather than private settings, milieus where people can recognize that their suffering has common roots and is shared. Additionally, there are issues connected with historical memory and amnesia, the refusal of national discourses to properly honor and teach the history of such events as slavery and the Native American genocide in the United States, the dictatorships and terror in Latin America, or the Holocaust in Europe. These require a public settling of psychological accounts that far exceeds the capacities of the individual clinical encounter.

Redrawing disciplinary boundaries

There are important psychologists and activists around the world who are improvising new practices and theories in order to cope with this climactic change. They are often ignored by more mainstream professionals and funding sources. Much of psychology, because it aspires to be a science, lacks a connection to related contemporary interdisciplinary work in the humanities as well as to innovative projects being carried out by progressive cultural workers who are not professional psychologists. This artificial damming of potential tributaries to psychology has left a desert surrounding a discipline which has hoped to see itself as a scientific rather than an interdisciplinary and interpretive endeavor.

When rivers are dammed, whole areas are deprived of nourishment while others are flooded over. Biodiversity is diminished, and often a single invading species colonizes what was once a rich forest or wetlands environment where many species flourished. In psychology, the process of damming off examples of transformation from activist communities and questions from interdisciplinary and critical theory has led to a situation where universalist and Eurocentric ideas have crowded out the possibility of multiple indigenous psychologies that could be linked in enriching dialogues. We find ourselves often trying to break the dam surrounding the academic discipline of psychology, linking psychological theories, research, and practices to community and arts projects around the world. Working in this desert border area we have found assisted regeneration—a model from environmental restoration—helpful in thinking about restorative psychological and community work.

Practices of assisted regeneration

Contemporary environmentalists speak of assisted regeneration, a process by which humans collaborate to serve biodiversity within devastated environments. The idea of assisted regeneration serves as a metaphor for the work we want to do in psychology and in this book. Grounded in a sense of place, differing according to location, local culture, and social fabric, assisted regeneration in ecology must mean different things in different ecosystems.

Eileen and Joan Bradley invented the Bradley Method of bush regeneration in Australia. The method is applicable in places where overgrazing or clear-cutting has produced tracts of land that are stripped of life and turning into desert. It is also useful in places where exotic plants or lawns have been imported and now require large amounts of water, which is no longer affordable. The method requires that we search for areas where there are still elements remaining of the local biodiversity we wish to foster. The first step may be to fence off an area to work with, to keep cows, goats, or people at bay. We need to be able to identify all the species of plants that are present, and be able to recognize them both in their mature form and as seedlings. Then gradually over time, we strengthen the diversity of sustainable species, even new and hybrid species that begin to emerge, while cutting back on invading or colonizing species. The method is based on a deep trust in the regenerative capacities of nature, and the patience to wait for small changes to create larger ones (Seed, 2001). Ideally, each year more species emerge, and some begin a succession that creates conditions for others to appear. The microclimate gradually changes as some species begin to repair the soil with shade and leaf mulch, and then eventually climax species may begin to emerge that have not been seen in the area for hundreds of years.

We want to strengthen efforts of assisted regeneration for the theorizing and practice of psychology, focusing on areas at the edge of the discipline where new conversations might develop. What we are attempting to uproot are Western and universalizing assumptions that include the notion that experts trained in the traditions where these assumptions go unquestioned can be placed in charge of the well-being of others. In practice, what we are attempting to protect and build on are cases where individuals and communities have found local, creative, and participatory solutions to problematic conditions and institutions by transforming their psychological relationships to self and other, sometimes in dialogue with psychologists who are transgressing academic boundaries. These projects are ones that regenerate hope and a sense of agency through the birthing of novel psychological spaces for creative dialogue. We want to be able to recognize such efforts both as seedlings just beginning and in their more mature form, where they have begun processes of transformation which begin to affect whole communities and regions, even national policies and governments.

Association of Maya Ixil Women, Guatemala

An example of the sort of project we have been studying is one that has been created in the aftermath of many years of war and violence in Guatemala by a group of women in the Ixil region, who formed an organization called Association of Maya Ixil Women—New Dawn (ADMI). In dialogue with various consultants, public educators, cultural workers, and activists, including peace psychologist M. Brinton Lykes, the group created and coordinated a library, several development projects, an educational program for children, and an ongoing participatory action research project to collect testimony about the effects of the war on women and children in their region. As the women met to document their lives with photographs and share their histories and stories, their voices constructed a community narrative that went beyond a report on "facts":

> They embed their register of the number of deaths in a set of interrogations that situate their understanding of the event within the context of their rights as human beings and as indigenous peoples. They express sorrow and outrage alongside their solidarity with those who were killed and their families. The innocence of the victims starkly implicates the murderers in an unjust war. Equally important, the women analysts tell us about their rituals for mourning their losses and commemorating the lives of the deceased families, rituals that were also disrupted by the war. Thus the "facts" are embedded in past practices and reflect the symbolic

systems that are ruptured in the war's wake. The women of ADMI stand with those who have been killed while affirming their commitment to struggle for a better and more just peace. The end of the war was an occasion to recover lost bodies and to rethread ritual practices within a contemporary context, thereby reclaiming not only loved ones but also the stories of the past and the challenges they pose for the future.

(Lykes, Blanche, & Hamber, 2003, p. 4)

This work with women suffering from the impact of war went far beyond an attempt to treat individual victims suffering from trauma. It began to heal rifts in the community, and reconstitute a sense of value in a shared future. Some women involved with the project learned new skills in technology, became consultants in other communities, spoke publicly in national forums, wrote grant proposals, began economic development projects, and joined national and regional efforts to build a more just society. In an environment notable for rigid class and ethnic boundaries, this work has created a transnational rupture through which the technologies of social science research, and some of the privileges of the elite to participate in international human rights discourse, have been claimed by rural women with only a fifth- or sixth-grade education. Their voices have evolved through engagement with international media, and are not simply "authentic" testimonies of the "marginalized" but the outcome of an unfolding collaborative process of dialogue and representation. While violence and repression continues against individuals and communities doing human rights work in Guatemala, ADMI publicly bears witness in the international arena to its effects.

The Green Belt Movement, Kenya

Wangari Maathai and the Green Belt Movement instituted a very different project with similar values in Kenya. The Green Belt Movement began with the fortunate encounter in 1977 of Maathai, working with a group of Kenyans interested in environmental issues, and the National Council of Women of Kenya (NCWK). The NCWK had emerged from the period of colonialism as an organization representing all sectors of Kenyan women that had previously been segregated along racial and ethnic lines. Discussions and seminars were being arranged by the organization through which Kenyan women could begin to critically analyze their own situation. Rural women identified their needs for firewood, clean drinking water, balanced diets, shelter, and income. This signaled the dwindling of resources to sustain their families. Maathai, a biologist, was invited to speak to the group about problems of deforestation and desertification in Kenya that had concerned her for years, and was then elected to work on the Executive Committee on issues of environment and habitat. During a NCWK seminar attended by Maathai, members of the group discussed the growing problems of malnutrition in Kenya due to the transition to a globalized market economy in rural areas, where less and less food for domestic consumption was being grown. A process of discussion, experimentation, and innovation within the NCWK led to a national campaign of tree planting to begin to address the needs identified by the rural women. Through the careful learning of cultivation, planting, and tending of seedlings, many uneducated rural women were able to earn an income.

Part of the initial difficulty of inertia in embracing the work was psychological. Many of the poor women felt they lacked not only capital but also knowledge and skills to address their challenges. They were conditioned to believe that solutions to their problems must come from outside. They had located the source of power outside of themselves, but had not yet understood the larger context that was affecting their daily lives. Becoming aware of the injustices in international economic arrangements allowed them to see the connection between their dwindling food supplies and economic policies that were not taking their well-being into account. Their development of critical consciousness in citizen education programs importantly included a growing awareness about the link between environmental degradation and increased poverty and violence. Critical consciousness involves decoding the social lies that naturalize the status quo, while searching for alternative interpretations of one's situation. Maathai understood that the planting of trees could also be the planting of ideas and the development of understanding. "When you have the understanding," says Maathai, "you have the energy, you are restless. When you don't, you go to sleep" (2003).

The campaign was embedded within a tradition of historic cultural pride, taking the term "harambee spirit," which had been popularized during the first government after independence means "let's all pull together." Each year they organized a "Save the Land Harambee" celebration. In the first, and many other such local celebrations, trees were planted in honor of local and national leaders who had made important contributions to the liberation of Kenya but whose historic roles were not being honored and taught. The empowering activity of tree planting and tending allowed the women to connect their actions with the solving of the issues they had identified as problematic. In addition to holding their governments accountable for abuses of power, corruption, and environmental mismanagement, they made a shift in holding themselves accountable to bring into being the leadership values of justice, integrity, and trust that they wished to see in their national leaders.

Today, the women of the Green Belt Movement have planted and nurtured over 30 million trees, created 6000 income-producing tree-nurseries in Kenya, and provided jobs for 100,000 people, mostly women. The project is an international model being replicated all over the world. When Maathai won a Nobel Prize in 2004 for her work, she communicated the reciprocal relation between healing the earth and healing ourselves: "We are called to assist the Earth to heal her wounds and in the process heal our own."

Restoration of the environment proceeded hand in hand with psychological, community, and political restoration. The Green Belt Movement includes as its accomplishments the empowerment of thousands of individuals and rural communities, community mobilization and inspiration, an improved image of the capacities of women, increased advocacy and networking activities, survival of the movement in spite of political persecution, extensive historical documentation and recognition of its work, and movement toward democracy. The Green Belt Movement proceeded toward a deeper understanding of the interdependence of environmental preservation with democratic and peaceful processes of government, and was part of laying the foundation for a peaceful transition to democracy in Kenya in 2002. Maathai and her collaborators call on African leaders to build fair, democratic, and just societies, in which the creativity and energy of their citizens can flourish, linking macropolitical context with the intimate well-being of each person. Maathai survived beatings, imprisonment, divorce, and death threats, all occasioned by her activism. In 2002 she was elected to the Kenyan parliament with 98 per cent of the vote.

Dynamics of liberatory work

When we look at these two different projects through the lens of liberation psychology we can see a series of related values and themes emerge inflected by local conditions. Each project has organized a psychological space on multiple fronts that opens a dialogue through and beyond individual suffering. Each project evolved in its scope and purpose as the experience and identities of the women participating in it began to transform. Beginning with an analysis of the history, needs, and conditions of daily life for women in the past and present, the work continued with an interrogation of causes and a critical analysis of political, religious, economic, and gender dynamics impacting personal history. Photography, monuments, performance, theater, art, media, and other forms of documentation were utilized to begin to give voice to issues haunting the present that have not yet found a public articulation (see Chapter 12). New relationships were formed, as well as new possibilities and hope for community and solidarity. Discussions evolved toward economic projects that could affect survival and psychological well-being, and the transformation of conditions for the next generation. These discussions took place in an environment where ongoing violence continued, and the group began to take up the question of how to prevent further violence and transform the larger social and political context. Small communities began to link with others to share experience and technologies, to build a public record of their work, and to educate others about the conditions affecting them.

What places these projects in the field of psychology is that central to their success is a group of individuals who are going through a process of re-imagining their lives, evolving as narrators and protagonists of their own history. Their projects are not one-issue campaigns, though many of the single projects they take up are critical. Yet more important than any individual action is the process of psychological development through which participants grow stronger in their capacities for survival, critical analysis, emergence of new ideas, flexibility of action, community building, and the process of hopeful self-organization. One of the goals of such projects is not homogeneity of thought or agreement on all issues, but the psychological capacity to bear a dialogue with difference, to tolerate conflicting experiences and points of view, while still finding common ground and constructing a shared future (see Chapter 10). In both projects, people from different ethnic backgrounds and with different political positions, without full agreement on many issues, were able to work together to transform their futures. Returning to the image of assisted regeneration in devastated areas, we note the renewed vitality and vibrancy of the individuals and communities that have engaged in the work of ADMI and the Green Belt Movement. Small local changes have seeded changes in neighboring communities. The ideas that organize their work have acted like pollen in distant places.

Symbolic interruptions

One way in which successful liberation psychology practices can be particularly effective and insightful is by inventing projects that symbolically interrupt repressive government discourse and public amnesia about suffering. Though the projects operate at a local level, they often have a national or even international significance. Perhaps the most famous of such practices was begun by Gandhi's salt march to Dandi in 1930 (Gandhi, 1972). The British colonial government had imposed a salt tax in early 1930 that prevented the sale or production of salt by anyone in India except the British. Of course, everyone in India used and needed salt, and those living along the coastal zones were used to collecting it themselves. Gandhi urged his followers to use nonviolent civil disobedience to continue making salt for themselves. He began a 78-mile walk for 23 days from Sabarmati to Dandi, collecting thousands of people to accompany him on the way. Salt was sold illegally all over the country. Over 60,000 people were arrested in a month, including Gandhi. The international press followed the march closely.

Typical of many liberation psychology projects, the salt march and its nonviolent resistance enabled local groups to see the relevance of resistance to their lives. They were able to participate cooperatively at the local level, breaking out of passivity and despair. The issue was important enough to mobilize a massive following, but at the same time innocuous enough not to alienate centrist parties. It broke apart the facade of control and dominance maintained by the British. Finally, it was bold, clever, and satisfyingly contrary in refusing colonial domination at both a symbolic and practical level, turning the tide in the independence movement.

A contemporary project with similar potentials is the Arlington West Memorial organized in Santa Barbara and Santa Monica by Veterans for Peace (VFP). Each Sunday the group erects a memorial of crosses on the beach, one for each American soldier killed in Iraq, as well as a monument to the now over 600,000 Iraqis who have died. As the number of crosses has grown, more and more local volunteers have come to set them up and take them down each Sunday. A rich process of dialogue and critique about the war, along with personal mourning and reflection, has evolved as thousands of tourists arrive and discover the sites. Families and friends of the dead soldiers come to place names and mementos on the crosses and take part in the process. Veterans for Peace has invited other local community groups to put up similar monuments, and the project has been covered extensively in the national press. While at first glance, the project may appear innocuous and local, it was conceived at a time when the U.S. government was denying the costs of war and preventing the publication of photographs of coffins of soldiers returning to the United States from Iraq. By intervening to symbolically represent the personal and physical costs of war, the VFP has interrupted the lies, distortions, and cover-ups at the national level, contributing to the growth of a massive antiwar effort.

Both the Kenyan and the Guatemalan projects we discussed above also have this quality of beginning as somewhat innocuous local projects while at the same time developing critical symbolic interventions in a repressive national discourse. In Guatemala, there has never been an accounting of the violence and terror imposed by the government on indigenous communities between 1960 and 1996. This included 150,000 deaths, 580 massacres, and the destruction of 440 villages. Over a million people were internally displaced, renting the fabric of local cultures. By collecting stories, creating photographic exhibits, and speaking publicly, the Ixil women are contributing to a countrywide effort to break the silence and demand an accounting and public truth telling about what happened. Because women are organizing themselves, the project also breaks open gender and ethnic stereotypes in a country where indigenous women rarely have opportunities to speak publicly about their experiences. Similarly in Kenya, by focusing on poor rural women as expert agents for economic and environmental change, the project reversed stereotypes. It also interrupted the silence about the corrupt and antidemocratic practices of the government.

Though individual therapy in a clinical setting was not the goal of any of these projects, each has had a profound effect on the psychology of the individuals participating. Through many months of testimony, analysis, discussion, and action, symbolic identity constructions were interrupted and individuals transformed. In fact, organizers of such projects have argued that individual therapy might be counterproductive in such settings. According to Dr. Roberto Cabrera (1998b) of the Human Rights Office of the Archdiocese of Guatemala,

> Just retrieving the victims' memories is a worthless re-experience of pain. It should be a social and political space, where society as a whole dares to construct a common history, dares to accept the responsibility of what happened and will be willing to adopt the changes to secure that such atrocities will never happen again.
>
> (p. 3)

Cabrera believes that remembering should lead to dreaming social action projects for the future: "There is no point to look back if it does not help to dream a better future" (p. 3).

In rural locations where individuals have not been exposed to an education based on assumptions of individualism and competitiveness, it is particularly important to strengthen communal traditions after violent disruptions. Identity is constructed in part through cultural symbols that can be both wounded and repaired.

By placing these diverse projects alongside one another, we are helping to collect the practices and construct the theory for the field of liberation psychology. The vitality of these multiple streams of work demonstrates the successes of these ingenious and creative participatory projects that nourish communities that have been stunted, separated from one another, terrorized, controlled, and colonized. Psychology needs to learn important forms of knowledge that develop in the streets, in the arts, and in rural settings—often in the heat of struggle—from experiences in communities where people resist oppression by organizing in creative ways. The river of psychologies of liberation also draws from other contributing streams of thought including liberation theology, Theater of the Oppressed, feminist leadership, collaborative arts, dynamic depth psychologies, critical community psychology, peace psychology, (post)colonial studies, engaged spirituality, queer theory, participatory and critical research, performance studies, and other interdisciplinary work in the humanities. Each involves a turn away from a colonial, ethnocentric Euro-American psychology posing as universal, as it orients toward multiple indigenous psychologies arising in processes of transformation and dialogue with one another. As we bear witness to the confluence of work that can be characterized as psychologies of liberation, shared principles emerge. Rather than offer an exhaustive survey of the history of each tributary, or give a thorough history of practitioners, our hope is to describe the basic principles of such work and to trace the outlines of the kinds of research and community practices that are developing out of this theoretical perspective, and contributing back to it.

2
Beyond Ideology: Dialogue

Could a liberation psychology emerge in the United States to address the connection between unconscious mental processes and socioeconomic forces that determine the crises facing humankind in the present era? Is it possible that a socially engaged psychology can take its place alongside the struggles for a humane social order?

(Nancy Hollander, 1997, p. 234)

In 1989, Ignacio Martín-Baró, a Jesuit and a psychologist, was assassinated along with seven others by the Atlacatl Battalion, a U.S.-trained Salvadoran death squad, at the University of Central America (UCA) in San Salvador, where he headed the psychology department and was the academic vice-rector. Martín-Baró was a Spanish priest, educated at the University of Chicago, who aligned himself with the poor in Latin America in the years after the Medellín Conference. It was at this meeting in 1968 that the Latin American Bishops articulated the outlines of a liberation theology and its commitment to serve the poor. As a priest of the small pueblo of Jayaque, west of San Salvador, Martín-Baró could observe the psychological suffering, terror, and hunger of those brutally oppressed by the elite who ruled El Salvador. During his years in Latin America, a powerful popular movement had developed, mobilizing thousands of people to imagine alternatives to their present conditions. Through participatory processes and stunning courage and tenacity, they organized community groups to resist terror and silencing. Martín-Baró used his position as a leading academic to form a National Institute of Public Opinion that published research information about current events as seen by anonymous ordinary people, in the cities and countryside, who would have been killed if they had publicly expressed their opinions or shared their experiences. In this way, as well as through his numerous books and articles on the psychology of repression and prejudice, and dreams of social transformation, Martín-Baró, along with other colleagues at the

UCA, dangerously challenged the ideologies of a government invested in silence about human rights abuses and poverty.

After Martín-Baró's death, Adrianne Aron and Shawn Corne of the Committee for Health Rights in Central America (CHRICA) collected, translated, and published in English twelve of his articles previously only available in Spanish. In this work, *Writings for a liberation psychology*, he expressed the yearnings, experience, and wounds of the powerless in Central America. He called for psychology to critically examine itself so that it could be a force for transformation rather than for conformity to status quo cultural arrangements that contribute to injustice, poverty, violence, and war.

Martín-Baró's critique of Eurocentric psychologies

Martín-Baró was critical of European and American psychology, and what he saw as its Latin American imitators. He resisted the emphasis on individualism and hedonism in virtually every school of psychology, all of which assumed that the unit of psychological analysis was a freestanding, autonomous individual whose single most important goal was personal happiness or satisfaction. Nowhere in this construction could you make sense of the commitment to sacrifice, solidarity, social justice, and community building that had cost over 80,000 Salvadorans their lives and displaced 40 per cent of the population. Most psychological theories of the 1970s and 1980s were a historical and universalist, assuming that the fundamental realities of personality and psychopathology were the same across times and cultures. They had a homeostatic vision, which assumed the persistence of essential social structures rather than their transformation. Many psychological theories leaned toward a sterile scientism, focusing solely on quantifiable variables measurable in laboratory situations rather than an analysis of lived experience.

Martín-Baró's thinking led him to anticipate poststructuralist and (post)colonial critical theory. He had a sophisticated understanding of the implications of the cultural construction of knowledge, and the evolving, local, and provisional character of all frames of reference and identifications. He imagined mental health, not through modernist or humanistic theories that lay out fixed universal characteristics of humanity that are to be reached by all. Instead he created provisional goals, or what Butler (in McLaren & Lankshear, 1994) has called "contingent universalities" (p. 211). These allow the capacity to differ and break from dominant modes of understanding self and society, as well as from past understandings in one's local context. Agreeing with Salvatore Maddi, Martín-Baró (1994) understood that "the healing power of any psychotherapeutic method depends on the dosage of its break with the dominant culture," which he described as "the veil of lies we move about in" (p. 120). In part, the construction of a more just society is "a mental health problem," requiring us to "work hard to find theoretical models and methods of intervention that allow us, as a community and as individuals, to break with the culture of vitiated social relations and put other, more humanizing relations in their place" (p. 120). His interdependent goals for liberation psychology were "healthy, free, and creative minds" in a "free, dynamic, and just social body," where "people have sown enough seeds of life to be able to trust in the possibility of a tomorrow" (p. 121).

The sensibility here is a recognition of our limitations of knowing at any moment, while not giving up our desire and responsibility to plant and nurture seeds of life. We want to create together situations that lead to a rebuilding of positive and joyful modes of interdependence, and the creation of new forms of attachment in which the humanity of each individual is acknowledged. Here is a program for an ongoing revolution, where the central goal is not a fixed and future utopia known in advance, for which we have to sacrifice in the present, but rather a continuing practice of dialogue and restoration with the goal of building more humane communities.

Martín-Baró's radical proposals

Martín-Baró envisioned a psychology that would acknowledge the psychological wounding caused by war, racism, poverty, and violence; a psychology that would support historical memory and critical reflection; a psychology that would aid the emergence of the sorts of subjectivity through which people felt they could creatively make sense of and respond to the world. When individuals have been taught silence and accommodation by the institutions around them, the outcome is a sense of fatalism about life conditions. The way things are seems inevitable. One's failure seems one's own fault. Desires for different ways of being in relation to oneself and others are crushed by a sense of oneself as powerless. The crucial question of liberation psychology, then, involves the transformation of fatalism into critical consciousness, an awakening of agency and the power to perform our roles differently, and a quickening of imaginations of desire. In order to effect such changes, we need to learn how to create safe and protected spaces where people can experiment with stepping outside inherited scripts and unconsciously assumed identifications to consider alternative performances. What we reach for, according to Martín-Baró, "is an opening— an opening against all closure, flexibility against everything fixed, elasticity against rigidity, a readiness to act against all stagnation" (p. 183). Who we are in the present contains a kernel of something ideal in the future: "hunger for change, affirmation of what is new, life in hope" (p. 183). The discipline of psychology should be able to support this opening and to learn from those who are already doing so.

In his essay "Toward a liberation psychology", Martín-Baró (1994) laid out the following essential prerequisites for the development of a liberation psychology:

1. *Psychology needs a new goal.* Psychologists need to stop thinking about personal careers and publication in academic journals, and instead focus on the needs and sufferings of the majorities who are numbed by oppressive life circumstances. In the past, by considering psychological problems as primarily individual, "psychology has often contributed to obscuring the relationship between personal estrangement and social oppression, presenting the pathology of persons as if it were something removed from history and society, and behavioral disorders as if they played themselves out entirely in the individual plane" (p. 27). Instead, liberation psychology should illuminate the links between an individual's psychological suffering and the social, economic, and political contexts in which he or she lives. We need to learn to connect psychic fragmentation and apathy that force people "to learn submission and expect nothing from life" with the social structures, discourses, and ideologies that create subjects in states of "marginalized dependency" and "oppressive misery," while "snatching away their ability to define their own lives" (pp. 26–7).

2. *Psychology needs a new epistemology.* Martín-Baró proposes a dialogical and evolving form of truth, one that is "not to be found, but made" (p. 27). Here there is a stress on the possibilities for critical and utopian imagination that can continually rework and re-think experience in liberatory ways. The psychologist does not function as an expert who fixes individuals beset by psychopathology. Martín-Baró's vision draws from the theories of Paulo Freire, whose literacy work in Brazil and Chile began with a different sense of pedagogy, a pedagogy "of" the oppressed, not "for" the oppressed. According to Martín-Baró: "It was the very person, the very same community, that constituted the subject of its own conscienticizing literacy, that in community dialogue with the educator had to learn to read its reality and write its historical word" (p. 28). Here the role of the psychologist becomes that of a convener, a witness, a coparticipant, a mirror, and a holder of faith for a process through which those who have been silenced may discover their own capacities for historical memory, critical analysis, utopian imagination, and transformative social action. The psychologist might bring to the table theories and histories that have been developed in the past, but they will be "relativized" and "critically revised" in each local arena where they may or may not apply. Truth in this new epistemology is democratized. Each participant evolves a sense of meaningful voice; a way of making sense of the world that is both valued and provisional within the larger context of community listening and discernment. Psychologists relinquish their role as authorities and experts who have the final word; but developing new

capacities for listening, questioning, and facilitation of group processes enriches their roles.

3. *Psychology needs a new praxis.* Martín-Baró develops an orientation toward pragmatism, suggesting we learn through a communal process of discovering perspectives, imagining different strategies, trying them out, and then evaluating failures and success. Drawing from the work of Fals Borda (1988) on participatory research, a practice that transforms researchers as much as it transforms reality, Martín-Baró proposes a profound re-orientation of psychological practice through which yesterday's universalizing "experts" begin to learn from organic histories with local participants. Citing the spectacular failure of much social science planning for development projects, school reform, and workplace organization, which "meant in practice taking the perspective of those in power and acting from a position of dominance" (p. 29), Martín-Baró (1994) argues for psychological research that arises between people out of their common concerns and toward their common desires. He develops a radical proposal: to transform and humanize repressive or failing human institutions, all of the people who participate in them must also be transformed and humanized through participatory dialogue and creative imagination about alternatives. Such praxis nurtures individuals' dreaming, while creating together, what Paulo Freire described as "a world in which it will be easier to love" (Freire, 1989, p. 24).

The call to liberation psychologies

In the brief period since Martín-Baró's death, his call for a liberation psychology has served as a rallying cry to place into conversation a number of liberatory psychologies and other interdisciplinary efforts and participatory practices that have arisen in the United States and throughout the world. We are working out a creative genealogy, an interpretive link among ideas that are similar, yet may or may not be in dialogue. We are seeing the outlines of a new way of thinking in diverse arenas. We believe a new discipline (or interdiscipline) and a new vision of community are being forged in multiple locations out of the ashes of the confrontations of the Cold War, from critical (post)colonial articulations, and the moral failures of both neoliberal economies and revolutionary political projects.

Whether its practice is accomplished in individual therapies, in small groups or larger community wide and intercommunity efforts, liberation psychologies understand that the health of individuals and the health of communities, the health of those who suffer from oppression and those who inflict it—categories which sometimes overlap in our complex world—are inextricably intertwined. The fall of the Berlin Wall, which took place in the same month as Martín-Baró's assassination, symbolized the waning of the strength of old oppositions. On one side of the wall, there was corporate greed, neocolonialism, government corruption, deregulation, privatization, outsourcing, unemployment, and alienation in supposedly democratic countries; and on the other side, rigid hierarchy and brutal secret police in "dictatorships of the proletariat" or just plain dictatorships with all pretense stripped away. Both options have led to a globalization of capital that is stripping bare the earth and its cultures.

This has produced among many a profound suspicion of both the Left and the Right, of hypocritical "master narratives" that lay out grand schemes for progress, while benefiting only an elite. In the past, both the Left and the Right have operated according to hierarchical principles that promoted discipline and silencing rather than dialogue and initiative. Repressive practices in institutions interacted with authoritarian approaches to family life, gender relations, and childrearing. Commitments to abstract utopias in the future were able to foreclose emancipatory educational practices in the present. As a result of this historical experience, liberation psychologies place less emphasis on political platforms leading to long-term goals, and more emphasis on processes of inclusion, reflection, transformation, investigation, dialogue, decision making, and responsibility. Local projects of participatory dialogue and resistance, new initiatives for self-sustaining alternatives, and the fertilizing of revisioning desired futures are emerging. They are developing in contexts where there is a deeper appreciation of the ways that our own capacities for self-delusion and amnesia, apathy and numbness, even collusion, can make us part of the problems we are trying to solve. Some of the problems that need to be addressed are economic and political, but they are also psychological, because transformations are needed in thinking, symbolizing, relating, and imagining.

Breaking open the paradigms through which we think is a difficult and painful process, which needs to be understood psychologically and midwifed in relationship. It requires a moral re-orientation within psychology, an advocacy that psychology be placed in the service of the restoration of individuals, communities, and habitats that have been numbed or maimed by the multiple collective traumas and injustices that mark our historical past and the living present. Through the lens of liberation psychologies, we can begin to articulate hoped for changes as well as name the losses— psychological, interpersonal, symbolic, economic, and environmental—that whole communities have suffered due to colonialism and its present incarnation as neoliberal policy.

Marginalization and liberation

Liberation psychology moves in two opposite directions. One motion is deconstructive and critical, looking backward at what we have been doing and thinking that is dysfunctional, dissociative, and destructive; the other motion is moving forward, toward new capacities for imagining, voicing, connecting, empathizing, and celebrating self and other in community. Liberation psychology develops what Chela Sandoval (2000) has called "oppositional consciousness" (p. 54), a capacity to search for and reflect upon the polarizations, distances, gaps, or marginalizations both in the world and in ourselves. We bring attention to moments when we find ourselves thinking I am (or we are) like this and they are the opposite (or profoundly different). We begin to wonder about the construction of these differences, searching for ways to reposition our energies to explore and mediate boundaries of separation.

One polarization that is central to our work, and one of the themes of dominant culture with which we need to break, is the discourse that has created a vast imaginary difference between a homogenized privileged North and an homogenized impoverished South of the globe. A closer and less ideological exploration of both human culture and natural environment in these regions yields a far more complex situation, and, at the personal level, surprising possibilities for reconstituting bonds. As a result of our many years of experience in community work both in the United States and Latin America, we can report that in both regions, people are struggling to find meaningful ways of life in a climate where globalization is rapidly impoverishing public institutions, environments, and cultural identity and diversity. Throughout the world, each country has visionaries and idealists imagining solutions, and each has intractable pockets of poverty and violence, many children (both rich and poor) without a sense of a meaningful future, and countless adults using alcohol, medications, and passive entertainment to suppress feelings of depression and alienation as well as hunger, both physical and spiritual. There are many different forms of oppression, silence, and suffering, all painful and all linked to cultural systems where my silence and your silence reinforce each other. Agonies of doubts and symptoms may be suffered by the most economically privileged, side by side with the distress and demoralization of the poor. Contemporary trauma theory shows that both torturers and their victims, as well as the government commissioners who examine human rights violations, the bystanders who "didn't know," and the journalists who report on these subjects, all can suffer a contagion of unbearable, fragmenting, and dehumanizing states while participating in unjust and violent social systems (see Chapters 4, 5, 6, and 7). Psychological distress differs according to cultural location, while forming an interlocking mosaic of despair.

We have discovered that the set of universalizing, modernist ideas referenced by notions of "the West," or "Westernization," or "the Western Mind" (or "American" or "Americanization") are, in psychological terms, an idealized and false unity, a discourse of manic defense covering over a complicated situation in which massive numbers of people think otherwise or have serious doubts about business as usual. Being "from the West" or "Westernized" is a state of mind with which one can identify or dis-identify in any geographical location, depending on the complexity of one's conscious differentiation. When we propose psychologies of liberation grounded in local conditions and local dialogues within a framework of interdependence, the tasks of remembering, regenerating, and re-thinking community initiatives belong equally to all people. Although psychologies of liberation developed in a coherent form first in Latin America, they shed light on and provide perspectives for all of us. In this period of globalization, corporations and privatization are creating situations where the well-being of local communities, whether in Los Angeles, Cochabamba, or Calcutta, is being sacrificed to profit-making schemes by distant investors. While it is inevitable that confronting such issues will produce conflict both within and between groups, liberation psychology's commitment is to maintain transparent dialogue practices that allow us to witness and challenge dissonant views in the hopes of evolving transformative solutions, common ground, and new solidarities wherever that is possible.

Colonialism as institution and structural metaphor

Over the years a larger picture has emerged that allows us to see a metaphorical parallel among communities, environments, hearts, and minds living in situations of colonialism, a picture linking the damage sustained and the solutions possible. Historical colonialism was the process through which one group invaded the territory of another group and took over its resources, squeezing out local forms and replacing them with homogenizing influences. As its corollary, colonialism has an ideology of denial, pretending that the situation is normal and natural, a survival of the fittest in a marketplace of goods and ideas, the best of all possible worlds. The resultant suffering is silenced under a rhetoric of development and progress.

The outcome of colonialism has been a controlling or blocking of interconnectivity and interdependence in related arenas: the environment (where rivers are dammed, channeled, or drained and natural geographies replaced with grids), in societies (where communities are divided in a pseudologic of superiority/inferiority), in economies (where resources like trees, coal, or oil are extracted as rapidly and brutally as possible without regard for surrounding destruction and pollution), and thought (where knowledge is organized under the rubrics of specialization, expertise, and compartmentalization, affected by racism and Eurocentrism).

Colonialism, globalization, and development planning are ways of thinking as well as ways of life, and we need to find their alternatives, islands where other ways of life are explored through the resurgence of interconnectivity at local levels, creating dialogue among diverse points of view and projects of counter-development and liberation. When we take the idea of colonialism out of its location in history texts as a period of conquest located in the past, and begin to think of it as a metaphor for a way to live in the environment, certain general patterns appear. Before colonialism, there were environments of interpenetrating local biodiversities with cyclic retreats and advances, in which human groups integrated and competed; after colonialism, there was large-scale monoculture, control of land and resources by distant privileged elites who exploit and fragment local communities while polluting and destroying ecosystems. Before colonialism, there were many diverse cultural worlds, each its own center of meaning making and language arts, with Europe at the periphery. After colonialism, cultures were ranked on a kind of "great chain of being" according to European notions of culture and development, with Europe at the center. As a corollary, individual subjectivities were ranked as to how completely they could think through decontextualized universals in European languages. One way to think about liberation psychologies is as an evolving and multiple set of projects of decolonization.

Much of Euro-American psychology has incorporated status quo ideas of taming nature through progress and development, of individualism and competition among separate bounded, self-determining identities cut off from and rising above environment, culture, and community. Psychologies of liberation throughout the world struggle to disentangle their ideas and work from these colonial mindsets, posing a different range of values and ideals.

Ruth Behar (1996) has called for "an anthropology that breaks your heart," a way of entering into encounter not at a safe objectifying distance, but up close, where one begins to feel and articulate all the contradictory and ambivalent affects of engagement. She imagines that it will involve new forms of criticism that are "rigorous, yet not disinterested," as well as a mapping of an "intermediate space we can't quite define yet, a borderland between passion and intellect, analysis and subjectivity, ethnography and autobiography, art and life" (p. 174). Similarly, we need a psychology that breaks our hearts, because only that kind of psychology could awaken us to our entanglements in strategies of dissociation, to the despairs of trauma, to grief from mourning, and to potential joy in restoration and healing. Only such a psychology could move us from a fatalism that unconsciously yields to the status quo, to tentative hope for gradual transformation of ourselves and for the communities where we are standing and placing our advocacies. In the next chapter, we will explore how liberation psychologists are rethinking development—both psychological and economic—by a shift in emphasis from the idea of progress to that of liberation.

3
Beyond Development: Liberation

Peace, justice, love, and freedom are not private realities; they are not only internal attitudes. They are social realities, implying a historical liberation.

(Gutiérrez, 1988, p. 167)

Development as a preconception

Most Euro-American psychological theories are oriented around values concerning individual development, and most Euro-American economic theories are centered on material development. In these theories, culturally preferred ways of being are stationed as endpoints, with sequential stages of change laid out like stepping-stones on a path toward them. A lattice of implicit and critically unexamined cultural values structures developmental psychology (Kaplan, 1983a, 1983b). Its discourse often colludes with the language of "progress" that we have come to expect from psychology's roots in the nineteenth century. Economic development planning has assumed that individuals want the same level of material infrastructure that exists in Euro-American urban environments.

Gustavo Esteva (1992), Mexican grassroots activist and self-described "deprofessionalized intellectual," has traced the fate of the term "development". The early use of the term "development" was to characterize a plant or animal reaching its natural, complete, or full-fledged form. Its meaning was extended between 1759 and 1859. "Development" began to be used to describe social and economic changes, carrying over the connotations from biology of development as growth, evolution, and maturation. "Development" and "evolution" were used interchangeably, as the former extended its sense from the attainment of the appropriate form to what was considered the perfect or ideal form. Now cultures could be judged and ranked according to the degree to which they met the standards of Euro-American ideals, as though the latter were God-given natural law. This discourse of "development" became foundational to rationalizations for colonialism. It is out of this soil that Euro-American psychology sprang, with some of its theorists collapsing the so-called "primitive" thinking of indigenous peoples with the thought of children and schizophrenics (Werner, 1940).

Theories of psychological development, presented as biological facts of unfolding natural processes, were often complicit with the colonial agenda. They described the starting point as the kind of *participation mystique* taken to be common to diverse "primitive" peoples outside of Europe, and the ideal endpoint of development as forms of rationality and individualism lauded in Euro-American thought. The term "participation mystique" suggested that "primitive" peoples mistakenly think that nature is alive and related to them. It inferred they could not draw as clear a line as Europeans between their own bounded individual identity and the objective world around them. The efficient rationalism of scientific and industrial societies was lauded over supposedly inferior qualities used to describe the thought of indigenous societies: "presymbolic," "affect laden," "concrete," and "superstitious."

Underdevelopment

Esteva (1992) describes another use of the term "development" during the Cold War. After World War II the United States and the Soviet Union competed for the allegiance of nonaligned countries. In his inauguration speech in 1949, Truman announced a "program of development" to make "the benefits of our scientific advances and industrial progress available for the progress of underdeveloped areas" (Truman, in Esteva, 1992, p. 6). This division of the world into those cultures to be admired and emulated, and those found to be inferior was all too familiar from the discourse of colonialism. Now development was promoted as a benign process of granting gifts from the "developed" to the "underdeveloped." The yardstick was economic—gross national product—leaving out of the equation who might benefit from these transactions as well as all other varied measures of human well-being. Resistance to this "program of development" was often squelched by military action.

Esteva (2006b) remembers the personal impact Truman's declaration had on him as a Mexican youth with both Spanish colonial and indigenous roots to his family:

> I got underdevelopment when I was thirteen years old, when President Truman took office and coined the word "underdevelopment." I was one of the two billion people who that very day became underdeveloped. We were not. We were a different kind of people and suddenly we all became underdeveloped. If you become underdeveloped, it's a very humiliating condition. Very undignified condition. You cannot trust your nose. You need to trust the experts that will bring you to development. You cannot dream your dreams because they are already dreamt. That is the model to go.

Esteva confesses that for many the seduction of trying to replicate in Mexico the United States as represented in the Hollywood movies of the times was irresistible. The lived legacy of this rush to development, says Esteva (1994), is that

> for two-thirds of the people on earth, th[e] positive meaning of the word "development"—profoundly rooted after two centuries of its social construction—is a reminder of *what they are not*. It is a reminder of an undesirable, undignified condition. To escape from it, they need to be enslaved to others' experiences and dreams.
>
> (p. 6)

Psychologies of liberation reject the hidden agendas wrapped in this history of theorizing about development. They chose "liberation" (or peace psychology or critical psychology) as the term to characterize the spirit and goal of their work rather than "development," seeking new ground for their own aspirations. Exploring the desires that provide alternative orientations, we will look at several critiques of "development" from the viewpoints of liberation theology, engaged Buddhism, and theories of post-development and counter-development.

Liberation theology's critique of development

Liberation psychology, as Martín-Baró conceived it, flowed out of liberation theology's confrontation with the elite in Latin America. Historically the Catholic Church had largely served the interests of wealthy landowners and businessmen. Liberation theologians announced a commitment to the oppressed, the poor, and the marginalized, which they understood to be consistent with the Gospels (Rivers, 2005). For liberation theology, sin became defined as the absence of brotherhood and love in our relationships with others, and as well as with God (Gutiérrez, 1988, p. 167). It became synonymous with the exploitation and domination of others. Liberation theology in Latin America often drew its inspiration from the Old Testament book of Exodus, the story of the Hebrews' struggle from slavery in Egypt, their long wandering in the desert, and their mythic longing for a home free from oppression and injustice. In 1968, at the Second General Conference of Latin American Bishops at Medellín, Colombia, liberation theology was initiated with an invocation of the Exodus story that united faith and social liberation, and reclaimed the political dimension of the Gospels (Puleo, 1994). Confronting slavery, the book of Exodus is also important to African-American Christians and the Black liberation theology movement in the United States (Cone, 1972). In opposition to development initiatives framed by the powerful from the North, "genuine development" was defined as the transition from less human to more human conditions for each and every person (Berryman, 1987). For Gutiérrez, the Peruvian priest who founded liberation theology, faith in God requires our acting on behalf of justice, because God, as described in the book of Exodus and Jesus's teachings, is seen as encouraging and desiring liberation from oppression (Ellis, 1987).

In response to the forceful and often violent exportation and imposition of Euro-American economic and political agendas, liberation theologians and other (post)colonial writers rejected the colonial term "development" to characterize community improvement. They offered in return an analysis called dependency theory. They argued that "development" too often implies adopting an interlinked economic and cultural system that precipitated the development of *under*development. The Southern hemisphere directly witnessed that increased foreign investment often meant the trading away of natural resources at low prices, the violent displacement of communities, destruction of local cultures, and the importation of manufactured goods at unmanageably high prices. This undermined local economies leading to increased poverty and forced migration. This sort of development has rarely meant that technological education was shared and managerial positions offered. Instead, it has seen local communities as sources of cheap labor for goods to be exported to wealthier countries, and as impediments to the stripping of exportable natural resources. The term "development" has too often covered over the experience of inequality and dependence that has been generated by others' economic gain (Goizueta, 1988). As we know from the U.S. government's covert participation in the "dirty wars" in Latin America, weaker countries that resisted the seizing of their resources by those from stronger countries became prey to military and paramilitary intervention in their internal politics, so that the leadership friendly to foreign investors could be instated. In such scenarios, the capital of one group builds itself by depleting the capital of another. In dependent relationships, need does not draw resources from where they are stored or hoarded, and the draining of wealth and natural resources continues toward utter depletion (Hyde, 1983). From this perspective, dependence can be defined as "the assimilation of one nation or region within another's sphere of influence to such a degree that the development or lack thereof is governed, controlled, and determined by the development of the latter" (Goizueta, 1988, p. 7).

Argentine liberation philosopher, Enrique Dussel (in Goizueta, 1988) argued, "it is necessary to be able to *undertake one's own path of development,* different from the European (because up to the present we have been the other face of the same system, but the exploited, dominated, dependent face)" (p. 230). In contradistinction to development practices, where foreign "experts" dictate projects and priorities that often benefit the elite, the process that came to be called liberation in Latin America requires people in local communities to recognize and articulate their own interests, aspirations, and hopes. Desires that have been silenced or destroyed need to re-emerge through reflection, dialogue, and action with others, awakening an imagination that can begin to believe that transformation is even possible. Only then can people work in solidarity with one another to move toward the actualization of their commonly held desires. In Latin America, "liberation" was chosen by many as a better term for the goals of community and individual transformation than the tainted term "development." Ideally, liberation suggests interdependence. The liberation of one is inextricably tied to the liberation of all; everyone involved will change in the process. Liberation implies interconnectedness between personal, social, economic, and political realms. For many it is also connected to spiritual liberation.

In the book of Exodus, the beginning of an attempt to become liberated is likened to entering the desert. One leaves behind the certainties of oppression and domination, and takes on the uncertainty of being neither a community of slaves nor a community of the emancipated. Liberation is depicted as a long process filled with challenges, doubts, and potential backsliding. There is a period of pilgrimage, trial and error, where exploration, confusion, and the experience of being lost dominate. There can be a period where one's sense of subjectivity is broken and remade. One may go through a spiritual conversion in such a setting. In some interpretations, Moses was unable to go forward to enter the "promised land" because he was unable to adequately support such a transformative process.

One finds orientation in one's wandering in the desert through utopic imagining, nourishing a capacity to believe in a better future. Dussel (1985), working from one meaning of "utopia," says that this imagining is "the affirmation of 'that-which-has-no-place,'" because it has been denied value, including the denied value of the poor and exploited. Utopia is an imagining built from what and who has been excluded. From Exodus we learn that to break from bondage, to enter into, and survive the desert between slavery and liberation, one must carry close to the heart an image of the land of milk and honey: "A land wherein thou shalt eat bread without scarceness, thou shalt not lack anything" (Deuteronomy 8:7–9). The biblical prophets imagine a utopian New Jerusalem: "And my people shall build houses and inhabit them; and they shall plant vineyards, and eat the fruit of them; They shall not build and another inhabit; They shall not plant and another eat" (Isaiah 65:21–2). "They shall enjoy the work of their hands. They shall not labor in vain" (Isaiah 65:22–3). "They shall sit every man under his vine and his fig tree; and none shall make them afraid" (Micah 4:4). Contemporary liberation theologians such as Rubem Alves imagine communities of liberation that are filled with "an erotic exuberance for life," with "the beauty of the overflowing of love" (quoted in Puleo, 1994, pp. 191, 194). From the perspective of liberation theology, one desires the release of the other from objectification, so that he/she is the center of his/her own world, rather than determined by another's (Goizueta, 1988). Such a release of the other is also understood as a liberation of the self. Perfection does not consist in a "realization of *my* 'potential being,' but in a love that first loves the Other: love-in-justice" (Goizueta, 1988, p. 72).

Euro-American psychologists have generally focused on the development of the individual within the local context of the family, largely ignoring community, cultural, historical, and environmental contexts. Psychologies of liberation seek to bring into focus these forgotten contexts, seeing the individual as existing within this wider web of relationships. Liberation, unlike development, requires co-liberation within each of these interlocking contexts. The "other" becomes an equally important term to the "self," shifting our theorizing and practice in radical directions, which we shall explore later.

Engaged Buddhist critiques of development

Vietnamese monk and engaged Buddhist Thich Nhat Hanh (1988) teaches that liberation or emancipation means putting an end to the roots of afflictions and sorrows by transforming them. Like liberation theology, engaged Buddhists have realized that a structural analysis of the causes of suffering is necessary to grasp their roots. In various forms of engaged Buddhism in Asia, such as the Sarvodaya Shramadana Movement in Sri Lanka (Macy, 1983) and the dhammic socialism proposed by Thai Buddhist Bhikkhu Buddhadasa and his followers (Aitken, 1998; Puntarigvivat, 1994), the discourse of "economic development" has been critiqued, as it has in Latin America by liberation theologians and philosophers. The Thai Buddhist liberationist Sulak Sivaraksa (1992, 1994), a lay follower of Buddhadasa, says that we have been taught that development has to do with the increase and subsequent satisfaction of desires. He argues that from a spiritual standpoint, development requires that desires be seen through and reduced.

Sivaraksa (1992) posits the realization of peace as the telos for individuals and communities. He outlines four interconnected levels of freedom that are seen as indispensable for the development of peace and happiness: physical, social, emotional, and intellectual. These are interdependent, not achievable in isolation from one another. Whereas capitalism encourages increased material accumulation and power, fixed attachments and investments, Buddhism sees these as fostering greed, hate, and competition. Such greed and competition work against the cooperation, compassion, and loving kindness needed for individual and group happiness and peace. The Buddhist goals of liberation—equality, love, freedom, and peace—are furthered as the members of a community reduce selfishness and attachment. "To do so, two realizations are necessary: an inner realization concerning greed, hatred, and delusion, and an outer realization concerning the import these tendencies have on society and the planet" (Sivaraksa, 1992, p. 47).

Puntarigvivat (1994) argues that Buddhism's original focus on personal liberation from the suffering arising from cycles of birth, old age, sickness, and death now requires a focus on social liberation. The co-promotion of social and personal liberation, he proposes, requires Buddhism to have a structural vision, which includes an understanding of social, economic, and political conditions.

Like liberation theology, dhammic socialism also arises as a response to global capitalism, rejecting its terms and seeking its own compass points in equality, love, freedom, and peace. It also focuses on how greed, desire, and hatred create many of the social problems we suffer from such as poverty, violence, militarism, and war. Greed is understood as both a personal practice and as ingredient to oppressive social structures, which encourage social and economic dependence. According to Puntarigvivat (1994), socialism in Thai means the restraint of each member of the society for the benefit of the community. In lieu of capitalism, engaged Buddhists propose a socialism that promotes local self-sufficiency, political decentralization, participatory democracy, and the creation of work that promotes human dignity and freedom (Puntarigvivat, 1994). In this generative context, relatively freed from market dependency, cultural and spiritual values can be nourished in individuals and communities. Buddhist economics attempts to minimize the use of natural resources, and encourages simple living, so that, as Schumacher (1973) recommended in his classic work, *Small is beautiful: Economics as if people mattered*, consumption is a means to well-being, not a measure of it. Here it is hoped that human beings produce according to their capacities and consume according to their needs, not according to their artificially stimulated desires. Surpluses are shared for the well-being of all, rather than hoarded by individuals for personal gain and enjoyment.

Engaged Buddhism and dhammic socialism counter a focus on individual development with one on "dependent co-arising," stressing the interdependence of personal, communal, and ecological liberation. Here the fulfillment of one's own true nature entails a distancing from seeing in terms of a separate "me" and "mine" and attention to the realization of the potential of others (Swearer, 1994). The concept of dependent co-arising suggests that all beings emerge from a process of interrelated innovation. Acts of disregard toward others diminish the lived world we share. Thus, the process of liberation involves movement from greed and self-centeredness to nonattachment, selflessness, and the capacity to be other-regarding of both sentient and nonsentient beings and nature.

In engaged Buddhism the practice of the Four Abodes—loving kindness toward self and others (*Metta*), compassion (*Karuna*), sympathetic joy (*Nudita*), and equanimity (*Upekkha*)—are cultivated in mindfulness meditation, and in one's relations with others and the community. The awakening of individuals is linked to the awakening of communities (*sanghas*) and societies. It is understood that without social liberation, personal liberation is limited, and vice versa. In his study, *Bhikkhu Buddhadasa's dhammic socialism in dialogue with Latin American liberation theology*, Puntarigvivat (1994) likens engaged Buddhists' emphasis on the sangha with liberation theology's focus on the base community. Whereas sanghas are led by charismatic monk leaders, and focus first on sustainability, self-governance, and self-sufficiency (*swaraj*) and secondly on resistance to injustice, the Latin American and Filipino base communities, more lay based, focus first on economic and political equality. American engaged Buddhist Robert Aitken (1998) likens these affinity groups to those of the Catholic Worker movement, the "society of societies" of European anarchism, and North American utopian societies of the nineteenth century. He cites Buddhist Peace Foundation communities in the Bay Area of California as present embodiments of the base community idea in the United States.

In examining the legacies of Bhikkhu Buddhadasa, Swearer (1994) emphasizes the importance of *anurak*, often translated as "conservation" or "protection." Buddhadasa focuses on nurturing empathy toward not only people but also for the forest and all things of the natural world. This empathy enables a relationship between humans and the environment that is not based on human use of the environment, but in "having at the very core of one's being the quality of caring for all things in the world in their natural conditions" (Swearer, 1994, p. 15).

One cares for the forest because one empathizes with the forest, just as one cares for another because one has become empathic toward his or her being and concerns. This empathy becomes possible as boundaries between self and other become redrawn through experiences of dependent co-arising. *Anurak*, in this sense, is fundamentally linked with nonattachment or liberation from preoccupation with self, a freedom that is central to Buddhadasa's thought. "We truly care for our total environment and for our fellow human beings only when we have overcome selfishness and those qualities which empower it, e.g. desire, greed, hatred. There is a persistent linkage ... among non-attachment, selfishness, and the capacity to be truly other-regarding" (Swearer, 1994, p. 15).

Puntarigvivat shares an example of a rural base community in Thailand led by Pha Khamkhun, a monk, where *anurak* is evident as they pursued increasing sustainability. As this community broke away from single cash crops and developed integrated farming, they created agricultural banks and community cooperatives. They succeeded in protecting their small local forest from illegal logging. These changes promoted a greater cultural independence and community self-determination. Communities from Kerala to Chiapas are involved in similar efforts to disengage from agendas of development that have degraded their culture and the environment, disrupted communal arrangements, and contributed to forced migration. These changes both promote and depend on psychological shifts from passivity, fatalism, and disempowerment to a re-invigorated empathic engagement, renewed hope, and a sense of agency in solidarity with others.

In Pali, "development" means disorderliness or confusion. In Buddhism it can refer to either progress or regress (Sivaraksa, 1992). This is resonant with one meaning of the Latin root of "development," *progresio*, which can also mean madness. In Buddhist thought, we are understood to live in states of delusional entrapment in collective ideas of the dominant culture. In Mahayana Buddhism, liberation is seen as freedom from unconscious identification with conventional views of reality (Queen & King, 1996). The potential for liberation involves breaking the bonds of these social constructions and entering into realms of emptiness or freedom where one is freer of fixed identifications and able to critically assess dominant construals of reality.

Participatory communication and post-development

By the middle of the 1980s, many Europeans and Americans who were working in the field of international development also began to have questions about their development work. Large-scale development projects were impoverishing masses of people, disrupting local cultures, and creating new local elites who joined with international investors in repressing dissent. Many expensive small-scale development projects were simply failing. These problems have spurred the evolution of a new stream of thought summarized as "post-development" (Rahnema & Bawtree, 1997). Thierry Verhelst (1987) of *The South–North Network on Cultures and Development*, after working for many years as a senior project officer with a Belgian development agency, summed it up this way:

> Today, poverty, malnutrition, and violation of human rights are even more widespread in the Third World than they were in the past. Most of the many development strategies and projects have ended in failure. This undeniable fact calls for a critical examination of the theories and analysis employed up to now, as well as the development strategies and projects arising from them.
>
> (p. 156)

Verhelst calls for a halt to the excessively extroverted and materialistic concept of progress, which has dominated development work for decades. Instead, regenerating self-reliance and indigenous thought and culture should be the starting points.

> Self-reliance must be understood as an act of emancipation from all harmful forms of extraversion and dependence. For each people or local community, it is a question of preserving or reclaiming their liberty and, ultimately their identity. ... In short, the cultural approach is synonymous with the human approach in all its complexity and richness. Respect for a local culture implies respect for the men and women who are both its trustees and its creators. Stressing the cultural dimension of development means placing human beings at the center of all analyses and initiatives.
>
> (pp. 160–1)

The first steps of transformation that Verhelst describes are resonant with liberation psychology. They are steps toward introversion to create an open space of community in which dialogue may begin. This crucial process needs to be protected:

> Intercultural solidarity implies respect for a temporary "withdrawal into oneself". If need be, funding agencies must shield communities from the development and progress that threatens them. Above all intercultural solidarity means support for all forms of research whose goal are local regeneration, resistance to deculturation and the positive affirmation of cultural identity. One should not always seek immediate effectiveness, optimal productivity, or results that are concrete and quantifiable.
>
> (p. 159)

By the end of the 1990s, the Communication for Development Group (CDG, 2001) within the Food and Agricultural Organization (FAO) of the United Nations had reached a very similar conclusion. They noted that although the 1996 World Food Summit had set as a goal to reduce by half the number of hungry people in the world by 2015, the number of malnourished in two-thirds of the countries being tracked had actually increased by 60 million in five years. According to Benor and Cleaver (in CDG, 2001): "The continent of Africa is littered with five-year projects, abandoned on 'completion' by farmers" (p. 3). Food development projects were failing and people were starving even though the best technologies were being applied. The CDG thought they understood why:

> The importance of popular participation in planning and executing projects was largely postulated during the 1970s ... In a ground-breaking article on developmental communication, Rogers (1996) suggested that the passing of the dominant paradigm of top-down planning would signal a shift toward self-development wherein villagers and urban poor would be the priority audiences, and self-reliance and building on local resources would be emphasized. ... Despite these early predictions, rural communications systems continued to service the transfer of technology or "TOT" model in which information passed from researchers to farmers through the extension system (Ramirez, 1995). At least a decade would pass before participatory methodologies began to gain acceptance.
>
> (p. 5)

According to the CDG, a growing number of development specialists and agencies are now beginning to see that any change in food production practices has to arise through collaboration and participation at the local level:

> During these three decades, the role of communication has undergone a 180 degree shift from a one-way top-down transfer of messages from

extension to farmers, to a social process which starts with farmers and brings together both groups in a two-way sharing of information among communication equals—in short participatory communication.

(p. 2)

By the year 2000 major funding sources were essentially recommending the compass points of liberation psychologies we have been describing as key to transforming world hunger and social suffering, and they began to promote projects based on participatory communication and participatory action research (see Chapters 12 and 13). According to the Rockefeller Foundation (in CDG, 2001):

Access to and control of information sources are essential for poor people to participate fully in decisions affecting their lives and communities. Sustained social change is impossible without their full participation.

(p. 2)

The FAO (in CDG, 2001) now suggests forms of local regeneration as the starting point for rural projects that attempt to initiate change in food production. They recommend the following requirements as a result of "hard lessons learned for the road ahead" (p. 2):

1. Participatory communication has to be built in from the start because local farmers "are often the most qualified to decide how or if, a given project's planning and objectives applies at the local level" (p. 2).
2. Indigenous knowledge and practice need to be the starting points.
3. Funding for the necessary collaborative communication needs to be included from the beginning.
4. Such projects take time and often require 10–15 years of participatory communication and education.
5. Projects should begin at the level of local communities, so that each can build from their own strengths and opportunities.
6. Particular attention should be paid to gender roles, as women produce 60–80 per cent of household food. Projects should address social, economic, cultural, and time constraints for women in local situations.
7. Methods need to be created for evaluating participatory communication methodologies that still seem to many a waste of time. Building baseline quantitative and qualitative measures into projects and using representative samples will help to give donors hard evidence of the necessity of these methods.
8. Researchers, educators, farmers, experts, and communicators should work as a collaborative team, taking turns in leading and learning to increase possibilities for sustainability.

Through hard experience of failures in the field, many former development agencies are evolving such methodologies of post-development where the key issue is no longer what experts advise but what local communities want and need. As this work evolves, its contours begin to coincide more and more with liberation psychologies.

Counter-development

Esteva and Prakash (1998) suggest that many communities may not want large-scale development. Instead of unlimited "progress," social majorities in local settings around the world may prefer "humility" and "austerity" through which they protect their commons and community from the chronic and insatiable sense of inequity, scarcity, and envy that modern development has produced. They may decide to maintain their cultural values through a sense of proportionality, harmony, and appropriateness of human scale. Esteva and Prakash (1998) suggest that "In its essence, austerity means bringing common sense back into political life," so that what is preserved above all is a "graceful playfulness" allowing a recovery of "the sense of community in personal relationships" (p. 204).

By rejecting development as a term to describe the overarching *telos* of psychological and economic life, we are in conversation with many others who are rethinking an old paradigm of dehumanizing material "progress", which has dominated public planning and education for centuries. We join Helena Norberg-Hodge (1991) in advocating for what she calls "counter-development." While living in Ladakh, she observed individuals and communities being bombarded by messages to emulate an energy and capital-intensive Western lifestyle that derogated their own culture, and undercut sustainability through the acquisitive individualism it fostered.

Ironically, while the ideals of economic development were being promoted in Asia, Africa, and Latin America, visionaries were beginning to proclaim the untenability of continuing along the same path in the "developed" world. Many environmentalists were realizing the massive pollution and destruction of the environment in the United States and Europe that resulted from unregulated corporate and industrial expansion.

Sociologists were noting the deterioration of family- and community-support structures, and psychologists the emptiness, loneliness, and sense of fatalism experienced by many across economic divides. While people in Ladakh are being presented with an impossibly glamorous vision of globalization by corporate advertising as well as film and television scripts that emphasize "the life styles of the rich and famous," the failure of this vision to create meaningful lives in the very countries that have spawned these images has yet to be fully grasped. At the same time, many in the West who support development are also not yet aware of its destructive effects.

Norberg-Hodge (1991) notes: "The majority of taxpayers are largely unaware of the impact of projects they are helping to fund. At most, perhaps, they hear of the building of roads and hospitals in impoverished regions, and assume this constitutes an improvement" (p. 158). They are unaware of the bargains struck under the guise of development. For instance, urgent health needs may be temporarily addressed, as rights to natural resources are sold out from under a community. Many people think of buying foreign-made goods as supporting workers, unaware of the exploitation and the relative lack of labor standards and workplace and environmental safeguards they suffer.

> They tend to believe that they can best support poor countries by buying their products, without realizing that rural communities in the Third World might be better off in the long term growing food for themselves and local markets, rather than coffee, cocoa, and rice for markets in the West. Very little is heard of communities that are relatively independent economically and would prefer to stay that way, like the Chipko women, who hug trees in the Himalayan foothills to prevent logging companies from felling them.
>
> (pp. 158–9)

In rural Asia, where transnational corporations have sold expensive pesticides and hybrid seeds as a solution to hunger produced by the export of natural resources and the degradation of the environment, many people are unaware that there is a profound concern among people in the West about toxic chemical residues, industrial foods, and poor air and water quality. They do not know that our cities suffer from traffic gridlocks, crowding, alienation, unemployment, and violence as a result of "progress" and "development" that has already occurred. Norberg-Hodge calls this version of progress "the development hoax."

When she traveled back to the United States, Norberg-Hodge saw people creating sustainable farming practices and experimenting with modes of being in community that had been orienting roots of communal life in Ladakh, but which were now being thrown over in a hopeless effort to emulate Western practices. While Ladakhis were trying to distance themselves from their own culture that had been pronounced as inferior by development rhetoric, others elsewhere were trying to discover sustainable practices to move toward a different future than the ecocide being predicted. As a result of this destructive information gap, Norberg-Hodge proposes another form of liberation psychology, an enormous investment in dialogue and information sharing between regions under the stress of "development" and those regions considered "developed." Rather than the infliction of exported practices and values in a pseudosharing, each side needs to learn about what forms of communal life are being fragmented, wasted, and destroyed and what in each locale is treasured as valuable and satisfying. We all need to learn more about alternatives—sustainable traditions of traditional agriculture and new experiments with permaculture, organic farming, bioregionalism, solar power, and windmills. According to Norberg-Hodge (1991):

> The primary goal of "counter-development" would be to provide people with the means to make fully informed choices about their own future. Using every possible form of communication, from satellite television to storytelling, we need to publicize the fact that today's capital and energy-intensive trends are simply unsustainable. Ultimately the goal would be to promote self-respect and self-reliance, thereby protecting life sustaining diversity and creating the conditions for locally based truly sustainable development.
>
> (p. 160)

Psychological counter-development

In the framework of liberation psychology, we want to apply this concept of counter-development to psychological life as well. The development hoax of psychological life is the idea of the "normal" well-adjusted and happy adult, a "Catch-22" situation. To be happy and well adjusted is a false ideal in many life circumstances. When the wealthiest 20 per cent of the world's people use 86 per cent of the goods, and earn 74 times the income of the poorest 20 per cent, it may be that those who are worried, anxious, sleepless, or depressed are having the most compassionate, healthy, and realistic responses. We need to discern with others what we regularly silence about the misgivings and doubts our lives and actions create; and to explore what kinds of negative affects and symptoms we suffer as a result of what we assume are our own individual problems. Again and again in our participatory work with groups, people awaken to the fact that some of the most deeply repressed and shameful feelings of failure and fear are shared by most people in the group and therefore must in some way be related to their social and cultural context. These are painful and liberatory moments as people break with dominant modes of thought to discover new forms of solidarity and kinship. There are ample periods of joyful insight as people begin a process of creative work that yields images of renewal and new possibilities for making a difference. As psychologists, we are proposing that there is a mirroring effect between political and economic institutions and psychic constructs. The oppression and domination in a culture are echoed in the skewed and polarized dynamics of thought and feeling. While some might hope that his/her individual development can be won in the face of contributing to or being a silent bystander to others' oppression and suffering, we will argue that in either instance psychological well-being is grossly compromised, in ways about which we have become desensitized (see Chapter 5).

From development to liberation

Sachs (1992) and Esteva (1992) argue that it is time to dismantle the mental structure and language of "development," including that which is still attached to it in the form of opposition, such as "underdevelopment" and "counter-development." We intend "liberation" as a holistic term that urges us to consider the links between economic, political, sociocultural, spiritual, and psychological transformation. In its holistic intent, it helps us to resist thinking that one could be psychologically liberated or individuated while economically or culturally enslaved or knowingly or unknowingly curtailing of the freedom of others. Liberation psychology links the interior with the exterior, widening its focus to include community, holding "self" and "other," body and soul together. In doing so, our encounters and treatment of others are as carefully reflected upon as our relation to ourselves. The self is seen to be diminished if the other—person, nature, or group—is only grasped as a means to one's own gratification: objectified, appropriated, and de-animated. There is a sustained attempt to witness the thoughts and feelings of the other, drawing back from attributions and projections upon the other that serve the ends of the self (see Chapter 10). Liberation psychologies try to understand how and why others in the community as well as parts of the self are silenced or unheard. They nurture milieus that encourage a restoration of voice. They seek to understand the psychologies of ego-defense that yield greed, hatred, violence, or amnesia about the suffering of self and others.

Contested history of the term "liberation"

We are aware that the concept of "liberation" also has a contested history from which we need to differentiate our efforts, and our present decision to use it. In a historical time when "liberation" is used as a misnomer for military occupation, when the desire of the victor is proclaimed to be the desire of the oppressed, it is necessary to further clarify our usage of the term "liberation." We do not intend by the term "liberation" any of the earlier historical meanings that suggest that a group can be "liberated" by another group working on its behalf. Sometimes "liberation" has been used with the sense of doing something *for* others: "freeing" them, or "helping" them to become not what they desire for themselves but what their "helpers" desire. This usage carries implications of "missionary" work, with the inequalities of power that have characterized colonial relationships. The "liberators" in this scenario have already arrived at some pre-established height in a hierarchy of their own construction. They have become more complete and advanced people who are carrying to the "underprivileged" messages of faith, rationality, adaptation, or "development." Such a euphemism for cultural invasion is not what we are talking about by using the term "liberation." Neither are we speaking of simplistic attempts to escape into a reductive binary of oppressed and oppressors, neglecting the reality that at different moments, one finds oneself on different sides of this fence. We are not describing processes that can be won through violence and military superiority.

Our use of the word "liberation" is intended differently. We propose instead a way of understanding the psychological maiming that affects all involved in oppressive practices—different wounds to our humanity, but wounds, nevertheless. Liberation must involve insight, restoration, and an opening for greater humanity for victims as well as perpetrators, bystanders, and witnesses—a theme to which we shall return in Chapters 4, 5, 6, and 7.

Liberation as jailbreak

We want to talk about a type of liberation that people can do *with* one another, but that no one can do *for* another; a kind of jailbreak in which we find the fullness of ourselves and our communities. One begins this participatory project with a sense of all that is still unknown in self and other. In this scenario, what is imprisoned in silence, yearning, and marginalization, will have a chance to escape into image, language, symbol, performance, and action. "Expertise" will be in the negative: learning how to empty oneself of already learned identifications and specializations to create space for listening and imagining, where one can dream new scripts and alternative ways of being in the world. This space is dialogical, welcoming conversation where monologue has reigned, within oneself and between oneself and others. One does this together with others, recovering sources of creativity and power, entering community rather than standing aside as bystanders or detached reporters. This space is co-creative. The rules one has lived by, the identities one has imagined as one's own origin, and the identities of others one imagined as different, begin to shift and transform in this understanding of liberation. Liberation psychologies begin at the edge of what has already been known and named. They begin with a wandering in the desert where one questions and deconstructs in dialogue the fixed compass that has been orienting one's identifications.

Liberation psychologies join communal traditions in diverse places where there exists longing for basic needs to be met reliably, where children might enjoy peaceful childhoods and supportive education, where issues of importance can be engaged dialogically, where those at the margins can be welcomed and supported, where difficult and conflictual issues can be worked through, and where the earth is protected and restored. Here the potential liveliness within each of us is set free and enjoyed in the "milk and honey" of conversation, the arts, and loving relationships with each another. The incarnation of these longings begins with a wandering in the desert as one attempts to sort through the ways of colonial thinking that bind one to an old order. Each person educated within dominant culture will have to go through a process of critical discernment—what Freire called "conscientization," and the liberation theologian Kolvenbach (2000) called "conversion"—as we attempt to grasp what it is we actually suffer from (see Chapters 4, 5, 6, and 7) and begin to articulate what has previously been unsayable (see Chapters 8, 9, and 10).

Liberation and the new commons

Many individuals and communities have embraced this challenge, and are now embarked on creating what Esteva (1992) and others have called the "new commons." Often carved out of hostile territory, they have rejected development's reduction of their humanity to economic terms, and are taking steps to affirm their dignity. Reducing their dependence on foreign markets, they have sought to reorder their priorities and values to ones that can sustain their hearts, souls, and bodies. Esteva (2006a) hears a shift in the way community is being spoken about, from a group asking for rights to be granted from above to a group linked by mutual obligations. The fulfilling of these obligations brings forth the new in the present.

Like the assisted regeneration of struggling landscapes in the midst of encroaching desertification, these communities have sought to place some protective fencing between themselves and that which encroaches upon them. Through oral history and dialogue they have taken an inventory of those cultural values and practices that are present, in both mature form and as seedlings, and those that have been lost and need to be refound. Just as in assisted regeneration, such processes of liberation—upon which the emergence of new commons depends—are born in a deep faith in our regenerative capacities.

Liberation psychologies set goals beyond and in place of development. Their aspirations are for networks of renewed communities in dialogue and solidarity, made up of individuals who have broken with the colonial and hierarchical ideologies of the past, and are attempting together to discern peaceful and sustainable paths forward. The first steps toward these outcomes involve turning toward the psychological wounds—the symptoms and signs of suffering—caused by current social arrangements for everyone involved. This will be the work of the next four chapters.

Part II Psychic Wounds of Colonialism and Globalization

Shortly before his early death, Frantz Fanon (1967a) wrote: "Today, I believe in the possibility of love; that is why I endeavor to trace its imperfections; its perversions" (p. 42). Fanon and Memmi described these perversions as they developed during the national liberation struggle in Algeria in the late 1950s, analyzing the psychic amputations and mutilations of the self that colonial dynamics set in motion. While globalization has rearranged how power and privilege operate, this has not benefited the majority of the peoples of the world; on the contrary, pernicious wounds occasioned by inequity, injustice, and violence continue to be inflicted, often in new forms and intensities. A starting point for psychologies of liberation is creating awareness of how much of our most intimate psychological orientation and suffering are connected with the historical and cultural contexts in which we live and the ways we have learned to think about them.

Psychologies of liberation sometimes draw on concepts developed by psychologies of the unconscious (depth psychologies), extending them to make links with historical and environmental conditions. In this section of the book, we will explore how this linkage can enhance the understanding of the suffering and symptoms that are reactions to living in situations of violence and inequity. Understanding psyches within the context of ideology, culture, and history can help us to break with the past, and provide fuel for efforts to create a world that is less wounding in the present and future. In order to make good use of psychologies of the unconscious, it is also important to understand why they have often failed to make the links required by liberation psychologies. Part of the work of liberation psychologies has been to free the theoretical contributions of psychoanalysis from the clinical consulting room, as well as from an exclusive focus on interiority, in order to bring such interiority back into community life where it originated (Chapter 4).

With the help of concepts from depth psychology, we analyze the unconscious effects of colonialism and globalization in Chapters 5, 6, and 7. Since the beginning of the eighteenth century, there have arisen detailed descriptions, whole phenomenologies, of the tragic psychic effects of violence. The preponderance of such work has focused on the psychology of victims of oppression (Chapter 7). While this effort has been crucial, it is also necessary to understand the psychic outcomes of being bystanders to injustice, of attempting to live daily life detached from the violence around one by defending against knowing about it too fully or allowing its presence to change the way life is led (Chapter 5). In addition, the psychic structures of those perpetrating violence and oppression need to be understood to undo the cycles of misery they put into motion for others, cycles which further deform themselves, their families, and accomplices (Chapter 6).

The narratives of coherent history and identity of a modernist nation shatter under the weight of unmourned violence. Public discourse is recognized as being shot through with ideology, lies, and silence about the past that cannot be spoken. Collective accounts no longer match up with daily life, and we enter the pastiche of experience that is now called the postmodern. Chela Sandoval (2000) calls this situation "a violently fragmented condition." Yet she suggests that the idea of solid identity in resonance with official history was always a fantasy reserved for the privileged. The process of colonialism was always played out against a backdrop of the fragmented experience, "the shattered minds and bodies" (p. 32) of all those marginalized by power and position – the colonized, enslaved, or disenfranchised. Today, in the process of globalization this process of disintegration reaches even the privileged according to Sandoval:

> If ... first world citizen-subjects are increasingly "unable to unify past, present, and future" of their own psychic lives, then citizen-subjects are entering the emotional state of peoples whose native territories were replaced, their bodies subordinated to other dominants, their futures unclear.
>
> (p. 33)

Where do the psychic states of bystanders, perpetrators, and victims overlap, and where do their experiences sharply divide? Shoshana Felman (1992), in her discussion of the documentary *Shoah*, maps these locations in relation to the Holocaust. She reflects on how the Holocaust was a "historical assault on seeing" (p. 209), which took different forms for victims, perpetrators, and bystanders. In the film, a story is related that points to what often could not be seen by the very victims of the Holocaust. An old Jewish man in a railway car, on route to a death camp, asks a boy outside the window where they are. The boy replied with a gesture, drawing his finger across his throat. Reportedly, the Jews who saw this gesture could not figure out what it meant. Felman comments that the Jews "see but they do not understand the purpose and destination of what they see: overwhelmed by loss and by deception, they are blind to the significance of what they witness" (p. 208). What could be seen exceeds what is seen, "due to the inherent blinding nature of the occurrence" (p. 255). She contrasts this with the Nazis' relation to seeing. Here there is enormous effort to make the visible invisible, to keep the camps and what was transpiring in them unseen. A chilling expression of this is the Gestapo's plan to reopen each mass grave and to burn the corpses. The witnesses to the extermination are already dead, yet, says Felman, the "corpses still continue to materially witness their own murderers. The scheme of the erasure of the witnesses must therefore be completed by the literal erasure—by the very burning—of the bodies. The witness must, quite literally, burn out, and burn out of sight" (p. 226). The effort and need to know, once deprived of what might have been seen, collapses and is replaced by an air of normality. Perpetrators need an enormous number of active and passive allies and accomplices to collude with their attempt to render the possibly seen unseeable.

The last position Felman describes is that of the bystander. Using the stance of some Poles who lived near the death camps, Felman describes this position: "The Poles, unlike the Jews, *do* see but, as bystanders, they do not quite *look*, they avoid looking directly, and thus they overlook at once their responsibility and their complicity as witnesses:"

> You couldn't look there. You couldn't talk to a Jew. Even going by on the road, you couldn't look there.
> *Did they look anyway?*
> Yes, vans came and the Jews were moved farther off. You could see them, but on the sly. In sidelong glances.
>
> (in Felman, 1992, p. 208)

Understanding these three positions, each "an amputation of seeing" (Felman, 1992), is a critical part of liberation psychologies. Each position breeds distinctive psychic configurations, evidenced by what cannot be seen and heard. Yet as distinctive as they are, they are not always discrete. For instance, during the Holocaust, it was possible that an inmate of a death camp could be involved in all three stances, as victim, bystander, and, at times, accomplice to the perpetrators. On the other hand, it was also possible for very ordinary people to resist the amputation of their sight so that they could be witnesses to what was happening. They managed to reject the safety and neutrality of bystanding, as well as the destructive power of perpetrating violence on others. Liberation psychologies have to understand these alternative actions as well.

While extermination camps are very extreme conditions, today many people live within systems that may victimize them at certain junctions, and at others provide them with privileges borne of the victimization of others, all the while being bystanders to ongoing atrocities and oppressions. Psychically one may be fraught with varying conscious and unconscious approaches to seeing, which include avoiding seeing, efforts to keep the seen invisible, and interpretive dodges that allow one not to fully understand the meanings of what one sees. It is also important to note that there are many people who see clearly, witness and resist oppression, and who stand up for truth and justice in very difficult and sometimes dangerous situations.

In Chapter 4, we explore part of the history of depth psychology, attempting to make use of some of its most powerful insights while at the same time explaining its own erasures of seeing in historical context (Watkins, 2000a). We reflect on the ways in which depth psychology has worked with psychological symptoms that mark and announce problematic aspects of one's life: personal and communal. The systematic misreading of psychological symptoms, by sufferers as well as the therapists who assist them, help to sustain the current arrangements one is part of, despite the fact that these arrangements themselves cause psychological misery. While it is most often clear to victims of oppression that their circumstances need to change, the psychic costs of bystanding and perpetrating violence and oppression are less well recognized (Staub, 1993). Without such recognition, efforts to change oppressive cultural arrangements will be stalemated. For this reason, we begin with the positions of bystanding and perpetration in Chapters 5 and 6, continuing in Chapter 7 to the psychic wounds associated with suffering collective trauma of various kinds. This work is necessarily provisional, as we, the authors, doubtless suffer from some of the same conditions we are writing about, and are unable to assume fully the kind of distance that would lend greater perspective. Immersed in a period of rapid globalization, we cannot in any complete way name the psychic wounds that are developing in our midst. We are caught in an unavoidable tension, that of finding ourselves still learning from earlier writers such as Fanon and Memmi, who came from a modernist mind-set and described the mutilations of the self caused by colonial relations, while at the same time developing a (post)colonial point of view on subjectivities within the context of globalization.

4
Symptoms and Psychologies in Cultural Context

> Our lives begin to end the day we become silent about things that matter.
>
> (Martin Luther King, Jr.)

Symptoms as memorials in depth psychologies

Liberation psychologies teach that environments of injustice, violence, and repression have powerful psychological effects on everyone, whether they are registered consciously or unconsciously. When there is no public language or space to discuss these effects, they may turn into painful somatic symptoms of seemingly unknown origin that are misattributed to other factors. Such misattribution makes it impossible to address the roots of these symptoms.

All forms of depth psychology share the idea that human consciousness is shot through with possibilities for dissociation, that is, the unconscious elimination of painful knowledge from conscious awareness. Such unconscious strategies range from psychic numbing, disavowal, doubling, and splitting of consciousness to the development of somatic symptoms, and, ultimately, projection of painful affects onto others. The notion of dissociation helps us to understand that what one is currently aware of may leave out of consciousness many issues that are deeply troubling.

There is little in life that is more intimate and private than the suffering of symptoms, such as sleeplessness, depression, tension, anxiety, disabling fears, and unexpected bodily pains. Interrupting the flow of daily lives, they arrest attention, even when one cannot penetrate their reasons. Reading symptoms, struggling to hear their messages, is fraught with difficulty for it is the very nature of psychological symptoms to mark and to hide meanings at the same moment. The symptom provides a trace, a vestige, of what cannot yet be fully seen, leading archetypal psychologist James Hillman (1975) to say that "the eye and the wound are the same" (p. 107).

53

Peter Shabad (2000) introduces the idea of symptoms as memorials in his essay "The most intimate of creations: Symptoms as memorials to one's lonely suffering." He says, "[s]ymptoms may be viewed as self-created communicative actions intended to build a lasting monument once and for all to one's experience of suffering" (p. 207).

Insofar as the symptom memorializes something that must at the same moment be hidden, it holds in its heart that which has not yet been seen and understood. Premature erasure of symptoms by drugs can destroy a fragile, potential bridge, leaving the site of where we are struggling in our lives utterly disconnected from the meanings and understandings that we desperately need to orient us.

At their best, depth psychologies built on an understanding of unconscious processes have understood the importance of apprenticing to and learning from a symptom, of following it to the unsaid and unseen. They have taken care to learn how to walk the bridge between symptoms and their meanings, moving toward rather than away from the knowledge that symptoms bear. A radical practice in depth therapies of all kinds—such as psychoanalytic, Jungian, Adlerian, Reichian, and existential-phenomenological—is to wait patiently with a symptom, countering the ego's efforts to flee from the uncomfortable and the disturbing. At times one waits with what has been so muted that it has fallen into the body and given rise to physical illness and pain.

Within depth psychological traditions, there has been disagreement about the appropriate way to interpret and work with symptoms, reflecting controversy over how the psychological is formed and affected, and about the relationship between cultural context and psyche. Drive theories have understood symptoms as arising from the vicissitudes of conflicting internal needs. Object relations theorists have traced symptoms back to early difficulties in the child's affective relationship to the mother or primary caretaker. Those taking an archetypal view have seen symptoms arising out of the struggle of archetypal dominants. For Jungians, the issue may be seen as one of blocked life paths. Yet, often depth psychologists fail to make links between the inner lives of individuals and the outer environments in which their symptoms and identities evolve. Many practitioners take a universalist approach to psychological dynamics, obscuring the local cultural constructions of identity in which symptoms occur.

From our perspective, waiting and listening to symptoms must have a triple orientation: toward the symptom, toward the listener's theoretical and ideological commitments, and toward surrounding social and institutional contexts. We want to nourish this triple listening, aware that psychological theories can interpret symptoms and states too narrowly. This is particularly so when the theories themselves are marked by the social amnesia so characteristic of the individualistic paradigm common to capitalist societies. Russell Jacoby (1975) defines social amnesia as "society's repression of remembrance of its own past" (p. 5). It is produced through the process of social reification, the formation of ideologies that are favored by current social arrangements. These frameworks of understanding help to preserve the status quo distribution of social and economic power. The illusion is promoted that the ideologies that have been constructed are "natural," inevitable, and preferable. Such processes of reification create their own historical narratives. This contributes to "memory [being] driven out of the mind by the social and economic dynamics" of the society (Jacoby, 1975, p. 4). We will see in the examples below how social amnesia contributes to the misreading of symptoms—psychological and physical.

As part of the theoretical basis for liberation psychologies, we want to be able to draw on the insights of psychologies of the unconscious, but not always in their current form. In this chapter, we will look at how depth understandings of the relations between psyche and the surrounding culture were partially lost in the extension of psychoanalysis from pre–World War II Europe to postwar America. Part of the labor of psychologies of liberation today is to restore and extend an understanding of how institutional contexts and ideological constructs affect psychological health and symptoms of distress. We want to use methodologies and theories of depth psychology to approach psychological symptomatology, but first we need to understand depth psychology's own connections to the social conditions where it developed (Watkins, 2000b).

Early psychoanalysis and social justice

It would be difficult to tell from much of the contemporary mainstream practice of depth psychologies in America that psychoanalysis was conceived in an atmosphere of acute consciousness of social inequalities and their impact on mental health and the provision of psychological treatment. In its early chapters, psychoanalysis understood the deleterious effects of bourgeois conventionality on psychic vitality, and carefully challenged it while also being politically astute about psychoanalysis' need for mainstream support of its practices. In *Freud's free clinics: Psychoanalysis and social justice, 1918–1938*, Elizabeth Danto (2005) chronicles this now rarely considered early history of the psychoanalytic movement, forged in the aftermath of the economic and social devastation of World War I.

Many early psychoanalytic practitioners were engaged Marxists, socialists, or social democrats, whose practice of depth psychology issued from hopes of liberation on both social and psychological fronts, fronts which were seen as inextricably intertwined. Prominent members of the early psychoanalytic movement who were Marxists included Erich Fromm, Otto Fenichel, Gustav Landauer, Annie Reich; socialists included Bruno Bettleheim, Greta Bibring, Helene Deutsch, Ernst Simmel, and Siegfried Bernfeld; communists included Edith Jacobson, Marie Langer, and Wilhelm Reich; and social democrats included Karen Horney, Paul Federn, and Sigmund Freud (Danto, 2005, p. 9).

In the early period of psychoanalysis forged in Red Vienna, psychoanalysts were personally involved in initiatives for free clinics for psychoanalytic treatment, free clinics for reproductive health care and education for women, experimental schools for children of the poor, the kindergarten movement, school-based treatment centers for children traumatized by war and poverty, settlement house psychology classes for workers, the first child guidance clinics, and suicide prevention centers. They paid attention to building conditions for peace and stability in Austria and Europe, initiatives to help women struggle against various forms of domination and control, and architectural initiatives for public housing that would help build urban families' sense of community, understood to undergird psychological health (Danto, 2005). Their advocacy for children issued from the extensive needs of children after World War I, psychoanalytic insight into the importance of early childhood development for later psychological health, and awareness of the traumatizing effects of poverty on child development.

The whitening of psychoanalysis and the loss of "night vision"

When Freud was invited to give his first lectures in America at Clark University in 1909, he hesitated to accept, suspicious about the fate of psychoanalysis in the cultural landscape of America. He grew contemptuous of medicalized analysis in the United States that was politically conservative and generative of excessive affluence for its practitioners (Danto, 2005, p. 13). Freud's critique presciently foreshadowed the changes psychoanalysis would undergo in its transplantation to the United States.

Many Jewish émigré analysts sought refuge in America to escape death-dealing anti-Semitism in Europe followed by the Holocaust. Russell Jacoby (1983) argues that the transplanted analysts suppressed their history of social and political engagement in Europe to avoid delays in the United States' naturalization process. Many felt this suppression continued to be necessary because of the political climate in America as the Cold War deepened and McCarthyism erupted. Those with allegiances to Marxism and socialism were afraid they would be seen as communists, as indeed many were.

Altman, psychoanalyst and author of *The analyst in the inner city: Race, class, and culture through a psychoanalytic lens* (1995), argues that when Jewish psychoanalytic émigrés came to America before and during World War II, they were confronted with joining a White profession in America. Many in Europe saw Jews as Black (Gilman, 1993). Edward Said argues in *Freud and the non-European* (2004) that Freud himself understood Jews as non-European. Upon coming to America, many displaced Jewish analysts adopted "unreflectingly a Northern European value system and [sought] upper-class social status" (Altman, 2004, p. 808). To be assimilated into the psychoanalytic establishment, Jewish analysts, Altman argues, underwent a whitening.

Given the personal, familial, and cultural tragedies that had befallen them in Europe, this adaptation is understandable. However, it was to have grave consequences for the practice of depth psychologies in America. Psychoanalysis became whitened and myopic, often indifferent to racial and cultural issues, and unreflective of its own cultural location within a multi-cultural society (Altman, 1995).

Some psychoanalysts were to establish ego psychology, which adopted Northern European and Calvinist undertones, "emphasizing tolerance for frustration and abstention from gratification" (p. 810). Institutes jockeyed for societal prestige by joining the medical establishment and discouraging or outlawing lay analysis done by those without a medical degree, a practice that had encouraged interdisciplinary work and provision of analysis to the economically disadvantaged in Berlin and Vienna. Economic privilege in part was sought by flight from the kinds of public and socialist initiatives popular in Vienna to private practice models that uncritically embraced capitalism and its brutal divisions in the provision of health care.

As psychoanalysis retreated from interest in and commitment to social justice, it took refuge in disease models that undergird the need for individual treatment. The elimination of lay analysis against Freud's wishes, pushed psychoanalysis away from cultural criticism toward medicalized practice. Economic stresses on the health-care system forced a wide adoption of the disease model in the second half of the twentieth century, requiring diagnosis of psychopathology and systematic treatment of it in order to gain payment from third-party insurance. A principal problem with this model is that it locates pathology within individuals, looking only to the most local context of intimate and familial relations for understanding.

Altman (1995) laments that because so many analysts "went White" and pursued privilege, psychoanalysis gave up some of its night vision, trading subversive insight for conformity to the status quo. Altman (2004) describes psychoanalytic's "night vision" as its ability to critique society and to examine its intrapsychic implications from the position of an outsider and critic. Such vision allows us to begin to see what of our psychological suffering is linked with the culture(s) in which we reside. Jacoby (1975) argues that the trade of night vision for professional security has laced American depth practices with social amnesia. To the extent that depth practitioners identify with aspects of White American culture that are not conducive to psychological health, their treatment colludes with the very forces that cause distress. Insofar as psychology itself conserves the elision of slavery and the Native American genocide, it contributes to the defensive structure of the American psyche, rather than to a radical movement that could help develop insight into the psychological legacy of these two founding tragedies. Psychoanalyst Harry Stack Sullivan courageously tried to address the racism and militarism of America, and found himself ostracized by his own colleagues and plagued by financial worries during the final decades of his life (Cushman, 1995). Other analysts in the cultural school of psycho-analysis, such as Fromm and Horney, worked with psychoanalytic insights, reading from them not universal truths but situated conflicts, descriptive of the impact of culture on psyche. The heart of the psychoanalytic movement in the United States ostracized both Fromm and Horney. Wilhelm Reich, radical advocate for women's reproductive rights and to whom we are indebted for inspiring many approaches to psyche/soma healing, was arrested and imprisoned toward the end of his life, on charges of violating interstate commerce laws. He died in an American penitentiary.

Others, such as Fenichel, took their radical cultural ideas underground. Jacoby (1983) chronicles how vague wording began to replace earlier Leftist convictions, as some European analysts felt pressure to disclaim their past advocacy for social change.

Theorists working with depth psychological insights on issues of libera-tion, such as Fanon, Memmi, Césaire, Freire, Martín-Baró, Anzaldúa, Castillo, Morales, Griffin, Sandoval, Montero, Lira, and Dussel, have gone unclaimed as depth psychological theorists in the United States. African-American writ-ers on liberation and psychic decolonization who could have contributed mightily to a distinctly American and multicultural depth psychology, such as DuBois, Douglas, Wright, King, hooks, Cone, and Lorde have been placed outside the canon of a White depth psychology.

To see symptoms in terms of surrounding cultural discourses requires one to confront what has been normalized and taken for granted in the envi-ronment. To question this is to imperil one's own standing within the sta-tus quo. The effort to understand symptoms in the light of cultural construction was too transgressive for most psychoanalysts. Emerging from the Holocaust and the world wars, many psychoanalysts in America, sought refuge in interpretative systems that did not open out into the deep and tragic disarray of the twentieth century, circumscribing the focus of their practice and the understanding of symptoms. This circumscription was consistent with an individualistic sense of the psyche as self-contained and private. It was also a self-protective move. Interpreting symptoms in relation to community and cultural life connects psychological healing with social and cultural transformation. To do so would position depth psychological practice as a countercultural discipline, sacrificing mainstream support and secure financial viability (Cushman, 1995).

In her book *Love in a time of hate: Liberation psychology in Latin America*, Nancy Caro Hollander (1997) has documented the agonizing struggles over the future of psychoanalysis that occurred in urban centers in Latin America. During and after the Holocaust and World War II, many European psychoanalysts also emigrated to Latin America. As in North America there was also a retreat from social and political engagement. During the Dirty Wars in Latin America, some analysts were sadly confronted by a growing awareness of the social nightmare that was unfolding as sons and daughters of patients, friends, and even their own children were disappeared and tortured. During the late 1960s and early 1970s Latin American psychoanalysts argued over the role depth psychologies should play during periods of state terror. Within the Argentine Psychoanalytic Association (APA), newer members with social justice concerns began to dissent from the posture of political neutrality that was officially maintained.

> The dissidents accused the APA of becoming a self-enclosed safe house for an elite professional sector bound to maintain its privilege and thus its alignment with the ruling class and the existing social order. ... They demanded a return to the broader social questions that had once preoccupied psychoanalysts interested in the relationship between individual and social repression.
>
> (pp. 62–3)

Many dissidents broke with the APA in 1971, going on to work with all social classes in hospitals, community clinics, and trade unions. However, as the dictatorships in the Southern Cone became more established, most activist psychologists were arrested or forced into exile. Marie Langer (1992), who began her practice of psychoanalysis in Vienna, fled into exile in Mexico. She was then asked to help construct a mental health system in revolutionary Nicaragua. Her work began to distill those parts of psychoanalysis that could be useful to paraprofessional mental health workers who were aware of the need to contextualize the psychological within the sociopolitical. Today in a neoliberal postdictatorial period, those who survived continue working with the legacies of state terror, to demand accountability, and to develop forms of grassroots democracy and social restoration.

Ignoring and misreading of symptoms

The refusal to listen to symptoms in relation to culture and history by both psychologists and their clients occurs in many parts of the world. When we are not able to follow the symptom into its surrounding context, or when it is too dangerous to do so in authoritarian environments, we often misinterpret its protest and negate its voice. Perhaps we can see this most clearly in extreme examples.

The following of symptom always runs the risk of being foreclosed prematurely, causing one to mistakenly see in the unfamiliar and disturbing the familiar and safe idea. Phillip Cushman (1995) tells a story about how this happened with Melanie Klein's analytic treatment of her own son, Erich. As a psychoanalyst, Klein, an analysand and student of psychoanalyst Karl Abraham, began a move in psychoanalysis away from drive and instinct theory toward object relations theory, the latter focusing on our human interactions and our internalization of them. This move, furthered by Mrs. Klein, was not completed by her, as we shall see. Klein was born into a Jewish family and lived in Germany and Hungary between the two world wars. She was one of the first to begin psychoanalytic treatment of children. For experience in doing work with children, she attempted to treat her own anxious and phobic son, Erich. She wrote about his "case" using a pseudo-nym, disguising his identity as her son.

Klein elicited her son's fantasies through play, and interpreted them to him in an Oedipal light, explaining to him that his anxiety was caused by his wishes to have intercourse with her. Klein's treatment of her son was not working. Erich became more anxious, developing a phobia about going out-side. Redoubling her interpretive efforts had no ameliorating effect.

> For instance, in response to his phobia about venturing outside, she asked him to describe a street that was particularly frightening to him. He answered that the street was one that was filled with young toughs who tormented him. Klein ignored this fact and realized that the street was lined with large trees. She interpreted the trees as phalluses and explained to Erich that this meant that he was desiring his mother, and his anxiety was no doubt caused by the castration anxiety that inevitably followed this desire.
>
> (Cushman, 1995, p. 201)

Klein saw his symptom of anxiety as arising from inherent psychic struc-tures and collective dramas. What is most striking about Mrs. Klein's mis-reading of her son's phobia about going outside is her failure to connect his internal experience of anxiety with the social and political climate of his world. Years later Erich's older brother explained to him that the very street Erich most worried about was visited by youths who tormented him, "bullies [in] an anti-Semitic gang that routinely attacked Jewish children" (Cushman, 1995, p. 201). To complicate the matter of coming to know that which is difficult to know, Klein had never told her son that he was of Jewish descent.

The phobic symptom warned and protected against what could not be directly known and thus said. Like dream images, symptoms may resist enclosure into single understandings, inadequate to their call. They can persevere in their protest, continuing to disable, giving one the opportunity to submit to their tutelage, until one has heard their multiple messages; but there is also the possibility that they may collapse into mute collusion with the status quo.

In China during periods of political oppression and chronic hunger, neurasthenia or generalized malaise was explained as a biological condition and treated with drugs, silencing the protest of the body and the mind, and thus contributing to the maintenance of oppressive political power structures (Shulman-Lorenz, 1997a). In Brazil, those affected by hunger might explain their weakness as *nervos,* or nervous exhaustion, rather than confront social policies that produced food shortages. In a chilling example of misreading symptoms, anthropologist Nancy Scheper-Hughes (1995a) describes how in Northeast Brazil, there was a systematic avoidance of discussion about infant starvation and dehydration, which in some areas resulted in infant mortality rates as high as 40 per cent. Tragically, rather than following symptoms to accurately understand the situations of infant illness, Scheper-Hughes found them often misattributed to an inborn aversion to life (at least in discussions with the visiting American researcher). In the poorest areas of the Northeast, sickly infants, regarded as not having the "knack for living," were left to die in the corners of their households due to the impossible economic situations of their families. This discourse protects against the full onslaught of awareness regarding the ravages of poverty that assault so many families, mitigates against a loss of face, and works against a confrontation with one's sense of powerlessness to protect one's own children. To properly read the infants' symptoms of starvation and dehydration would require the possibly dangerous acknowledgment of how unjust land ownership and wealth distribution result in tragic inadequacies of food and clean water, even for the youngest of a society's members. To alleviate these symptoms would require that the protest of the symptom be taken to a public arena that is itself dis-eased. Too often this may seem impossible for the poorest.

Yet, ignored symptoms can often gather force like a recurring dream that finally breaks into a nightmare to gain attention. After the nuclear meltdown at Chernobyl, Adolf Harash traveled there to provide trauma treatment for the survivors. He chillingly related the frequency with which workers at the former plant confided that they had been visited by dreams and nightmares about the "accident" before it happened. Most had never told anyone about these symptomatic dreams, pushing them to the side. To voice misgivings about plant safety was felt to be disloyal to the government. To heed nightmares as potential sources of knowledge was a disavowed practice in Soviet life at that time (Watkins, 1992). The position of bystander, to which we soon turn, often entails bystanding in relation to not only an objective situation that asks for our attention but also an ignoring of how this situation gives rise to unbidden thoughts, dreams, images, and feelings within. One becomes a bystander to one's own psychic reality, disabling one's capacity to change the situations of which one is a part.

In faithfully submitting to the tutelage of symptoms, Hillman emerged from several decades in the psychotherapeutic consulting room to admit, like others before him, that psychological distress cannot be cordoned off from the distresses of the world of which one is a part.

My practice tells me that I can no longer distinguish clearly between neurosis of self and neurosis of world, psychopathology of self and psychopathology of world. Moreover, it tells me that to place neurosis and psychopathology solely in personal reality is a delusional repression of what is actually, realistically, being experienced. This further implies that my theories of neurosis and categories of psychopathology must be radically extended if they are not to foster the very pathologies that my job is to ameliorate.

(Hillman, 1992, p. 93)

The most radical spirit of psychoanalysis requires that one follow symptoms across the boundaries of paradigms and familiar interpretations, if called; that one take note of what one begins to see that would ordinarily cause one to retreat to a narrower lens. Liberation psychologies throughout the world ask that one forsake the safety of the narrowly construed "psychological," by placing oneself in dialogue situations with others that break open one's normalized assumptions, allowing one to see the interconnections between the psychological, the historical, the socioeconomic, and the spiritual. Without this transgression of disciplinary boundaries, an individual suffering pathology is unable to ferret out the ways in which his symptoms speak of the effects of the larger context that create suffering for others as well as himself. Without this transgression, doing psychotherapy becomes limited to working out personal solutions and accommodations to much larger social issues, without affecting or even clarifying consciousness about the wider context that may require insight and transformation to prevent further psychological suffering.

Loosened from a myopic individualistic paradigm, one can begin to wonder where the dis-ease is that gives rise to symptoms (Watkins, 1992; Shulman-Lorenz, 1997a). Might not many personal symptoms signal cultural pathology (Selig, 2003)? Arthur Kleinman (1988), a psychiatrist and anthropologist, works cross-culturally and epidemiologically to shine light on how our psychological disorders reflect cultural pathology. Cross-cultural studies of psychopathology allow us to see that the *Diagnostic and statistical manual*, which American psychiatry has developed to describe and export its understanding of psychological syndromes, portrays as "character disorders" syndromes that turn out to be relational disorders of the West and the North: paranoid, schizoid, antisocial, borderline, histrionic, avoidant, dependent, obsessive-compulsive, and narcissistic disorders. Dysthymic disorder, anorexia, and agoraphobia may not be valid cross-cultural categories (Kleinman, 1988). That the cultural differences provoked by gender profoundly impact mental health is amply displayed by the greater frequency in women of the following "disorders": borderline, histrionic, dependent, agoraphobia, major depression, panic disorder, somatization disorder, somatoform disorder, conversion disorder, pain disorder, dissociative identity disorder, anorexia, and bulimia.

In addition, the course and prognosis of various disorders is directly affected by cultural context. The most stunning example of this is schizophrenia that is eight times more prevalent in social situations where there is limited social belonging and a high sense of fatalism (Shulman-Lorenz, 1997a). Despite American psychopharmacological sophistication, many sufferers of schizophrenia in America endure a course of the illness that is more severe and chronic than similar sufferers in Third World countries such as India, where the disorder is seen as acute (not chronic) and the individual is not isolated from the community and deprived of work (Kleinman, 1988). Shulman-Lorenz (1997a) notes further that those suffering from schizophrenia and other serious diagnoses fare better in cultures where there is a greater tolerance and acceptance of their symptomatology, where personality may be seen as less fixed and personhood as less bounded and separate, and where there are healing rituals that include the community in calling one back to health.

Epidemiological studies reveal the impact of each of the following cultural pathologies on the increased incidence of psychopathology: poverty, the effects of Western capitalism on Third World countries and the poor and working classes within First World countries, urbanization, population mobility, family fragmentation, class inequities, poor and inadequate housing and education, gender inequities, racism, homophobia, torture, rapid social change and social disintegration, war, genocide, forced migration, unemployment, and failures of social- and community-support structures (Kleinman, 1988). The fact that "most mental disorders have their highest prevalence rates in the lowest socioeconomic class" (Kleinman, 1988, p. 54), where there is least access to security, resources, adequate food and housing, and health care, should give added weight to liberation psychologies' "preferential option for the poor." The very construction of the concept of "mental disorder" contributes to a serious misreading of social conditions as personal problems.

Theodor Adorno spoke of psyche as "the distillation of history" (in Jacoby, 1975). To approach psychological symptoms, liberation psychologies ask one to open up one's lens to the last 500 years of history that has been marked by the rise of colonialism, its parallel in hierarchical and dissociative ways of thinking, and its current transmutation into neocolonialism and exploitative forms of transnational capitalism (Shulman-Lorenz & Watkins, 2002a, 2003). We propose that it is this wider historical landscape, marked by tragic dismissals and assaults levied by one group on another, which has shaped the societal context in which our individual personalities have been formed. In the following three chapters, we will take up the task of linking psychological and somatic symptoms with both ideologies and social structures, building on the work of many liberation psychologists who have forged these connections.

5
From Bystanding toward Engaged Witness

> The emptier our hearts become, the greater will be our crimes. ... It is a terrible and inexorable law that one cannot deny the humanity of another without diminishing one's own: in the face of one's victim, one sees oneself.
>
> (James Baldwin, 1961, p. 66)

Bystanding

While many of those oppressed have described the intrapsychic wounds that are spawned by the dislocations and culture-cides of colonialism and globalization, those who have profited most from colonialism and transnational capitalism have had disincentives to reflect on the psychological correlates of being involved in oppressive structures. In large-scale industrialized societies, it has been hardest to recognize, describe, and begin to address the pathologies of bystanding. These pathologies are often normalized. Their cultural roots are unacknowledged; their dynamics largely unexamined; and their societal function unnamed. Bystanding allows status quo distributions of power and privilege to go unchecked, giving rise to what Arno Gruen (2007) has called the "insanity of normality." To question the psychic damage exacted through bystanding often requires unflinching examination of the psychic cost of privilege. Perhaps, if the mutilations of self that bystanding entails were more widely recognized, the courage could be gathered to confront the situations to which one otherwise capitulates. For those in colonizing cultures, colonial ideologies have contributed to dissociating the personal from the political, building a sense of private interiority that is strangely disconnected from historical and cultural context.

While there is a long history of individuals and activist organizations that have compassionately witnessed and taken a stand against oppression and marginalization in colonizing countries, many people have also been deeply socialized to be bystanders, taking retreat in a focus on the personal and a pursuit of happiness carried out within a very narrow range of life with family and friends. For those raised in educational systems that stress individualism, it becomes difficult to formulate ideas about the way one's own social environment and those of others affect one's well-being. Many cannot imagine themselves speaking out publicly or rocking the boat by asking painful and difficult questions. Bystanders may have been taught that protest is ineffective, that authorities know better, that getting to the roots of unjust power is impossible, and that the systems that manufacture injustice and violence are beyond one's control. Bystanders avoid talking with others with different points of view that might challenge their normalized perspectives.

Who and what profits from this level of psychic disenfranchisement? What psychic toll is paid by such retreat from necessary outcry and creative efforts to shape the environments in which one lives? What feelings lay unclaimed? Habitual bystanding is pernicious because its psychological toll goes so unacknowledged. It is as though there is a chronic illness of which one is unaware. To heal it, one must begin to experience it. Yet it is this very difficulty in experiencing it that is part of the illness. It is only by looking compassionately and deeply at oneself in dialogue with others—and not through the prism of guilt—that one can begin to make out the contours of the landscape one is living in.

To break out of bystanding is sometimes dangerous to the status quo in one's familial, work, and community relationships. It takes courage. It can result in the loss of jobs, marriages, friends, cultural capital, freedoms, and even lives. Ervin Staub (2003) describes moral courage as the "ability and willingness to act according to one's important values even in the face of opposition, disapproval, and the danger of ostracism" (p. 8). Yet, not to break with bystanding is injurious to one's sense of self and of solidarity with others. Psychically being a bystander to injustice and violence breeds disconnection, passivity, fatalism, a sense of futility, and failures in empathic connection.

Bystanding leads to very particular and intense symptomology that we want to explore in the light of depth psychologies. In the next part of this chapter, we will describe 12 symptoms of socially sanctioned bystanding that have been widely reported but rarely analyzed in connection with structural issues in social and economic environments. We will analyze the functions of these symptoms to mask privilege and history, to normalize violence, and to defend the status quo, as well as their capacity to anesthetize individuals from painful knowledge in ways that are sometimes adaptive, but more often devitalizing. In the final sections of this chapter, we discuss paths out of bystanding that allow one to be active learners and witnesses to the suffering that has attempted to announce itself in symptoms.

When bystanding intersects with privilege, the psychic costs are often offset by various kinds of profit from the current arrangements of power. In a chilling contrast between economically and educationally privileged White American and African-American teen girls at risk for high school dropout and teenage pregnancy, Taylor, Gilligan, and Sullivan (1995) observe that the former have been taught to precociously comply to normative gender expectations for them to be nice, quiet, good girls, with the promise of reaping the rewards of privilege later. Precocious compliance is a term used by object relations psychoanalyst Winnicott (1971) to describe the efforts of young children to conform to their depressed mother's need for them to be cheerful, well-behaved, and attentive to mother's emotional needs. Here we are opening up the usage of the term to include processes of adapting to cultural expectations. In both instances, one is conforming in order to achieve other ends—for the young child the love of the mother, for the White middle- to-upper-class teen girl love and economic and educational privileges. The teens surrender their dissenting voices to steer clear of conflict, often losing a sense of their own thoughts and feelings in the process. Many of the African-American girls in the study, however, exercised their voices, but felt as though few wanted to hear their experience, condemning them in the process as unruly and disruptive. These girls experienced few rewards for bystanding and remaining silent, but neither did they experience rewards for speaking out. In Chapter 11, we will address the critical need for communities of resistance to support those attempting to heal from the variety of wounds we are describing in this part of the book (Part II). The formation of such communities is crucial for the breaking of habits of bystanding and the emergence of needed solidarities.

Psychic wounds of bystanding

When studied from the point of view of liberation psychologies, bystanding can be seen to develop its own symptoms and pathologies linked to the socioeconomic environment. These include:

The severing of the self

The bystander to injustices and violence comes to think of his or her welfare as determined by his own (in)adequacy and (in)actions. In America, although there are multiple subcultures with communitarian values, many people are educated within an individualistic paradigm of selfhood, a paradigm that has distinct implications for mental health, developmental theorizing, and social action (Watkins, 1992). When one is thinking within an individualistic paradigm, development entails a progressive differentiation of self from other, and a corresponding strengthening of ego boundaries between self and other. Independence and self-sufficiency become laudable states, pushing interdependency and reliance on others into the realm of pathology. At the same time, the self that construes itself as independent can be unconsciously compliant to social expectations, rejecting connection to others who may speak what the severed self cannot say.

The boundary that is marked between self and other is joined by boundaries between self and community, self and nature. When the self's boundaries are experienced as fixed and firm, nature becomes a domain to pass through on the way to where one is going; a resource to be used and not a landscape of potential relations. Sadly, the same becomes true of one's neighborhood, where anonymity can remain after years of residence. While in place, one is dis-placed, with all the instability attendant with rootlessness that results from the incapacity for receiving nurture from earth and neighbors. The severed self—construed outside the web of interdependence—sees itself in a distorted light, encapsulated in its own present, seemingly unperturbed by a wider history of which one is a part.

Preoccupation with personal survival and success

When people are preoccupied by a sense of responsibility for their own successes and failures, they do not focus on the fact that the playing field is tilted—one side has Himalayan-size cliffs to climb over and the other side helps one slide toward success. Failure to succeed that has a context of lack of adequate access to resources is seen as personal failure; just as success in a context of privilege is lauded as wholly personal and "deserved." The sense of inferiority or superiority that results is illusory, while the advantages and disadvantages that are amassed are not. For instance, the fact of being White in America continues to confer economic advantages issuing from America's history of slavery.

One may assert oneself within extremely local situations such as intimate relations to fend off feelings of ineffectiveness. The low voter turnout rate in the United States (50 per cent in presidential elections) bespeaks the sense of futility in entering the political context. The lack of Bush administration response to early protests against U. S. invasions of Afghanistan and Iraq profoundly demoralized protest movements in the United States, and left many people feeling even more deeply that government decisions are made not only in places to which ordinary citizens have no access, but also upon which they have little influence.

Comparative neurosis

The ego of this kind of individualistic self strives for mastery and control of one's own thoughts and feelings and of immediate external situations. Control is achieved through the creation and scaling of hierarchy, providing access to resources to those on top. This kind of ego judges self in relation to others, and engages in competition to separate self from others in a vertical fashion, dividing others and parts of oneself along axes of presumed superiority and inferiority. Such a self suffers a neurosis of comparison, continuously assessing oneself in relation to others: who is smarter, more or less attractive, or who holds more power.

Loneliness

Such comparative practices distance one from the possibility of authentic relation to others. The other is someone to be outdone, or is the one who has outdone us. Security gained by fighting one's way to an elevated position vis-à-vis
the other is paid for by isolation and loneliness. The workplace may become a
site of potential self-elevation, rather than a potential community of unfolding
relations. The insecure individualistic self who is intent on amassing resources
for its own survival and enjoyment, on striving to aggrandize the self, paradoxically at the very same moment is impoverished one through cutting the
self off from multiple kinds of relations with self, others, and nature. The holding, containing, restorative potentialities within interdependent relations—
internal and external—are rarely experienced. As it construes its well-being to
be dependent only on its own efforts, such a striving self finds itself in a cycle
of exhausting pursuits and then in almost frantic efforts at recuperation.

Narcissism

In the extreme, this oscillation between feelings of inferiority and superiority results in pathological narcissism. Such narcissism results in a tragic
disfigurement of psyche that robs a person of any lasting sense of fulfillment
as well as the capacity to stably maintain mutual loving relationships, so
ferocious is the need to be and appear better than others and so deep is the
abyss of feelings of inadequacy.

The psychoanalyst Karen Horney (1950) lamented that the compulsive
drive for success that arises in a competitive culture does not secure peace of
mind, inner security, or joy. On the contrary, a person indiscriminately and
compulsively seeks praise, glory, and affirmation. Like the hungry ghost in
Tibetan mythologies, a being with a wide empty belly and tiny mouth, it
can never feel a sense of satiation or fulfillment. In its quest for excessive
admiration and glory, the drive to excel is split from the discernment of
what is meaningful, abandoning the self's search for deeper life purpose, and
cutting the self off from the vitality and spontaneity that lie available at the
heart of meaning. The severed self recreates its own abandonment over and
over again. Intense needs for admiration stand in where mutual relationships are absent. Preoccupations with grandiose fantasies about the self,
longings for "unlimited success, power, brilliance, beauty, or ideal love"
(*Diagnostic and statistical manual of mental disorders*, 1994, p. 661) are provoked,
but ultimately fail in filling intra- and interpersonal voids.

The degrading of others

The bystander rationalizes his or her remove from resisting injustice by both
subtle and overt dehumanization of the victims of injustice. Colonial conquest, the Holocaust, slavery throughout the Americas, current racial and ethnic hatreds and genocides reveal the deepest mutilations of the self. In all
these situations, and in their shadows, the empathic pathways hopefully built

in childhood through loving and caring exchanges, pathways that allow us freedom to enter into the experience of others, is channeled toward those with whom we are similar. It is truncated when encountering those from whom we see ourselves as different. Can one really believe that one's capacity for empathy goes undamaged in such a situation? Can one feel the effect on one's compassion of living in multiple relations each day where others are treated in an instrumental way, reduced to how the other can serve the self?

The colonial self, profiting from the oppression of others, creates a view of others that justifies oppression. The other is inferior, impulsive, undeveloped, unable to perform abstract thinking, locked in superstitious thought. Others need colonial stewardship to ensure their survival. The other is never seen in his or her specificity but "drawn in anonymous collectivity" (Memmi, 1965, p. 85). Fantasies of colonial superiority, intelligence, disciplined work ethic, logical thought, resourcefulness, and scientific thinking elevate the colonial self and justify control of others' resources. This colonial self splits off its own inferiorized, underdeveloped, and vulnerable aspects. This binary splitting, whereby one pole is lauded and the other degraded, falls into the psyches of both colonizer and colonized, creating caricatures of identity, and misreadings of history. Intelligence becomes severed from feeling, intuition, and imagination. Work becomes disassociated from spontaneity, vitality, and generativity (Martín-Baró, 1994).

Flinders (1998) argues that patriarchy organizes not only society but also assumptions about what constitutes a self. The first assumption is that there is not enough for everyone. "For one group to be fully 'authorized,' others have to be subordinate to them—'commodified' and 'reified' in one way or another, or simply silenced" (p. 108).

In current transnational capitalism, practices that undermine local economies, leading to increasing poverty and massive dislocations of populations, are called "progress" from the point of view of those who profit. Colonialism's stories of others as inferior, backward, and primitive mitigate against direct perceptions of structural and literal violence perpetrated against those others. This causes a dissociation within the self between the dominant cultural narrative and other empathic feelings or transgressive knowings that must now be defended against. Disassociations within cultural history become translated into psychic dissociations. The projective field that reduces the personhood of others acts as an obscuring cloud, allowing one not to experience human suffering. The work of healing begins when we ask what of our own sufferings, thoughts, feelings, and perceptions have been "disappeared" in this process.

Fear of oneself, of the abject

To experience the self in terms of multiple and conflicting narratives has further implications. Once one becomes split in terms of claimed superior and disowned inferior parts, two processes result. What is designated as inferior is projected onto others—seen as belonging to others—if one identifies with the superior position. Secondly, what is seen as inferior also arises as a possibility within the self; that is, once split, and even projected, it threatens the self internally by being a position into which one might fall. Psychoanalyst Julia Kristeva (1982) calls this part of our personality "the abject" and underscores our fear of owning it. This fear may cause intense anxiety. Kristeva links the abject with the unclean, vomit, sewage, and shame. She suggests that we spit out painful parts of ourselves in establishing an individualistic identity, constantly enforcing the border between our established "proper" self and others who must carry all the split-off feelings. "It is thus not lack of cleanliness or health that causes abjection, but what disturbs identity, system, order" (p. 4). The resultant personality is a "stray" who is always disoriented and dejected, asking where one is instead of who one is, questioning one's identity and solidarity in a constructed landscape that is "divisible, foldable, and catastrophic" (p. 8). Yet, this straying leaves open the possibility that in a flash the whole system may become visible in "a time of oblivion and thunder, of veiled infinity and the moment when revelation bursts forth" (p. 9). Then "the clean and proper (in the sense of incorporated and incorporable) becomes filthy," and "the sought after turns into the banished, fascination into shame" (pp. 8–9).

In the abject state, not only is the multiplicity of relations in the world denied, but so too are relations among the multiplicity of the self. One turns a deaf ear to what signals ambivalence and unsought after complexity.

The empty self

In lieu of fully perceiving and addressing the determining forces of his or her time, the bystander adopts a myopic viewpoint. This is maintained by a constriction of the boundaries of the self, and a firming of these boundaries in an attempt to avoid unbidden perceptions and feelings. Within this narrowed self, some semblance of control can be exercised and enjoyed. As Cushman (1995) assesses, the underside of mastery and boundedness is emptiness. This firmly bounded self is cut off from a free flow of energies across both interpersonal and intrapsychic boundaries, as well as exchanges with those who offer differences through their perceptions and experiences. It is separated from the wider community and its history and rituals that confer meaning on life's difficulties, joys, and transitions. This self engages with others lost in amnesia about the past, entering what Casey (1992) calls "a double oblivion," forgetting that one has forgotten.

It is little wonder, says Cushman (1995) that such a self suffers from pervasive feelings of emptiness and meaninglessness, with feelings of unreality, low self-esteem, and despair. Such a self is suffused with real and symbolic losses of community, tradition, and shared meaning. Bereft of a community with which to acknowledge and mourn these losses, the empty self experiences its own yearning as personal inadequacy and struggles to fill itself in the ways offered by the culture that has produced it: conspicuous consumption and consumerism, drug and alcohol abuse and addiction, personal rituals of bearing emptiness such as anorexia, entertainment celebrity and guru fixations, gambling, passive forms of entertainment, and even psychotherapy. Cushman (1995) describes a cultural terrain that is "oriented to purchasing and consuming rather than to moral striving; to individual transcendence rather than to community salvation; to isolated relationships rather than to community activism; to an individualistic mysticism rather than to political change" (p. 78).

The empty self in America is a "perfect complement to an economy that must stave off economic stagnation by arranging for the continual purchase and consumption of surplus goods," says Cushman (1995, p. 6). The advertising industry has pitched itself to this hunger, surrounding us with thousands of images that would have us believe that life will be made better by hundreds of small and large purchases that transform and adorn ourselves and our homes. Self-liberation, says Cushman, is sought after through consumption. "The empty self is configured to fit *our* particular [American] culture; it makes for a great deal of abundance and stimulation, isolation and loneliness" (Cushman, 1995, p. 7). Attention to surface appearance and to attracting the attention of others replaces deeper mutuality, sharing, and respect. Sloan (1996) warns us that by providing for material wants, capitalism "deflates most of the resistance that would stem from remaining gross inequalities" (p. 3). We are bought off, losing sight of larger configurations of power and injustice.

The replacement of being with having

Decades ago the psychoanalyst and social critic Erich Fromm (1976) saw how the rise of industrialism and secularism in the West had contributed to replacing values associated with *being* with values dedicated to *having*, plunging us into violence, wars, and genocides to protect what has come to be seen as necessary, unquestionable assets. The silent symptom of feelings of emptiness that prompt addictive consumption churns a mighty global industrial machine in an attempt to forge a sense of fulfillment. The fleeting relief of having can never replace the deeper joys of being that elude one as lives become centered on various consumptions. Perilous indeed are the cultures of violence that arise as the inevitable outcome of personal and cultural strivings to possess, pitting neighbors, neighborhoods, regions, and countries against one another. Freire (1989), following Fromm, described the grip of materialism as inanimating "everything and everyone it encounters, in its eagerness to possess," spreading an atmosphere of necrophilia (p. 45). Lewis Hyde (1983) describes the desire to consume as "a kind of lust":

We long to have the world flow through us like air or food. We are thirsty and hungry for something that can only be carried inside bodies. But consumer goods merely bait this lust, they do not satisfy it. The consumer of commodities is invited to a meal without passion, a consumption that leads to neither satiation nor fire. He is a stranger seduced into feeding on the drippings of someone else's capital without benefit of its inner nourishment, and he is hungry at the end of the meal, depressed and weary as we all feel when lust has dragged us from the house and led us to nothing.

(p. 10)

Greed and false feelings of entitlement

Quaker John Woolman's advice two centuries ago still holds: "May we look upon our treasures, and the furniture of our houses, and [our] garment ... and try whether the seeds of war have any nourishment in [these] possessions ..." (quoted in Moulton, 1989, p. 255). The bloody and tear-soaked side of shopping are routinely hidden and mystified beyond common comprehension. Misreading of everyday symptoms of emptiness are crafted and supported by the most sophisticated use of psychology—advertising. Low-paid wageworkers, separated from their families by long hours and often thousands of miles, workers who suffer dangerous working conditions with little or no environmental safeguards, are out of view. This self's sense of internal emptiness that turns to consuming to quell its pangs of hunger and to assuage its sense of meaninglessness, unwittingly feeds us on the fruits of misery of those pressed into the manufacture of consumer items. Unfair labor practices are taken even further from our direct view, across borders into *maquiladores* and sweat shops around the world. The hunger for meaning of those who disproportionately consume has become indelibly linked through consumerism with the literal hunger and struggle of millions who put their life's labor into items consumed impossibly far from their own struggling families, homes, and communities.

Out of view also are the history of capitalism and the role of slavery and low-paid workers to the amassing of capital that continues to privilege Whiteness, generations after abolition. What within the frame of individualism is experienced as personal reward for a job well done disintegrates under scrutiny in the bright light of recovered history. Without clear insight regarding the historical roots of one's bounty and its exacting toll on others, it is difficult to see the perversions of having. Since the cause of many wars and much violence and environmental destruction is greed, it is particularly important to name this correctly.

False entitlement is generated from a misreading of history. It flows into psychic recesses that fuel personal consumption. A sense of false entitlement is often shared with one's community, gated against claims from others' readings of history and sense of injustices in the present. False entitlement is a self-sustaining illusion where one does not reflect on the conundrum that the "more" one has, the "more" one presumes is deserved.

Psychic numbing

According to Hillman (1992), "the question of evil, like the question of ugliness, refers primarily to the anaesthetized heart, the heart that has no reaction to what it faces, thereby turning the variegated sensuous face of the world into monotony, sameness, oneness" (p. 64). Lifton (1967) named this affective anesthesia "psychic numbing." Such closing down of feelings interrupts processes of identifying with others. In extraordinary situations, this can be adaptive; in ordinary life, it is crippling. For instance, survivors of Hiroshima described observing the suffering and death of others, but experiencing this at a distance from themselves: "I see you dying; but I am not related to you or your death" (p. 500). Psychic numbing "begins as a defense against exposure to death, but ends up inundating the organism with death imagery" (p. 503). Defended against at the front door, death enters within from behind, casting a pale of neurasthenic symptoms: fatigue, depressive feelings, bodily complaints, and insomnia. The world itself appears diminished. Not only is the integrity of affects surrendered, but also the complex cognitive understandings that rely on affects, compromising our capacity to understand what is happening intrapsychically and in the world around us. One pretends to not see and to not know what one does in fact see and know. One lives daily life from the surface, failing to question distortions and lies, and living without the benefit of deeper potential understandings. Habitual practices of bystanding fortify psychic numbing and compromise spontaneous processes of symbol formation that feed psychic life. Lifton (2007) suggests that we find ourselves in an age of psychic numbing. As we shall demonstrate in Chapters 6 and 7, bystanders, perpetrators, and victims all suffer psychic numbing, but the moral significance of the numbing varies. The psychic numbing generated by bystanding constitutes a wordless bargain, an exchange of vitality for a distance from deep disturbance. One lives in a narrow preserve where there is a semblance of stability, distraction, and security, removing one from tangling with questions and situations that induce feelings of impotence and inadequacy.

The obsessive-compulsive rehearsal of violence

A psychically benumbed person is immune to low levels of violence. Only when violence is heightened does arousal begin. Sadly, such arousal may even be welcomed as a contrast to feelings of inner deadness. Symbolically, violence viewed from afar may memorialize in the outer world the kind of dissociative splitting in the inner world that has killed off capacities for feeling. How else can we explain the television and film industries' addiction to stories that involve murder, theft, destruction, mutilation, disappearance, and warfare? Each night, millions obsessively watch as fictional medical, forensic, police, and military personnel attempt to restore the status quo after violence has breached normal daily life. Bombarded by violence in the news, television, movies, and video games, children and adults have become accustomed to imagery of death and destruction. The lines blur between fabricated violence in media, actual violence reported in the news, and violence directly witnessed. When these distinctions are dim, a passive stance is adopted that includes little or no protest to desperate destructions of human well-being: the use of landmines, torture, cluster bombs, aerial bombing of cities, destruction of water systems, and contamination by depleted uranium in munitions; all the while continuing the development of nuclear arsenals. Saturated with these images, many simply accept domestic violence, child abuse, and authoritarian environments as unremarkable.

Aimé Césaire (1972), surrealist poet and one of the founders of the Negritude Movement (the first diasporic Black pride movement that developed before World War II) argued that Europeans were overcome by fascism because they had become so habituated to its practices through colonialism. Before the violence of Nazism was inflicted on them,

> they were its accomplices ... they absolved it, shut their eyes to it, legitimized it, because, until then, it had been applied to only non-European peoples; that they have cultivated that Nazism, that they are responsible for it, and that before engulfing the whole of Western, Christian civilization in its reddened waters, it oozes, seeps and trickles from every crack.
>
> (p. 36)

There is a vicious connection between bystanding and the normalization of violence. The less one interrupts violence and injustice, the more others, and perhaps even oneself, will end up in its sites. In the present, those who suffer it directly feel increasingly hopeless and futile, and are more likely to resort to violence, raging against the impossibility of peaceful daily life. As Fanon warned, terror is the weapon of choice of those who have been convinced of their impotence. Within the violence perpetrated by others, we can find the blossoming of the seeds cast by habits of bystanding.

Dissociation

A widespread survival strategy to avoid painful emotional states is the unconscious creation of a multiplicity of disconnected narratives and part selves within any one personality. In Western psychology, these states of dissociation, splitting, and, at times, even amnesia have been named in a variety of ways: conscious and unconscious by Freud; paranoid, schizoid, and depressive positions by Klein; ego and shadow by Jung; and imaginary and symbolic by Lacan. All describe parts of us that accept and identify with ideologies created in the context of local cultural construction, and other parts that may contain images, narratives, or threads of meaning that have been disowned and may rupture comfortable fantasies. People differ in the degree to which there is dialogue between these parts of the personality and the degree to which disowned aspects of the personality stage protests through symptoms.

In contemporary cross-cultural medical anthropology, dissociative strategies have been located all over the world under the heading of culture-bound reactive syndromes (Peters, 1998): *koro*, impotence panic, in China; *latah*, a startle reaction, in Indonesia; *susto*, a fright or soul loss, in Central America; and *wiitiko*, a frenzy, in First Nations Canadians. Such reactive syndromes require energy to be sustained, but serve the function of expressing deep distress. In cultural environments where such distress can be heard and witnessed, healers may interpret symptoms as calls to put something right in the environment. The whole community may come together to dialogue about and heal the breach. But where such symptoms cannot be heard and interpreted, there may be a descent into a chronic state of psychological dissociation and the lonely suffering of symptoms that compromise vitality, creativity, eros, and compassion.

A reading of culture can be done from looking closely at the fault lines within the psyches of people sharing a common community. Liberation and depth psychologies help one to understand that one must direct attention to the margins of psychic life: to what is excluded or held at bay, to what intrudes unbidden, to the multiple voices and fragmented images that arise autonomously in psychic life. This kind of looking allows one to see what is unconscious in a particular culture. Erich Fromm (1960) spoke of the "unconscious" as including everything that a particular culture disavows. To work on coming to understand what has been cast out is thus not only a work that entails personal knowledge, but as well a growing insight into the dictates and fixed ideas of one's evolving sociocultural milieu that determine what is exiled. Communities and individuals are affected differently by their positionality within a particular historical period and cultural discourse. Thus different configurations of psychic life and symptom must be followed to the soil of the cultural environment in which they arise with particular attention given to one's social positionality in relation to the relevant situations.

Mending dissociation

During 500 years of colonialism, the dissociative strategies encountered in many distinct cultural locations have been hardened into extremely rigid, destructive, and pathological complexes, affecting both individual personalities and whole communities. Currently these hardened cultural complexes organize many European and American educational institutions and social discourse in ways that generate bystanding, preventing the working through and mourning of the painful past, and mitigating against engagement with the pressing issues of our time. Bystanding has generated crises of overlooking, of not focusing, of abnegating deep seeing, where many have become blind to webs of interdependence. One attempts to live in a world without seeing it clearly. How can one be at home in such a world out of focus? How can one not feel disconnected, even unreal? How can one have a sense of caring, when one so continuously fails to see, and, thus, respond, to the needs of others?

To discuss psychological symptoms in this way is a transgressive act. Even within psychological theories we are taught to forget, to not see, to be unable to connect the inside with the outside. Yet our relations to events—past and present, personal, historical, and cultural—do shape us (Griffin, 1992). They do so as much in the perversity of our relations to them as in the content of the events themselves.

To begin to face the legacy of a rigid dissociative complex requires a defeat of a striving, individualistic ego with its attempts to control history, and to avoid painful memories. It requires that one begin to come to terms with what Hillman (2002) has called "the terrible consequences of winning". It is in the recovery of cultural memory, in the listening to previously unheard feelings, symptoms, and narratives that internal dissociations can begin to heal. This may require very protected forms of encounter with others in safe spaces where new feelings and thoughts can be explored without censure. To hold history in ways that can inform the present, we must nurture capacities for grief and mourning, for truth and reconciliation. We know that mourning is aided by the availability of support and rapport. Part of the sadness that must be faced is how one may have prevented some of one's deepest knowings from informing the major decisions in one's life, perpetuating misery in one's own life as well as that of others, even those at a distance.

To move from passive bystanding to active witnessing is a healing process on many levels—personal, interpersonal, community, intercommunity, and, sometimes, between humans and the natural and built environments. To move toward engaged witness is to reclaim history and to look for one's place in it; it is to look forward into the future for one's own role in creating it. "What process of change can move a people that doesn't know who it is, nor where it came from? If it doesn't know who it is, how can it know what it deserves to be?" asks Uruguayan writer Eduardo Galeano (quoted in Morales, 1998, p. 24).

In a complex, interlinked, global system, it is not possible for us each to actively witness across countless distant situations. It *is* possible to begin habits of witness and response to oppressive situations and events around us in our daily life (Weingarten, 2003). It is also possible to attend to where our biographies allow us particular sensitivity and potential understanding. In many cases, it is precisely where one has falsely separated oneself that one needs to begin a process of mending.

Sewing together what has been torn is a pilgrimage. Small steps of engagement build on one another, yielding a life cloth that is less hopeless, alienated, lonely, infused with futility, meaninglessness, and sterility. Psychologies of liberation insist that the self not be the basic unit of analysis in psychology. The other in its manifestations must be equally valued, as one mends a torn fabric of interdependence. What do these spontaneous calls for restoration look like in a fieldwork program based on liberation psychology?

One student who had rejected Chicano identity began to dream of recovering lost books in Mexico. She initiated a dialogue project on the role of the border experience for women who have grown up with one foot in Mexico and another in the United States (Villareal, 2004).

Suzan Still drove past a state prison each day to and from work. In her thoughts the prison suggested that she stop and engage. After ignoring this insinuation for many months, it intensified, and she began to explore that possibility. She became a creative writing teacher there, and in her relations to the prisoners she found a sense of joy and community that surprised her. This experience led to work in the prison abolition movement (Still, 1998, 1999).

A third student began to wonder what journey brought her African-American family to a New England town. She researched ancestral migrations, family stories, and relations to land, re-linking her family to lost histories and landscapes. This personal quest is blossoming into a dissertation study by Marcella DeVeaux on the psychological effects of multiple displacements on African-Americans.

Betsy Perluss, at the time a school counselor on Catalina Island, noticed her high school students' alienation from and lack of relationship to local histories and landscapes. She developed a summer experiential curriculum that fostered the students' relationships to the places of the island, its land, creatures, and stories. They studied the history of the oppression of the indigenous population of the island, and explored some of their stories. Here psychological well-being was enhanced as the relationship between self and place was deepened, including a fuller sense of the interwoven human histories of the groups that have shared the place where one stands (Perluss, 1998).

During her graduate studies, Ann Shine, a White descendant of Thomas Jefferson and a member of the Monticello Association, dreamed that a Black woman with a terrible condition of low-blood sugar came to tell her she had a responsibility. In the dream, Shine realized that part of her work was to help find the place where the woman's ancestors were buried to aid in her healing. This dream occurred as descendants of Sally Hemings began to come to the annual meeting of the Monticello Association. Hemings, a Black slave, was a lover of Jefferson and the mother of their children together. Shine (2001) studied the variety of responses that occurred ranging from rejection, to attempts at dialogue across difference, to friendly welcome, as she herself joined memorials for the slaves at Monticello, including those found buried under the visitor parking lot.

Many activists have begun restoration projects to rejoin broken connections. Meditating on the kind of bystanding that occurred during the Holocaust led Dennis Rivers (2006) to begin a movement for citizens to let the U.S. government know that should the United States ever be attacked by a nuclear device they do not license the government to strike back in their name. They are aware of the total environmental destruction that would be caused by such a response. Rivers felt moved to draft and deliver such a document in order to save his own heart from numbness and denial. Aware of people's tendency to "blot out qualms of conscience through addictions, violent entertainment, drugs, alcohol, overwork so that 'I don't feel much about the world around me,'" he poses the question, "what is left of my life after I do that?" (Rivers, 2006). To move from bystanding entailed his deep acknowledgment that the U.S. arsenal of nuclear weapons belongs to Americans: "They have been created to defend me, and they have been created with my tax dollars and the assumption of my consent. My silence on this matter gradually becomes my consent to be 'defended' in this way." Rivers's (2006) Web site enlists others into witness and action regarding the elimination of nuclear arsenals, exploring the possible paths beyond the global culture of violence.

The hunger to witness in cultures of bystanding can be found in many places. The civil war in Liberia displaced thousands to the United States, with Staten Island and Minneapolis receiving the preponderance of the refugees in the United States. When the Liberian government launched its truth and reconciliation process, it decided to include members from the Liberian diaspora. After the call went out for volunteers in the United States to take human rights testimony—a time-consuming long-term commitment—1500 people in Minneapolis came forward. In the documenting of human rights violations, many White middle-class Americans bore witness to violence and forced displacement that ruptured a more distanced and abstract understanding of what Liberians have suffered.

The desire to witness emerges in strange ways. It is a healing practice that can be engaged intentionally, but it is also one that erupts spontaneously calling our attention to certain events and situations and not others. Sometimes it emerges from the center of one's concerns as a call to deepen participation. At other times something from the margin of one's awareness whispers insistently asking for our attention. Each is a process of reconciliation necessary to the healing of a bystander stance. None of us can take on the entire complexity of the situations we live in, but each of us is called very particularly by aspects that we are sensitized to by our own biography and temperament. Time after time we have witnessed the emergence of joy in individuals who have newly placed themselves in complicated, difficult circumstances. The joy comes from the mending one's being so deeply thirsts for. Accepting the interdependent web of which one is a part paradoxically does not deplete, but provides membership in a gift economy where it is possible to draw sustenance from beyond narrowly defined selves (Hyde, 1983): "Our generosity may leave us empty, but our emptiness then pulls gently at the whole until the thing in motion returns to replenish us" (p. 23).

Symptom as a tunnel that connects the outside to the inside

Felman (1992) describes the difficulty of testimony of the Holocaust, as it was an event that attempted to erase its own witnesses.

> Inside the crematorium, "on the other side of the gate" where "everything disappeared and everything got quiet," there is loss: of voice, of life, of knowledge, of awareness, of truth, of the capacity to feel, of the capacity to speak. The truth of this loss constitutes precisely what it means to be inside the Holocaust. But the loss also defines an impossibility of testifying from inside to the truth of that inside.
>
> (p. 231)

Where witness is possible, Felman says, one must know "the tunnel that connects the outside to the inside ... guiding us into a singular and unforgettable experience of a *seeing*" (p. 238). One must try to communicate "the abyssal *lostness* of the inside, without being either crushed by the abyss or overwhelmed by the pathos, *without losing the outside*" (p. 239).

It is only from such witness and the actions that arise from it that the dissociations within individuals, as well as between self and other, on the levels of family and community, can be mended. Such tunneling presupposes contexts in which dialogical capacities can be developed and nurtured. Through the ensuing dialogue, it will be possible to see more clearly the cultural ideologies that shape one's world, one's sense of others, and one's daily experience, including the suffering of symptoms. Subcomandante Marcos (2002), a spokesperson for the Zapatistas' indigenous rights movement in Chiapas, Mexico, urges us to counter processes of social amnesia with attempts "to open a crack in history" (p. 212), a break with naturalized narratives that block understanding of how suffering in the present came about and is sustained.

> "That's what we are," I said to myself, fallen stars that barely scratch the sky of history with a scrawl. ... 30 years ago, a few people scratched history, and knowing this, they began calling to many others so that by dint of scribbling, scratching, and scrawling they would end up rending the veil of history, so that light would finally be seen. That, and nothing else, is the struggle we are making. And so if you ask us what we want, we will unashamedly answer: "To open a crack in history."
>
> (p. 212)

Symptoms announce a need to relinquish ideas one has identified with that preclude an understanding of what causes psychological suffering. When cracks in the structure of these ideas occur, one can begin to search for alternate understandings. Psychologies of liberation invite bystanders to travel the tunnel that connects the inside to the outside, issuing a challenge to identify and disrupt processes of social amnesia. To enter this tunnel requires the development of relational capacities through play, dialogue, the arts, and empathic engagements. The therapeutic must be re-imagined to include the emergence from bystanding into dialogical participation and engaged witness (see Chapter 10). It requires a re-imagining of subjectivity-in-relation (see Chapter 9).

There is a collusion between bystanding and perpetration that is often difficult to discern. Perpetrators rely on and are encouraged by the silence of bystanders. In a sculpture installation by Morackis and Serrano, *Border Dynamics*, figures lean against and support a dividing wall—in this case a replica of a piece of the border wall built by the United States at the U.S./Mexico border. It is held up not only by figures who actively and forcefully reinforce it, but by those who turn their back to it, lean against it and look elsewhere—their weight mindlessly supporting it. With the implicit collusion of bystanding, a grievous situation can be passively supported by inaction, the omission of witness, and the stifling of creative resistance. In the next chapter, we address active perpetration of violence and injustice and the psychic amputations experienced by individuals who have entered routines of dehumanizing and destroying others, which are rationalized by the ideologies they have embraced.

6
Pathologies of Perpetration

> As Gandhi was to so clearly formulate through his own life, freedom is indivisible, not only in the popular sense that the oppressed of the world are one, but also in the unpopular sense that the oppressor too is caught in the culture of oppression.
>
> (Nandy, 1983, p. 6)

Many may think it strange to be concerned about the psychodynamics and suffering of perpetrators of violence. There is often a fear that if we try to "understand" and "explain" violent behavior, we somehow excuse the perpetrator from moral responsibility, and diminish the emotional horror of the crimes. That is not our aim. The perpetrator of violence is ultimately responsible for his or her actions. At the same time, the historical, cultural, and political context may press powerful ideologies upon the potential perpetrator that instigate, sustain, and justify violence. As Lifton (1983) has stressed, a "critical examination of ideologies and institutions in their interaction with styles of self-process" in perpetrators is necessary as a "prophylaxis against genocidal directions of the self" (p. 500). To focus on the individual alone will mislead us and weaken our grasp of how perpetration of violence unfolds within particular communities and cultures. There are three crucial tasks for psychologies of liberation regarding perpetration: (1) to understand the intrapsychic dynamics of the perpetrator in societal context; (2) to study and facilitate processes of sharing remembrance and acknowledgment, at times apology and forgiveness, or reconciliation and restoration in post-conflict situations (Chapter 15); and (3) to help communities promote the kinds of critical thinking, empathic bonds, and dialogical relations that mitigate against violence (Chapters 10 and 11).

We want to address the contextualized psychodynamics of perpetrators as well as the long-term psychological and community consequences of their actions. As members or descendents of members of groups that have either experienced or perpetrated injustice and violence, many of us are faced with comprehending these consequences. Because of the growing number of civil wars, it is increasingly likely that most of us will live—or already live—in communities side by side with perpetrators, or even more likely, their allies, accomplices, families, and descendents. In Guatemala, after the Civil Patrols of the 1980s, in Chile and Argentina after the "dirty wars," in South Africa after apartheid, in Mississippi after Klan violence, in South Dakota after the Wounded Knee Massacre, community members on opposite sides of a violent struggle have to face each other daily while reconstructing their worlds. Unprecedented worldwide migration places together in cities families whose histories interlocked in deadly colonial conflicts and imperial wars in distant locations: from Moslem Algerians in Paris to Vietnamese in Los Angeles.

The children and grandchildren of perpetrators have important work to do to break the cycle of identifications and projections that would allow such enmities to continue indefinitely. They need to discover how their parents' and grandparents' capacity for compassion for the suffering of others transformed into a cold and rigid opposition between "us and them", which allowed multiple levels of violation. This often means asking difficult questions that have never been asked.

The first step in such a process is finding out what happened in one's own family and community in the past from multiple points of view. While investigating, we need to hold the tension between our awareness that even in extreme circumstances all people retain a possibility to refuse to act criminally on moral, religious, or emotional grounds whatever the consequences—often death—and on the other hand, that there are situations that are so authoritarian and coercive, that it can become extremely difficult to think and act independently. In such situations, neat divisions of victims from perpetrators may prove impossible. This is tragically illustrated in Uganda and Sudan where children have been kidnapped by paramilitary groups, beaten and tortured until they commit murder, often of their own family members (Briggs, 2005). In such cases, a complex dialogue and set of rituals must evolve that both acknowledge wounds and accept responsibility for wounding. In Uganda this is happening through traditional *Matoput* rituals of restorative justice and reconciliation of the returning youth with their families and villages.

What most of us will be looking at in the future, if not already in the present, are situations in which the children, other relatives, and associates of victims and those of the perpetrators will face each other in dialogue. They will begin with memories and narratives that construct historical events through alarmingly different perspectives. In order to build a common future of peace and security, new solidarities will have to be formed out of the ashes of a violent past. This is very difficult and painful work, and will require learning how to re-imagine differences. As Audre Lorde (1984) said: "The master's tools will never dismantle the master's house" (p. 110). Lorde advocated confrontation across difference:

> Difference must be not merely tolerated, but seen as a fund of necessary polarities between which our creativity can spark like a dialectic. Only then does the necessity for interdependency become unthreatening. Only within that interdependency of different strengths, acknowledged and equal, can the power to seek new ways of being in the world generate, as well as the courage and sustenance to act where there are no charters.
>
> Within the interdependence of mutual (nondominant) differences lies that security which enables us to descend into the chaos of knowledge and return with true visions of our future, along with the concomitant power to effect those changes which can bring that future into being. Difference is that raw and powerful connection from which our personal power is forged.
>
> (pp. 112–3)

When we look at the history of large groupings of people, we can see a constant recurrence of rigid boundary building: we people are like this and you people are like that. In order to break with this form of polarized thinking and the destructive actions it yields, we must create spaces for encountering difference without dominance. In such spaces, we need to be able to take two kinds of risks that are uncommon and difficult—to differ from those we identify with and to listen to those we do not understand. Thus, we look toward the lives of perpetrators and their associates to begin a process that over many years might lead toward new forms of peacemaking in the future.

In this chapter, we will explore the psychological and social outcome of violence on perpetrators and their families as well as future generations living in environments created by terror. While it is common knowledge that perpetrators of violence do terrible things to their victims, it is less well understood how they too are deformed and constricted by what they do, further engendering harmful ways of living. Because many of us are the inheritors of histories of violence, we will necessarily have to consider reflexively how our own collective past may be silenced by truncated understandings and discourses.

Breaking with silences about the past

In most cases, perpetration of violence functions in an environment that paradoxically mixes silence and anonymity with the announcing of danger and terror. This mix can be accomplished through various means, such as the intentional circulation of photographs of torture by the French secret forces during the Algerian revolution, and, more recently, by American leaks of such pictures from Abu Ghraib prison in Iraq. Announcement of a terrorizing and dangerous situation insures that people understand the risk of dissent to themselves and to their family members, silencing many in the population it is aimed at. Blanketing violence in a shroud of anonymity and secrecy is the first step toward creating situations in which perpetrators are free to act because few know who is responsible. In addition, even if one did know, there is no reliable space for people to be held accountable. Because speaking out is often dangerous in immediate situations of violence, particularly the kinds of extrajudicial killing done by death squads or secret societies such as the mafia or the Klan, they generate waves of internal hushing, often for many years, as each individual is forced to assess the risks of breaking the unspoken yet shared code of silence. Certain kinds of violence are not mentioned in public in some communities for decades or even generations after they occur because the police and government institutions that supported them are still in power. Lynchings, cross burnings, disappearances, murders, or collaboration can be dangerous to investigate even many years later.

In reports from the Truth and Reconciliation Commission in South Africa and research into the lives of those committing atrocities in Nazi Germany, Chile, Brazil, Argentina, and Guatemala, a picture is beginning to emerge of the psychological lives of perpetrators of violence and their effects on the surrounding communities. When exploring the psychology of violence and the mentality of violence workers, one may enter spaces that shatter ideas about any norms that might exist in the landscape of internal life. One may meet a difference so profound that it is difficult to know how to react. Yet as long as knowing is avoided, there is collusion in the ignorance and silence that allows violence to continue.

Doubling, derealization, and disavowal

In the late 1960s, after Robert Jay Lifton's interviews with Japanese survivors of the U.S. atomic bombing of Hiroshima, a rabbi commented to him: "Hiroshima is your path, as a Jew, to the Holocaust." Lifton came to understand that many people find research into their own family and community histories too painful, and are led instead to explore the suffering of others. This insight freed him to directly investigate the Holocaust. His path led him to a study not of survivors, but of some of its perpetrators, namely Nazi doctors.

From his analysis of interviews with Nazi doctors involved in the daily workings of the death camps, Lifton (1986) began to understand a psychological process central to their perpetration of evil: *doubling*, a form of dissociation. Unlike splitting, where a part of oneself becomes hidden, abandoned, and no longer responsive to the environment, doubling entails "the division of the self into two functioning wholes, so that a part-self acts as an entire self" (p. 417). In the case of doctors who joined the Nazi cause, the individual maintained his/her prior self in order to continue seeing oneself as humane, while taking on a killing self that is experienced as necessary to one's own psychological survival in a death-dealing environment. Doubling of the self allows one enough detachment from one's prior self to be able to minimize psychological discomfort and responsibility about actions and thoughts that would otherwise be prohibited by it. Such doubling protects one from feelings of guilt associated with the violation of the ethical principles one was originally committed to.

What Lifton calls the "Auschwitz self" allowed a doctor to adapt to and accomplish his genocidal tasks, while his prior self allowed him to see himself as a caring physician, husband, and father. The doubling gave rise to lived contradictions. For instance, one day a doctor might be in charge of asking all pregnant women to step forward for an extra meal ration. In doing so, he might feel related to his prior healing self, attempting to improve the nutrition of a pregnant woman and her unborn child. Beneath this moment, however, lay another unclaimed meaning: now these women had unknowingly identified themselves to be gassed the following day. The doubling by which the doctors protected themselves from such a direct awareness of their role in atrocity, required derealization, disavowal, and reversal. In derealization, one "divest[s] oneself from the actuality of what one is a part of, not experiencing it as 'real'" (Lifton, 1986, p. 442). Even years later when Lifton interviewed the Nazi doctors, the effects of this derealization were still present. One doctor suggested: "That world is not this world." Another described Auschwitz as "another planet." Such diminishment of the substantiality of a lived moment in the present requires a concomitant diminishment of a sense of the reality of one's own being. Through disavowal one backs away from one's own perceptions, feelings, and the process of giving meaning to them, further reducing one's humanity. These processes combine to yield what Lifton describes as psychic numbing, a diminished capacity or inclination to feel. Derealization and numbness fatally weaken the line that separates us from evil doing. Once the reality of violence is derealized, mindless repetitions of violence become increasingly possible.

Through doubling, one could alternate between the rewards of being a healing doctor (one's prior self) and the rewards of a healing-killing doctor in participating in the healing of the German people. In this state of psychic division, a deadly reversal of meaning became possible: murder was seen as "cleansing," medical tortures as "research." The Auschwitz self believed it had its own sense of morality to which the individual remained loyal. Acts of killing and genocide were experienced as positive moral acts, linked to the "cleansing" and "regeneration" of the race. Lifton is clear that the doctors knew what they were doing, but had been able to disavow the contradictory meanings of their deadly actions. For instance, they knew they were involved in selecting and sorting of "inmates," but did not see this as murder.

Given the heroic vision held out to them—as cultivators of the genes and as physicians to the Volk, and as militarized healers combining the

life-death power of shaman and general—any cruelty they might per-
petrate was all too readily drowned in hubris. And their medical hubris
was furthered by their role in the sterilization and "euthanasia" projects within a vision of curing the ills of the Nordic race and the German
people.

(p. 427)

Once set in motion, the Auschwitz self required the further committing of
atrocity in order to protect the self from coming to see itself as a killer:
"[A]trocity begets atrocity: continuing to kill becomes necessary in order to
justify the killing and to view it as other than it is" (Lifton, 1986, p. 213).
Central to the splitting off of the Auschwitz self was identification with and
loyalty to the prevailing Nazi ideology and mission that justified everything
for this self (Lifton, 1986). When Alexander Mitscherlich (1975) returned
from the Nuremberg trials against German doctors who were complicit with
Nazi exterminations, he was emphatic that it was not a matter of a few bad
apples. Rather, he argued, the ideology of Nazism was allowed to corrupt the
medical profession, encouraging the perpetration of violence by those
responsible for healing. The embrace of Nazi ideology set the stage for the
dehumanization of others that allowed the doctors to treat Jewish prisoners
like vermin or laboratory animals. The self-evacuating effects of this doubling on one of the cruelest of Nazi doctors, Mengele, is described by an
inmate Jewish doctor: He "never looked into your eyes ... [or] show[ed] any
signs of enjoyment ... [but] seemed always ... [to have] something else on
his mind other than what he was doing, even when he was speaking to you"
(Lifton, 1986, p. 376).

Effects of psychic splitting on families

Such psychic splitting takes an enormous amount of energy to maintain,
and in the long run, few people are able to kill or torture without bringing
some kind of suffering on themselves and their families. Eric Santner (1990)
documents the long-term inability in Europe to acknowledge participation
in and to mourn over the events of the Holocaust during the period after
World War II. Because the violence was surrounded by a culture of silence
and denial, many perpetrators became cut off from their families. Santner
cites interviews of the children of the Nazis by Peter Sichrovsky, which
yield shocking insights into the multigenerational dynamics of alienation
yielded by a silenced past. One interview recounts the story of Suzanne,
who discovered as a result of research for a homework assignment done by
her son that her family's apartment had been taken over from a family of
Jews on the night they were deported to Auschwitz, where her father had
worked as a guard. This led to a long process of awakening from psychic

numbness about the war as she began to recall her relationship to it and to her father.

> He used words like "murderers" and "criminals." He never offered excuses and never claimed that the things we read about in the papers or in books weren't true. But as to guilt, he never considered himself guilty. He never, not once, said that he had made a mistake or that he had been partner to a crime. He was simply a victim of circumstances. And I, I always believed anything he told me.
>
> (quoted in Santner, 1990, p. 44)

Only with the outrage and questioning of the third generation, in this case, her son Dieter, did Suzanne begin to analyze the family dynamics that had yielded her own passivity in the face of the stark contradictions in her father's relation to the past.

> In retrospect, the terrifying thing about him was his objectivity. His reports and descriptions, his careful recapitulation of events. I never saw him shed a tear, never heard him break off in the middle, halt, unable to continue talking. Only these monotonous litanies; almost as though he were reading from a script.
>
> (quoted in Santner, 1990, p. 44)

In the case of postwar Germany, Santner thinks that the second and third generation, the children and grandchildren of Nazis, inherited some of the sufferings that their Nazi parents had been unable to experience directly. On the one hand, they were cut off from their parents through silences, omissions, contradictions, and ambivalence. On the other hand, they felt a need to rescue them from what they saw as a kind of victimhood in defeat. According to Santner (1990):

> The core dilemma is that the cultural reservoir has been poisoned, and few totems seem to exist which would not evoke such traumatic ambivalence that only a global foreclosure of all symbolic legacies would prevent further contamination. ... In numerous cases the parents were available to the children only on the condition that the children contribute to the restitution of the parents' damaged selves and thereby enter into complicity with their defense mechanisms and their inability or refusal to mourn.
>
> (pp. 45–6)

The German defeat was so painful and shocking for most surviving Nazi officers that they could never let go of their military discipline to mourn the past. As a result their children also learned not to speak about the war, and most conspired to move heroically forward into a reconstruction, tragically unmindful of the past and its psychological and societal correlates in the present.

The work of cultural anamnesis

Anamnesis is a psychoanalytic term that refers to a process of reflecting on and emotionally working through one's relationship to past events with another. Santner (1990) cites Christa Wolf's (1980) work in her novel *Kindheitsmuster* as the kind of anamnesis and mourning that second-generation German writers have occasionally been able to do successfully in literature. Wolf gives us a painful picture of German family life during and after World War II. She chronicles the way that anxieties, tensions, doubts, conflicts, and fears that could not be spoken began to be built up as symptoms, "forgotten by consciousness, but remembered by the body" (Santner, 1990, p. 157). "The body then functions in this novel as a sort of writing tablet and mnemonic device of the unconscious" (Santner, 1990, p. 157). The symptoms become in Wolf's words, "stabilized rock formations ... a fly in a piece of amber ... the fleeting track of a bird in once spongy sediments, hardened and immortalized by propitious stratification" (quoted in Santner, 1990, p. 157). The work of those who want to unearth the meanings of such symptoms is compared to the work of a paleontologist: "to learn to deal with petrified remains, to read from calcified imprints about the existence of early living forms which one can no longer observe" (p. 157).

Wolf remembers small details of her childhood:

> The childhood nights at the end of the long summer vacation. Sleepless, but as yet without the headaches, which are now going to attack you without fail. Analgesic caffeine to suppress pain and sleep. My head is splitting—who was it that always used those words.
>
> (p. 157)

She catches glimpses of her own crippling deformation in the past:

> Nelly couldn't help it: the charred buildings made her sad. But she didn't know she was feeling sad, because she wasn't supposed to feel sad. She had long ago begun to cheat herself out of her true feelings.
>
> (p. 158)

The author catalogues these symptoms to begin to catch glimpses of the traces of humanity and empathy that were distorted and finally destroyed by the culture of fascism during the war, and thus to begin to regain a grounding for her own capacities for solidarity and compassion in the present.

But Santner (1990) cautions that there are cases where it can simply be impossible to make these links:

> In numerous instances it may be that no amount of paleological memory-work will hit on the fossilized traces of a once vital and intact solidarity with the victim. It may be the case, in other words, that the breach in solidarity with the victims was so thorough ... that there is no residual empathetic potential that could in any sense be recuperated. In these instances a boundary has been crossed from which there is no return, not even by way of the unconscious. In short, these are cases in which all elegiac resources fail.
>
> (p. 160)

Anamnesis is a difficult project, especially when dialogue about the past has been cut off, and it feels like breaking a taboo to begin questioning, recollecting, and naming all that went unspoken for years. Nevertheless, the future hinges on the courage to begin such a project at the boundary between the said and the unsaid.

Killing one's own humanity

One eloquent account of struggle with that critical boundary is provided by South African psychologist Pumla Gobodo-Madikizela (2003). As a member of the Human Rights Violations Committee of South Africa's Truth and Reconciliation Commission, which attempted to document the violence committed during apartheid, she had the opportunity to observe many encounters between families of victims and the government officials responsible for killing their loved ones. She interviewed Eugene de Kock in the Pretoria maximum-security prison, where he was serving a 212-year sentence for crimes against humanity committed while working as a commanding officer of state-sanctioned death squads under apartheid. After hearing his testimony and the response from family members of those he killed, she became interested in questions of remorse and forgiveness.

In general, perpetrators whose lives are stopped by regime change or military defeat, or both, those who are tried publicly and forced to hear testimony against them, and especially those who serve time in prison, are far more likely to begin a process of reflection, mourning, and remorse than those who continue their lives unchanged and are never named in public. In the latter situation, which is the case for the majority of the former Afrikaans armed services and police in South Africa, the ongoing conscious position is "I was following orders in a war against enemies." Any doubts or remorse must be expressed unconsciously through symptoms.

The situation of de Kock, by contrast, was a unique one of total defeat. Although he was considered "the most brutal of apartheid's covert police

operatives, and nicknamed 'prime evil'" (p. 4), Gobodo-Madikizela, who visited him many times, found him wrestling with his past.

> His world was a cold world, where eyes of death stared accusingly at him,
> a world littered with corpses and graves—graves of the unknown dead,
> dismembered or blown-up bodies. But for all the horrific singularity of
> his acts, de Kock was a desperate soul seeking to affirm to himself that he
> was still part of the human universe.
>
> (p. 47)

In her questioning about his past, Gobodo-Madikizela located a time
when de Kock seemed deeply troubled by what he was doing. On her
second visit to the prison, she asked de Kock what was his worst memory of
his past. He described a border raid, one of many, after which, while driving
home, he began to feel increasingly uncomfortable. In an almost psychotic
episode, he began to imagine an odd smell coming from his body that
required shower after shower, dumping all of the clothes he had worn into
the garbage. For Gobodo-Madikizela, the fantasy of a smell of blood or death
was a last assertion of conscience, empathy, and ultimately humanity being
expressed through body symptoms.

> It was a haunting story vividly told. In my mind it painted a clear picture
> of someone struggling with guilt, with a shadow that would not leave
> him and that he had tried to deny for too long. A human being died that
> night in the murder operation. This reality seemed to hang between us.
> At that moment I thought I saw a man finally acknowledging the debt he
> owed to his conscience.
>
> (p. 51)

What is being suggested in this story is that when a violence perpetrator
repeatedly kills or tortures others in secret extrajudicial activities, he kills or
silences almost all of the positive feeling capacities that belong to the realm
of the human in himself, and becomes a kind of killing machine. While
killing others, he also kills off all those affects in himself that connect to
others through shared emotional life.

This insight is confirmed in the work of Frantz Fanon (1965). As a psychiatrist at the main mental hospital in Algeria, Fanon found himself treating the sequelae of torture in both those who had been victims and those
who had been perpetrators, observing what Felman (1992) described as
"amputations of seeing" in both groups. He wrote: "What we Algerians
want to discover is the man behind the colonizer; this man who is both
the organizer and the victim of a system that has choked him and reduced
him to silence" (p. 32). Fanon (1967a) observed the effects of violence on
its perpetrators, in the French Foreign Legion serving in Algeria, who

developed symptoms we have come to think of as post-traumatic stress syndrome:

> In the course of the first quarter of 1956, cases of insanity among the police became frequent. The disturbances they manifested in the home (threatening to kill their wives, inflicting severe injuries on their children, insomnia, nightmares, continual threats of suicide), and professional misconduct (coming to blows with colleagues, neglect of duty, lack of energy, disrespectful attitudes toward their superiors) often required medical attention, assignment to a different service, or more frequently, a transfer back to France.
>
> (p. 66)

These symptoms stand in for conscious compassion for one's victims. For such compassion to finally break through often requires a shift in the dynamics of power. Stripped of the distance of authority and role, the perpetrator may be able to allow the experiences of his victims and/or their loved ones to enter his being. Extrapolating from Lifton's (1986) report of those who carried out face-to-face shooting of Jews in Eastern Europe, 20 per cent of perpetrators of violence will suffer psychological decompensation: severe anxiety, nightmares, tremors, and bodily complaints.

Isolation and burnout in perpetrators

A similar story has emerged in the work of Huggins, Haritos-Fatouros, and Zimbardo (2002), who studied police torturers and murderers in Brazil. Their research showed that police in Brazil suffered to an extreme degree from something like what has been called "burnout" in helping professions. The symptoms are generally,

> feelings of being overextended and depleted of emotional resources (emotional exhaustion); a negative, cynical or detached response to other people and the job (depersonalization); and a decline in feelings of productivity at work (a sense of ineffectiveness and failure). The experience of burnout has been linked to several negative outcomes, including problems at work (e.g. employee turnover, absenteeism, interpersonal conflict); troubles with family life (e.g. emotional distancing, interpersonal conflict, violence, divorce); and reduced physical and mental well-being (e.g. insomnia, alcohol and drug abuse, depression).
>
> (p. 211)

Because torturers and death squad members generally hide the work they do from friends, family, and coworkers—often claiming they are merely civil servants or government workers—they frequently become cut off not only from the humanity of their victims but also from others more generally.

> Social and professional isolation, combined with emotional or physical health problems, therefore tend to characterize the most burned out police, who complained of feeling they were losing their mind as well as of excessive drinking, insomnia, physical pains, marital breakups, and feelings of professional and social rejection and isolation.
>
> (p. 228)

Whereas helping professionals experience "burnout" from a fatigue of compassion and the effects of vicarious traumatization, perpetrators "burnout" from a persistent overriding of possible empathetic response. The whole police system was set up so that

> their training programs, social and work organization, and social-psychological dynamics are so organized as to discourage and punish any collegiality that could create the moral introspection that not only might call atrocity into question but might also mitigate the effects of burnout. Atrocity systems operate by nurturing operatives' unthinking reactions, thriving on secrecy and political and juridical impunity and gaining sustenance from fraud and disguise.
>
> (p. 229)

While many of these men later justify the violence they did in Brazil during the dictatorship, it is clear from the research that their destructive actions had a massive effect on the families and communities surrounding them. An atmosphere of danger, a not so subtle "don't ask, don't tell" habit pervades relationships with perpetrators in a way that breaks down the democratic fabric of society. What is built up as a result is an atrocity environment, where violence becomes a normalized part of the scene.

Huggins, Haritos-Fatouros, and Zimbardo (2002) found that many torturers in Brazil were not born psychopaths but fairly ordinary, unsophisticated people, usually from rural areas, who entered the atrocity-producing environment. Here they encountered a system that distorted all relationships. The system was fueled by paranoia, a sense that there was a powerful, subversive alien other threatening to undermine ordinary innocent civilians through acts of aggression. Within their police and military training, a grueling experience of hazing and victimization taught recruits to obey orders without thinking about implications. The units they entered were loosely organized in independent cells with little oversight, yet with support and approval from higher up in a hierarchy. At the top, there were powerful facilitators high up in the government who secretly gave orders and arranged funding but who would not be punished should any acts of terror come to light publicly. As we know from situations in Brazil, Rwanda, and the United States, paranoia about the other upon which violence and murder thrive can be fed from the highest levels of government.

According to Huggins, Haritos-Fatouros, and Zimbardo (2002), the perpetrators of atrocity they studied were encouraged and validated by three sets of facilitators:

> (1) international governments and their representatives, along with the international corporations that supply atrocity technologies and resources; (2) national governments that provide the ideology, the cast of auxiliary actors, and the system of rewards and sanctions as well as the legal and financial structure that supports and excuses atrocity; and (3) bystander communities, both in the perpetrators' society and in the broader world, who watch the play unfold in silence.
>
> (p. 261)

Because of the crucial role of ordinary citizen bystanders in this analysis, we see the facilitation of witnessing where only bystanding existed as a central goal of liberation psychology.

The normalization of violence

How easy it is to get sucked up into an atrocity environment, where one is constantly surrounded by reports of extreme violence so that one becomes inured to it. This was shockingly illustrated recently in the United States through disclosures about torture at Guantanamo and Abu Ghraib prisons, and other secret locations throughout the world. Officials at the highest level of government became engaged in a debate about how much torture and how much pain—described callously by Vice President Cheney as "a dunk in the water"—would be acceptable, given that national security was threatened by an alien "enemy." Meanwhile, the lowest-level soldiers were prosecuted as rogue actors, while mid-level officers claimed to know nothing about what was going on. Few suggested that Cheney, Rumsfeld, and Bush should be held responsible, and for the majority, the discussion of torture methodologies was treated as a completely "normal" public debate about policy. Citizens who were appalled felt little sense that their protest would be listened to or even acknowledged. Governmental unresponsiveness to protest contributes to many citizens "tuning out" of national debate from a sense of futility.

Yet atrocity environments have devastating effects on communities as well as individuals over the long term. Habits of silence and repetitive formulaic thinking set in. As the past slips away unprocessed and unmourned, communities lose the capacity to reflect on current events with any depth of understanding or affect. This leads the way toward what Argentine writer Elizabeth Jelin (2003) has called "social catastrophes."

> ... these catastrophes can involve a rupture between individual memory and collective and public practices. This happens when due to political conditions, collective practices are dominated by ritualization, repetition, deformation, or distortion, silence, or lies. They can also involve silences and fault lines in the process of intergenerational transmission.
>
> (pp. 21–2)

According to Rene Kaes (quoted in Jelin, 2003), a social catastrophe involves:

> the annihilation (or perversion) of the imaginary and symbolic systems inherent in social and transgenerational institutions, affecting the basic prescriptions regulating shared representations, prohibitions, structuring contracts, inter-subjective places and practices. ... Situations of social catastrophe bring about ruptures in the psychic work of attachment, representation, and articulation. ... As Freud emphasized, while natural catastrophes promote social solidarity, social catastrophes disaggregate and divide the social body.
>
> (p. 136)

The normalization of violence is a social catastrophe with far-reaching effects for individuals and communities. Social capacities gradually diminish in ways that are unmarked, because the whole enterprise is covered over with silence and secrecy that itself becomes normalized. People draw farther away from each other, increasing social distances and creating barriers to easy exchange of ideas. Other people seem more threatening, making it seem right to draw into small closed communities of like-minded associates with similar aspirations.

Diminished subjectivity in the absence of collective memory

When the past is frozen in silences that divide individuals and communities, it can become extremely difficult for people to interpret, represent, and express the effects of historical events on their own lives. "Experience" is partly the result of symbolic and interpretive work done by individuals and communities through the mediation of language, organized within a shared cultural interpretive framework. Subjectivity and memory are structured through language as a social and symbolic vehicle. Memory is therefore partly a social process. Jelin (2003) speaks of the "labor of memory" as an active and productive process through which individuals and groups in dialogue assign meaning to the past and orient themselves toward the future through constantly evolving interpretive frameworks.

When events in atrocity environments are silenced over many years, lively interpretive work comes to a halt, and is replaced by the stifling lies and official histories created by powerful public institutions to obscure the truth about what happened. Subjectivity becomes diminished when individuals can no longer freely explore alternate narratives in public conversations. The disruption of social relations by atrocity generating environments increases the vulnerability of the psyche and the likelihood that violations will be experienced as traumatic. When words have been denied and/or enlisted for propaganda, a gap is created.

> This provokes a hole in the ability to represent symbolically the event. There are no words and therefore there cannot be memories. Memory remains disarticulated and only painful traces, pathologies, and silences come to the surface. Trauma alters the temporality of other psychic processes and memory cannot handle them. It is unable to recover, convey, or communicate that which has been lived through.
>
> (p. 23)

Diminished subjectivity affects the families and allies of perpetrators as much or even more than the families and allies of victims, who are more likely to be haunted by the past than to silence it completely (see Chapter 7). Perpetrators are forced to live a constricted present and future if they are unwilling or unable to recollect the past.

After living through a period of historical violence in which an atrocity environment has developed, the families of perpetrators, accomplices, collaborators, and allies as well as bystanders need to learn how to remember the past, to develop the capacity to encounter traces of the past in the present for the sake of a more peaceful future. The question here is how to create new kinds of social spaces and dialogue that raise the discussion of the past beyond the inevitable clash of conflicting representations of violence that can then be denied or claimed as patriotic acts. The conversations about the past need to be entered into with the future in mind, being careful to navigate beyond the polarities that undergirded violent irruptions in the past. In the absence of such spaces for conversation, the narratives of coherent history and identity of a modernist nation begin to shatter under the weight of trauma.

Regardless of how far the groups that tacitly or openly support atrocity environments are from the violence they condoned, toxic psychic effects gradually seep back toward them. Writing after World War II about the long-term effects of the brutality of colonialism in Africa, Martinican Aimé Césaire (1972) described this process:

> First we must study how colonization works to *decivilize* the colonizer, to *brutalize* him in the true sense of the word, to degrade him, to awaken

him to buried instincts, to covetousness, violence, race hatred, and moral relativism; and we must show that each time a head is cut off or an eye put out in Vietnam and in France they accept the fact, each time a Madagascan is tortured and in France they accept the fact, civilization acquires another dead weight, a universal regression sets in, a gangrene sets in, a center of infection begins to spread; and that at the end of all these treaties that have been violated, all these lies that have been propagated, all these punitive expeditions that have been tolerated, all these prisoners that have been tied up and "interrogated", all these patriots who have been tortured, at the end of all the racial pride that has been encouraged, all the boastfulness that has been displayed, a poison has been distilled into the veins of Europe, and slowly but surely, the continent proceeds toward *savagery*.

And then one fine day the bourgeoisie is awakened by a terrific boomerang effect: the gestapos are busy, the prisons fill up, the torturers standing around the racks invent, refine, discuss.

(p. 35–6)

To begin to reverse such histories is a daunting task, but a critical one. The maimed subjectivity of perpetrators and their allies, and those who have been co-opted by the social scripts they put in motion brings them to a crossroads. They can attempt to retreat to shattered historical fantasies of coherence through a kind of amnesia and willful innocence. Then they perform as the model citizens who forget what should not be spoken, policing the familiar borders that lead to boundaries of them and us. But maintaining secrets and lies can be difficult. That there is an epidemic of feelings of depression, alienation, and emptiness, and a concomitant dependence on alcohol, antidepressants, and other legal and illegal drugs is a clue that many have walked on this path.

Yet there are other possibilities arising. The same circumstance of fragmentation and desubjectification we have described can also lead to new options. When the hold of official narratives weakens, when one experiences oneself as shot through with contradictions and opposing desires, spaces open for drift and rupture. Sandoval (2000) likens such openings to a hermeneutics of love—moments when new empathies, attachments, and solidarities may form outside the rules of control. Held less firmly in the network of dominant ideology, "a cruising, migrant, improvisational mode of subjectivity" may develop that can cause "an explosion of meaning"(p. 178). Surprises of empathy can suddenly break through old attachments.

Awakening from violence

Sometimes, after participating in violence, perpetrators begin to gradually question their experiences. In the Middle East, an organization called Combatants for Peace has arisen among former Israeli and Palestinian military through such a transformation. One of the founders, Yonatan Shapira, a war hero who served in Gaza, describes in an interview how he unaccountably began to go though a process that led to the realization that he was a perpetrator of terror:

> You know, it's a long process, and through the process you suffer ... they ordered a F-16 with a one ton bomb, that shot—that dropped this bomb on the house of a Hamas leader in Gaza strip, killing with him 14 innocent civilians, 14 innocent people, including nine babies. And although I didn't drop this bomb and I didn't shoot in my life anyone but I felt that this, me being part of this system that is causing this harm and this suffering and this killing to innocent people, it's just the same like being a terrorist in another organization. And those kids that were killed by the Palestinian fighter are just the same.
>
> (Combatants for Peace, 2006)

In 2005, Israeli and Palestinian combatants, ranging in age between 20 and 60, began to meet in secret and were stunned to discover the commonality of their doubts and experiences. Bassam Aramim, a former Fatah fighter, and another group cofounder, also expresses the uncanniness of the experience:

> It's a paradox. You hear a man talking about how he shot, killed, damaged your neighbor's house. But you feel empathy for him. You realize that we are all from the same background, but just from different sides. The soldier wanted to protect his people, and so did we. But we've all discovered we were wrong in how we did it.
>
> (Thomas, 2006)

These experiences have led the combatants to reflect on the education and values that led to their participation in what they now see as acts of terrorism. Yonatan Shapira puts it this way:

> In history lessons, I didn't learn about the occupation. I learned those beautiful peace and bereavement songs. I learned about the beautiful values, about democracy, peace, justice equality, freedom, and it took me many years to figure out and to know that at the same time that I was sitting in the classroom, learning all those beautiful values, my country, my military was occupying and oppressing millions of Palestinians, millions of people that were living without all those beautiful values.
>
> (Combatants for Peace, 2006)

Shapira was shocked to see a wedding one day as he landed a Black Hawk helicopter at a hospital with the injured from a terror attack:

> And it took me a while to understand that not just these guys down in the wedding were disconnected from reality, but also in the cockpit here inside me was a lot of ignorance, a lot of things that I didn't know.

And then you start to figure out and to learn and to find out all this half-side history lesson that you didn't get. And I realized that in order to change and not just to find a solution for myself, for my soul, for my being able to live with myself, I have to do something publicly.

(Combatants for Peace, 2006)

Such turnabouts can take years to arrive at the point of being able and willing to speak. Combatants for Peace has caused an enormous rupture in Israeli and Palestinian circles as they continue to recruit and speak out publicly. Now nearly one hundred members strong, their lives are in danger from both sides and they have difficulty finding places to meet. Nevertheless, their work is a courageous call for peace and dialogue in a powerfully polarized environment.

The long process of thinking through one's role as a perpetrator can lead to a complete re-evaluation of social norms in one's home country and to a reshaping of one's solidarities. From his conversations with Vietnam veterans, Lifton (2007) says that during the commission of atrocities, perpetrators quickly accept or construct meanings that minimize the contradictions between their values and their actions. To confront one's participation in atrocities, one must allow these hastily constructed meanings to explode, and begin to evolve an alternative survival mission, in the hope of restoring personal meaning and connection. Sometimes this can lead to despair and even suicide, unless a new life orientation can be developed. Rather than rationalize one's actions, this alternate pilgrimage requires that one radically call into question the formerly accepted meanings of the deadly enterprise of which one has been a part. This requires a process of de-ideologization that is best accomplished in the company of others also engaged in it, even if at different stages. Ben Chitty (1998) of the Vietnam Veterans Against War in the United States made this assessment years later with the support of fellow veterans:

By the time we were drafted or enlisted to fight in Vietnam, we had already been indoctrinated for that war since childhood by the mythology of America. One myth we soaked up was "cowboys and Indians"— the long saga telling how white Europeans carved a great nation out of a land inhabited by savages. But when we went to war, it wasn't much like the movies. Not much of a script ... The victims weren't grateful. Death wasn't noble ...

After returning home, Chitty began to see the war as a teacher of "hard lessons." As he thought about who profited from the war and what the Vietnamese must have endured, he began to think he had been fighting on the wrong side. A deeper exploration into American history allowed him to link colonial wars, slavery, and Native American genocide to the war in

Vietnam. This led to more profound questions about "the American way of life" where class and racial differences and marginalization are the norm. Veterans began to see "from a different angle, at the edge of the empire" that they had previously enforced.

> Then when we looked again at our own history, our war in Indochina turned out to be an all-American war. The Dominican Republic, Korea, Puerto Rico, Nicaragua, Haiti, the Philippines, Cuba, Mexico: American soldiers fought in all these countries, occupying some, annexing others, installing puppet regimes in the rest, extending or defending an empire. A bitter irony—we had wanted to serve: we wanted to be patriots. African Americans whose parents couldn't vote; Chicanos and Puerto Ricans whose culture dissolved into assimilated poverty. Poor and working-class whites tracked into the draft instead of college or the National Guard. Native Americans proving they too were "real" Americans. The real war— it turned out—was here at home too, and we had been on the wrong side.
>
> (Chitty, 1998)

Such painful reflections may take years to process and evolve into articulate language. Other Vietnam veterans discerned bits and pieces of Chitty's analysis without ever finding the strength to think these ideas through to their bitter end. Many were lost to alcohol, drugs, violence, and suicide, before finding a path into public dialogue. This loss has been a national tragedy.

The critical education Chitty wrenched from the violence he found himself part of perpetuating was not offered to him as a young person before going to war. If a society is to work against the dynamics that generate atrocities, it must provide educational pathways to support children and adults in becoming aware of the collective norms they have identified with. Jung saw such a process of awareness and dis-identification with unacceptable norms as crucial to the individuation process and the avoidance of fascism. Such a critical education teaches the "underside of history" (Dussel, 1975). Insofar as greed and lust for power generate propaganda and the machinery of war, such an education must help us see through the superficial rationalizations that are offered to defend violence as a needed option.

Exposing our own histories

The testimony of these soldiers points to the failures of formal education systems to disrupt official histories. Some—such as Myles Horton, founder of Highlander Research and Education Center—have argued that mainstream academic institutions and public education systems are hopelessly conservative, requiring the creation of informal learning environments where the histories of marginalized communities can be taught and analyzed. Facing a violent past requires shining a light of inquiry on painful chapters of one's own collective history, wherever one lives.

Official histories gain their imprimatur in formal academic institutions, and are disseminated far and wide through state-sponsored educational curricula. It is crucial that academic institutions open themselves to ruptures of official history through welcoming dissonant voices. For almost a century in the United States, African-American, Mexican-American, and Asian-American scholars and their allies protested the erasure of the history of violence against their communities from curricula in American schools. They struggled to have their communities' experiences included in the study of history, literature, and the arts.

At first, such efforts in universities were ignored and rejected. Later they were given token status: perhaps a single scholar in a department, or a separate isolated program, was able to offer materials as a kind of side dish to the main meal that was the "real" discipline. Many scholars were fired or failed to be hired or promoted during the long years when these interests were seen to be irrelevant to mainstream concerns—"not part of our discipline." Yet many of these insistent and often lonely scholars continued to unearth silences and absences. Today, at several American universities, including Emory University and the Universities of Alabama and North Carolina projects are finally underway to restore a fuller story of the past. At Brown University, where President Ruth Simmons is a great-granddaughter of slaves, a committee has worked for three years to study the university's connection with slavery and make recommendations for action. The Final Report of the committee stated:

> We cannot change the past. But an institution can hold itself accountable for the past accepting its burdens and responsibilities along with its benefits and privileges. ... In the present instance this means acknowledging and taking responsibility for Brown's part in grievous crimes.
> (Brown University's Debt to Slavery, 2006)

Omar Bartov, a committee member and Holocaust scholar, said after the report was published that the official history of Brown would now have to be entirely rewritten. President Simmons has asked the entire Brown community to discuss the report and give feedback before final recommendations are made. This is new ground for a major university, and an important model for the kind of work children, grandchildren, and even great-grandchildren of perpetrators and victims will have to do to begin a re-membering of the past and settling with it in a way that could change the future.

Unfortunately the vast majority of scholars who care about these issues and are working in the academic world are trying to function in institutions where their work is marginalized and considered irrelevant to their disciplines. Mainstream scholars who actively or passively resist studying their own discipline's collusion with histories of violence reinscribe the silencing and the divides perpetrators put into place through their actions.

Some state and local governments are also beginning to see the need for frank acknowledgments of violence perpetrated in the past. Recently the state of Virginia began discussing the state's history as part of the preparations for the yearlong commemoration of the 400th anniversary of the founding of Jamestown. Democratic delegate A. Donald Mc Eachin, also a great-grandson of slaves, sponsored a resolution in the House of Delegates that would put the issues on the table. The resolution, which passed unanimously, stated:

> The general assembly hereby expresses its profound regret for the commonwealth's role in sanctioning the immoral institution of human slavery, in the historic wrongs visited upon native peoples, and in all other forms of discrimination and injustice that have been rooted in racial and cultural bias and misunderstanding.
>
> (Virginia Faces Role in Slavery, 2007).

While the resolution does not suggest any institutional changes or offer reparations, it is an important first step toward more mature and inclusive conversations about Virginian history. According to McEachin, "Virginia had nothing to do with the end of slavery. It had everything to do with the beginning ..."(Virginia Faces Role in Slavery, 2007). This acknowledgment will be critical to altering the way history is taught in the South.

The refusal of violence

Sometimes the break with atrocity is a refusal to be who one is supposed to be, a bodily revulsion to expectations that does not happen years afterwards, but in the midst of the action. A recent film, *The Lives of Others* (2007) portrays a STASI officer in East Germany in the 1980s, slowly losing confidence in the whole paradigm of state security while working in an atmosphere of corruption and petty power manipulation. The character is assigned to spy on a group of writers and theater activists who have created passionate, intellectual, and engaged lives, and discovers by comparison how dry and empty is the cultural landscape of state bureaucracy and his own life. In the end, he defies orders and protects the writers by falsifying his surveillance reports, losing his position and status in the system shortly before the fall of the Berlin Wall undermined the entire structure. The film suggests that such structures of violence may be crumbling from within at the same time that they are resisted from without. While it is unclear how realistic such a fantasy about rapid transformation in East Germany might be, the film presents a useful model of a perpetrator of violence as capable of humanity, refusal, and redemption. It holds out the possibility of saying no as a valid option, regardless of the consequences.

Refusal to participate is a more than occasional strategy for those co-opted into structures of violence. For example, a group of Israeli Defense Force reservists involved in the occupation of Palestine refused the roles that had been required of them. They circulated leaflets in the military that offered to others a path to refusal, emphasizing that the occupation breeds violence, and that soldiers have a role in stopping it:

> When you take part in extrajudicial killings ("liquidation," in the army's terms), when you take part in demolishing residential homes, when you open fire at unarmed civilian population or residential homes, when you uproot orchards, when you interdict food supplies or medical treatment, *you are taking part in actions defined in international conventions (such as the 4th Geneva Convention) and in Israeli law, as war crimes.*

They appealed directly to the conscience of soldiers:

> Do you consider such war crimes justifiable?
> Don't acts of "liquidation" provoke suicide bombings?
> Is it justifiable to demolish the homes and vandalize the property of entire families?
> Can one justify the killing of children, women, old people—or, overall, of unarmed civilians?
> What are the "security" grounds to justify starving entire villages and depriving the sick of medical care?
> Soldier: don't these daily acts of repression, which are part of the routine of the occupation—curfew and blockade, land confiscation, preventing people from working or studying, the run-around and humiliation at the road-blocks and the violent searches in Palestinian homes—fuel hatred of us?
> *End the occupation—End the cycle of bloodshed!*

Some of these men were imprisoned, others removed from the army. The list of signatories has grown to over 550 (Courage to Refuse, n.d.).

Personally, the reservists are often torn apart by competing sentiments. One said:

> I didn't want to refuse orders. I didn't look forward to this moment. If there had been any way to avoid it, I think I would have chosen it. ... But there are times when there is no other choice but to refuse. That "no choice" is the personal aspect of refusal. My red line isn't yours, and vice versa. But traversing that red line is a surrender of your personality, your uniqueness, your values, and above all, the dictates of your conscience.

The Refuseniks have received international support that has helped them bear the alienation they suffer from many in their homeland. One peace organization that supports them, *Yesh Gevul* ("There is a limit!"), says that while anyone who decides to refuse reaches his decision on his own, they will then find a helping hand extending to them unreserved moral and material backing in the form of information, financial support for their families while the soldiers are imprisoned, and pickets at the military prisons where they are held.

The option of refusal is always a possibility for perpetrators of violence who come to believe that their actions are wrong. As resistance to the war in Iraq grows in the United States, Internet Web sites are allowing U.S. soldiers in Iraq and Iraq veterans at home to begin a broad ranging discussion of refusal. Web sites like http://soldiersvoices.net and http://www.ivaw.org are allowing a public discussion of war experience and the ethics of occupation.

Lt. Ehren Watada is the first commissioned officer to publicly refuse deployment to Iraq. He spoke at a national convention for Veterans for Peace in August 2006 surrounded on stage by 50 Iraq veterans who were supporting him. He suggested that "to stop an illegal and unjust war, the soldiers can refuse to stop fighting it" (Watada, 2006). Lt. Watada argued that there were two crucial elements necessary for such a refusal. First the soldier must go through a very difficult process of breaking out of military socialization and facing ostracism by peers. They need to understand the history and context of the war in Iraq, and face what the war will involve for them personally:

> Though the American soldier wants to do right, the illegitimacy of the occupation itself, the politics of the administration, and rules of engagement of desperate field commanders will ultimately force them to be party to war crimes.
>
> (Watada, 2006)

Second, according to Watada, ordinary people in the Untied States need to find ways to support those who refuse military service, along with their families. Those who refuse should not have to face a life of loneliness and isolation, and if they are imprisoned their families should not have to face hunger and homelessness.

> I tell you this because you must know that to stop this war, for the soldiers to stop fighting it, they must have the unconditional support of the people. I have seen this support with my own eyes. For me it was a leap of faith. For other soldiers, they do not have that luxury. They must know it and you must show it to them. Convince them that no matter how long they sit in prison, no matter how long this country takes to right itself, their families will have a roof over their heads, food in their stomachs, opportunities and education.
>
> (Watada, 2006)

Lt. Watada is calling bystanders to be active witnesses in stopping immoral wars. As we write, it is still not clear what the outcome of his refusal will be.

While refusal is increasingly discussed, in part due to the Internet, violence and terror are unfortunately on the rise throughout the world. New generations of victims are being created, and the need to understand the wounds of such experiences is more crucial than ever. In the next chapter, we turn to an analysis of the outcomes of terror on victims and their families.

7
Mourning and Witness after Collective Trauma

> How can one pose the task of mourning—which is always, in a sense, the task of actively forgetting—when all is immersed in passive forgetting, that brand of oblivion that ignores itself as such, not suspecting that it is the product of a powerful repressive operation?
>
> (Avelar, 1999, pp. 1–2)

Each historical community holds what Eviatar Zerubavel (2003) calls a "time-map," a social construction marking what is seen as important for that community. Not everything that happens is remembered. Some events fall into oblivion, while others are stressed in official histories. Those who have been marginalized and oppressed by dominant hierarchies often find that the issues they need to explore about the past are nowhere represented in official histories and when spoken about cannot be heard by those from the dominant culture. As transnational migration is affecting enormous numbers of people today, many of us carry multiple time maps and discourses, and need social spaces in which to negotiate complex identities that are both emergent and hybrid. In this chapter, we are addressing the wounds of victims of collective trauma, and the way victims maintain collective memories of the past that either enable or disallow various types of knowing, identity, and dialogue. We are attempting in this chapter to link the literature on fatalism in Latin America and colonialism in Africa with the literature on trauma that has developed largely in European and American contexts. The former has tended to focus on collective wounds, that is, trauma shared by a group, while much of the American and European literature on trauma has tended to focus on individual and familial abuse. We believe that by bringing these theoretical perspectives together, both psychological and sociological effects can be seen more clearly in their interrelationships. The silences, distortions, displacements, and amnesias within families about traumatic events echo larger societal patterns of misremembering and forgetting (Griffin, 1992).

Because many people in the world are living under military dictatorships or in violent and dangerous environments only thinly masked as democratic societies, the whole issue of speaking about the past and wrongs is permeated with considerations of safety and reprisal. In many countries, such as Argentina, Burma, Mexico, or Guatemala, if people attempt to raise issues about human rights violations, they can still "disappear"—that is, be kidnapped and murdered by extralegal military groups that may or may not be directly associated with governments. In the years after periods of terror, it may not be clear what is safe or dangerous. Remembering the assassinations of Martin Luther King, Jr. and Medgar Evers, and knowing that the Ku Klux Klan is still active, people often make uneasy jokes about Black leaders such as Barack Obama or Jesse Jackson being targeted if they speak too freely. Even where immediate danger has receded, built-up habits of fear and silence persist. Many people do not know how to be supportive witnesses to stories of terror and atrocity they are hearing for the first time. Automatic protective mechanisms of denial, shock, and dissociation may enter initial responses to such information, making it difficult for victims to overcome their own habits of reluctance or fear about speaking. Even if we were attempting to discover the facts about a single instance of violence, for example, an experience of childhood abuse or incest in a certain community, inconvenient questions might quickly lead to issues no one wanted to confront. Where was the mother or grandmother? Was she subjected to domestic violence? What was the role of women in that community? Were they free to speak without reprisals? The whole issue of remembering the past is thickly covered over with questions that bear on current circumstances and cultural conditions. We cannot assume an open field of safety and empathic witness exists already; in fact learning how to construct conditions for respectful and safe listening environments is part of the work of addressing traumatic experience.

Collective trauma

The key characteristic of traumatogenic events, whether a sudden shocking disaster or a slow insidious development, is that they bring about a calamitous emotional rupture in our sense of self-identity and community, disconnecting us from the ways of thinking, speaking, acting, and relating through which we previously made sense of the world. When trauma affects a whole community, particularly if the calamity was avoidable and human error or neglect played a role as in an oil spill, destructive social forces may set in, driving people apart. Researcher Kai Erikson (1994) calls this "a new species of trouble" (p. 22). While such calamities as earthquakes, mudslides, and floods have always been part of the context of human life, what is new in Erikson's view are large-scale toxic events that are human caused such as chemical explosions, groundwater contamination, and nuclear accidents. These events cause despair, a sense that no one cares and that one's life is expendable. Collective trauma, he writes, is a "blow to the basic tissues of social life," creating a "gradual realization that the community no longer exists as an effective source of support and that an important part of the self has disappeared" (1976, p. 154). Individuals begin to feel as if they are completely on their own, and a sense of distrust about the world often develops. The individualism and isolation felt to be the norm in modern urban environments may in fact be the end product of the traumatic disruption of communities over time.

As trauma research has deepened over the last 15 years, many people have come to suspect that a state of traumatization leading to numbness and a sense of defeat and hopelessness can be brought on by conditions associated with cultural marginalization, such as racism, poverty, forced displacement and migration, violence, and inadequate health care and education (Kleinman, 1988). Of course many people and communities that experience marginalization have resources of resilience that allow them to cope with and transform their realities; but others do not, and fall into cycles of despondency.

According to Erikson (1994), both chronic and acute conditions can induce trauma.

A chronic disaster is one that gathers force slowly and insidiously, creeping around one's defenses rather than smashing through them. People are unable to mobilize their normal defenses against the threat, sometimes because they have elected consciously or unconsciously to ignore it, sometimes because they have been misinformed about it, and sometimes because they cannot do anything to avoid it in any case. It has long been recognized for example that living in conditions of chronic poverty is often traumatizing, and if one looks carefully at the faces as well as the clinic records of people who live in institutions or hang out on the vacant corners of skid row or enlist in the migrant labor force or eke out a living in urban slums, one can scarcely avoid seeing the familiar symptoms of trauma—a numbness of spirit, a susceptibility to anxiety and rage and depression, a sense of helplessness, an inability to concentrate, a loss of various motor skills, a heightened apprehension about the physical and social environment, a preoccupation with death, a retreat into dependency, and a general loss of ego functions. One can find those symptoms wherever people feel left out of things, abandoned, and separated from the life around them. From that point of view, being too poor to participate in the promise of the culture or too old to take a meaningful place in the structure of the community can be counted as a kind of disaster.

(p. 21)

Psychologies of liberation work with this expanded notion of trauma, seeking to restore the links between individuals and the larger community and culture.

Effects of collective trauma

When we speak of trauma, we are referring to the psychological effects of certain events on persons and communities rather than the events that initiated these effects. According to the American Psychiatric Association's *Diagnostic and statistical manual of mental disorders* (1994), these psychological effects include the re-experiencing of the trauma in intrusive thoughts, recurring nightmares, and physiological reactivity when exposed to cues that symbolize an aspect of the traumatic situation. Victims of trauma find themselves in a world apart, struggling to avoid intrusive thoughts, feelings, and memories for fear of being overwhelmed. While longing for calm, they are beset with states of hyperarousal and are unable to fall or remain asleep. They have difficulty concentrating, are easily startled, and are hypervigilant in efforts to make sure trauma is not revisited. When we discuss traumatic events we are referring to the events that initiated, not caused, the psychological effects, because many other conditions need to be present in the social context for such events to generate the symptoms of psychological trauma. Not all people exposed to disastrous events experience symptoms of trauma.

While sharing historical and personal narratives in testimony or dialogue processes is an important form of bearing witness, trauma often makes this initially impossible. In addition, recounting of trauma often exacerbates symptoms because the telling itself may retraumatize, erasing the boundaries between the past and the present, the remembered and the presently experienced. Trauma marks efforts at dialogue with silences, gaps, absences, eruptions of emotion, and the impossibility of completeness. Events such as incest, domestic abuse, homophobic and racist violence, state terror, or industrial disaster, especially when they occur without public witness, can create ruptures in experience so profound for some that it may prove impossible to form any type of narrative frame to link earlier life with the postrupture condition. Some children who survive such violent ruptures may not remember the events that occurred at all and may never really be sure what happened. Some adults who have endured traumatic situations as victims (or, remarkably, as perpetrators, collaborators, or bystanders, which we discussed in the previous sections) lose the capacity to witness what has occurred for many years afterward or sometimes forever. It may be that after traumatic disruption there is a need for routine, for the reliability of normalization for years after such experiences; but even where this is successful, symptoms related to the periods of trauma may reappear again and again.

The therapeutic fantasy shared by many psychologies appears to be that there is a lost narrative of the traumatic past locked like an abscess within the psyche. Dissociated, but still accessible to the narrating ego, attempts to remember the past are the basis for much work of individual counseling. The metaphors guiding this work involve something like draining an abscess while filling in the gaps through narrating a gradual recollection of events.

Unfortunately, for many who have suffered traumatizing events, the greatest stamp of the past may be the feeling of having been overwhelmed, so that the occasion itself was a kind of absence of oneself, a missing-in-action experience. The poet Mary Oliver (1986) writes of the adult who suffered incest as a child as "a tree that will never come to leaf, in your dreams she's a watch you dropped on the dark stones till no one could gather the fragments" (p. 12). In this case, what remains are only fragments of the experience rather than a linear narrative that could be reconstructed. This creates certain problems for the process of remembering and mourning under conditions of trauma. The attempt to establish a factual narrative about past traumatic events may retraumatize victims by causing the same dissociated states in the present that marked the experience of the original event.

Once collective psychological sequela of trauma have set in, it becomes very difficult to form a picture of the significance of the everyday events within their historical period, or even to give personal testimony about what happened. Though the murder of millions of Jews in Germany took place in the 1940s, it was only in the 1960s after the Eichmann trial that the Holocaust was widely discussed and memorialized outside of the Jewish community. Before that there was a great deal of visceral resistance to personal testimony and historical reconstruction. Only isolated events could be recounted, but not linked to a larger picture. Those whose families were affected were often haunted by dreams and images of tattooed numbers, trains, and piles of shoes and suitcases, which they felt could never be spoken of to others. Discomfort could more often be expressed in symptoms or iconic images than in public discussion.

We need to differentiate between profound collective trauma that is so total and devastating that no public space for witness and community restoration could be preserved, and those types of suffering and victimization where resistance, action, witness, and testimony were maintained inspite of brutal conditions in atrocity environments. Where public action and witness could be sustained, there may have been terrible suffering, but it did not completely disintegrate into characteristic traumatic effects. Where no adaptive action is possible, and adults experience a situation of violence about which there is nothing they can do, helplessness, psychic freezing, numbing, and dissociation are likely to set in.

Henry Krystal (1995) has written about his long-term work with adult concentration camp survivors from Germany, whose responses are characteristic of traumatized adults. In general, the survivors exhibited severe alexithymia, an inability to respond emotionally and cognitively to events in the present, along with anhedonia, an inability to feel and express happiness.

Survivors also tended to use operative thinking, "an overly exaggerated emphasis on the mundane details of the 'things' in one's life, and a severe impairment in the capacity for wish fulfillment fantasy" (p. 79).

According to Krystal (1995):

> The adult traumatic state is initiated by the recognition of inevitable danger, and the surrendering to it. Thereupon the affective state changes from the signal of avoidable danger (anxiety) to a surrender pattern which is the common pattern of "freezing," "playing possum" or "panic inaction" which is common throughout the animal kingdom. ...
>
> With the surrender to what is perceived as inevitable, inescapable, immediate danger, an affective process is initiated, which Stern (1951) has called "catatonoid reaction." Briefly, it consists of a paralysis of initiative, followed by *varying degrees of immobilization leading to automatic obedience. At the same time there is a "numbing" process by which all affective and pain responses are blocked.* ... [T]he next aspect of the traumatic process is the *progressive constriction of cognitive processes, including memory and problem solving, until a mere vestige of the self-observing ego is preserved. This process may culminate in psychogenic death.*
>
> (pp. 80–1)

Adults who have undergone such an experience are often incapable of acting assertively, and may seem dull or obtuse and unable to express emotion. They may be anxious and need to speak repetitively about the past, while at other times they cannot bear to do so. They tend to screen anxieties through excessive concern about health and illness. Krystal found that the majority of the survivors he had come into contact with over many years of work did not do well: "unable to grieve effectively, most survivors become severely depressed, become ill, and die early. While they are alive, they live in constant pain" (p. 97).

It was only in 1980, when post-traumatic stress was listed in the third edition of the *Diagnostic and statistical manual of mental disorders*—the bible of psychiatric diagnoses—that it was officially recognized as a way of thinking about the catastrophic effects of certain experiences. At first the term "post-traumatic stress" was applied to those showing dramatic symptoms of flashbacks, memory gaps, and intruding, overwhelming images. The early identified sufferers of this syndrome were soldiers, train wreck survivors, then, eventually, victims of domestic abuse. In the last 25 years, a slow flood tide of recognition has covered the fields of psychiatry and clinical psychology, as the diagnoses of traumatic stress gathered up victims of violence suffered in homes, neighborhoods, and devastated environments. Some clearly link traumatic psychological suffering with social violence. Others, caught in a medical model of treating individuals, delink the individual from social, political, or environmental contexts that give rise to post-traumatic symptoms.

Recent work in the psychology of trauma and memory has expanded the implications of trauma to encompass our understandings of how we construct self and other, history, community, and culture at the most basic levels (Avelar, 1999; Edkins, 2003; Jelin, 2003; Marks, 2000). In these understandings, trauma affects what we talk about with each other, and what we are silent about.

Fatalism

While the first generation of Holocaust survivors are a discrete and distinctive cohort, a parallel set of psychological patterns has been found to be widespread among the poor and dispossessed who have suffered the violence of colonialism and globalization. In Latin America, a similar traumatic syndrome has been identified as fatalism. Ignacio Martín-Baró (1994) focused on the symptom of fatalism among the dispossessed in Latin America, seeing it as the root of the "forced siesta, a state of semi-wakefulness that keeps [the people of Latin America] at the margins of their own history, where they are forced to participate in processes that others control" (p. 199). By the term "fatalism," Martín-Baró sought to describe the way in which the poorest come to experience their lives as predetermined at birth by cosmic or spiritual forces deemed out of their control. It is a stance where one submits to unfolding fate, without any sense of being able to effect it. The passive and submissive behavior that results from such a worldview conforms and adapts, taking up a stance of resignation in which one's fate and the suffering inevitably embedded in it can—at best— be borne with dignity. As one struggles with meeting daily difficulties through such a fatalistic stance, hopelessness creates myopia, narrowing time to the present. Memory is lost and any sense of being able to plan and affect the future in the light of one's desires is abandoned in pessimism.

Through looking at studies about Latin American fatalism, Martín-Baró found that it was seen as passed on from parent to child, contributing to the maintenance of poverty. When the causes of this fatalistic stance are not critically questioned, the oppressed are blamed for bringing about their misery. Martín-Baró (1994) argued differently:

> Fatalism is a way for people to make sense of a world they have found closed and beyond their control: it is an attitude caused and continually reinforced by the oppressive functioning of overall social structures. Marginalized children in *favelas*, or *champas*, or other shantytowns of Latin America internalize fatalism not so much because they inherit it from their parents as because it is the fruit of their own experience with society. Day by day they learn their efforts in school get them nowhere; the street does not reward them well for their premature efforts at selling newspapers, taking care of cars, or shining shoes; and therefore it is better not to dream or set goals they will never be able to reach. They learn

to be resigned and submissive, not so much as the result of the transmission of values through a closed subculture as through the everyday
demonstration of how impossible and useless it is to strive to change
their situation, when that environment itself forms part of an overall
oppressive social system. Hence, just as marginalization is caused by a
socioeconomic system to which the marginalized, as marginalized people, belong, the attitudes and values of a culture of poverty are being continually caused and reinforced by the normal functioning of this social
system, which includes the poor as members.

(pp. 210–11)

Martín-Baró thought that those suffering from fatalism had correctly seen
how impossible it was to effect their situation through their own efforts, but
that they had misdiagnosed the cause of this state of affairs. Fatalism is
symptomatic of the internalization of social domination. To see this relationship disrupts a rationale by which minority rule by a powerful elite is
justified. It disrupts the docility of people's efforts to accept their fates given
at birth as inevitable, the "will of God", making minority rule possible.

Hence we can see that even though fatalism is a personal syndrome, it
correlates psychologically with particular social structures. ... there is a
correlation between objective and subjective structures, between the
demands of social systems and the character traits of individuals. ... the
organization and functioning of each social system favors some attitudes
while impeding others and rewards some kinds of behavior while pro-
hibiting and punishing others.

(p. 213)

Symptoms of fatalism are depressive feelings of inferiority, worthlessness,
and hopelessness about the larger context of daily life, lack of a sense of
agency, of the impossibility of effecting a future or of even being able to
hope for a future different from the present, the abandonment of the past,
and, too often, the erupting of violence born of futility. Within such a
psychology, immersion in the present, whenever possible, brings the relief
of immediate activity. Such symptoms are borne individually, while created
socially and shared communally.

The genius of educators such as Paulo Freire was to understand that the
addressing of the kind of memories and symptoms noted above needs to
occur not in the privacy of an office, in a dyadic relationship, but among
others who are suffering similarly. In the context of small Christian Base
Communities organized by liberation theologists, one could see that one's
"fate" was shared, and together people could begin to try to read personal
experience in the light of history. The recovery of historical memory
through the sharing of stories and pictures begins to allow a more complex

view of how things have become the way they are. Only through understanding the origins and functioning of what one has accepted as inevitable
and normal, can one begin to imagine a way to intervene creatively to
change one's situation in the course of time with the support of others.

Internal colonization

A syndrome very similar to that of fatalism was identified as one of the
effects of the violence of European colonialism on some of the indigenous
populations of Africa.

Psychiatrist Frantz Fanon, born in Martinique, became one of the most
important theorists of Africa's struggle for liberation. While speaking to the
psychological dynamics of "the black man," his theorizing rang true for others who were caught in the dehumanizing racist objectifications that
marked colonialism. To understand the inferiority complex that fuels a
sense of impotence, he turned our attention to what he calls a "double
process" that begins in economic terms and becomes internalized. This
sense of inferiority becomes "epidermalized", as people reduce others to
their skin color. He argued that next to the ontogenetic approach of Freud,
we must create a sociogeny, an analysis of cultural context, to understand
the colonized subject's alienation.

According to Fanon (1967a), for the colonized to become free psychologically they must "free [themselves] of the arsenal of complexes that has been
developed by the colonial environment" (p. 30). A central part of the arsenal
has to do with the equation of whiteness with beauty and intelligence: "In the
man of color there is a constant effort to run away from his own individuality,
to annihilate his own presence" (p. 60). What is needed, says Fanon, "is to
hold oneself, like a sliver, to the heart of the world, to interrupt if necessary
the rhythm of the world, to upset, if necessary, the chain of command, but in
any case, and most assuredly, *to stand up to the world*" (p. 78).

> Every colonized people—in other words, every people in whose soul an
> inferiority complex has been created by the death and burial of its local
> cultural originality—finds itself face to face with the language of the
> civilizing nation; that is, with the culture of the mother country. The
> colonized is elevated above his jungle status in proportion to his adoption
> of the mother country's cultural standards.
>
> (p. 18)

He is clear that it was the European's feeling of superiority that co-creates
the feeling of inferiority of the colonized.

> I begin to suffer from not being a white man to the degree that the white
> man imposes discrimination on me, makes me a colonized native, robs
> me of all worth, all individuality, tells me that I am a parasite on the

world, that I must bring myself as quickly as possible into step with the white world.

(Fanon, 1967a, p. 98)

The colonialist "reaches the point of no longer being able to imagine a time occurring without him. His irruption into the history of the colonized people is deified, transformed into absolute necessity" (Fanon, 1967b, p. 159). With this irruption comes the loss of local histories and languages, of indigenous traditions and rituals that offered community cohesiveness, pride, and resilience. One possible outcome of such an enforced sense of inferiority is violence. Fanon is clear: "Terror is the weapon of choice of the impotent" (1967, p. 9).

Albert Memmi, born in Tunisia in 1920, philosopher and novelist, is the author of *The colonizer and the colonized*. As a Jew in French-colonized Tunisia, he found himself able to describe phenomenologically interlocking portraits of both the colonizer and the colonized. Memmi describes how colonization *disfigures* both the colonized and the colonizer. For the colonized, colonialism constitutes a "social and historical *mutilation*," severing a people from their own history, culture, and language; substituting the oppressors' holidays and costumes. Both past and future are denied, locking the colonized into a present reality of being perceived as subservient, weak, backward, and evil. Indeed, one becomes painted in a dehumanized fashion to justify the oppressor's dominance and exploitation. There is an illusion created that the colonized can be assimilated into the society of the oppressors, enjoying the rewards of the dominant system. Once assimilation is rejected by the colonizers, the colonized are left to recover their own dignity, terminating earlier efforts of imitation and self-denial.

Resistance to Westernization

Amin Maalouf (2000), a Lebanese Christian, sums up the resistance to Westernization that is part of the effect of the traumatic displacements of globalization. In doing so, he awakens our awareness to how the shadow of the West's quest for superiority falls across the psyches of others.

It is all the easier to imagine the reactions of the various non-Western peoples whose every step, for many generations has already been accompanied by a sense of defeat and self-betrayal. They have had to admit that their ways were out of date, that everything they produced was worthless compared with what was produced by the West, that their attachment to traditional medicine was superstitious, their military glory just a memory, the great men they had been brought up to revere—the poets, scholars, saints and travelers—disregarded by the rest of the world, their religion suspected of barbarism, their language now studied by only a handful of specialists, while they had to learn other people's languages if they wanted to survive and work and remain in contact with the rest of mankind. Whenever they speak with a Westerner it is always in his language, almost never in their own ...

Yes, at every turn they meet with disappointment, disillusion or humiliation. How can their personalities fail to be damaged? How can they not feel their identities are threatened? That they are living in a world that belongs to others and obeys rules made by others, a world where they are orphans, strangers, intruders or pariahs.

(pp. 74–5)

Maalouf understands that the rise of religious fanaticism was not the Middle East's first response to colonialism. It was not until other paths, such as democratic rather than authoritarian, corrupt, and inept nationalisms, were blocked that "beards and veils started to burgeon as signs of protest" in the 1970s (Maalouf, 2000, p. 82). Reclaiming and identifying with aspects of a culture that has been besieged and weakened helps embolden identities disfigured by colonialism and globalization (Jurgensmayer, 2000), satisfying needs for identity, affiliation, spirituality, action, and revolt (Maalouf, 2000).

In *Decolonization and the decolonized*, Memmi (2006) explains how cultures under attack identify more adamantly with their traditions, losing the ability to discern which elements should be revised or questioned. In reaction to cultural assaults, that which has been demeaned is held in high esteem regardless of the desirability of a particular practice. Fundamentalism is thus fueled.

Belated memories

One of the hallmarks of collective trauma is that the memory and understanding of it is always belated, constructed after the fact. According to Dori Laub (Felman & Laub, 1992), writing about the Holocaust, "The degree to which bearing witness was required, entailed such an outstanding measure of awareness and of comprehension of the event—of its dimensions, consequences, and above all of its radical *otherness* to all known frames of reference—that it was beyond the limits of human ability (and willingness) to grasp, to transmit, or to imagine" (p. 84). Laub suggests that this inability to witness is a universal and "human" failing, but we would rather place such unknowing within the framework of colonialism, where for centuries colonists managed to avoid seeing the suffering they imposed on the colonies. Where violence and inequity have become normalized, a kind of amnesia sets in among the privileged that is part of the pathology of collective trauma. Where there is no framework of cultural reference within which to place testimonies about traumatic events, no one is listening for the stories of victims, thereby reinforcing the conditions that contribute to breaks in narrative. Polarization becomes permanently embedded, and the privileged begin to think of the marginalized as unalterably other and alien or as delinquent troublemakers. The task of remembering in situations of collective trauma is one that then becomes the work of subsequent genera-tions, a work that echoes through the families of both victims and perpe-trators as a sacred task.

Witness as a powerful defense against collective trauma

It is not always the case that people in situations of violence find themselves completely helpless. Concentration camps are extreme cases of isolation, control, and silencing, and are perhaps the most totalized atrocity environ-ments. Colonial conquest also provided unique opportunities for white set-tlers to alienate and dominate others whom they perceived as markedly different. There are other situations of violence that are more complicated, and that allow for more fluidity and possibilities for action for the oppressed who have been amazingly resilient and creative in developing forms of pub-lic witness.

After the military coup in Chile in 1973 that brought Pinochet to power for 17 years, thousands of people were arrested, tortured, murdered, and dis-appeared. Nevertheless, during the early years of the dictatorship, people found startling ways of speaking out against the violence in acts of cultural resistance. Writing about these activities, Chilean journalist Ariel Dorfman (1978) suggested that even though the dictatorship had made a brutal assault on educational institutions, the media, and cultural producers such as musicians, artists, and actors, there was still an active semi-legal cultural resistance in process, particularly under the wing of parish churches and union federations, which were barely tolerated by the military.

> There exist song festivals, concerts in churches and universities, neigh-borhood newspapers, painting and poetry workshops, folkloric peñas ("clubs"), artistic encounters, amateur theatrical works, books of carefully drawn but insolent content. The mere act of joining together, of listening in a group, of contemplating one another's faces, of learning once again how to organize activities together, even if they are cultural or sporting, is a fundamental way for the people to exercise and legitimize their right to associate with one another, to move and to express themselves. It is precisely the popular, massive character of these manifestations that limits the possibilities of repressing or even keeping watch over them. Nor is it easy for any regime—not even one like that of Chile, notorious for its stupidity and savageness—to prohibit the workers from singing or listening to song; from playing soccer or watching others play. Culture has an especially mobilizing and energizing effect upon a *pueblo* that has been subjected to a law of passivity determined to repress it. Shared art is one way of uniting mutilated hands, of sending forth a heart which never stopped beating but which has not been well heard by all. What's more, the mere organization of a cultural event is a victory, a preliminary step

to further organizing, to making more contacts, to pushing one more inch beyond the limits that the authorities can tolerate.

The culture that expresses itself publicly is not only a means of keeping a voice alive, of exercising the vocal chords, of preparing oneself for songs and messages to come; it is also a way in which to mount a counter-culture. For example there are songs that through the use of double meanings have taken on an ambiguous heaviness, reflecting inexpressible desires, alluding to two things at a time. A vast secret language has thus been created; a language which the military knows but cannot admit or repress.

(pp. 192–3)

Throughout the years of the dictatorship, thousands of people participated in small ways resisting the military through various clandestine means: writing slogans and graffiti on currency, buses, and walls; distributing forbidden music tapes, books, and newspapers; creating underground films, posters, and poetry; and organizing popular workshops in theater, music, and the arts. Of course many cultural workers were arrested, tortured, placed in concentration camps, killed, or forced into exile. Eventually, some of this work developed in exile and was then smuggled back, fanning the flames of resistance and bearing witness abroad to the brutality of the dictatorship. Dorfman was impressed with the creativity of the resistance.

The first point that attracts the attention of anyone who tries to describe this resistance—whose existence the dictatorship itself recognizes—is the extraordinary wealth of levels and *vias*, channels and paths, spaces and breaches, which the Chileans have learned to open, utilize or invent in order to maintain contact. By these varied means they continue to work together—in the "now" that precedes "tomorrow"—for a democratic alternative.

(p. 192)

Because the deep-rooted resistance continued on home ground in spite of the military dictatorship, many Chileans were able to witness the atrocities of the dictatorship both at home and abroad. Thus a rich array of valued narratives and memorials in music, art, and literature continued to be produced and widely distributed for many years, while unacknowledged in national public discourse.

We can observe a similar pattern in South Africa where during the long years of the anti-apartheid struggle, a secret language of song, dance, literature, and art continued to comment publicly on events, holding out hope for a different future (see Chapter 12). While in both Chile and South Africa there was profound suffering as a result of brutal state terror, we would suggest that public witness allowed many to survive it without the specific symptoms of trauma. In fact, many people were able to supply detailed and often outstandingly expressive accounts of what had happened to their families and communities both at the time and years later. These testimonies in both South Africa and Chile were able to generate enormous international solidarity movements that hastened the defeat of their oppressive regimes.

The postdictatorial period in Chile, and also in Argentina, Peru, Uruguay, Guatemala, and other countries, however, was very different from that of South Africa where the opposition forces were the majority, and the anti-apartheid organizations were able to take over the government after years of struggle. The Truth and Reconciliation Commission of South Africa placed on public record much of the sordid story of police and government violence during the apartheid period. The Commission called the whole nation to face up to its past and begin a new chapter for the future (see Chapter 15). In contrast, in Chile, Argentina, Peru, and Uruguay, where opposition forces were defeated, the inability of public national discourse to integrate the history and effects of dictatorship became traumatic through silences in public accountings. The circumstances of the detainment of the disappeared have still not been explained, their bodies have not been located, and most of those responsible have not been named or brought to justice for these crimes. There has not yet been a complete national public acceptance of the events and effects of the military dictatorships in Latin America. Nor has there been a public accounting in the United States of the illegal counter-insurgency activities organized by the CIA that contributed to these events. The silences have allowed the recycling of many of the central players from that period, such as Cheney, Bush, Abrams, Kissinger, Haig, Negroponte, Poindexter, Gates, Allen, and Addington into anti-democratic and semi-legal schemes for kidnapping and torture as well as for amassing wealth related to the wars in Afghanistan and Iraq.

The result of these long-term silences has been to change the quality of social relations in Chile, Argentina, Peru, and Uruguay, where according to Chilean psychologist Elizabeth Lira (2001), a climate of mistrust, fear, and polarization has been created.

> Political repression delineated the exclusion of one sector of society by making it the target of violence. The predominant ideological argument centers around division and social polarization. One group is termed the "others," "the enemies," "subversives," "criminals," "terrorists," or any other equivalent term, endowing such individuals with a "negative identity" (Erikson, 1985), which makes it possible to strip them of their human condition.
>
> (p. 112)

The victims of such dehumanization in a context of polarization and silencing may begin to feel a sense of derealization and depersonalization.

It becomes, according to Lira, a "collective mental health need" to establish publicly that violence happened, and in the case of torture victims, "that it happened to me" (p. 113).

> This need becomes more evident in a country when a society denies that such things happen, when political repression is concealed, when the "normality" of daily life distorts social perceptions of the catastrophe, and traumatic experiences of a political origin appear to be nothing more than private and personal experiences.
>
> (p. 113)

After years of living in such an environment, and as a whole new generation has come of age in a climate of repression, Lira feels that Chilean society has been changed dramatically by the traumatic effects of violence:

> From a psychosocial perspective, the repression affected the daily life of Chilean society, which was characterized by a rigid social frame-work, sociopolitical polarization, and constrained life, and ruptured the commonly held sense of everyday life. It was also expressed in weakened personal autonomy and self-confidence. This was augmented by a most devastating psychosocial characteristic, the "devaluation of human life".
>
> (p. 113)

As a result, history remains an "open wound" that keeps traumatic memories alive and is continually aggravated by calls to forget the past and move on. The symptoms Lira describes, when left unheeded, become "insurmountable obstacles to peaceful social coexistence and to political reconciliation" (p. 113). This became painfully obvious during the funeral of Augusto Pinochet, when huge crowds demonstrated to denounce his leadership, while thousands of others who saw him as a national hero, mourned his passing.

The work of mourning

During the postdictatorial period in Chile, according to Idelber Avelar (1999), the environment of the neoliberal market economy promotes forgetting of the past and the constant replacement of the old with the new. The old is obsolete in this logic and needs to be dislodged by the latest, newest set of commodities. Those interested in mourning and memory are accused of being fixated in the past, unwilling to move forward into the brave new world of globalization. The work of mourning is thus always operating against the grain of globalization, refusing the blank slate of an ahistorical present in favor of emblems and allegorical ruins of a lost past.

> In incessantly producing the new and discarding the old, the market also creates an array of leftovers that point toward the past, as if demanding restitution for what has been lost and forgotten.
>
> (Avelar, 1999, p. 2)

For those still mourning the losses of the past, these leftovers draw painful attention to all that was left unaccomplished in the past. The texts, sites, memorials, and art objects that embody this work of mourning, "carry the seeds of a messianic energy ... that looks back at the pile of debris, ruins, and defeats of the past in an effort to redeem them" (p. 3).

> Unlike the replacement of old by new commodities, the substitution proper to the work of mourning always includes the persistence of an unmourned, unresolved remainder, which is the very index of the interminability of mourning.
>
> (p. 5)

These remainders become important metonymic memorials of lost ways of life: a certain song stands in for the hope and optimism before a defeat, a picture recollects a feeling of community, a ritual recreates a fragment of a former time, a particular meal comes to embody the tastes and smells of lost familiarity, a way of dress re-performs a seemingly unrecoverable period of dignity and autonomy. It is this ability of remainders of the past to carry iconically another way of being that makes them so explosively meaningful for victims of trauma.

During and after the dictatorships in Argentina and Chile, *Las Madres de Los Desaparecidos* (the Mothers of the Disappeared), *Los Familiares de Los Desaparecidos* (Families of the Disappeared), and later the *Los Hijos de Los Desaparecidos* (the Children of the Disappeared) spent years holding up pictures of lost loved ones in public plazas. These acts of resistance carried the memories of specific families, but they also spoke volumes about what the dictatorship had destroyed. The persistence of these iconic performances by family members, along with many other voices demanding an accounting, carried on the work of mourning against the grain of forgetfulness. The photographs of lost family members never accounted for became allegories of an entire period of losses that had never been publicly acknowledged. Eventually mourners spearheaded the retrieval and reconstruction of public cultural memories about the violence of the 1970s that many others wanted to forget. It was only with the arrest of Pinochet in London in 1998 that the process of public accounting in Chile of the violent and repressive period after the military coup of 1973 rose to a new level. Most recently, the election of President Bachelet, whose father was tortured and murdered by the dictatorship, and who was herself arrested with her mother and taken to the Villa Grimaldi torture center in Santiago, has been an important validation of collective recollection in the present.

Isolation of memory in buried crypts

In some situations, such as that of Burma, it has been completely impossible to publicly discuss violent events of recent history without harsh reprisals. When public discourse is absolutely forbidden, the effects can be extreme. Psychoanalysts Abraham and Torok (1994), Hungarian Jewish refugees in post–World War II France, argue that the traumatic is found in every experience we cannot digest, verbalize, symbolize, or think when the surrounding family and collective culture are unprepared to witness painful events and help us transform them into speakable and recognizable experiences. Such events break apart psychic webs of identity, isolating individuals whose experience of coherence has been torn apart. Bits and pieces of symptom and image from such events become buried in what Abraham and Torok call a psychic "crypt" creating a psychological geography far more complicated than that imagined by early depth psychologists.

It is not simply a matter of events that were experienced becoming "repressed" because they are counter to an ego ideal. Rather, traumatic events are never actually experienced at all. The construction of experience happens after the trauma through a symbolic and imaginative process within dialogue spaces provided by culture and community. In order to tell one's story, there needs to be a participatory public space of listening and recollection, a quiet and essentially sacred space where the dead and the violated can be memorialized and honored. Such sacred spaces of recovery do not rely only on words, for the unsaid will exceed the sayable. After particularly painful testimony in Truth and Reconciliation hearings in South Africa, Bishop Tutu often stopped proceedings for a period of silence, prayer, or song, to honor the dead and respect the survivors, a period of silence in which to absorb the shameful history that had been suffered through. In such spaces of recollection, we enter as we would a spiritual ritual, with humility and an attitude of contemplation, open to grace or transformation through new insights. In spaces of recollection, we can publicly begin to speak or to express through the arts what has not yet been acknowledged. We take an active role in trying to make sense of our history and context.

When such potential spaces are lacking because no one is prepared to witness what has occurred, isolated and unprocessed islands of unbearable image and symptom go on living in what Abraham and Torok called "anasemic" effects, parts of the psyche that are unknown because they are not linked with narratives and symbols of self-identity. These crypts form a living kernel surrounded by a symbolic shell made up of our remembered and symbolized personality. We are then haunted by enigmatic symptoms, images, and feelings emanating from the phantom kernel. Children whose parents have been traumatized—and we also think friends, neighbors, witnesses, and other family members—experience the trauma victim's secret crypt as an uncomfortable absence, a verbal silence alongside powerful images that creates what Abraham and Torok called "enclaves," or isolated parts of the self full of mute fantasies about the absence that is never spoken. Writing about the experiences of children of the survivors of the Holocaust like herself, Helen Epstein (1979) explained: "There were documents, evidence of our part in a history so powerful that whenever I tried to read about it in books, I could not take it in" (p. 11).

Non-redemptive mourning

Claudia Bernardi (in Godoy, 1999), an Argentine artist and human rights activist, has assisted her sister, a forensic examiner, at the exhumation of mass graves in Guatemala, El Salvador, and Ethiopia. She writes: "Something really major happens when you go down a well to find over one hundred children murdered. At that point ... the membrane which divides lucidity from madness ... is stretched." The states of despair and suffering that open in those who witness such events are an extension of the original crimes which have destroyed the capacity of participants to sort past, present, and future. According to Bernardi, the Argentine dictatorship intended this long-term consequence:

> What they wanted was not to kill so many thousand people ... it was to create an atmosphere to last into the future, an atmosphere of bleak individuality, of hopelessness, ugliness, even a lack of remembering what integrity is about. And they almost succeeded.
>
> (in Godoy, 1999)

After the violence of state terror, the years of repressive silence, the personal suffering and fear, "there is an enormous temptation to become ugly, dry up in the heart ..." Involved in such processes, it no longer makes sense to talk about healing. For Bernardi, the idea of healing "has dangerous ramifications because from certain things there is no healing possible ... I know where the wound is, and I don't want to forget it, to make it less" (Bernardi, in Godoy, 1999).

Bernardi creates art "as an antidote for the solitude" engendered by suffering. There is no representational attempt here to document facts or present any kind of historical realism. She applies multiple pigments to wet paper and runs them through a press again and again. Between and over the layers of color she engraves images with a quill. The effect is of a ghost world, shifting and disappearing like the past and our memories of it. We see here a ritual of bodily engagement that we could think of as the creation of an altar, an honoring of remains—of the dead, of history, of memory—without any attempt to cover them over with a finished narrative. Bernardi's compassionate work touches a chord for many people whose lives were changed by terror. It opens a way to thinking about how to mourn a traumatic past. Here is the development of a non-redemptive mourning, not intended to finish with the past and return to "normal life," but rather to keep the past from slipping away in a present that continues to deny it.

Mourning without understanding

In a very different project with a similar strategy, filmmaker Claude Lanzmann created a nine-and-a-half-hour film on the Holocaust called *Shoah*, which at the time of its release in France in 1985 was called the film event of the century. The film never attempts to give a cohesive historical account of the Holocaust, but moves back and forth from a series of abstract questions asked by Lanzmann, who appears in the film, to stories and images of very particular concrete details and memory fragments. The effect of the film on many viewers is devastating, because it shatters any possibility to be coherent in response to the historical event; and in this way it is faithfully transmitting the fragmenting and unintelligible character of this history as it was lived. Lanzmann (1995) is very clear about his refusal to attempt an overview of these events that would structure them as knowable:

> There is an absolute obscenity in the very project of understanding. Not to understand was my iron law during all the eleven years of production of *Shoah*. I clung to this refusal of understanding as the only possible ethical and at the same time the only possible operative attitude. This blindness was for me the vital condition of creation. Blindness has to be understood here as the purest mode of looking, of the gaze, the only way not to turn away from a reality which is literally blinding.
>
> (p. 204)

Trauma theorist and film critic Shoshana Felman (in Caruth, 1995) links *Shoah* to the psychological theories of Lacanian psychoanalysis. She likens the "bodily and physical presence" of Lanzmann on the screen to that of a psychoanalyst with his "depth of silence, and in the efficacy of his speech" (p. 202). Both the filmmaker and the psychoanalyst are on a quest, "a search for truth through an act of talking, through dialogue, through the act of interlocution" (p. 202). Both initiate a quest for memory, but only through circumambulating memories, events, and images in the present repetitively, in nonlinear fashion, and over a long period of time. Each is stranded among concrete fragments of detail from the memories being offered: Abraham Bomba is staged cutting hair in a Tel Aviv barbershop as he recounts to Lanzmann his shaving the heads of Jewish women in the room next to the gas chamber at Auschwitz. The gap between Auschwitz and Tel Aviv is clear, at the same time it is undermined through recollection that cannot be complete.

Many recent films are working within a similar ethical and aesthetic strategy. For example, Tranh Anh Hung's film trilogy on Vietnam, *The Scent of Green Papaya* (1993), *Cyclo* (1995), and *Vertical Ray of the Sun* (2001) represent attempts to gather into the present a way of life that has been destroyed, on the basis of fragments of scent, touch, image, and sound linked to the past through synaesthetic memories. Julie Dash's film *Daughters of the Dust* (1991) links food, dialogue, weather, and wind with its disruptions to the intrusion of the past, spirits, and ancestors into the present. Marlon Riggs's final work *Black is ... Black Ain't* (1994) presents the ritual of a family gathering cooking gumbo and remembering the dead as a way to recapitulate and reconnect the diverse and shattering experiences of the African diaspora.

Each of these works of art is developing a new understanding of postmodern rituals of bodily witness that are very different in function from legal notions of testimony and truth, personal mourning, or dialogue practices. In Freudian psychology, melancholia is portrayed as an inability to mourn, and the resolution of mourning as a letting go of the past in order to get on with the present. However after traumatic events, particularly those that are connected with large-scale forms of social injustice, where people have been wronged and lives have been destroyed in ways and for motives that are completely unconscionable, it is unlikely that victims want to entirely forget. Often, a way of life has been disrupted and remains buried in memory as a lost object that must be protected against contemporary values. Where this has occurred, there is a recurring need for a work of allegory through which the crypt can be literalized in the social world: "the erection of an *exterior* tomb where the brutal literalization of the internal tomb can be metaphorized" (Avelar, 1999, p. 9). This work of exposing the tomb of silenced wounds and narratives can never be completed:

> There is a *belatedness* proper to this endeavor, for it establishes a salvific relation with an object irrevocably lost. This is an engagement that cannot but be perpetually catching up with its own inadequacy, aware that all witnessing is a retrospective construction that must elaborate its legitimacy discursively, in the midst of a war in which the most powerful voice threatens to be that of forgetfulness.
>
> (Avelar, 1999, p. 3)

The mourning involved in such belated engagement is non-redemptive mourning that does not want to give up the past and redeem the present, but will require performances of remembrance over and over again.

Post-memory and non-redemptive mourning

In situations of collective trauma where there continues to be little public space for memory, victims often adopt a strategy of non-redemptive mourning, a process of remembering that does not have closure as its aim. Marianne Hirsch (1997) has written about "post-memory," the memory of those who did not directly go through the traumatic event, but nevertheless continue a haunted, restless, and searching relationship to it through photographs, images, and fragmentary sources, a memory "shot through with holes" (p. 23). According to psychoanalytic theory, post-memory, trauma, and marginalization produce an unstable splitting in the personality. On the one hand, post-memory can lead to dissociation and separation, a "manic defense" against recognition and mourning. To the personality defending itself through dissociation, the marginalized trauma victim becomes a source of contamination, a catastrophic threat to the ideal of the known personality in a safe and comfortable world. Then—as in post-Katrina New Orleans—victims may be labeled as delinquents, sinners, looters, or losers who brought tragedy on themselves through their own failures and deficits. Their plight is essentially severed from nonvictims who bear no responsibility for their well-being. As long as bystanders do not enter a space where hearts may be touched by human accounts and images of suffering, they can automatically renew a mythology that normalizes "business as usual," even in extreme circumstances.

In order to empathetically recognize those who have been marginalized and traumatized as "like me" or "not other," one necessarily opens floodgates within one's own personality to recognize all those symptoms of one's own suffering that have been denied. To confront the crypt in the other is to confront the crypt or enclave in oneself. In this flood, one might begin to see the way that one normally lives within an automatic bubble of defensive strategies designed to deny the unpredictability of the world, creating a feeling of safety. When one lives surrounded by people suffering chronic stress, poverty, or marginalization that has developed over centuries, dissociative strategies will allow the shutting out of feelings of empathy and connectedness. One can avoid any knowledge about the way one's own choices affect their situation.

Post-memory can be a source of separative forces fleeing from the sites of tragedy. On the other hand, where one finds oneself in spaces of recollection and begins to witness stories and see images that slide in painfully beneath the radar, post-memory can lead to identifications with victims, creating difficult feelings of disorganization and helplessness, a flooding of emotion, and a sense of shame and degradation that may cause confusion and fatalism. One may lose one's footing, and in this interstitial space begin to experience the collapse of the illusion that things are going normally and comfortably in the world. This is an event Lacanian psychoanalysts imagine as the shock of the "Real" interrupting automatic imaginaries.

Yet, it is through these ruptures nurtured in spaces of recollection that revelations can happen, as one begins to hear into the uncanny silences that have shaped daily lives. One may at last become troubled and unsettled about injustices that seemed "natural" and "normal" and this troubling can open to a new kind of listening, where one becomes aware of silences and gaps as much as to speech, to what is underneath and left out of stories as much as to their manifest plots. New forms of creativity, dialogue, action, and gesture become possible as people develop defiant ways to speak about lives that disturb accepted myths and histories (see Chapters 11 and 12).

Here, then, is a source of binding forces that break through barriers. When conditions are right, when public spaces of recollection are created, when catastrophe is placed in historical context, symptom and image are allowed to speak ruined parts of the past and the self. When translated into works of art or halting narratives strengthened by community support, witnesses, bystanders, perpetrators, accomplices, and victims (or more likely their children and grandchildren) may begin to join together to accept responsibility for a different future. By participating together to memorialize and address injury, we may wake the dead in our own personalities. Frozen myths and identities can be recreated anew. Here is the possibility to emerge into revelatory forms of community support and public dialogue. From these encounters, one can begin asking questions about building ethical communities.

Constructing spaces of recollection

> Seeking to see, to know, to take in all that is, as it is. To meet all that exists. It is by such a sacrament that wounds will heal us. Any healing will require us to witness all our histories where they converge, the history of empires and emancipations, of slave ships as well as underground railroads; it requires us to listen back into the muted cries of the beaten, burned, forgotten and also to hear the ring of speech among us, meeting the miracle of that.
>
> (Griffin, 1995, pp. 152–3)

The work of constructing spaces of recollection begins with a critical deconstruction of the fantasy that it is possible to understand experience fully. One begins by acknowledging what Toni Morrison (2004) calls the "unspoken and unaccounted for" in our communities, histories, and personal narratives. Yet according to Laura Marks (2000), writing about films as spaces of recollection,

> ... once this deconstruction has been accomplished, no simple truth is uncovered. There is a moment of suspension that occurs in these works after the official discourse has been (if only momentarily) dismantled and before the emerging discourse finds its voice. This is a moment of silence, an act of mourning for the terrible fact that histories are lost for good. Yet this moment is also enormously suggestive and productive. It is where these works begin to call upon other forms of cultural knowledge: it is where the

knowledges embedded in fetish-like objects, bodily memory, and the memory of the senses ... are found. This process of discovery is like scavenging in a tide pool for the small, speaking objects that are briefly revealed there before the water rushes in again.

(p. 26)

Cognitive psychology has identified a form of iconic memory that precedes narrative memory in childhood development. Narrative memory always has a plot line: this happened first and then that happened. In iconic memory, an object, a smell, a sound, or an image may trigger a set of associations for which no narrative structure yet exists. So the sound of the opening of the refrigerator door or the smell of food cooking may bring a rush of interest and energy to a small child who still has no idea how these events are organized. Poetry and fiction often make use of this form of memory when they use the literary device of metonymy in their work. Metonymy allows something nearby an object, or associated with it, to bring the object to consciousness. For example, in Julie Dash's film, *Daughters of the Dust*, wind in a cemetery functions to suggest spirits, ancestors, or divine intention and intervention. Such images are iconic in that there is no language to describe the links being made.

In trauma work, people often retain bits of iconic memory related to the event that are not anchored in any narrative memory about the event. The image of a train, a body, a suitcase, the sound of a door, a storm, or water, a photograph or piece of jewelry, the smell of certain food, the visual pattern on a pillowcase or wallpaper may bring a rush of associations, feelings, and partial memories out of a lost past. These have been described as "radioactive fossils" by Deleuze and as "aura" by Benjamin (in Marks, 2000, pp. 113, 188). Writing on radioactive fossils and aura in film, Marks (2000) says that

Aura is the sense an object gives that it can speak to us of the past, without ever letting us completely decipher it. It is a brush with involuntary memory, memory that can only be arrived at through a shock. We return again and again to the auratic object, still thirsty because it can never completely satisfy our desire to recover that memory.

(p. 81)

When attempting to develop public spaces of recollection, one is essentially creating an opening where people may bring forward iconic images related to past trauma. Entering into these spaces may require more silence than dialogue, a kind of hospitality or empathetic witness for which the primary ritual is presence or touch. Essentially, spaces of recollection are a way of constructing altars or memorials to what has been ruined in the past (see Chapter 12). The iconic objects or images that are brought forward in such spaces activate the memories and affects of individuals, while at the same time maintaining a significance that is collective and historical. For example, artifacts such as a photograph of Steven Biko, Salvador Allende, or Rosa Parks; a song by Bob Marley, Mercedes Sosa, or Miriam Makeba; or a Bible, a Torah, or a Koran may have a powerful metonymic significance for members of certain communities, especially those with a crypt or a post-memory from a traumatic past, while at the same time people from other communities of memory may have no response at all, or even a negative and dissociative response. Thus we cannot assume that people enter spaces of recollection as freestanding individuals equally capable of dialogue across difference. Spaces of recollection are an opening, a *kairos*, for those who have or want to find a key.

Clearing away frozen identities

In the best-case scenario, the space to encounter such iconic artifacts may lead in time to a process of remembrance and imaginative recollection of the past, an intergenerational and intercommunal recovery of multiple perspectives and frames of reference. This work of memory restores historical context to traumatic events. Where there is appropriate witness and response from the community, spaces of recollection can knit together alienated individuals and recreate communities capable of holding the truths of the past so that they can be used to fuel transformation and mobilization.

Yet when we are dealing with unmourned historical issues of collective trauma, such as the genocide of Native Americans or slavery in the United States, where one group continues to benefit at the expense of another, there will be many individuals who do not want to remember or mourn the past. The outcome of creating spaces of recollection for those individuals will therefore involve rupture, as unwanted and rejected icons appear to disrupt expected rituals, accustomed privileges, and an unreflected upon sense of superiority.

For those able to open to such disruption, Eric Santner (2001) suggests an evolution of psychoanalytic theory, a new "ecumenical framework for living with difference," a "psychotheology" that would involve rethinking our subjectivity (p. 9). Working in the lineage of Lacan and Žižek, he proposes that all forms of identity be seen as a kind of collectively imposed deadness, stuckness, or automatism that stereotypes our responses in the present. Trauma, in this view, is frozen identity in a frozen past:

> We might say that the mode of verification of a trauma is not some form of recovered memory—some form of historical knowledge—but rather a way of acknowledging a distinctive automaticity at the heart of one's being.
>
> (p. 40)

The "revelation" of Santner's psychotheology is then the "clearing away" of defensive fantasies that "keep us at a kind of distance from everyday life ...

from the possibilities for new possibilities that are all the time breaking out within it. ... new possibilities of community *here and now*" (pp. 100–1).

When one recognizes the possibility that historical amnesia, manic defense, and normative deafness may be central to the way one knows the world, one can begin to think about their deadening effects. Interruptions may then be revelatory by producing moments of undeadness that wake us up. Santner says that by turning toward this undeadness, we become called to bear responsibility, and to open possibilities for freedom. This implies that we need to create spaces of recollection that loosen defenses and open processes for "states of emergence of the new" (Santner, 2001, p. 137). Beyond the police order of normative thought there is always a remnant, an opening to the uniqueness of a moment that has not yet been mapped where there are "new possibilities for being together, which is in the end the very heart of politics" (p. 146).

An aesthetics of interruption

The sensibility we have been describing has emerged in the last decades in a number of fields as an ethics and aesthetics of interruption. Its telos is to produce a process that will cause participants to return to a silenced, traumatic crypt where there has been a frozen and forsaken possibility of imaginative understanding and mourning. The return is staged within a community setting where the rules have changed: what was not heard must now be heard, what was "normal" will be seen as a cover-up, what was dead is to be resurrected in imagination and returned to life. Such work is not a regular mourning process that requires a period of grieving and then a return to daily activities. It is different from individual scenarios of therapy, where in the long run, the point is to get on with life. Within the ethics and aesthetics of interruption, mourning is non-redemptive in the sense that it will need to be done in ritual space over and over again because there is no possible closure about what has been lost within the current climate where so many are invested in forgetting.

The ethics and aesthetics of interruption express a deep-seated human need to make collective meaning of life experience. Denied social witness, these needs will not disappear, but will go underground and re-emerge in symptomatic rage and destructiveness, substituting other kinds of interruption for needed mourning and witness. How satisfying the falling towers of the World Trade Center looked to those whose cultures and communities, whose very identity and psychic viability, were broken by centuries of colonialism, racism, denigration, violence, and American imperialism. Unless we can make public spaces of recollection to honor marginalized suffering in another way, there will be more and more displays of reactive violence, attempting to create for others the experiences one has suffered oneself. Abdul Rantisi, the Palestinian founder of Hamas, assassinated by Israeli forces, explained before his death that Hamas is attempting to "morally educate": by actually experiencing violence themselves, he hoped Israelis would be better able to understand the Palestinian experience of Israeli occupation. Spaces of recollection work against such cycles of violence, interrupting them and posing in their stead other processes through which empathy can be built.

Re-thinking multicultural encounters

Much of the work of diversity training and multicultural awareness undertaken in the academic context of the last 25 years has been based on the notion that people as individuals are capable of dialogue about traumatic events of collective history. It may be that the lessons of the approaches to trauma theory we have cited suggest that these conversations will be far more difficult than originally imagined. Embedded within iconic and constructed social landscapes, many people profoundly idealize and identify with the community of memory within which they have developed their sense of themselves. Where larger community dialogue practices have disintegrated, particularly in urban settings, many of these constructions have come to signify a "we" that is deemed completely different from others who are presumed unable to understand their way of life, suffering, worldview, or memories, and whom they fear feel no ethical obligations toward them. For others, complex memories and identities-in-process are still forming and require creative unfolding. Part of the work of liberation psychologies is to build intercommunity spaces of recollection and to support the formation of new types of critical subjectivity that might allow us to enter into them. A catalogue of the effects of collective trauma and colonialism is part of the work of building new spaces for dialogue.

When individuals are born into communities that have suffered a traumatic past, that past continues to haunt the present, demanding expression and return. There is no possibility of closure, and the linear narratives of a complete and official national history need to be broken open again and again for unsettled retellings and memorializing of unfinished history. Such needs are in direct opposition to those of others in the community whose historical positions have placed them on the side of forgetting. It is our hope that as intercommunity spaces of recollection are created, the psychic and communal damage from such forgetting will become more apparent. Here inclusiveness becomes tantamount if one is to hope that bystanders can move toward witnessing, and that some perpetrators (or their families or accomplices) will be moved to regret their actions, to speak truthfully and to apologize for their violent pasts. Such confrontations will inevitably involve rupturing encounters, which is the subject of the following chapter.

Part III Springs for Creative Restoration

At the heart of psychologies of liberation is the prophetic vision of individuals living together in a peaceful network of just and joyful communities, where past violence and marginalization can be acknowledged and mourned, where conflict can be experienced and resolved, where the diversity of cultures, species, and habitats is appreciated and protected, and where dialogue and love can flourish. Although we live in a world that is painfully distant from this utopian vision, we can begin to walk in the direction of its incarnation. The embodiment of such a vision depends upon the nurture of individuals' and communities' capacities for critically understanding how the everyday world we live in is created and sustained, including its historical roots and dynamics of power. From this critical understanding, individuals and groups can grow experiments in transformation that help them claim a greater sense of agency and empowerment with which to engage with their world effectively and creatively. One can begin practices of democracy that allow participation in public dialogue and the opening of spaces for hearing into difference and disagreement. Unfortunately, all human beings have an enormous capacity to live in states of denial, dissociation, forgetfulness, and identification with ideologies of the dominant culture. It can be extremely painful to develop a critical consciousness, to unlearn what one has been taught over a lifetime.

As psychologists, we are interested in the methodologies and theories that can assist in cultivating environments where capacities for creative engagement with one's circumstances can be nurtured. While the potential settings for such nurturance are diverse, certain common elements need to be present in order for people to begin processes of intrapsychic and interpsychic transformation. In Part III, we will describe the orientations that guide such methodologies, before going on to address the methodologies themselves in Part IV. In Chapter 8, we analyze four narrative approaches to experiences of rupture. We trace the decline of liminal spaces where narratives may be revisioned as a result of globalization and the effect of this decline on diminishing support for people to use rupture for psychological transformation. A contemporary reconstructing of liminal spaces is one needed spring of creative restoration. Another is a shifting in how one conceives of and practices identity. In Chapter 9, we explore ideas of nomadic identity as a possibility for re-imagining selfhood in two ways: first, to enhance one's ability to step aside from styles of selfhood that contribute to polarization, violence, and oppression, and, second, to contribute positively to the possible function of identity as a plurality of sites for connecting with oneself and others. Chapter 10 will explore work that strengthens capacities for dialogue and critical consciousness. Each of these three chapters contribute needed elements for restoring psychological and social environments that can support processes of resymbolization and renarrativization that have declined through the collective trauma that was explored in Part II.

8
Rupture and Hospitality

> It is also about transforming language, creating alterna-
> tives, asking ourselves questions about what types of
> images subvert, pose critical alternatives, and transform
> our worldviews and move us away from dualistic thinking
> about good and bad. Making space for the transgressive
> image, the outlaw rebel vision, is essential to any effort to
> create a context for transformation. And even then little
> progress is made if we transform images without shifting
> paradigms, changing perspectives, ways of looking.
>
> (bell hooks, 1992, p. 4)

Habitual thinking

If liberation psychologies begin with wandering in the desert attempting to
break with dominant modes of consciousness to create new possibilities for
community life, we need to identify and name the "stations of the cross" of
this type of pilgrimage. In this section on habitual thinking, we are addressing how people living in relatively stable circumstances transform the ways
they think in response to environmental surprises or discrepancies that challenge their current paradigms. How do we learn to change the sedimented
ways we understand the world, and how do we evolve new and more creative responses when unexpected events interrupt a settled way of life and
override our defenses? Can we become aware of how much of what we do is
an automatic acceptance of surrounding habits of "normal" social life in our
own communities? How flexible can we be in considering those things that
do not fit within our expectations? How might it change our thinking to
consider human beings not as freestanding individual units but as embedded in, defined by, performing, and co-creating structures (or vortices) of
cultural discourse, practice, and assumptions?

One of the key tasks in liberation psychology is to analyze how people
defend or break with old dominant ideas and find (or fail to find) a language

133

for new ones. Work in both clinical psychology and trauma theory focuses on this phenomenon. Because our attachments to ways of thinking are partly unconscious, the psychology of the unconscious becomes relevant. Environmentalists have used the horrible image of frogs in water that is slowly being heated, ignoring the temperature change because it is too gradual, in order to explain how it is that we go on polluting even now that we know what the long-range toxic outcomes are likely to be. One of the most troubling aspects of contemporary life is that large numbers of people can see there are human, cultural, and ecological crises underway, yet it seems almost impossible to change business as usual in most of the discourses, ways of thinking, practices, and economies that are contributing to the unfolding disaster. Of course there are issues of power involved, but it is also the case that many people go along unthinkingly and unconsciously with arrangements they could change. We need to understand better than we do why people are not the "rational" consumers that political economy or sociology has sometimes assumed them to be. An analysis of contemporary affairs can produce many examples of people who vote for candidates who do not represent their economic interests, support institutions that are repressive and exploitive, and identify with leaders who are dishonest, abusive, and manipulative. Sometimes people later awaken to a realization that they have lived in a kind of trance, in exile from their own needs and desires, as they embraced structures that seemed to give their lives meaning and coherence. These awakenings are often excruciatingly painful.

Unexpected rupture

Most major life transformations for individuals begin with a spontaneous yet still manageable rupture, a shocking break in routine. Here, we mean more than an unexpected event. Rupture is the sort of happening that challenges all of one's capacity to make sense of life. No frameworks of understanding developed up to the point of rupture are able to completely explain or contain the new situation. We could give as examples personal tragedies such as untimely death in a family or a car crash that leaves its victims disabled. Ruptures can also be positive, such as those caused by falling in love unexpectedly or encountering a person with a fascinating and entirely unique point of view that changes the way one thinks about the world. In addition, there are endogenous ruptures, such as states of depression or debilitating disease, provoking a spiritual crisis that can descend without warning on a previously well-adapted adult. Though no precipitating cause can be found in a definite event, the effect can completely undermine one's usual life. For those involved, these types of occurrences, whether endogenous or causal, positive or negative, are so unexpected, so out of the ordinary, that they disrupt a sense that the world is familiar. One may be thrust into a radical space of pilgrimage, a searching for meaning and orientation from a location "betwixt and between" seemingly stable states.

We need to mark the difference here between a traumatic rupture, one which has global and devastating long-term effects on a personality (as discussed in the previous chapter), and a kind of difficult but negotiable rupture that initiates a period of transformation and rethinking that in the end can be thought of as creating new strengths. Manageable rupture may at times be painful, but if surrounding conditions allow for support and experimentation, there is a possibility for a widening of the personality and the development of a more critical and creative consciousness.

In the previous chapter, we began from the point of view of whole communities undergoing historical crisis. After such traumatic experiences, everything changes for individuals trying to negotiate daily life. Here we consider the problem of transformation from the point of view of individuals who are trying to cope with the unexpected while the world around them remains more or less the same. While such individuals may turn out to have been the canaries in a coal mine, registering social upheaval before it appeared on the radar of others, they often feel very isolated and alone.

Liminal spaces

Often in the aftermath of rupture, if there is a safe and containing space to retreat to, and understanding witnesses to dialogue with, people find themselves in a kind of thoughtful ruminative process in which they have little interest at all in the things that previously engaged them. This space has been named and theorized in a number of different fields. In psychoanalytic theory, particularly that of D.W. Winnicott, the process has been called "regression," and is believed to be central to healing. Here regression does not signify a return to a childhood or infantile state; it indicates a stepping back from busy or manic doing toward a slower more reflective stance. Certain forms of adaptation to life are seen by Winnicott (1989) as responses that are organized toward "invulnerability," that is, toward not being disappointed again by a hurtful and unreliable surrounding environment. Regression is the moment in which one can find a space to mourn, to "abandon invulnerability and to become a sufferer" (p. 199).

Writing about the multiple ruptures of being both bilingual and bicultural in racist society as well a lesbian in a homophobic society, Gloria Anzaldúa (1987) has been an articulate chronicler and phenomenologist of the betwixt and between. She calls such a state of regression *"nepantla"*, the Aztec preconquest word meaning a netherworld between the living and the dead, also used to describe the result of the Aztec's confusing and ultimately devastating encounter with European culture. When we enter *nepantla*, we begin another way of seeing that Anzaldúa calls *"la facultad"*:

> Fear develops the proximity sense of *la facultad*. But there is a deeper sensing that is another aspect of this faculty. It is anything that breaks

into one's everyday mode of perception, that causes a break in one's defenses and resistance, anything that takes one from one's habitual grounding, causes the depths to open up, causes a shift in perception. This shift in perception deepens the way we see concrete objects and people; the senses become so acute and piercing that we can see through things, view events in depth, a piercing that reaches the underworld (the realm of the soul). As we plunge vertically, the break, with its accompanying new seeing, makes us pay attention to the soul, and we are thus carried into awareness—an experiencing of soul (Self).

(p. 61)

For Anzaldúa, such states are critical for transformation. In *nepantla* we find ourselves at sea in oppositional whirlpools of narrative and script. We do not know to which we belong and become what Anzaldúa calls a *"mestiza"*, a focal point or fulcrum "where phenomena tend to collide."

It is where the possibility of uniting all that is separate occurs. This assembly is not one where severed pieces merely come together. Nor is it a balancing of opposing powers. In attempting to work out a synthesis, the self has added a third element which is greater than the sum of its severed parts. That third element is a new consciousness—a *mestiza* consciousness—and though it is a source of intense pain, its energy comes from continual creative motion that keeps breaking down the unitary aspect of each new paradigm.

En unas pocas centurias, the future will belong to the *mestiza*. Because the future depends on the breaking down of paradigms, it depends on the straddling of two or more cultures. By creating a new mythos—that is, a change in the way we perceive reality, the way we see ourselves, and the ways we behave— *la mestiza* creates a new consciousness.

(pp. 101–2)

For those who have been silenced or marginalized, that is, the majority under globalization, entering this future may be critical to gaining a capacity for creative response to life. Becoming *mestiza* means discovering other ideals such as the *orisha Eshu*, "Yoruba God of uncertainty, who blesses her choice of path" (p. 80). *Eshu* is the guardian of the spirit world between the living and the dead, human, and *orisha* or god. In taking up this challenge *la mestiza* "has gone from being the sacrificial goat to becoming the officiating priestess at the crossroads"(p. 80). Here, Anzaldúa is suggesting we can make a shift from feeling overwhelmed by rupture toward a willingness to explore its context.

Basing his ideas on earlier work by van Gennep, anthropologist Victor Turner (1977) called the betwixt and between state "liminality." In his studies of sub-Saharan cultures, he came to the conclusion that many small-scale cultures intentionally organize periods in community life in which the entire group, or a portion of it, undergoes a break with daily roles and routine structures. The initiating occasion for the break might be a puberty crisis, marriage ceremony, death, or seasonal astronomical, agricultural, or herding event. During a specified period of time and under the leadership of ritual specialists, the whole community might play at role reversals, tell stories or myths, enter altered states through use of drugs or alcohol, or perform inherited or spontaneous dance or song cycles. Everything that could not be spoken or thought while maintaining structure can be creatively worked with and aired. During the liminal period, the group might be stripped of rank and class privileges and characteristics and meet as equal and unique human beings. "Thus," says Turner (1977) "liminality is frequently likened to death, to being in the womb, to invisibility, to darkness, to bisexuality, to the wilderness, and to an eclipse of the sun or moon" (p. 94).

One of the outcomes of the periods of liminality was that they were likely to generate cohesive community bonds that could form the basis for legitimacy when the community passed again to a stage of reaggregation. There would be a sense in the group of being bound together in a sacred fellowship that Turner named *"communitas,"* "a relationship between concrete, historical, idiosyncratic individuals. These individuals were not segmented into roles and statuses but confronted one another in the manner of Martin Buber's 'I and Thou'" (p. 132). For Turner, periodic experiences of liminality and *communitas* in small-scale cultures provided the social glue that allowed the structure of that society to cohere and evolve in inclusive ways.

Loss of liminal spaces

Unfortunately, one of the outcomes of industrialization and urbanization has been to fragment and uproot many of the communities that developed these types of rituals. In large urban settings today, there are people living in states of anomie and alienation where they do not even know their neighbors, much less form bonds of *communitas*. The typical urban worker has instead "vacation" or "holiday" which in most cases is carried out alone or with one companion or a small nuclear family. Public events are mostly based on spectatorship rather than participation, with church services, concerts, theater, and civic ceremonies organized hierarchically so that performers and speakers are set apart from passive audiences who watch while seated in rows, often not speaking at all to those alongside them.

In ways of life where there is rarely an organized period of liminality, maintaining structures and routines of work and householding may become permanently exhausting and stressful. "Burnout," boredom, depression, psychosomatic illness, and addiction to legal and illegal drugs or alcohol increase as attempts to remain in a fixed structure become ever more unrelieved. Such situations contribute to the possibility that increasingly brittle rigidity will be broken apart by some sort of rupture. Without community, living tradition, and ritual specialists with a theory and practice of liminality, many individuals are on their own trying to figure out how to navigate rupture. There are ways of framing the experience of rupture that can guarantee that it will be a chronically debilitating experience rather than an opportunity for growth, integration, *communitas*, or transformation.

Renormalization

During a period of rupture and liminality, one may notice for the very first time the contingent, culturally constructed character of the life ideals and routines that had been carried out up until that time as if they were the only reasonable possibility. After events such as divorce, job loss, moving, retirement, military service, or the end of child rearing that leaves an "empty nest," many people report a sense of floating in a space of meaninglessness and alienation without orientation. After a collective rupture such as genocide, war, or a sudden event of toxic pollution, the sense of the annihilation of a way of life may be total, and there may be so little possibility for restoration that the situation hardens into trauma. The structure that previously gave stable meanings to one's life and actions may all at once seem fragile and temporary, even lost. Feelings of confusion and anomie that arise in such periods can seem terrifying, and sometimes people going through them wonder if they are going insane or are going to be permanently incapacitated. At first, they cannot imagine any way of going forward. No wonder then that there is a strong temptation to deny the experience, to numb one's feelings with medications or alcohol, to continue with rigid routines out of sheer willpower even when they no longer make sense. Especially if one is surrounded by professionals, friends, and cultural messages that encourage one to "get over it," to "keep busy," to "not dwell on the past," the social support for exploration and discernment closes off and there is no psychological space to process the rupture. In this case, there is a desperate calcification of one's point of view that Jung called a retrogressive restoration of the persona. Melanie Klein called it manic defense. In this mode, experimentation, play, imagination, and spontaneity seem dangerous, and there is a general withdrawal and shutting down in relationship to the new and unknown. Discipline and loyalty to the past may become everything for it is all that seems possible.

In psychological life, renormalization is the constant refusal to explore what unexpectedly occurs in the environment through rupture, chance, accident, or contact with an unknown "other." It produces structures of rigidity and authority in individuals, families, and communities that mitigate against needed collapse and opening to vulnerability. The outcome can be an incapacity to bear an empathetic response to oneself, a failure that can become extended to those one loves, as well as to those outside one's usual social circles. One can pretend that nothing unusual is occurring during an extreme crisis. In families there are many examples of this failure to see where everyone maintains a pretense that alcoholism, incest, abuse, or forms of mental illness are simply not happening when in fact someone in the family is slowly being destroyed. Renormalization leads unconsciously to social narcissism, a complete identification with those perceived to be most like oneself, and an alienation and dissociation from those who appear different. Polarized identities—we are good and upright, they are bad and delinquent—are rigidified in this scenario.

Fouad Ajami (2001) gave us a brilliant example of renormalization when he analyzed the press conference of the father of Mohamed Atta, who is believed to have organized the attacks on the World Trade Center on 9/11, and who flew one of the planes into it. The elder Atta, an Egyptian lawyer and strict Muslim who denied that his son could ever have been involved in such a misdeed, claimed: "We keep our doors closed and that is why my two daughters and my son are morally and academically excellent." In fact, the elder Atta was worried his son was too weak: "He was so gentle. I used to tell him 'Toughen up, boy'." But such brittle renormalization often fails for those who are constrained by rigid authority. Ajami saw it this way:

> On the crowded campuses where Atta and his peers received an education—an education that put off the moment of reckoning with a country that had little if any room for them, little if any hope—there emerged an anxious, belligerent piety. Growing numbers of young women took to conservative Islamic dress—at times the veil, more often the head cover. While the secularists sneered, it became a powerful trend, a fashion in its own right. It was a way of marking a zone of privacy, a declaration of moral limits. Young men picked up the faith as well, growing their beards long and finding their way into Islamist political movements and religious cells. A cultural war erupted in Egypt. A stranger who knew the ways of this land could see the stresses of the place growing more acute by the day.
>
> The sermons of the country—religious and political, the words of those who monitored and dominated its cultural life—insisted on a false harmony, held on to the image of the good, stable society that kept the troubles and "perversions" of the world at bay. But the outwardly obedient sons and daughters were in the throes of a seething rebellion.
>
> (Ajami, 2001, p. 19)

When parents, teachers, and other authority figures cannot bear witness to the struggles and suffering that their own and other children are going through because it ruptures their sense of harmony and order, children are pushed toward fatalism and sometimes even suicide. Around the world, the rate of suicide and suicide terrorism, among adolescents is rising. In 1999, on Hitler's birthday, Eric Harris and Dylan Klebold killed or wounded 23 people at their school in Littleton, Colorado, before killing themselves. For over a year before the event, they had planned to bring guns and homemade bombs to their school and to commit suicide. Yet most of the adults in their environment, including the sheriff's department and neighbors who could hear them doing some kind of construction in a garage, had no idea what they were up to and clearly were not in adequate communication with the boys. While many of the students at the school noted the boys' anger, referring to them as the "trenchcoat mafia," and though there was even a picture of them in the school yearbook in their black trench coats, the school principal never heard of the trenchcoat mafia until the day of the shooting. The boys, along with many other students, had been teased, bullied, and harassed for years at the school; but these ruptures of their dignity and sense of self-worth were continually renormalized by most adults who saw that kind of school hazing as a regular part of the culture they had no responsibility to address. In an alleged suicide note, Eric Harris was clear about whom he thought was responsible for his agony:

By now, it's over. If you are reading this, my mission is complete. ... Your children who have ridiculed me, who have chosen not to accept me, who have treated me like I am not worth their time are dead. THEY ARE FUCKING DEAD ...

Surely you will try to blame it on the clothes I wear, the music I listen to, or the way I choose to present myself, but no. Do not hide behind my choices. You need to face the fact that this comes as a result of YOUR CHOICES.

Parents and teachers, you fucked up. You have taught these kids to not accept what is different. YOU ARE IN THE WRONG. I have taken their lives and my own—but it was your doing. Teachers, parents, LET THIS MASSACRE BE ON YOUR SHOULDERS UNTIL THE DAY YOU DIE.

(Harris, 1999)

As the victims of normalized violence, Harris and Klebold saw all too clearly that their suffering was invisible to others. Although this does not excuse or rationalize their murderous rampage, it points to the underlying problems of renormalization, especially blindness to the suffering of others.

Narrative framing

In a world undergoing rapid upheaval because of the rate of expansion of globalization, the origination of new conditions and technologies that rupture old expectations is far more common than it was several hundred years ago. In earlier times, the majority of the world's people would have remained in the same 100-mile territory for their entire lives, rarely meeting anyone who had traveled further or spoke another language. Today most people live, study, or work in environments where people from around the globe are interacting with them every day. We are bathed in a sea of media images from all quarters. Meeting the new through strategies of renormalization places us at odds with ourselves and the world, requiring structures of dissociation and the expenditure of ever-greater energy to maintain order and a comfortable authority over uncomfortable ruptures.

Ruptures have always been part of life. The critical issues are how they are framed and understood, what narrative context they are placed in, and the degree of flexibility or defensiveness of the social and personal environment with which they are met. If an event has turned one's life upside down, it makes a big difference whether one imaginatively embeds the event as a need for a paradigm change, a failure of chemical balance in the brain, a hysterical symptom, a result of social trauma, a punishment from God, or an incorrect relationship to the spirit world. Some of these narratives turn one against oneself, like a chronic form of autoimmune response. Some attempt to rally through medication and/or will a control that has already been lost. Some narratives project reactions outward toward others who need to be punished or destroyed; other narratives promote dialogue, experimentation, and innovation. Beneath efforts of renormalization, we want to explore four common types of narrative framing and talk about their general effects: narratives of dissociation, narratives of fatalism, narratives of messianic reversal, and narratives of participation. There are also situations without a narrative frame that are the outcome of trauma that we have addressed in the previous chapter. The larger question is how we might learn to consciously intensify the contexts in which unproductive frames might transform. Of course, narrative frameworks evolve unconsciously as circumstances change. A functional adult placed in a concentration camp or prison will very rapidly alter perceptions of the world. It is very likely that most people have different parts of their personalities embedded in different narrative frames. That is, there may be parts of myself and the world that I am fatalistic about, parts that I am constantly renormalizing because I cannot bear to face their dissolution, parts of intention that I have exaggerated hopes for, and other parts where I am able to face change with an experimental attitude. When we become aware of the narrative frameworks we are embedded in, when dialogue with others causes us to question the logic of our narrative frameworks, we open up possibilities for evolution and transformation.

When we speak of narrative framing, we are talking about a complex process that is not simply an individual choice. A narrative frame is a cultural nexus with its own particular set of imaginings about the world. It links a social, economic, and political environment at a certain moment in history with a group of individuals who have to function performatively in that milieu, either reproducing older scripts, challenging them, or creatively reworking them through innovative choices. Every individual is operating in the environment simultaneously, reacting to and influencing narratives in ways that may be partly conscious and partly unconscious. Complex and unpredictable patterns are always emerging from this interaction. Some narrative frames promote lots of possibilities for interaction and creative imagination; others create information hierarchies where interaction is highly limited and compartmentalized. The more controlled environment will offer fewer opportunities to explore and express affect, symptom, and emergent thought. More and more of one's possible reactions will be forced into exile or unconsciousness as options for speech become more rigidly closed off. Then it will become impossible for the majority to speak of certain kinds of suffering and certain kinds of yearning, while those in control of the hierarchies maintain the possibility for an infantile absolutism, where only their own suffering and desire can be stated and valued. In this context, liberation psychology would represent a desire for a democratic equalization of options for expression. By organizing spaces for liminal encounters, the possibilities can be maximized for the evolution of frameworks. Liberation psychology allows us to be conscious of a diversity of narrative frameworks that may be ruptured and transformed through dialogical encounters.

Narratives of dissociation

Narratives of dissociation again and again deny and split off anything new, unexpected, or "unnatural" that has occurred. Though it was clear that the Littleton shootings were partly a response to years of bullying, hazing, and scapegoating toward Harris and Klebold, many teachers, parents, and administrators continued to see this type of behavior as a normal part of school life that children should learn to survive. Though there had been shotguns and pipe bomb makings out in the open in their bedrooms, their parents had not noticed anything out of the ordinary. Harris and Klebold had attended a year of a court-ordered juvenile diversion program after stealing a car a year earlier, including a course on anger management, all of which they passed with flying colors and had their records wiped clean. Many schools responded to this and other school shootings with tougher security measures and armed guards rather than any type of dialogue with a goal of changing school culture. It is clear with hindsight that the adults surrounding the high school completely failed to grasp and respond to the intensity of the experience that was rupturing their environment.

Narratives of dissociation may sometimes work to keep order in situations of chaotic dynamism; but the downside of this strategy is the complete loss of a capacity to come to grips with profound change as it is occurring. People who are using strategies of dissociation have affective responses to new elements developing in their environment, but cannot form narratives to contain them and link them into previous experience, so they remain unaware of their own intuitions and intimations of rupture.

Strangely, another difficulty with narratives of dissociation is that they may have a negative effect on the immune system and health in general among some populations in the United States. Realizing the inflection of local cultural constructions on concepts of body and self, we could not say these effects would be felt in all cultural locations everywhere. In a recent volume on dialogue between anthropologists and the new field of psychoneuroimmunology entitled *Social and cultural lives of immune systems* (Wilce, 2003), several authors discuss the findings of Dr. Samuel Mann that show a correlation in the United States between high blood pressure and repressed emotions. It used to be thought that high blood pressure developed in situations of stress, but this has been shown not to be the case. The link is between high blood pressure and the process of keeping emotions outside of conscious awareness. "These include denial, dissociation, repression, alexithymia, defensiveness, isolation of affect and others" (Mann, 2003, p. 194).

People who develop such defensive strategies learn to repress painful and potentially overwhelming affects in early childhood when they have no support for understanding emotionally difficult and, even, traumatic events. These strategies are protective at the time, but later become habits that are maintained over decades. Given the levels of bullying and social harassment in primary school cultures, and of neglect and abuse within families, such strategies may be widespread in the United States, where many children do not have adequate emotional support for dealing with attitudes and institutions that threaten their self-esteem on a daily and long-term basis.

If people are not aware of what they are feeling or experiencing, they cannot talk about their experience with others. Yet there is evidence that, for some cultural settings, it is exactly the process of sharing stressful experience in an environment that is experienced as safe, that contributes to health (though emotional support might mean different things in different cultural contexts). According to Mann (2003):

Evolution provided us with the ability to keep emotions from awareness when we need to. It also provided us with the ability to face these emotions by deriving strength through emotional and spiritual support. There is growing evidence that emotional support has important effects on physical health. Recent studies have documented that emotional support is more relevant to survival in the months and years following myocardial infarction than are any of the traditional risk factors such as cholesterol, blood pressure, or smoking. [F]amilies within each society vary in the degree of emotional support available for its members. ... [W]hen ... severe emotional stress is borne in isolation ... it is often barred from awareness ... with a different set of consequences for our health. ... Although medical research is beginning to document the medical benefits of emotional support, the breakdown of both the nuclear and extended family, geographic mobility, and the breakneck pace of life, act in concert to reduce its availability. A "be happy" philosophy also diverts attention from unwanted emotions to passive entertainment and diversions, instead of promoting their processing in an atmosphere of emotional support.

(p. 199)

Narratives of dissociation are extremely difficult to challenge. People whose experience is embedded in a frame of dissociation may only go through a profound change when they or someone they are very close to are confronted with their own mortality, or in the throes of an extreme moral, physical, or spiritual crisis. After that, everything depends on locating a social and psychological space where exploration of the unknown can be supported and witnessed, and that often requires leaving behind what is familiar to search for alternative forms of community.

Narratives of fatalism

A different type of social experience might lead people to embed their experience in narratives of fatalism, in which there is no hope for the situation to change. Here the situation originates not from individual early childhood trauma but from having to live over a long period of time in a debilitating or dangerous social setting from which there is no escape. Living in poverty, in violent neighborhoods, in prison, or in situations of repeated domestic violence or state terror might produce such conditions.

The work of Belenky, Bond, and Weinstock (1999) with rural women in Vermont is fascinating to consider in relation to this. They interviewed women participants before and after being in a "Listening Partners" group, where a supportive and empowering group milieu was developed (see Chapter 11). Before participating in the group, most of the women experienced their lives within fatalistic narrative frames. For example, one said: "I feel isolated, away from everything because I don't have a phone and I don't have a car during the day. Even though my family is around, it's like nobody ever has time to come to the house during the day because everybody else works" (pp. 99–100). Most of the participants at the beginning of the project reported having few friends, a lack of control over their lives, and a sense of being controlled by others. They believed their own thoughts and feelings held little value and felt powerless to affect their own lives. They had no sense of the potential strength of their own voices.

The Listening Partners program convened the women weekly as a circle of learners in small groups with staff support. The lives of a control group of nonparticipants were also studied during the same period. Outcomes of the project showed that it is possible to shift narratives of fatalism, encouraging more active participation in decision making and more complex ways of understanding the world that awaken possibilities for transforming one's situation in concert with others.

Narratives of fatalism can be changed with an altered environment of social support and dialogue. Unlike narratives of dissociation, there does not have to be an acute crisis to mobilize change. Narratives of fatalism provide adaptation to handle a history of ruptures that one has suffered without sufficient support or power to transform them. It is the experience of ongoing rupture that the individual was powerless to prevent that has precipitated the "playing possum" that narratives of fatalism represent. Where the surrounding social environment can be changed to provide safety, witness, and resources, the narratives of fatalism may begin to evolve.

Narratives of messianic transformation

Another type of narrative framing that rupture may precipitate is the narrative of messianic reversal. Fifty years ago, such narratives would have been thought to be relatively rare, the classic example being the "cargo cults" of Southeast Asia. On various islands, groups of inhabitants experiencing extreme rupture from invasion, began to line beaches or runways because they were imagining that the gods were going to send them large amounts of cargo on planes or ships—gifts from the gods that would completely reverse their situations of poverty.

Today, these kinds of fixed fantasies of millennial upheaval have become widespread in the world, giving us an index of how many people's lives and livelihoods have been affected by globalization. Often these frameworks are a defense from a sense that the world is changing too rapidly, that one's footing and sense of meaning are slipping away more rapidly than they can be shored up. Millennial frameworks give the world an order, a logic that makes it bearable to see cherished investments and institutions eroded. In a shocking article by journalist Bill Moyers, written after he received Harvard Medical School's Global Environment Citizen Award, he reported that 59 per cent of Americans believe that the prophecies found in the book of Revelation are going to come true and 25 per cent believe that the Bible predicted the 9/11 attacks. Large numbers of people in the United States are apparently living with a messianic narrative predicting the imminent return of Jesus Christ. According to Moyers (2004), they believe:

[O]nce Israel has occupied the rest of its 'biblical lands,' legions of the anti-Christ will attack it, triggering a final showdown in the valley of Armageddon. As the Jews who have not been converted are burned, the messiah will return for the rapture. True believers will be lifted out of their clothes and transported to heaven, where, seated next to the right hand of God, they will watch their political and religious opponents suffer plagues of boils, sores, locusts, and frogs during the several years of tribulation that follow. ... I've reported on these people, following some of them from Texas to the West Bank. They are sincere, serious, and polite as they tell you they feel called to help bring the rapture on as fulfillment

of biblical prophecy. That is why they have declared solidarity with Israel
and the Jewish settlements and backed up their support with money and
volunteers.

It's why the invasion of Iraq for them was a warm-up act, predicted in
the Book of Revelations.

(pp. 1–2)

Moyers felt it was hard for him as a journalist to report a story like this with
any credibility because it is so fantastic, but he suggests that these beliefs are
affecting contemporary U.S. military and environmental policy:

Why care about the earth when the droughts, floods, famines, and
pestilence brought on by ecological collapse are signs of the apocalypse
foretold in the bible? Why care about global climate change when you
and yours will be rescued in the rapture? And why care about convert-
ing from oil to solar when the same God who performed the miracle of
the loaves and fishes can whip up a few billion barrels of light crude
with a word?

(p. 3)

For those involved in these messianic narratives, public policy is secondary
to such major dramatic scripts. Moyers (2004) believes that numerous people with these beliefs are at the highest level of government in the United
States, where "the delusional is no longer marginal" (p. 1). James Watt,
President Reagan's first Secretary of the Interior, articulated this policy
before Congress, suggesting that protecting natural resources was unimpor-
tant in light of the imminent return of Jesus Christ. In public testimony, he
said that after the last tree has fallen, Christ will return.

More and more people in the twenty-first century are developing messianic narratives in which they are embedding their life experience. For
instance, there is a widespread belief in the Islamic world that the
caliphate—the historical period in the first millennium when Islam had
its widest reach—is going to be restored with the help of Allah. This idea
has helped to organize large numbers of Islamic militants into combat or
terror missions to hasten the return of the caliphate. Similarly, White
Citizens Councils and the Ku Klux Klan have generated visions of the
future triumph and restoration of the "White Race." The current popular
folk myths about aliens who have come from outer space to colonize the
earth also find a diverse following.

Narratives of messianic reversal can be extremely dangerous because they
leave no room for contradictory facts or experiences to raise questions about
the beliefs involved. While in the past such views would have seemed to be
the scripts of isolated cult organizations, in times of rapid change and

insecurity about the future, they can develop contagiously and begin to influence large numbers of people. What is so frightening about such ideas is that historically—as in the Inquisition, the Crusades, and witch burnings— they run their course over a long period of time before people begin to emerge from them as if from a trance. People who are involved with narratives of messianic reversal are not interested in dialogue with those not intending initiation, and each new rupture seems only to add fuel to the fire. Nevertheless, there are always those who have doubts, with whom personal relationship, an unexpected taste of new pleasures or understand- ings, or a rush of old memories can contradict the presumed certainties of the present and have a transforming affect. Participation in environments that allow for ambiguity and divergence, that witness and support transfor- mation, may prove critical to developing less rigid and defensive frame- works of understanding.

Narratives of participation

Finally, instead of defending against the dislocation and liminality of rup- ture, one may be able to bear and contain the ambiguities, fears, uncer- tainty, and uncanniness of a pilgrimage. Ruptures may be embedded in narratives of participation that embrace exploration. In this type of journey, one will often feel disoriented and lost. Without a road map for transfor- mation, one is pressed to develop a capacity for engaging a process of trial and error, of improvising meanings for one's new experiences, meanings that may themselves prove inadequate. In such a process, there may be a dis- identification with and sacrifice of old ideals and a deconstruction of old ways of thinking. There may be a long period when contradictory ideas con- tend for space and adherence. Supportive and witnessing relationships will be crucial (see Chapter 10). In liminal space, one meets the unknown, the marginalized, the synchronistic, the other, the unconscious edge of one's former narratives. At this point, the possibility to try out new narratives, to reframe one's story, becomes critical. Through narratives of participation the center of gravity shifts from fear and defensiveness to curiosity, creativity, and celebration. One begins to take a stand to validate one's own affects and doubts while at the same time interrogating them. The effect of such a shift is that the area of questioning about the self, the world, and the use of nar- rative language begins to widen noticeably. We can no longer assume there will be an outcome of homogeneous accounts through dialogue. The frames of narratives of participation anticipate heterogeneity rather than accord. Emergent and hybrid cultural performances, where new imaginations enter the world, will be welcomed side by side with cultural traditions that can bridge between past and future. The difficulty of participatory frames is the process of discernment: how much to hold on to and how much to give up. There are times when previous commitments need to be constant, as in commitments to childrearing; and other times when old habits can be let go.

Holding contradictory impulses in dialogue may require long periods of uncertainty and reflection, slowing down response until a synthesis is reached.

Some anthropologists provide us descriptions of participatory framing from fieldwork that has required they inhabit more than one cultural framework at a time, often destabilizing their identification with their own cultural frames. Writing about how postmodern, (post)colonial, and feminist theory have dramatically altered anthropological writing and the identities of its writers, Iain Chambers (1994) suggests their work has become "a migrant's tale, the nomad's story" (p. 246). Over the years, many have become critical of their own starting points, forced by rupture to abandon old formulations of Eurocentrism, empire, and gender:

> It is to abandon the fixed geometry of sites and roots for the unstable cal-culations of transit. It is to embark on the winding and interminable path of heteronomy. This means to recognize in the homesickness of much contemporary critical thought not so much the melancholy conclusion of a thwarted rationalism but an opening toward a new horizon of ques-tions. For it is to contemplate crossing over to the 'other' side of the authorized tale, that other side of modernity, of the West, of History, and from there to consider that breach in contemporary culture that reveals an increasing number of people who are making a home in homelessness, there dwelling in diasporic identities and heterogeneous histories. Bearing witness to '… the pressure of dumbness, the accumulation of unrecorded life', I am pulled toward an insistent supplement whose silence cannot be filled with a ready meaning.
>
> (p. 246)

In narratives of participation, one is no longer completely congruent with fixed identifications. Past descriptions and attachments are held without rigidity, realizing that all narratives form tentatively around an unconscious gap, a limitation of language and current understandings, an opening where the future must enter to shatter complacent expectations. This rift in reality is also the space where one enters into relationship with others formerly excluded from one's habitual circles, and where one begins to listen for the creative formation of new sentiments.

After India exploded a nuclear bomb in 1998, Arundhati Roy questioned the widespread acceptance in India that nuclear weapons made India more secure, causing a critical uproar. In her talks afterward, she said:

> If protesting against having a nuclear bomb implanted in my brain is anti-Hindu and anti-national, then I secede. I hereby declare myself an independent mobile republic. I am a citizen of the earth. I own no territory. I have no flag.
>
> (quoted in Bearak, 1998, p. 4)

This type of secession from fixed identity, where one takes the space to raise new questions of the surrounding collective, is called "individuation" in Jungian psychology. Individuation is paradoxical, because at the same moment that one separates from identification with collective social narratives, there is the possibility of being in a deeper relationship with oneself and others. In such a process, one begins to listen more deeply, speak directly from the heart, encounter feeling fully, bear suffering in the self and other, and at the same time, experience the joyful and mysterious presence of other unknown souls. In postmodern discourse, this secession from fixed alliances is sometimes referred to as "nomadic identity" (see Chapter 9).

Through the mere fact of aliveness, however this is interpreted, each of us has some parts of the personality that are engaged with the world through narratives of participation. Aliveness is the animal and bodily capacity to be responsive to surrounding change. Without that aptitude, living beings starve and die. Aliveness is the key and the possibility for transformation in every human being, no matter what ideas or dogmas are currently dominating the landscape of consciousness. The question for liberation psychologies is how to create the kinds of environments that enlarge possibilities for aliveness.

Centrifugal and centripetal energies

When we encounter others embedded in narrative frames different from our own, we often talk at cross-purposes. It is not simply a matter of disagreeing on facts or interpretations, although this too will quickly become problematic. Rather, different narrative frames produce different stances toward facts and opposing attitudes in relationship to dialogue and exploration. When people with different narrative frames attempt to communicate, the effect may quickly induce centrifugal energies propelling discussions and people in opposing and polarizing directions. Such encounters can result in complete lack of understanding, cold formalism, the end of communication, or even enmity and violence. It is critically important to understand how situations can be created that are capable of centripetal force, that is, of bringing people together in ways that allow for divergence while melting unnecessary oppositions. Clearly, this can only happen where there is no threat of domination, violence, or reprisal. The work will inevitably be difficult, diplomatic, and creative, and only partially successful in many cases. The key to encounters that begin liberatory processes is to create environments where it is possible to get beneath already existent narrative frames in organized spaces that are safe and protected. The rules of engagement need to slow down knee-jerk reactions and professions of already-spoken dogmas in order to open processes where everyone begins to encounter and symbolize what is at the forgotten edges of consciousness and the forbidden or dangerous edges of conversation (see Chapter 10). Liminal spaces require as much silence as speaking, as well as bodily forms of response that cut beneath language.

Sometimes just agreeing to stand in the same room, or sit at the same table, or share a meal, is a step into a renewed relationship. Creative arts may be crucial in opening new dialogues (see Chapter 12). Entering into liminal space may entail stepping toward unconscious processes that work on us, processes that we cannot entirely control. Such encounters rupture policed borders of imagination that freeze responses into repetitive patterns. Liminal spaces can create a radical equality of imagination, where all can participate in shaping visions of liberation.

The goal of centripetal encounters in liminal space is the critical turn of each subject toward experiences of resymbolization and renarrativization. Sometimes this can involve mourning past losses and failures, but more often it is about surprising and unexpected images and insights arising spontaneously, a process that leads toward regeneration of life energies. This is less about recollection and more about making creative spaces for new visions, while letting go of rigid formulations that no longer serve. For example, each member of a group may be asked to create an image of their ideal for a community and also what they most fear. The images can be presented and arranged so that similar images are displayed side by side, often leading to surprising convergences. The group may divide into pairs to talk about their responses to the images, before coming back together to look for common and divergent themes. Because the images contain much information that is outside of narrative framing, they open a process of reflection and discernment allowing hidden and surprising aspects of self and other begin to be articulated. Here there is a hope for an intrapsychic dimension of democracy where the conflicts inherent in pluralism can begin to be encountered, tolerated, and symbolized within the subject.

An ethics of hospitality

Liberation psychology frankly places a value on widening the possibilities for transformative and participatory responses to rupture within liminal space. The basic call of the world to encounter other beings presents options for openings, difference, or newness as well as a future that by definition may be recognized as evolving in a direction distinct from the present. That is, to live within a time frame already presents countless possibilities for rupture that can be denied or embraced. Liberation psychology opts for hospitality and relatedness in ongoing and evolving situations of rupture within the limits of manageability.

In the past, much ethical thought has been founded on what Jacques Derrida (2003) has called "contracts of the same." In this form of ethics, one owes another kindness and respect as a result of natural and conventional identifications that are firmly held in place: "I owe you respect" because of what we share. For example, we are Christian, Jewish, American, Japanese, brothers, sisters, husband and wife, White, Black, or human. While creating ethical contracts based in the known, contracts of the same inevitably draw borders against what is not included or different defining what is on the other side as delinquent, abnormal, foreign, or even abject (see Chapter 5).

In liberation psychology, the stress changes to what is beyond the borders of contracts of the same. In this revaluation of ethics, we begin to ask what do individuals and communities owe events and beings that are unexpected and different from the same. In these encounters with the unknown we find rupturing realities that cannot be "understood" and assimilated into already-known narratives. They interrupt our conventional ways of thinking, forcing us to acknowledge and witness that for which we still have no narrative frame.

For Franz Rosenzweig, a German-Jewish writer, who worked with Martin Buber in Frankfurt in the 1920s, this encounter forces us to confront what he calls "a metaethical self." Here we discover a sort of liminality in the heart of our own experience of ourselves, and in the core of the Other that ruptures our expectations. We confront each other across a space of symbolic possibility that has not yet been filled up with conventional language, where a mysterious connectedness can be felt. According to Eric Santner (2001), the metaethical self is not "some sort of true self that, say, assumes a distance to the social roles of the personality; it is, rather a gap in the series of identifications that constitute it" (p. 73). Connecting Rosenzweig's work with Freud's, Santner suggests that the metaethical self means,

> exposure not simply to the thoughts, values, hopes, and memories of the Other, but also to the Other's touch of madness, to the way in which the Other is disoriented in the world, destitute, divested of an identity that firmly locates him or her in a delimited whole of some sort. ... To put it most simply, the Other to whom I am answerable *has an unconscious*, is the bearer of an irreducible and internal otherness, a locus of animation that belongs to no form of life.
>
> (p. 82)

Both self and other in this philosophy are partly unknown and mysterious, requiring a stance of openness to uncertain exploration. We approach the practice of understanding both ourselves and others in this philosophy as a process of revelation.

Communities of revelation

Ideas about identity and social space are grounded in the possibilities of imagination, in the streams of fantasy that rise up to either order or disrupt our comprehension of the world. Rosenzweig suggested a form of ethics that he called "absolute empiricism," a form of life built around the notion of ruptures and gaps as the quintessential core of life calling for constant awakenings to the otherness surrounding what we already know through familiar language. Awakenings would be a form of revelation, a moment when we realize that we are encased in tombs of inherited language and thinking from which we can revive in order to create fresh apprehensions of the unknown real. He proposed that our ethics be grounded through "communities of revelation." Such communities are "paradoxical in that they are constituted, from the start, in relation to the remnant, that is to a hindrance or leftover of the very forms of identification that normally sustain the psychic bonds of communities" (Santner, 2001, pp. 116–7). The remnant is all that in ourselves that remains unconscious and mysterious, all the potentialities for love and attachment that have the potential to surprise us, all of the feelings and reactions that may be called out through new encounters.

In order to participate in a community of revelation, one rejects generalizations about who belongs and who does not, in favor of an aliveness and openness. The world in which we participate is imagined as based in an evolving order that is larger, more generative and complex than personal consciousness and collective discourse. One has to dis-identify and dissociate with fixed understandings of both the self and the other, and sink down into spaces of doubt, questioning, and innovation to articulate the basic uncanniness (*unheimlichkeit*) of one's own insertion in life. Here one finds the site of forgotten memories and feelings, dreams, gaps in understanding, symptoms and discomforts, shame and reconciliation, which belong uniquely to one's own place in history. From this perspective, a stance committed to the certain and the familiar is a kind of exile from which one awakens to return home.

Relatedness and interdependence

The fundamental insights founding an ethics of liberation psychology are the notions of relatedness and interdependence. A utopian hope for peace and justice grounds itself in the idea that we can access a profound relatedness with all life-forms because we are historically embedded in the flesh of a biosphere. This insight has been developed repeatedly in liberation movements throughout the world in various local formulations. Brazilian theologian and ecofeminist Yvonne Gebara (1999) sees relatedness and connectivity as the founding reality of life.

> Within the perspective I seek to develop, relatedness is the primary reality: It is constitutive of all beings. It is more elementary than awareness of differences or than autonomy, individuality, or freedom. It is the foundational reality of all that is or can exist. It is the underlying fabric that is continually brought forth within the vital process in which we are

immersed. Its interwoven fibers do not exist separately, but only in perfect reciprocity with one another—in space, in time; in origin and into the future.

If we understand relatedness first of all as the constitutive relationship of communion we have with all beings, then we will have to acknowledge that the person is much more than the individuality recognized by my consciousness. Furthermore, my individuality does not end with my human characteristics and my network of human relationships. These no doubt have to do with my individuality as well, but it is much more than this, even if I am not aware of the fullness of being that brought me forth. My personal memory is very limited.

(p. 83)

Gebara (1999) presents her work as an "aspiration," a "con-spiracy," a "breathing with" the idea of relatedness through the intensity with which "the deer longs for running waters" (p. 215). Working and living in the poorest communities in northeastern Brazil, Gebara came to see that issues of unemployment, work, poverty, hunger, waste, and pollution are linked to styles of religious, economic, and cultural thinking. A failure to hear into the deep suffering of the marginalized represents a hardness of heart that is the opposite of relatedness. She presents her longing for an ethics of solidarity and communion as a yearning that prefigures the hope that we could find a way "to seek an atmosphere that is propitious for life" (p. 215).

If relatedness and interdependence are the foundational reality, then biodiversity is the fundamental challenge. This heterogeneity will be found among individuals, families, species, cultures, and religions creating an array of local tapestries, each different from the other. For Gebara, no one can regulate or dictate how they should be created.

Besides, a tapestry cannot be eternal, atemporal, or valid forever. It will lose its beauty and its aesthetic qualities. Ephemeral things enjoy the eternity of the present moment, and in this resides their evocative and inspirational task. Often the tapestry has to be rewoven, even if some of the old designs are copies—or even though we can manage to use some of the old threads that have not decayed. This is recreation, religious biodiversity, respect for new moments, creative inspiration, and the welcoming of new hands prepared to weave marvelous designs.

(p. 209)

This notion that we are forever in the process of co-creating a world together has been noted widely. Bishop Desmond Tutu (1999), commenting on the Truth and Reconciliation Commission of South Africa, has come to quite similar conclusions. "There is a movement," he writes, "not easily discernable, at the heart of things to reverse the awful centrifugal force of alienation, brokenness, division, hostility, and disharmony" (p. 265).

> Somewhere deep inside of us we seem to know that we are destined for something better. Now and again we catch a glimpse of the better thing for which we are meant—for example, when we work together to counter the effects of natural disasters and the world is galvanized by a spirit of compassion and an amazing outpouring of generosity; when for a little while we are bound together by bonds of a caring humanity, a universal sense of *ubuntu*, when victorious powers set up a Marshall Plan to help in the reconstruction of their former adversaries; when we establish a United Nations Organization where the peoples of the earth can parlay as they endeavor to avoid war; when we sign charters on the rights of children and of women; when we seek to ban the use of antipersonnel land mines; when we agree to outlaw torture and racism. Then we experience fleetingly that we are made for togetherness, for friendship, for community, for family, that we are created to live in a delicate network of interdependence.
>
> (pp. 264–5)

Bishop Tutu suggests that an impulse toward reconciliation was able to take root in South Africa because African culture was skilled at community building, drawing on an archive of inherited concepts and traditions that supported the constant reweaving of connectedness. He references the Nguni notion of *ubuntu* as a quality that is at the core of African conviviality:

> A person with *ubuntu* is open and available to others, affirming of others, does not feel threatened that others are able and good, for he and she has a proper self-assurance that comes from knowing that he or she belongs in a greater whole and is diminished when others are humiliated or diminished, when others are tortured or oppressed, or treated as if they were less than who they are.
>
> (p. 31)

This faith in the capacity of human beings to found their lives on relatedness and to rebuild communities that have been fragmented is central to liberation psychologies.

Undermining exiled consciousness

What happens to individuals who live in environments far from such traditions and visions of solidarity? What is the effect of living in a community permanently broken apart by the centrifugal forces of alienation and cruelty? At the level of individual consciousness, those who are educated in such locations learn what the early women's movement called "how not to speak." As discussed in Part II, we collude in silencing ourselves in situations of alienation and lose opportunities to listen to others. In our conscious lives, we live in exile from much of our own and others' experience, knowledge, and wisdom, covering over our uniqueness with collective niceties and narratives. Much falls into the area of the unsaid, and eventually becomes dissociated from consciousness, only to reappear in another form as symptom, affect, or illness. Nevertheless, the world surrounds us, and again and again offers us invitations to learn and evolve. All narrative frames are continually being undermined by what Argentine liberation philosopher Enrique Dussel (2003) calls "proximity," the originary bodily closeness of human beings:

> Proximity is security and warmth, the immediacy of flesh or of wine; it forgets afflictions and absorbs with pleasure what one deserves. Proximity is a feast—of liberation, not of exploitation, injustice or desecration. ... Archeologically timeless and eschatologically utopian, proximity is the most essential reality of a person, the beginning of the philosophical discourse of liberation, and metaphysics in its strict sense—real, reflective, and carefully thought out.
>
> (p. 21)

The world offers opportunities for new types of dialogue and the transformation of narrative frames every day. Because such transformation is mostly an unconscious process, it can happen without one's consent. Relatedness and love spring up spontaneously without rules, rupturing hardened narrative frames and throwing one into transformative liminal spaces whether desired or not. Then one may find oneself in proximity to other persons with whom one has to learn new forms of dialogue in order to communicate at all. For many, this will mean also a new relationship to oneself, because the kind of dialogue and relatedness we are proposing does not stop at identification with the other or assumptions that we are alike. Discerning what we share and the ways we differ is also part of learning about the outlines of one's own personality and sometimes leads to a change in perspective. Liberation psychology takes as its central task the creation of new spaces for allowing proxemics, relatedness, and *ubuntu* to bloom in relationship to both self and other. Through the cultivation of liminal spaces we may be graced with and challenged by in our communities, we need to maximize centripetal forces and minimize centrifugal forces.

Cultivation of liminal spaces

One task of liberation psychology, then, is to discern possibilities for rebuilding safe liminal spaces that can allow individuals carrying different narrative frameworks to encounter each other in cooperative efforts. Creating these spaces is an art and a craft. It may be done by professional psychologists, health experts, or social workers, but there are many others—community activists, cultural workers, elders, and religious leaders—who also do this work. It helps to have role models, to understand what others have tried and theorized in the past; but each local situation is also unique and requires complex symbolic understanding to find the framework and projects that allow entry and collaborative potential to multiple voices that may not yet be in harmony to let in conversation. We may need to enter potential liminal spaces without the idea that everyone can give a linear testimony about identity or past history, starting instead with photos, mementos, exploratory investigations, community interviews, theater projects, discussions of immediate needs and difficulties, or single-issue campaigns (see Chapter 12). For some there will be spiritual dimensions to the work of restoration of community. Capacities for dialogue will need to be built up to engage both supportive and difficult conversations (see Chapter 10).

It is often, though not always, the case that more mature people in a community have the moral authority to create and hold together liminal spaces. In traditional cultures, it is usually elders who maintain open sites for religious and social rituals because they are the most experienced in the processes involved. Because liminal spaces are experimental and transgressive, forming a safe container, "a free and protected space" (Kalff, 2003) is critical to success. The navigation of liminal space requires intelligent facilitation by those who can hold and protect without interfering, intruding, and controlling. Learning to understand, play, participate in, and model such a mentoring role is central to the work of liberation psychologies.

Generally, in reconstructed liminal spaces one needs to begin to excavate and symbolize iconic memories, lost affects, and emotional commitments existing beneath narrative frameworks. This archeology allows for a loosening of the already known and a beginning of wonder in the experience of the unspoken and uncanny, which everyone can share. The willingness to go beneath fixed narratives can provide a new basis for *communitas* where before there was only opposition. Often local community activists or cultural workers reconstruct liminal spaces through trial and error, and perceptiveness about what is missing. Each of these constructed spaces is a psychological space because it allows for individual emergence and liberation, but it is also a community space where cultural assumptions may be challenged and transformed and *communitas* experienced (see Chapter 11).

Methodologies used for reconstructing liminal spaces within already existent communities will be discussed in Part IV, Chapters 11, 12, and 15, which focus on public homeplaces, liberation arts, and processes of restoration and reconciliation. Methodologies for reconstructing liminal spaces used by psychologists or other researchers with groups convened through participatory action research, with its unique ethical challenges, will be analyzed in Chapters 13 and 14.

Openings for dialogue with others can only happen where there are counterbalancing possibilities for psychological openings within individual subjectivities, and vice versa. In such spaces, old and new, expected and unexpected begin to collide and form new patterns. Different roles can be tried on and new identities experimented with as solidarities and alliances are slowly built. Such paradoxically open yet contained liminal spaces contribute to the needed dissolutions of fixed and singular identities to which we now turn in Chapter 9.

9
Non-Subjects and Nomadic Consciousness

> *Soy un amasciento*, I am an act of kneading, of uniting and joining that not only has produced both a creature of darkness and a creature of light, but also a creature that questions the definitions of light and dark and gives them new meanings.
>
> (Anzaldúa, 1987, p. 103)

An ethics of subjectivity

The compass points we described for psychologies of liberation have their analogues on the personal, psychological level. Once departing from false universals, unconscious identification with dominant ideologies, and fixed schemas of development, an interior sense of self that finds alternative orientations becomes possible. Here the points of the compass function paradoxically, helping us let go of our usual ground. They do not fix our location but encourage presence, wandering, and even getting lost. Intrapsychically, these paradoxical markers encourage us to welcome what has been kept at bay: unbidden feelings, thoughts, and images; mourning for losses and absences; unsatisfied yearnings for what has not been born; and joy in unexpected places. Between ourselves and others we gain a new footing: to orient toward that which differs from our own experience, to what challenges our ego positions, and catches us by surprise. This re-orientation helps us to emerge from states of dissociation by allowing us to enter those parts of ourselves, our relationships, and our communities that have not been welcomed (Watkins, 2005).

Dion-Buffalo and Mohawk (in Esteva & Prakash, 1998) suggest that in the wake of colonialism and the onslaught of neoliberalism, one's task is neither to become good subjects who unquestioningly accept the premises of the West or bad subjects in revolt against the West's processes of colonization. The challenge is to become non-subjects, who are capable of acting and thinking in ways removed from unconsciously identifying with Western assumptions. To varying degrees, societies encourage members to participate in the repression or silencing of the unexpected and even parts of themselves that destabilize societally desired thoughts and behaviors. When we begin to listen for what has been discouraged and silenced, and turn to orient ourselves to what is unfamiliar, we begin to take up a transgressive relationship to those norms that has implications for our very experience of self. Following Deleuze and Guattari, Rosi Braidotti (1994) names as "nomadic" consciousness those ways of thinking that resist assimilation into dominant habits of representing the self, that have "forgotten to forget injustice and symbolic poverty: their memory is activated against the stream; they enact a rebellion of subjugated knowledges" (p. 25).

In Part II, we delineated the psychic fragmentation that ensues in environments of atrocity, injustice, and isolation. Here we are addressing the reclaiming of psychic multiplicity and complex identity as pathways to interconnectedness. The multiplicity of fragmentation and the multiplicity of identity we are addressing here are not to be confused. As Rose (in Said, 2004) points out, we do not want to be at risk "of idealizing the flaws and fissures of identity" that result from trauma.

> For trauma, far from generating freedom, openness to others as well as to the divided and unresolved fragments of a self, leads to a very different kind of fragmentation—one which is, in Freud's words, "devastating", and causes identities to batten down, to go exactly the other way: towards dogma, the dangers of coercive and coercing forms of faith.
>
> (pp. 75–6)

The undoing of this defensive battening will entail the work of mourning that has been addressed in Chapter. In this chapter, we will explore forms of participatory identity or nomadic consciousness that are guided by an ethics of hospitality toward the unknown in oneself and the other.

As the dislocations caused by migration fragment communities ever more, (post)colonial fiction has documented the confusions, joys, and terrors of living in situations where old life paths have failed, and new orientations are being sought. Brazilian novelist Clarice Lispector in her novel, *The apple in the dark* (1967), imagines the world of a man, Martim, whose life has imploded around him through its sense of meaningless routine:

> But with the passage of time, contrary to what might be expected, he had been turning into an abstract man. Like a fingernail that somehow manages never to get dirty: the dirt is only peripheral to the nail; and if the nail is cut, it does not even hurt, it grows again like a cactus. He had been turning into a huge man. Like an abstract fingernail. ...
>
> Yes, that's what had begun to happen. ... his soul had become abstract. ... His own body was abstract. ... Then you would go home to sleep in abstract beds, held up in the air by four legs; you made love with concentration,

and you slept like a fingernail that had grown too long. We were eternal
and gigantic. ...

(p. 39)

In Lispector's novel, Martim is thrown into a desert where he is lost and
must navigate without any compass or goal, with only his bodily senses of
touch and intuition to guide him:

> The man standing there could not perceive what law ruled the harsh wind
> and the silent sparkling of the stones. But having laid down the arms of
> man, he was giving himself over defenseless to the immense harmony of
> the wasteland. He too was pure, harmonious, and he too had no sense. ...
> Since the breeze was blowing from the left he deliberately turned away
> from the direction he had been following—and with great deliberation,
> with the care of a craftsman, he tried to walk in such a way that he would
> always feel the wind full in the face. His groping face was attempting to
> follow that open path in the air and the promise that it held.

(p. 44)

Here, Lispector is trying to describe the difference between living through a
conventional narrative of dissociation (like an abstract fingernail) and committing to an ethics of hospitality toward whatever arises in one's environment (facing the wind). She is attempting to imagine a new ethic beyond
compliance with authoritarian colonial hierarchies.

As an epigraph for the novel, she inscribes a passage from the Upanishads
that captures the idea of non-subjects:

> By creating all things, he entered into everything. By entering into all
> things, he became what has form and what is formless; he became what
> can be defined and what cannot be defined; he became what has support
> and what has no support; he became what is crude and what is delicate. He
> became every kind of thing: that is why wise men call him the Real One.

When on such a pilgrimage, one might use images and metaphors of a
destination to help orient. Here, however, we will offer images for re-imagining the pilgrim and his or her relation to what is encountered. In invok-
ing the metaphor of travel, we focus on the effects on identity of entering
and moving in liminal spaces. As one is thrown open to unexpected experiences, one can experiment with departing from the familiar, tolerating the
vulnerability of becoming lost, and even the possibility of becoming a
stranger to oneself (Seshadri-Crooks, 2002). We will work to imagine identity less as product and more as process, a practice marked by its gestures
toward otherness in oneself and others. At times this is thrust upon one; at
other times a sense of the impoverishment imposed by normative identity
and official history fuels a "radical desire for the dissolution of one's subjective certainty" (Seshadri-Crooks, 2002, p. 75).

For some, the first question will be, how it is possible to maintain current commitments to friends, family, and community while engaging in the processes of identity transformation suggested by becoming a non-subject. Re-imagining subjectivity does not entail a literal abandonment of home. Commitments may be strengthened by circumambulating various centers, searching for crevices in the foundations, unexplored neighborhoods, and vacant lots nearby. One imagines a journey, a retreat to the forest, followed by a return, through which a new attitude, cleansed from the baggage of dry and brittle husks, refreshes the spirit and allows an invigorated perspective. The journey may be imagined as a period in a protected enclosure, far from usual routines, where mysterious and uncertain transformation has the possibility of birthing something altogether different inside of oneself (Flinders, 1998). These effects cannot happen all at once, because they take time. Although one cannot change the past, one can develop new understandings of oneself and others in relation to it. The processes that cultivate non-subjects and nomadic consciousness involve schooling in deeper listening, in the widening of sensibilities, and in the expanding of expression that deepens relationships.

Morales (1998) imagines nomadic consciousness as "nightflying." Tracing the traumatic effects of centuries of violence against women framed as witch-hunting, she suggests a need to look deeply into the historical forces that have shaped our silences:

One of the common accusations against witches is nightflying: the ability to change shape or endow a household object, a pot or broom, with magical powers and soar above the landscape of daily life, with eyes that can penetrate the darkness and see what we are not supposed to see. From these forbidden heights one can see the lines of extinct roads and old riverbeds, the designs made by private landholdings, the relationships between water and growth, and the proximity or distances between people. Those who can see in the dark can uncover secrets: hidden comings and goings, deals and escapes, the undercover movements of troops, layers of life normally conducted out of sight.

(p. 49)

Nightflying allows us to include silences and absences in our thinking about what we encounter. We can listen not only for what people say and think, but also for what they omit and refuse.

In the work of Deleuze and Guattari (1987), the defensive and sedentary lifeways at the heart of agriculturally based societies are viewed as leading to a form of thinking that territorializes identities and ideas, defending them from encroachment like fences around fields. They propose "deterritorialization" as the form of being of nomads and non-subjects who rather than tear fences down, burrow under or go over or around fixed perimeters to explore in-between spaces, connections, and solidarities. By making territorial perimeters irrelevant, they defuse defensive energies little by little, disrupting conceptual, symbolic, and even literal boundaries.

On the path to non-subjecthood one comes to understand modes of practicing subjectivity that contribute to the strength of destructive normative ways of viewing oneself and others. In tandem, reflection on taken-for-granted habits of conducting the self and a concomitant conscious generativity regarding ways to practice oneself constitute an ethics of subjectivity.

Each day we reaffirm, challenge, or reconstruct the world by the myriad approaches we take toward selfhood. These practices have implications for the ways we hold our own experiences, for what we open to, as well as what we one foreclose. From the point of view of liberation psychologies, movements toward complex and heterogeneous identity are moral moves, as well as psychological and social ones. When complex identities are narrowed and reduced, it becomes easier for one group to act destructively against another. Philosopher Kelly Oliver (2001) observes that previous models of subjectivity have grounded identity in dualistic thinking that often, unwittingly, promotes such hostility toward others. The other is what one is not, or what one does not want to be and cannot accept about oneself. Thus to ground subjectivity differently, one must initiate processes of hosting one's repressed otherness as well as placing oneself in liminal environments where one can work through "whatever we might find threatening in relation to otherness and difference" (p. 10). She sees the possibility of grounding subjectivity not in exclusion but in relationship through difference. "Love is an ethics of otherness," Oliver (2001) says, "that thrives on the adventure of otherness. This means that love is an ethical and social responsibility to open personal and public space in which otherness and difference can be articulated. Love requires a commitment to the advent and nurturing of difference" (p. 20).

The claiming of one's hybridity and the turning toward others who refuse to experience identity in narrow ways retrieve multiple potential sites for solidarity, making binary oppositions of self and other less likely. The themes offered below are not in the spirit of fixed prescriptions for conduct, but for the nourishment of intrasubjective and intersubjective sensitivities and sensibilities that are critical to the making and sustaining of peace. An ethics of otherness does not imply premature forgiveness, but an openness to encounter and dialogue, even if the conversation is difficult and conflictual.

From fixed and stable to fluid and reflexive identities

Many in the West are used to thinking of identity as arising from normative processes of socialization. One speaks of a "core" of identity, of "fixed" identity, expecting that identity is "stable," and can be relied on for its continuity and unity, no matter how limiting these characteristics might also be. In a highly individualistic culture, one lauds "firm boundaries" that preclude any confusion about where one ends, and the world and others begin. Psychology has made pathologies out of experiences of "fluid boundaries," "unstable egos," "multiplicity" of selfhood, radical experiences of the inter-penetration of self/other/world, and "co-dependency."

Selves living under the sway of individualism believe they are more unfet-tered than others to physically migrate, leaving behind what have come to feel like unnecessary and restrictive bonds to family, community, and place. They may shed the past, using cultural amnesia as a springboard into an acquisitive future. Unfortunately, while experiencing such so-called freedom, individualistic selves can be better controlled when they lack solidarity with one another, better manipulated as a workforce, and more easily propagan-dized by corporate-controlled politics (Sloan, 1996). They can be taught that whatever limitations they experience are due to their own shortcomings and inadequacies, for they are tutored not to understand their own history in the light of the larger web of culture. The individualistic self conducts itself as though its neighborhood, community, and, perhaps, even family do not really matter. What counts are impressive showings in the array of competi-tive tasks that are presented as necessary to survival and to opportunities to succeed and excel in the mainstream culture. The capacity to separate and differentiate from others is understood as a triumph of psychological devel-opment, advocated by developmental theorizing and supported by norma-tive family and individual therapy, as well as families and schools.

This competitive self is rooted in visions of scarcity, a vision that leads to violence and disconnection due to struggles over resources presumed to be insufficient. Regina Schwartz (1997) sees this paradigm as a violent legacy of monotheism, and proposes instead an ideal of plenitude, with a corollary eth-ical imperative of generosity. But once the self is convinced it cannot rely on others, hoarding behavior appears rational and desirable, fueling con-sumerism and its associated norms. Separate selves can experience themselves as independent even from their bodies and from nature, both moving to mere backdrops to experience, and thereby as sites of potential exploitation.

Initially children do not manufacture their identities as much as they receive them, finding themselves in the eyes of those around them. Maalouf (2000), a French Lebanese Christian, says, "it is less a matter of our choosing our identities than that we find some of our identity constrained, strewn with obstacles" (p. 25). Selves living in the shadow of individualism, who find themselves exploited as objects to fuel the affluence or power of others, some-times suffer from introjecting negative images of themselves cast out from the center. In the preface to Fanon's (1963) *The wretched of the earth*, Sartre asserted that what matters is what one does with what others have done to us. One may become painfully aware of the projections one has identified with, pro-jections that cage one into fixed, as though unalterable identities. This process of reflexivity opens up a critical space in which it becomes possible to perform oneself in new ways, transforming the restrictiveness of binary divisions.

José Esteban Muñoz (1999) refers to such transformations as "disidentifications" that neither assimilate and identify with normative roles nor resist and oppose, but "wear down the coherency of borders" (p. 32). He sees such a strategy in Arturo Islas's novel *Migrant souls* (1990) where the character Miguel Chico navigates between his life as a gay intellectual at the University of Chicago and relationships with his cousins in a large Chicano family. The hybrid identity that emerges from this "shuttling between different identity vectors" repeats the history that already infuses his family myths:

> They were migrant, not immigrant souls. They simply and naturally went from one bloody side of the river to the other and into a land that just a few decades earlier had been Mexico. They became border Mexicans with American citizenship.
>
> (Islas, quoted in Muñoz, 1999, p. 32)

By reducing these borders to permeable spaces through migrancy, the family refuses the logic that created them and undermines the "rhetorics of normativity and normalization" that hold them in place (p. 34).

For Muñoz,

> Disidentification is about recycling and rethinking encoded meaning. The process of disidentification scrambles and reconstructs the encoded messages of a cultural text in a fashion that both exposes its encoded message's universalizing and exclusionary machinations and recircuits its workings to account for, include, and empower minority identities and identifications. Thus disidentification is a step further than cracking open the code of the majority; it proceeds to use this code as raw material for representing a disempowered politics or positionality that has been rendered unthinkable by the dominant culture.
>
> (p. 31)

Psychologies of liberation problematize identity, working with a set of understandings about identity that are radically different from those encountered in developmental psychology. They are careful not to universalize Euro-American notions of "identity." For instance, African psychologist Amini Mama says that she is not aware of a term for identity in any of the African languages she knows. As a young girl, she felt she received identity only when she left Africa to be schooled in England. "We recall distasteful colonial impositions that told us who we were: a race of kaffirs, natives, Negroes and Negresses." "I grew a more specifiable identity only when I went away to school in Europe. It was in an English boarding school that I was first compelled to claim and assert an identity, if only to correct the daily nonsense I was subjected to." This "nonsense" included the assumption that she had "an identity problem," being "reduced to being a 'colored girl,' or a 'black.' To be treated as an orphan, a refugee, or an immigrant" (Mama, 2002, p. 7).

To actively resist the introjection of such negative designations, the practices of liberation psychologies are aimed at nurturing the development of alternative ways of practicing subjectivity. These alternatives can arise through an exile from the "center" or mainstream—imposed, chosen, or happened upon through circumstances—which provides a "critical distance from all cultural identities, a restless opposition to all orthodoxies—both those of the colonizer and those of the colonized" (Nussbaum, 2001).

Advocating nomadic consciousness, Rosi Braidotti (2002) urges us to question fixed identities as much as possible, seeing them as "sedentary site[s] that produce reactive passions like greed, paranoia, and Oedipal jealousy and other forms of symbolic constipation" (p. 8). Identity that is de-centered can work to claim discarded fibers of affect and desire, yielding a hybridized subjectivity reflective of multiple roots, even if disjunctive, ambivalent, and contradictory.

Fixed, singular identities breed polarized perceptions of self and other, reducing the complexity of others into that which resembles the self or that which is different. Often those different are derogated as "inferior," and thus worthy of exclusion, exploitation, and ill-treatment. Most American high schools are breeding grounds for this kind of thinking, giving vast numbers of children archetypal experiences of insider and outsider statuses, of bullying and exclusion. The past century is laden with the horrors of annihilations and exploitations that result from such grivously dehumanizing polarizations, binary divisions of people into categories of "pure" and "impure," of human and inhuman.

Rather than imagining identity as achieved and fixed, psychologies of liberation point us toward becoming aware of how one practices and performs one's identities. They open one to re-imagine oneself in ways that can subvert the internalization of stereotypes and transgress limiting normalized scripts. One is encouraged to enjoy a self capable of improvising what has been desired but not lived, that brings into the world the kind of creativity and dialogue necessary to vibrant, peaceful, and just communities. For instance, both playful and serious stepping aside from fixed gender stereotypes in carnival or theater can open a space where a multiplicity of ways of engendering oneself can arise. Such transgressive moves may contribute to bringing awareness to and breaking the hold of unconscious identifications that are promoted in a culture.

From the singular center to the multiple peripheries

We live in a world of increasing complexity where rootlessness, forced and chosen migrations, and the deterioration of cohesive communities are on the rise, where the possibility of a consistent, stable, and highly bounded sense of identity is being openly questioned and is harder to live with. Deconstructionist and psychoanalytic theories challenge modernist ideas of a unified subject, inviting us to a view of human subjectivity that instead is complex, multiple and, often, contradictory. Nomadic consciousness involves recovering a multiplicity of selves that have slipped into the cracks, and which have become disavowed and unwitnessed by the dominant culture. According to Braidotti (2002), "Nomadic subjectivity is about the simultaneity of complex and multi-layered identities" where axes such as class, race, ethnicity, gender, and age interact with each other (p. 6). A nomadic identity affords us multiple interconnections, while steering clear of appropriation. It is "rather an emphatic proximity, intensive inter-connectedness" that allows us to think through and move across established categories and levels of experience (p. 5). The nomad does not take up residence within one fixed and central experience of identity, but can blur fixity, using ambiguity as a bridge to connect with multiple others and aspects of self.

When we resist the collapse of multiple potential partialities into a singular, more fixed identity, surprising and important alliances can occur. For instance, Moslem and Jewish parents of Palestinian and Israeli children killed in conflicts have created the Parents' Forum. Rather than split across religious, national, or ethnic identifications, these parents have reached out to each other based on their shared experiences of loss. From this common experience *and* their differences they are able to host together successful community forums aimed at peace building. The implication of their alliance for others caught in the conflicts is that if those who paid the ultimate price of losing a child at the hands of "the enemy" can talk to each other, so can the rest (Wilkinson, 2003).

Wounded cosmopolitanism

Contemporary studies at the interface of psychoanalysis and social theory have looked at what can be learned about subjectivity from the experience of hybrid subjects. Large numbers of people have already evolved forms of nomadic consciousness as a result of life situations that have required them to function in complex spaces with multiple points of view. As Du Bois (1903) first pointed out, the survival of the marginalized depends on a "double consciousness," a double vision that learns to see each encounter not only from one's own point of view, but also from the point of view of the oppressor. This studied doubleness creates what Homi Bhabha (2004) calls "wounded cosmopolitanism." Now, he argues, the "cosmopolitan" is more likely to be the migrant who has had to learn at least two languages and two cultures. The migrant maid in the kitchen, he asserts, is more cosmopolitan than the mistress or master in the study, who is working on extending power at the center. "[It] is from those who have suffered the sentence of history—subjugation, domination, diaspora, displacement—that we learn our most enduring lessons for living and thinking" (Bhabha, quoted in Sandoval, 2000, p. 1). Those who have been relegated to the periphery teach those in the center by their example about a different mode of practicing the self. As strategies for survival evolve in the everyday lives of the excluded, they begin a process of rehearsing and articulating the outlines for new sensitivities and attitudes that are suggested through their improvisations.

Without predetermined destinations

In exploring migrancy as a metaphor for the ethical attitude, we need to spawn a new subjectivity. Braidotti (2002) suggests that the nomadic style is about "transitions and passages without predetermined destinations or lost homelands" (p. 7). Seshadri-Crooks (2002) speaks of letting go of our mooring, of the need to undo "the quilting point of our subjectivity" (p. 75). Nomadic subjectivity abandons styles of being that are wholly ego dominated. Instead of entering into relations with others with one's own agenda, one enters with an openness to understand something new. One orients to that which surprises and pulls one into the unfamiliar—within oneself and one's relationships. It is an orientation toward discovery that occurs at the edges of the already known, rather than the promulgation of the already known. For this reason, it is characterized more by humility than hubris, more by questioning and listening than by dictation, and more by mischief than obedience. Its beauty lies in the patient discovery of common ground, surprising irruptions of laughter at limits seen through, as well as the ability to articulate and attempt to understand and respect differences.

It is an openness to the "unhomely" (or uncanny) where, according to Freud, what ought to remain hidden comes to light. Homi Bhabha (1994) describes it as times when our ordinary domesticity breaks open to reveal the disturbing history it has sought to contain: "[t]he borders between home and world become confused; and, uncannily, the private and the public become part of each other, forcing upon us a vision as divided as it is disorienting" (p. 9). To come to know oneself is to journey into the history of one's culture. As Susan Griffin (1992) puts it:

> We forget that we are history. We have kept the left hand from knowing the right. ... We are not used to associating our private lives with public events. Yet the histories of families cannot be separated from the histories of nations. To divide them is part of our denial.
>
> (p. 11)

To lose our homeland would be to loosen ourselves from the responsibilities of our originating locations, to pretend that they are histories that did not exist and do not have legacies in the present. By contrast, to explore without lost homelands means to ground our own formation in a historical context that has marked us deeply. Such exploration is extended to the sites of one's own psychic shaping. We learn to engage in what Mary Louise Pratt (1992) has called "autoethnography" and Fanon (1967) called a "scrutiny of the self," a self-reflective process of understanding our own social formation that is necessary to create the ideal conditions for a more human world (p. 23). This scrutiny and the resulting dis-identifications from destructive norms that ensue become acts of freedom.

One possible effect of trauma is to abandon what has become poisoned. This spontaneous self-protective move severs one from cultural roots, and contributes to a failure to understand the implications of them. Those in positions of cultural power by virtue of ethnicity, gender, or class often fail to see that their social location and the meanings of it for themselves and others may have emerged from a traumatic past. It has become "naturalized," taken for granted; one is identified with it and thus unable to reflect upon it.

Those who teach critical race theory on college campuses in the United States often attempt to create class projects that allow students to break open an unconscious compliance with dominant narratives through autoethnography. Each student in one class taught by Shulman-Lorenz (1997b) was asked to interview an unfamiliar subgroup on campus about their experiences at college. The class then pooled the reports to get a picture of the whole. Many students were shocked when their naiveté was shattered. One such class member who interviewed Native American students wrote:

> Before this assignment I didn't realize how non-diverse the campus was. I guess being a white male I thought of it as being very diverse. I didn't even realize that a group of people could possibly be unhappy with their social standing on the campus. Personally I feel responsible and I feel like I was once, although unintentionally, part of an aspect that was a part in making these students unhappy. I never bothered to learn about other cultures, or tried to understand what people from other cultures are faced with every day. I took my own standing for granted. ... The situation that Native American students here are faced with now is completely unsatisfactory. ... But looking back at them now, I see myself as blind. I never realized the difficulties faced by others.
>
> (p. 25)

Most psychologies of liberation articulate the need to learn to dis-identify from the unquestioned assumptions of one's social location, to shift away from a sedimented identity. This creation of an antagonism with oneself, ejecting "the introjected subject positions of dominant groups, allows affiliations and alliances outside of one's usual circles, and new forms of subjectivity"

(JanMohamed, 1993). One is often most blind regarding the position from which one is seeing. Given colonial histories, one must gain insight on the impact of ideas about ethnicity and nation on identity.

Interrogating Whiteness

If one sees oneself as White, a move toward nomadic consciousness involves understanding that identifying with being "White" is a constructed experience of recent history. In entering the United States, many immigrant groups became "whitened" to distinguish their fates from that of Native Americans and Blacks. Beneath the assumption of "being White" lies denial and amnesia regarding the multiple ethnic roots of all who live in America. Reversing this forgetfulness allows the claiming of one's own discarded pieces of identity that opens up possible points of contact with others. Such a re-membering entails seeing clearly the privileges that have accrued from the claim to Whiteness and the shadow of dispossession this casts on others. Braidotti (2002) says that to "rework whiteness in the era of postmodernity is *firstly* to situate it, de-naturalize it and embody and embed it. Secondly, nomadize it, or to de-stabilize it, to undo its hegemonic hold" (p. 6). One looks at the multiplicity of identities held within the interrelated categories of "White" and "Black," and studies the activity at the border gates of their division. For instance, when the Irish began to immigrate to the United States, those of British ancestry saw them as Black. Once they advanced in their efforts at assimilation, the Irish became incorporated under the umbrella of whiteness.

Nomadic identity resists an acculturation based on integration and assimilation and struggles for one issuing from negotiation and dialogue (Bhatia, 2003). This perspective challenges the "achievement" of racial or ethnic identity referred to in developmental research, as though identification with a single race or ethnicity is an ideal. The idea of "race" itself has been destabilized and is increasingly understood as a social construction without biological foundation. The fact that there is more genetic variation between two fruit flies than there is between two persons of different races helps to explode essentialism about race based on genetic fantasies.

For White Americans, the stability of identity is secured in part by surrounding oneself with the familiar, with those who are similar to oneself, restricting contact with people-of-color who might challenge one's narratives and identifications. For the affluent, security of identity is achieved by class apartheid that serves to protect the myth of the self-made person from critiques that their stature is due partly to privilege and a function of entitlement, rather than simply the deserved fruits of hard labor. Whiteness studies in the last decade have explored the lived experience of being White, interrogating how the idea of being "White" emerged, how identification with it has allowed individuals and groups to accrue benefits, and how it can be surrendered without falling into an ahistorical and naive color blindness (Roediger, 1999, 2005; Lipsitz, 1998).

A critical examination of Whiteness as a construct is also essential to those whom it has exiled from the center and treated with disdain, those who have suffered from Whites' assumption of authority and privilege. Fanon and Malcolm X advocated "new eyes" for a "new racial subject," "a new man," "released from nauseating mimicry," and the "self-mutilation enacted by efforts to be what one is not" (Marable, 2004). According to bell hooks (1994), the beginning processes of decolonization entail the "members of exploited and oppressed groups dar[ing] to critically interrogate" their locations, identities, and allegiances. Radical Black subjectivity is, hooks (1990) says, a "quest to find ways to construct self and identity that are oppositional and libratory" (p. 28).

Beyond national identities

"Nation," like "race," is a relatively new concept imposed on many disparate communities through the processes of colonialism (Bhabha, 1990). Philosopher Richard Kearney questions individuals' identification with nationality, seeing it as too broad to allow for local affiliations that safeguard indigenous languages and cultural experiences, while at the same time being too small to enable the kind of cross-cultural alliances that are necessary to peaceful relations and mutually beneficial initiatives.

In speaking of the Irish dilemma, Richard Kearney (1998b) writes:

> There is no such thing as primordial nationality. Every nation is a hybrid construct, an "imagined community" that can be re-imagined again in alternative versions. The challenge is to embrace the process of hybridization from which we derive and to which we are committed willy-nilly.
>
> (p. 13)

The challenge is also to be able to move between "multiple layers of compatible identification" (p. 13): a larger, deterritorializing identification that reflects transnational exchanges, a national level, a regional one that allows for the strengthening of participatory democracy, and, in many places, a local cultural one where indigenous languages and traditions are safeguarded. An example of this is found in the Zapatista communities in Chiapas, Mexico, where indigenous groups have linked together to create autonomous zones. These communities do not negate the boundaries of local and regional Mexican government, but overlap them. The Zapatistas have been clear that they are neither seceding from the Mexican government nor wholly relying on it. While working to safeguard indigenous languages and ways of life, they also seek solidarity with similar autonomous communities both within and outside of Mexico.

Imagining ourselves differently

In Braidotti's (1994) discussion of nomadism, she uses the term "figuration" to refer to a "style of thought that evokes or expresses ways out of the phallocentric vision of the subject" (p. 1). By this she means a movement away from the center, from dualistic conceptualizations and "monological mental habits" that mitigate against dialogical encounters with others and even with hidden aspects of oneself. The creation of and the living into a figuration is an affirmative deconstructive move, challenging taken-for-granted ideas of identity, and posing an alternative, politically informed subjectivity that is more mobile, complex, and shifting (Braidotti, 2002). The "as-if" quality of a figuration opens an improvisational space for more consciously performing identity rather than unconsciously enacting a set of unreflective identifications.

Other figurations proposed that are resonant with nomadic identities include diasporic identity, hybrid identity, the protean self (Lifton, 1993), creolization/transculturality (Hall, 1996; Gilroy, 1993), pilgrims, migratory identities, post-conventional identity (Santner, 1990), multiculturalist inclusive identity (Cross, 1991), and the ensembled self (Sampson, 1988, 1989). All of these "figurations" embrace ambiguity, complexity, and multiplicity, and encourage resistance to repressive and alienating cultural norms. In speaking of such hybridity, Anzaldúa and Keating (2002) say that it encourages us to pass

> beyond separate and easy identification, creating bridges that cross race and other classifications among different groups via intergenerational dialogue. Rather than legislating and restricting racial identities, it tries to make them more pliant and multiple. The personal and cultural narratives are not disinterested, objective questionings of identity politics, but impassioned and conflicted engagements in resistance.
>
> (p. 2)

Gloria Anzaldúa (1987) calls selves resonant with these figurations, "border crossers." She imagines a new tribalism arising from such transgressions, connecting people who embody unique complex configurations of identity, who share a penchant for inclusion (rather than exclusion), and are capable of empathic connections across differences. The *mestiza* consciousness of such border crossers explodes dictated dualities. She says that although the consciousness of the borderlands "is a source of intense pain, its energy comes from continual creative motion that keeps breaking down the unitary aspect of each paradigm" (p. 80).

> As a *mestiza* I have no country, my homeland cast me out; yet all countries are mine. ... I am cultureless because, as a feminist I challenge the

collective cultural/religious male-derived beliefs of Indo-Hispanics and Anglos; yet I am cultured because I am participating in the creation of yet another culture, a new story to explain the world and our participation in it, a new value system with images that connect us to each other and to the planet.

(pp. 102–3)

Lavie and Swendenburg (1996) describe borders as minefields for identity:

Living in the border means frequently experiencing the feeling of being trapped in an impossible in-between. Franco-Maghrebis who are denied the option of identifying with either France or Algeria and are harassed both by white racist extremists and Islamic xenophobes. ... Borders and diasporas are phenomena that blow up—both enlarge and explode—the hyphen: Arab-Jew, African-American, Franco-Maghrebis, and Black-British. Avoiding the dual axes of migration between distinct territorial entities, the hyphen becomes the third space.

(pp. 15–6)

Maalouf (2000) sees those able to claim complex identities as living "in a sort of frontier crisscrossed by ethnic, religious and other fault lines."

They have a special role to play in forging links, eliminating misunderstandings, making some parties more reasonable and others less belligerent, smoothing out difficulties, seeking compromise. Their role is to act as bridges, go-betweens, mediators between the various communities and cultures. And that is precisely why their dilemma is so significant: if they cannot sustain their multiple allegiances, if they are continually being pressed to take sides or ordered to stay within their own tribe, then all of us have reason to be uneasy about the way the world is going.

(pp. 4–5)

He imagines these "frontier dwellers" as a mortar that joins together and strengthens their societies. What is emphasized here is the way in which a culture can become more of a crossroads, providing sites for mixing and creating multiple contact zones (Hermans & Kempen, 1998).

The refiguring of identity needs to include the way we perceive the identities of others, as well as ourselves. Maalouf argues that we lay the seeds for violence when we confine others within a narrow identity that we hold in a humiliating and denigrating light that disregards the complexity of their affiliations. When the fluidity, malleability, and multiplicity of identity go unrecognized, dehumanizing the Other is more possible. "For it is often the way we look at other people that imprisons them within their own narrowest allegiances. And it is also the way we look at them that may set them free" (Maalouf, 2000, p. 22). In the throes of being narrowed to a singular identity that is denigrated, we make it more probable that others will violently assert their identity.

Playing with subjectivity: Chosen and practiced exile

The psychological task for those on the way to nomadic identity is to begin to see through one's own cultural locations and to stretch beyond their limits, leaving the comfort and familiarity one may have grown used to. In doing so one becomes more adept at entering into and creating dialogical spaces where individuals can share their cultural experience with one another. Our roots may be imagined as rhizomatic, allowing us to emerge into dialogue in multiple cultural contexts (Deleuze & Guattari, 1986).

The nomad, seen as "different" and cast out from or deserting of normative cultural centers, begins a pilgrimage, a creative foray into re-imagining and experiencing identity. If this exclusion or fall from the center can be embraced as not only necessary but desirable and interesting, even if undeserved or unexpected, then a potential transformation of one's own subjectivity can be sought. Each way one falls "out of grace" opens up potentials for new relationships with others and oneself, insights and avenues in life and work that one could not have anticipated. Said (2004) describes that finding oneself radically displaced gifts one with an awareness that is contrapuntal, giving one a plurality of vantage points from which one can view self and others. For example, White adoptive parents of biracial and mixed race children often find that their white peers and colleagues have dropped them from the privileged rank of Whiteness. Now, unexpectedly, they begin to see racism function from another vantage point than the one they grew up with. New awareness and solidarities become possible as they shift toward understanding multiple points of view.

When those already secure in asserting themselves within a fixed identity embark on the moral pilgrimage of nomadic consciousness, they begin to be able to play with subjectivity. Such play has both an external and internal level. The former involves building relationships with those one has grown accustomed to place outside ordinary circles. To do so this may, in time, involve changing one's neighborhood, workplace, place of worship, and work as a result of shifting alliances; or one may remain in place, opening the borders to those formerly excluded. It may involve learning a different language and sharing the lives and rituals of others. It requires that children also have access to multiple communities and individuals with whom they can be in dialogue. The internal component of "playing" with subjectivity has to do with learning to see the potential hybridity of one's cultural location, "detecting within it those chips of heterogeneity that it has been unable quite to dislodge" (Eagleton, quoted in Santner, 1990, p. 100). One's odyssey into understanding the multiple roots of one's own identity involves a growing comprehension of the processes of repression and exclusion that characterize the modes of one's presentation to others and ourselves. The consistency and coherence that identity is supposed to provide are not absent in nomadic figurations. They arise from the deepening of capacities for dialogue, improvisations, and resistance, all of which can contribute to resilience.

It is crucial that therapists working one-on-one with individuals undergoing such a journey also have a critical and dialogical understanding of dominant ideologies. They need to be able to resist singular interpretations, and to support the subjective discomfort of finding within oneself multiple histories and points of view that are still unsynthesized. The use of arts media through which emergent images of not yet formed ways of being can be improvised and rehearsed can often prove central to such transformative processes.

Non-subjects and turning toward history

What are the psychological conditions for history to awaken? How can those who have turned their backs on history turn toward it? Buffered by possessions and the habits of acquisition, it is possible to wrap oneself in a present that has no eyes or windows onto the past or future. To turn toward history, one can venture out of one's own neighborhood and family-bound sense of self to encounter others and their stories that are different from one's own. Only insofar as one enters into a relationship with what is different from one's own experience will one be able to look back at where one has been standing and see it as if for the first time.

The paradigm of the self required by the awakening to history is a self-in-relation to others and the world one is on the way toward, not in a quiet, passive manner, but as people attempting to strike out of the confines dictated by individualism, nationalism, racism, sexism, and other parochialisms. We are using the ideas of nomadic self, of border crosser, *mestiza*, of hybridity and wounded cosmopolitanism to indicate a direction for relationship to others and the world. The nomad, the *mestiza*, does not extract him or herself from history, but rather questions its normative scripts. Listening across borders, they encounter suppressed histories that complexify narratives. The practice of non-subjecthood returns us as well to a dialogical engagement with the natural world and one's own fleshly incarnation. Here what has been seen as a resource to be used appears to us in its own integrity, as well as deep vulnerability.

Beneath experiences of alienation lies a rich and complex root system. For those with a sense of existential homelessness, for those engaged in mourning the loss of simple and straightforward identity, the bearing of vulnerability left by the absence of hard-edged exclusionary definitions can work to expose the intertwining root system, which is everyone's legacy. Julia Kristeva

(1982) describes wanting her writing to exist "on the fragile border where identities do not exist or only barely so: double, fuzzy, heterogeneous, animal, metamorphosed, altered, abject" (p. 207). When we join her in this psychic place, we enjoy a vantage point from which we can see identities as they shift into greater definition. We can struggle to wonder aloud with each other about the functions for such sharper definitions, struggling in ourselves against those that may create the kind of binary oppositions from which the world suffers.

Martín-Baró's (1994) vision of *el pueblo* (the people) requires a transformation of self: "The self is open to becoming different, on a plane of equality with neither privileges or oppressive mechanisms" (p. 183). It requires "an opening toward the other, a readiness to let oneself be questioned by the other, as a separate being, to listen to his or her words, in dialogue; to confront reality in relationship to and with (but not over) him or her" (p. 183). We have been working to re-imagine subjectivity to help birth these capacities for dialogue with oneself and others, to which we now turn.

10
Dialogue

> Thus, a divine spark lives in every thing and being, but
> each spark is enclosed by an isolating shell. Only man can
> re-join it with the Origin: by holding holy converse with
> the thing and using it in a holy manner ...
>
> (Buber, 1970, pp. 5–6)

The development of dialogical capacities

To be a witness to the divine spark in each being requires a careful and sustained nurture of a dialogical stance. Moving from bystanding to compassionate engagement, facing one's own collusion with perpetration of violence and/or injustice, and healing from the wounds of oppression require the development of dialogical skills. They also entail the ethical clarity to seek out opportunities for dialogue and to work to nurture dialogical spaces (see Chapter 11).

In this chapter, we tease apart the components of our capacity for dialogue, and describe how dialogue with ourselves and others can be cultivated at different points across the life span through various practices. While dialogue is essential to liberation, the nurture of its practice is often neglected. Even though the absence and failure of dialogue are evident all around us, we too often unreflectively mis-assume that capacities for dialogue simply develop on their own. Capacities for dialogue require cultivation (Rivers, n.d.). Unfortunately, their development can easily be undermined. Dialogical practices are being systematically limited by globalization's erosion of human relations and community: the placing of multiple stresses on individuals and families, the fostering of hierarchical and objectifying models in education and the workplace, and the widespread support of racism and sexism in securing cheap labor and maintaining power (Sloan, 1996). Where hierarchical and monological patterns prevail, oppression triumphs.

In this chapter, we will travel to the work of theorists and practitioners who help us see developmentally into different aspects of dialogue's heart and complexity. Dialogical capacities that are necessary for restoring a sacred manner of relation between people are multiple: the allowing of self and other to freely arise and to be given a chance for expression; to allow the other to exist autonomously from myself; to patiently wait for relation to occur in an open horizon; to move toward difference not with denial or rejection but with vulnerability, curiosity, and a clear sense that it is in the encounter with otherness and multiplicity of perspectives that deeper and more complex meanings can emerge. Such dialogue presupposes the capacity to grant the other an interiority different from our own—one that is not diminished or dehumanized. It also requires the psychic agility to de-center and to try on the perspective and feelings of the other. It necessitates our ability to take a third-person perspective on the self, so that one can reflect on how one's actions and attitudes have affected the other and the situation of which we are a part. Obviously we are discussing in this section dialogue with others who share with us aims of reciprocity and mutuality.

As these capacities develop, the other emerges not only in how he or she is like us or can satisfy our needs, but as someone our actions affect. We can begin to see that the other's experience departs from our own, often in radical ways. In the chasm, where such departures differentiate self and other, there is a choice available to be open to the difference(s) present through attempts at dialogue and understanding. This is never only an opening toward the other's experience and reality. It signals as well a willingness to see and question the assumptions within one's own most cherished attitudes, beliefs, and commitments. To be able to deeply entertain the difference that the other poses, we must learn to at least temporarily dis-identify from our passionately held beliefs and be able to see what ideologies and assumptions they are based on. Through the grasping of the other's difference from us— be it intrapsychic other or interpersonal other—we come to see more clearly who we are.

Jung (1969) describes this relationship between inner dialogue and dialogue with others:

> The present day shows with appalling clarity how little able people are to let the other man's argument count, although this capacity is a fundamental and indispensable condition for any human community. Everyone who proposes to come to terms with himself must reckon with this basic problem. For, to the degree that he does not admit the validity of the other person, he denies the "other" within himself the right to exist—and vice versa. The capacity for inner dialogue is a touchstone for outer objectivity.
>
> (p. 187)

As such dialogue occurs there is a shift from our identifying unreflectively with our own standpoint to our being able to reflect upon the multiplicity of perspectives in a given situation.

Holding liberation as a telos of human development, requires us to study what mitigates against dialogue and what helps it flourish. It is clear that adulthood can be reached and traveled through without the development of adequate dialogical capacities. In this absence, "the other"—be it part of oneself, of one's neighbor or enemy, or an aspect of nature—can be silenced, used, abused, and, even, destroyed. Liberation depends on dialogue that allows both the other's and our own being, desires, and differences to come forth, to be listened to with attention and care. Through such dialogue, "the other" is at least in part released from objectification and projection, and becomes perceived more as the center of his or her own world, rather than wholly determined by ours (Goizueta, 1988). For this reason, liberation theology and psychology claim that "the other" must be as important to psychology as "the self."

As dialogical capacities become established in individuals and dialogical practices become part of group life, they can be used to develop a more critical awareness and, in time, an openness to imaginative processes that disrupt the practice of a restrictive "normal". The exemplars we turn to will establish signposts beyond this text for those who wish to study the cultivation of dialogue, and as well help us to see some of the threads that crisscross the development of dialogues with ourself and those we have with others.

Differentiating and coordinating the perspectives of self and other

How do children and adults learn to see that the other may have a different perspective? How do they learn to receive that other perspective, particularly when it is highly divergent from their own? How does one begin to see beyond the perspective of self and other to recognize and acknowledge the voices of the contexts of which we are a part, to take a systems perspective? How is the development of these dialogical capacities related to the capacity to play, to imagine, to reflect deeply and complexly, and to create? We will begin to approach these questions through the work of Robert Selman and Lynn Schultz (1990).

In psychotherapeutic work with children suffering from emotional difficulties, learning disabilities, and, often, the burdens of poverty and racism, Selman and Schultz, developmental and clinical psychologists, saw that individual and family therapy were often insufficient. While providing understanding support to a child's family, such therapy often fails to develop the child's capacity to have and be a friend. While the therapist's listening to the child encourages the child's self-expression, it does not directly nurture the child's ability to listen to another, to practice assuming his/her perspective, and to engage in an increasingly reciprocal and then mutual relationship. Selman and Schultz were moved by the loneliness of some of their child clients and improvised a therapy called "pair therapy" that would carefully nurture children's capacities for dialogue and connection, for collaborative relationship that fosters intimacy and autonomy. They were committed to help isolated children learn how to become a friend. It was hoped that through pair therapy, children isolated by their patterns of withdrawal or aggression would gain the capacity to create new mutual relationships.

Even though as adults we might not suffer from all the difficulties faced by these children, we will recognize ourselves and those around us in these children's struggles, particularly at challenging moments when our own and other's dialogical capacities regress to earlier stages. By being aware of the developmental steps in differentiating and coordinating the perspectives of self and other, we can more sensitively assist children to take the developmental step that is possible for them at a particular moment. The Russian developmentalist Lev Vygotsky (1962) called this next step the zone of proximal development, underscoring the futility of urging someone to engage in cognitive and affective tasks too far beyond the stretch of their present capacities.

Our development toward genuine dialogue is gradual and unassured. In part, it is dependent on our capacity to imagine the other as different from ourselves and to be able to perceive the other independently from our own needs to see him/her in certain ways. Selman and Schultz (1990) chart the young child's egocentric understanding of the other, where first the other is assumed to have similar feelings as the self. In the friendship of young children, the other is judged to be a friend by superficial appearance or sheer physical proximity. He is experienced as a flat two-dimensional self, with no psychological characteristics of his own. Interactions at such a developmental moment may well be better described as monological, where the other is not imagined as different from the self.

Selman and Schultz observed that interactive fantasy play is markedly absent in the history of children whose interpersonal understanding is at such an early level. These children do not understand that self and other can interpret the same event differently; i.e., the other is not understood to have an interiority different from the self's. They are unable to differentiate between an unintentional act of another and an intentional one. If one child accidentally knocks another down while running excitedly toward something else, the child who is injured believes that the running child intended harm. There is no capacity to differentiate the overt action from the hidden intent. At this stage, there is also little ability to differentiate physical from psychological characteristics of the person (i.e., if the person is deemed "pretty," then she is a "good" person). In short, the child is unable to differentiate and integrate the self's and other's points of view and to understand the relation between each other's thoughts, feelings, and wishes.

The capacity to differentiate and integrate the self's and others' points of view is at the core of dialogical capacity. As Selman and Schultz point out, a deficit in this ability shows both in problematic interpersonal relating and in an absence of the dialogues of pretend play. They describe how the seeds for interpersonal dialogue can be planted from the dialogues of play. In their pair therapy work with isolated children, they pair a submissive, withdrawn child with a child who is overcontrolling, sometimes downright bullying. The withdrawn child is prone to drop his own wishes (self-transforming style), rather than press the other for change, while the controlling child tenaciously hangs on to his own desires and perspectives putting pressure on the other to change (other-transforming style). Initially, each clings to his or her style, making impossible a deepening of relationship. Selman and Schultz share an image from a session with two boys where one traps the other in the up position on the seesaw. There is no movement! In pretend play these two boys initially replicate their roles on the seesaw:

> Andy initiated a fantasy in which he was the television/comic book char-acter "The Hulk," a large, powerful, fearsome mutant who is good inside, but who cannot control his feelings to let the good direct him. Paul then took a part as "Mini-Man," a being of his own creation who is smaller than anything else in the world and can hide in flowers. ... The play was a fantasy in which one boy had the power to control the thoughts and will of the other by virtue of a psychological "force field."
>
> (pp. 169–70)

With their roles personified, however, each boy is seduced into embodying both of the available roles. Paul experiments with putting up his force field, and then with "zapping" his partner, just as Andy relaxes his grip on power and enjoys the submissive position of "Mini-Man."

> Theoretically speaking we believe that this switching of roles in play is a key therapeutic process, in effect a way to *share experience*. Andy was able to relax his defenses and express the message that part of him was happy to be or even had a need to be controlled, taken care of, told what to do. He could abandon for the moment the tenderly held goals for which he generally fought so fiercely. ... And Paul, often too frightened to take the initiative in actual interactions, was able to take steps toward assuming the control that felt too risky in real life, despite its practical and emo-tional attractions. ... When it is just play, children can dress rehearse for changing roles on the stage of real-life interaction.
>
> (p. 171)

Here we see the interrelation between the dialogues of pretend play and those of social relationship. The dialogues of play seed the possibility of dia-logue in friendship. The dialogues of pretend play and those of social inter-action are creative of the self and liberatory of the self. George Herbert Mead (1934) described how the child begins to take on the voices of those around him, first those closest to him, and then those in one's neighborhood and community. We can see this increasing repertoire in pretend play. Through each empathic leap in the dialogues of play and relationship, through each re-embodiment of ourselves in play and imagination, we pass beyond our usual confines of self. Who you are becomes broadened by your transits beyond yourself, however momentary.

While children are playing, pair therapists take opportunities to facilitate the children's statement of their own perspectives, their listening to the other's perspective, and the unfolding of capacities to negotiate. At early stages of development, children do not see conflict as a potential site for negotiation. The child simply wants the other to do what he/she wants them to. In the middle of Andy and Paul's three years of pair therapy, a moment arose that amply demonstrates this. While Andy is still dominant, their power discrepancy is less extreme. Selman and Schultz (1990) describe a session where the boys wanted to play kickball, but found the gym already occupied by another boy and his therapist. While Paul concludes they simply cannot play, since others were there first, Andy shouts out "Hey, What are you doing here? You can't use this gym. We're going to play kickball here." Paul, ready to concede defeat, is embarrassed when Andy continues to assume that the others should leave because he wants them to. The therapist asks the boys to step to the side of the gym to consider what their options are and to listen to each other's ideas. This entails Andy's moving from a place of unilateral decree to problem solving in dialogue with others. For Paul, it requires not withdrawing to the point of silence. With the prompting of the therapist, Paul makes a suggestion: "We'll take half the court," and promptly moves to carry out this decision. "Here will be home plate," he announces as he sets down a base. Paul no sooner has the idea than he begins to act on it. There is no pause to consider others' reactions or even the feasibility of the idea itself.

> Therapist: "Paul, don't you think you might want to check out your idea with Andy, and with those guys there?"
> Paul is visibly annoyed. "Let's play. Come on, move it!"
> Therapist: "Oh, I see. You want to go right ahead and play. No more discussion." The therapist to help Paul deal with, rather than ignore, the real aspects of the situation, raises the realistic problem that the "outsiders" would then be playing basketball in the middle of their outfield. "I think the ball would go down there and it could hit them or get in their way."
> Paul emphatically denies this, "It will not! It won't hit them!"
> Andy, now dealing directly with Paul's idea: "We can't do this," he says. "The court's too short. I'm not playing that way."
> Therapist: "Well, then, is there something you can work out with them?"

Andy answers, "Well, we can tell them it's our time."

Paul (disdainfully): "It is not!"

Andy: "It is. They were here for a long time before, so we should have it now."

Paul challenges with irritation. "How do you know that?"

Andy: "Well, they were here when we got here, so it's our turn."

Paul counters, "You don't know how long they were here before us, dummy."

Andy turns away and ignores Paul's last insulting remark, but yells out to the others once again, "Hey you guys, it is our turn to use the gym."

Paul now blurts out in a frantic, desperate whine, "Cut that out!" At this point he moves to the side of the gym, drops down to sit on the floor, and hangs his head between his knees in a display of what seems to be both disgust and embarrassment.

Therapist in a calm voice to Andy: "It seems that Paul doesn't agree with you. Can you think of some way to work this out?"

Andy: "We could negotiate with them."

Therapist: "Paul, Andy has suggested that we try to negotiate."

Paul just waves this off with a hand gesture.

Therapist: "It seems that Paul would rather not try to deal with them directly."

Andy: "We could see if they would take turns using the court, they could have it for five minutes, then we would use it for five minutes."

Paul: "They won't go for that."

Andy: "Well, maybe we could ask them if they want to play."

Therapist: "Andy suggested asking them to play. What do you think, Paul?"

Paul: "I don't care. I just want to play."

Andy immediately carries out his idea by asking the others if they want to join in a game of kickball. As they accept, Andy and Paul excitedly call out what the sides will be.

(pp. 174–6)

In these few minutes of dialogue, we witness the fragility of human connection. Without the adult's holding open the possibility of dialogue, one person's assertion of entitlement and power, his ready assumption that his preferences, perspectives, and feelings are superior, perhaps shared, determine what will happen. The other person's perspective and feelings will be overrun and silenced. Moments like this happen each day in classrooms, on playgrounds, in families, and workplaces, between groups, and even nations. To move toward dialogue, however uncertainly, instead of exercising unilateral power, we must begin to see relationship with one another as a deep and abiding aim.

Andy is willing to move to the side, to reflect on other possibilities, to take into account Paul's hesitation and embarrassed rage because he wants a friend. The therapist as coach sets up the situation for dialogue: pulling the partners back into a reflective space, asking for ideas from both partners, suggesting working out the situation *with* each other, reflecting the feelings that have gone unnoticed, enlisting the perspectives of both boys. These facilitations of dialogue must be repeated many times for them to become part of the boys' own repertoire. Certainly many children are members of communities, families, and classrooms where the adults and older children present know how to nurture dialogue in everyday moments of life. For many, however, this nurture is absent. Children in classrooms run unilaterally and monologically by teachers and raised in homes and communities where dialogue is short-circuited by the imposition of abusive power cannot easily taste the nectar and engage in the challenge of dialogue.

Paul and Andy had the benefit of individual, family, and pair therapy, as well as attending a therapeutic school for three years. Against the backdrop of their difficult early lives, their emergence into moments of intimate sharing is all the more poignant. In the third year of their relational work with one another, we see them able to withstand the storm of each other's emotions, to venture into different roles with each other, and to begin to share around the deepest areas of their life concerns: missing their absent parents, and the fear of one boy that his mother does not miss or love him.

Andy arrives late for therapy and upset that he may miss a visit from his mother.

Andy, his voice laced with thick sniffles: "They probably won't let me go early, because they don't know about what I'm missing. They don't know I'm missing my mother,"

Paul spontaneously speaks to offer a kind of understanding, "Hey listen, Andy you miss your mother, I miss my father. The only time I get to see him is when I wake up pretty early. He comes home about midnight and I'm fast asleep."

Andy wipes his nose with his sleeve. His eyes are focused on Paul as he listens to him talk.

Paul talks on, "I hardly ever see my dad because he has to work overtime."

Andy offers in a calmer voice, "My father works almost every day. Matter of fact he works every night except Saturday, Sunday, and Friday. So I'm usually left with the babysitter. Tonight I'll be with the babysitter."

Paul says, "Yeah, Dad misses us. We miss him."

Andy's tone is low. "That's the problem—my mother doesn't miss me." Andy relates an incident from the past weekend, when he and his parents were going to go out together. As Andy tells it, he rode off on his bike telling his mother where he'd be, but his mother forgot to call him. "And when I came back my mom had gone to bed, and my dad had gone to sleep. And I was left alone." Paul says softly, "I'm sorry." After a brief pause, he adds, "By the way Andy, if you see any raffle tickets around, I've lost mine." Rather than being put off and hurt by this sudden change of subject on Paul's part, Andy immediately picks up on the new topic. "Let's go look for them in the after school room," he says.

(pp. 180–2)

Here the boys share aspects of their lives never divulged to their therapists. They deeply touch on these painful absences of presence and connection, remaining alongside of each other in tacit support. Their verbal dialogue melts into a wordless dialogue of being present with one another as they pursue a common activity.

Through the linking of one's own understanding and experience with that of another's, the meaning of conflict shifts from being a site for the satisfaction or frustration of one's own wishes to being seen as inevitable due to each person having his/her own needs, thoughts, feelings, and wishes. This sense of inevitability of conflict is balanced by the strengthening of one's capacity to take the perspective of the other, to express one's own perspective, and to work together toward common ground.

At the higher reaches of interpersonal understanding, Selman and Schultz describe a capacity for in-depth and societal perspective taking. Here the individual begins to see the impact of their membership in social groups on their perspectives. We will explore this capacity through an examination of the work of Carol Gilligan and her colleagues on the impact of gender on relationships and dialogue, and by looking at how dialogue is used in Freirean work with groups suffering from various forms of oppression.

Sustaining one's voice among others

For authentic dialogue to occur, it is necessary for one to be able to differentiate one's perspective from the other's and to allow the other a voice. However, one must also be able to maintain one's own voice amidst the fray of relationship. In turning their attention to normative development in preadolescent and adolescent American girls, primarily White and upper-middle-class girls, Brown and Gilligan (1992) found that the girls had achieved many of the relational and dialogical milestones that Selman and Schultz outlined.

As these girls grow older they become less dependent on external authorities, less egocentric or locked into their own experience or point of view, more differentiated from others in the sense of being able to distinguish their feelings and thoughts from those of other people, more autonomous in the sense of being able to rely on or to take responsibility for themselves, more appreciative of the complex interplay of voices and perspectives in any relationship, more aware of the diversity of human experience and the differences between societal and cultural groups.

Unfortunately, these capacities were not sufficient. They also found

> that this developmental progress goes hand in hand with evidence of a loss of voice, a struggle to authorize or take seriously their own experience—to listen to their own voices in conversation and respond to their feelings and thoughts—increased confusion, sometimes defensiveness, as well as evidence for the replacement of real with inauthentic or idealized relationships. If we consider responding to oneself, knowing one's feelings and thoughts, clarity, courage, openness, and free-flowing connections with others and the world as signs of psychological health, as we do, then these girls are in fact not developing, but are showing evidence of loss and struggle and signs of an impasse in their ability to act in the face of conflict.
>
> (Brown & Gilligan, 1992, p. 6)

In order to maintain the semblance of relationship, these girls were struggling with "a series of disconnections that seem at once adaptive and psychologically wounding, between psyche and body, voice and desire, thoughts and feelings, self and relationship" (Brown & Gilligan, 1992, p. 7). Too often girls were found stepping away from articulating their thoughts and feelings in conversations if these would bring them into conflict with others. What was initially conscious public disavowal of thoughts and feelings, over time became unconscious disavowal. Speaking haltingly, girls then expressed that they felt confused and unsure about what they thought and felt. Over time, many took themselves out of authentic relationship—with others and with themselves. They became unable to identify relational violations, and were thus more susceptible to abuse. Brown and Gilligan began to wonder if they were "witnessing the beginning of psychological splits and relational struggles well documented in the psychology of women" (1992, p. 106).

To encourage girls' resistance and resilience, Gilligan and her colleagues realized that it was not enough to help girls put into words for others their thoughts and feelings. For many, the fear of how their thoughts and feelings would be received had already metamorphosed into the girls' not listening to themselves. The women working with these girls tried to find ways to help the inner ear not go deaf, to revive a capacity to listen to the multiplicity within oneself. At the same time, they constructed a space to strengthen dialogue, a group where the girls could experience that others can survive their voice(s); that authentic dialogue is possible, not just false or idealized relations. Without such an experience of one's voice being received without the forfeiture of relationship, the ear cannot reawaken and the voice cannot speak—be it in "internal" dialogue or "external" dialogue.

Akin to Selman and Schultz's valuing of play, Gilligan's team moved toward supporting the girls' diary and journal writing, their dramatic and poetic writing, and their claiming their physical and metaphorical voices through Linklater's (1976) voice work. They encouraged small group communities which they called "Theater, Writing, and Outing Clubs" that were safe enough for girls to voice their dissent from one another without a loss of friendships and a sense of belonging. This alternative space provided community for resistance to the cultural messages aimed at these girls to forfeit their voices—particularly when divergent—in order to please and be in relationship.

The women working with the girls became clear that they had often participated in practices that unwittingly colluded with the girls' obscuring what they knew. It is possible to be calling for dialogue, while unconsciously limiting both the content of what can be shared and the manner in which it can be shared. For dialogue to more freely flow, there must be a deep receptivity to the disturbances it can create.

Taylor, Gilligan, and Sullivan (1995) became clearer about this as they studied African-American and Hispanic girls in inner-city Boston who were deemed "at-risk" for dropping out of high school and for teenage pregnancy. Unlike the primarily White and privileged girls and teens Gilligan's original work was based on, the girls in this study had little or no incentive to "modulate their voices to blend in or harmonize with the prevailing key" (p. 3). For girls of privilege, such restraint and accommodation carries the promise of societal rewards up ahead. For the disenfranchised, such self-restraint has no clear pay-offs. They found many of these girls of color were quite able to speak, to express their dissent. But, for the most part, they felt that few others listened and cared. Their raised voices at school were experienced as disruptive, and were discouraged by their teachers.

Not surprisingly, they found that a set of supportive relationships with women who were able to listen to them, and who were able to share their own stories, was critical to not only graduating from high school and postponing pregnancy, but to postsecondary schooling and vocational success, as well as emotional and psychological development more generally. But why was it so unusual for these girls to be deeply heard?

Listening to these girls, Taylor et al. (1995) say,

> is to invite disruption, disturbance, or dissolution of the status quo. To support the strengths, intelligence, resilience, and knowledge of girls, whose culture or class is marginalized by society is to support political, social, educational, and economic change. It may be easier to sacrifice girls than to support their development, and when girls sense this, it may be hard for them, with the best of intentions, not to give up on themselves and sacrifice their own hopes.

(pp. 202–3)

Dialogue—in the ideal sense—necessitates both the capacity to deeply receive the other and the capacity to receive oneself; to allow the other a voice *and* to allow the self a voice. Dialogue requires the experience of being listened into words. For dialogue not to appear futile, one's experience needs to be received by the other and honored and reflected in their words and deeds. In listening to the girls in their study, Taylor, Gilligan, and Sullivan learned how abandoned these girls felt by the educational system. Many shared how difficult it had been to go from elementary school where there was caring, personal supervision to secondary school where they felt unnoticed, anonymous, and unwanted. In the world of the large urban high school the girls often felt completely on their own, with little or no continuity of relationships with teachers and counselors. Too often their youthful aspirations for their futures were not met by willing adults who could help them avail themselves of opportunities, gathering the information and resources they needed to turn their dreams into reality.

While studying girls' adolescent development of voice and capacity to engage in dialogical relationships, the researchers realized that the very process of their research was itself potentially dialogical. The quality of their participation impacted whether the girls could come forward with their experiences. They backed into an essential learning: to deeply listen to another's pain and woundedness demands a response, often drawing one into participation alongside the other to address the sources of their suffering. Belenky, Bond, and Weinstock (1997) have struggled to take this step in their work with women whom they describe as "silenced" in dialogue with themselves and others.

Witness and dialogue

Belenky, Clinchy, Goldberger, and Tarule (1986), in *Women's ways of knowing: The development of self, voice, and mind*, vividly describe the interpenetration of intrapsychic and interpersonal dialogue as they articulate different ways of women's knowing. From interviews with women who had participated in both formal and informal learning environments, they described five ways of knowing and their relation to dialogue.

"Silenced knowing" in adulthood is linked to earlier family experiences of neglect and abuse. These women are passive and subdued, and engaging in subordinate roles in adulthood. Belenky et al. conclude from listening carefully to their biographies: "The ever-present fear of volcanic eruptions and catastrophic events leaves children speechless and numbed, unwilling to develop their capacities for hearing and knowing" (p. 159). These women experience themselves fatalistically, as mindless and voiceless. Their childhoods were not only lived in isolation from their family members and others outside the family, but most often were lived *without play*. The intersection of an absence of dialogue with others with an absence of play, which provides occasion for imaginal dialogue, is particularly damaging for these children as they grew to womanhood.

> In the ordinary course of development, the use of play metaphors gives way to language—a consensually validated symbol system—allowing for more precise communication of meanings between persons. Outer speech becomes increasingly internalized as it is transformed into inner speech. Impulsive behavior gives way to behavior that is guided by the actor's own symbolic representations of hopes, plans, and meanings. Without playing, conversing, listening to others, and drawing out their own voice, people fail to develop a sense that they can talk and think things through.
>
> (p. 33)

Moreover, the world of those who have been brought up through force and neglect, rather than with dialogue, becomes a place of simplistic dichotomies—good/bad, big/little, win/lose—forfeiting all subtle and complex texture.

Without the imaginal dialogues of play and substantive interpersonal dialogues, the child is constrained within a narrow band of reality (Watkins, 1986). Both play and dialogue allow the child to escape such confinement by visiting the perspectives of others, as well as fantasizing that which is beyond the given. "What is" and "who one is" become radically widened as we are able to de-center from a single perspective and set of experiences. Through the metaphorizing of play, one leaps past the given confines of "self" and "reality." The dialogues of play and the dialogues of social inter-action are both creative of a complex and multifaceted self and liberatory of the self. Through each empathic leap, through each re-embodiment of our-selves in play and fantasy, we pass beyond our usual borders and exceed the given. Working an issue through play—expressing it, addressing it from sev-eral perspectives, and taking the role of the others in play—is translated into the dialogues of though, bearing fruit in our everyday interactions. It should come as no surprise that the complexity and subtlety of a child's play, her flexibility in moving between the dramatis personae, can be seen in her capacity for reflection and her agile participation in interpersonal dialogue.

Childhoods that do not give opportunity for pretend play and its move-ment between imaginal dramatis personae, whose families discourage inter-personal dialogue, and whose schools limit the classroom experience to verbal exchanges that are unilateral and teacher initiated make it highly unlikely that children will learn the "give and take of dialogue" (Belenky et al., 1986, p. 34). For such children, and the adults into whom they grow, words have force only when uttered violently. They "tend to be action-oriented, with little insight into their own behaviors or motivations. Since they do not expect to be heard, they expect no response. The volume of their voices seems more important than the content. They lack verbal negotiating skills and do not expect conflicts to be resolved through non-violent means" (1986, p. 160). Those who do not escape silence pass the legacy of their early homes and schools on to their children:

> Mothers who have so little sense of their own minds and voices are unable to imagine such capacities in their children. Not being fully aware of the power of words for communicating meaning, they expect their children to know what is on their minds without the benefit of words. These parents do not tell their children what they mean by "good"— much less why. Nor do they ask their children to explain themselves.
>
> We observed these mothers "backhanding" their children whenever the child asked questions, even when the questions stemmed from genuine curiosity and desire for knowledge. It was as if the questions themselves were another example of the child's "talking back" and "disrespect." Such a mother finds the curious, thinking child's questions stressful, since she does not yet see herself as an authority who has anything to say or teach.
>
> (1986, pp. 163–4)

Interestingly, these women were not aware of any experience within themselves of dialogue with a self or of having an inner voice; nor did their words express a familiarity with introspection or a sense of their own consciousness. Those who were able to emerge from silence had the benefit of relationships or environments that provided a witnessing presence: schools that encouraged the cultivation of mind and an interaction with the arts, significant relationships outside the home despite the prohibition not to form them, and for a few, relationships forged "through the sheer power of their imaginations, by endowing their pets and imaginary playmates with those attributes that nourish the human potential" (1986, p. 163).

In the second way of knowing, which Belenky et al. (1986) describe as "received knowing," women experience others as the authorities, silencing their own voices to be better able to imbibe the wisdom of others. Lacking in trust for their own capacity to think through complexity, it is not surprising that they seek to eliminate ambiguity from their worlds. Parented and schooled in hierarchical models, these women are unused to testing their thoughts out loud in a supportive milieu. When provided such a milieu, they are heartened to hear others similar to themselves speak thoughts akin to their own, and to see others' positive reception of these thoughts. Through such vicarious experiences of having one's thoughts received and appreciated, received knowers can begin to assume more authorship for their thoughts and edge them into relational space.

In the third way of knowing, "subjective knowing," women listened closely to their own intuitions, distrustful of others' knowing. Fearful of others' dismissive response to their intuitive grasp of situations, many of these women grew isolated. Their knowing still had a quality of being received, though in this instance from within rather than through external authority. In the fourth way of knowing, "procedural knowing," women had experienced mentors who shared access to the modes of knowing of their discipline, giving them access to deriving their own understandings through available models.

When children grow up in families and schools where dialogue is encouraged, knowing becomes a creative act. When a mother openly presents her own experiences and thoughts, as well as facilitates the child's expression of her own, the young person becomes accustomed to the back and forth of thinking together. In what is clearly their preferred developmental telos, Belenky and her colleagues describe those who engage in this kind of "constructed knowing." In this fifth way of knowing, knowledge comes to be understood as contextual. It is recognized that there are multiple viewpoints to be had, but not all are equally adequate to revealing what one is trying to understand. These knowers are familiar with listening to their inner voices. Yet they know that even an inner voice may be wrong at times, for it too is perspectival. They are also adept at patient listening to the voices of others. Constructed knowers have a high tolerance for navigating contradiction and ambiguity.

Just as the child breaks the confines of the given through the dialogues of play, so too may the adult who can move between perspectives and systems of knowing. Liberated from unreflective obedience to external authority, to any one system of thought, and even to their own internal voices, these knowers have the dialogical tools to break the oppressive aspects not only of thought but also of social arrangements. Strikingly, their nurture, care, and engagement with their own voices, the voices of others, and ideas broaden out to their nurture and care of aspects of the world. They understand that cultural dialogue itself can be intervened in, affected, and transformed. Such work, however, cannot be undertaken when there is little or no awareness of the multiplicity of thought, little or no experience of being listened into speech, or of practice being an active participant in the give-and-take of dialogue, revealing as it does the perspectival nature of conventional truths. It requires ample experience of being listened into thought and the voicing of thought, and a strengthening of one's own witness to the thoughts of others. In Chapter 11, we will take up the creation of public homeplaces, where active witnessing of and engagement with multiple perspectives can contribute to building a community where expression, understanding, and vision can unfold.

Council and circle: Practicing self-expression and deep listening

[S]peaking and listening are a form of psychic breathing.

Gilligan, 1982, p. xvi)

Council and circle practices (Zimmerman & Coyle, 1996; Baldwin, 1998) draw on traditional ways of calling people to enter a circle with one another to mindfully listen to themselves and to one another. They provide basic, foundational ways of listening for feelings, thoughts, and visions that are living within us and others. Through a structured format that allows space for each participant to come forward as well as to listen quietly, children and adults can begin to disengage from monological practices, entering instead a dialogical rhythm. Council practice can be used in friendships, classrooms, families, organizations, and communities. Zimmerman and Coyle (1996) of the Ojai Foundation have crystallized the four basic intentions to guide group members in their presence with one another:

- Listen from the heart
- Speak from the heart
- Be of lean expression
- Speak spontaneously.

These intentions shift the energy of participants so that a space is created for deep communications to come forward. By passing a "talking piece" such as a stone, the opportunity to speak is made available to each participant. When it is a person's turn to hold the talking piece, it is his/her turn to share, or to pass and remain silent. Participants are asked not to interrupt, ask questions, debate, or discuss, but to listen as deeply as possible so that multiple and contradictory perspectives can communicate side by side.

Simple ritual beginnings and endings, such as lighting a candle at the beginning or shaking hands at the end, help to form the containing space of the circle. A brief period of silence at the beginning and between speakers allows the opportunity to listen with more concentration to self and others. To allow a form of shared leadership, often the convener of the circle rotates. An agreed upon query may initiate sharing, or the circle can more simply be used to hear into what is present in the group. Once available as a practice, a community can shift into council when deeper listening is called for around a particular topic. Even within seemingly homogenous circles, council allows a space for differences to come forward, making it possible for people to grow more comfortable in welcoming and making room for them. Its practices of empathic listening to and expression by all present are foundational to building democratic cultures of peace, grounded in mutual respect and understanding and shared leadership.

In council practices it is important that when issues are raised they are not simply left to wither on the table because no one responds to them. At one such use of council practice, we saw students of color and White allies raise issues about racism in school curriculum, while other students argued for the status quo. The council session had been planned in such a way that there was only time for each person to speak once before the meeting was ended. After everyone had spoken, they were thanked for their input and the meeting was over. A tremendous sense of frustration and rage hung in the air, and divided the group after the meeting. As a result of experiences of this kind, when we use this practice, we often combine it with a form of participatory research to be discussed further in Chapter 12. In this variation, we ask participants to carefully listen to each story as we go around the circle the first time in order to discern common threads of connection, and interesting or strong differences among the experiences being articulated. Then we go around the circle a second time to see what people have noticed. For example, in a class we asked students to speak about the kinds of unmet desires or stirrings that had led them to sign up for a graduate program in depth psychology and culture. As each person spoke, it became shockingly apparent that in 25 separate social environments, each student was feeling that important issues of their lives could never be addressed because they felt isolated and alone in their thinking. In the second round of speaking, the class began to see that these issues could not be merely personal or idiosyncratic; that there must be social, cultural, and contextual factors in American society that separate people and cut off social dialogue. During this round of the circle, the analysis of the class broke out of individualistic and personalistic reflections to begin to consider the interrelatedness of cultural and psychological factors in a more profound way. They began to question why they had taken for granted certain aspects of their social context, or assumed that what was happening to them was entirely an individual matter. The council ruptured old assumptions and left the students with a new set of questions, more ready to explore the materials being presented, the readings, and the council method. This combination of council practice with participatory research helps participants to break through into new understandings of themselves, each other, and the larger context.

From cultures of silence to liberatory dialogue: The work of Paulo Freire

The connections between coming to understand the context one is in, gaining voice to address this context, and being able to creatively engage in efforts to transform it, are thoughtfully articulated in the work of Paulo Freire. In cultures of silence, there is a suppression of voice, dialogue, and memory that obscures and normalizes the context to maintain status quo arrangements of power.

Paulo Freire grew up in Recife, in the northeast of Brazil, in a solidly middle-class family. Repercussions from the Depression in the United States suddenly threw many in Latin America into poverty, including Freire's family. Freire recalls that while sitting in his classroom as a young boy, unable to concentrate on his lessons due to hunger, he silently forged a commitment to work on issues of world hunger when he grew up. Indeed, he did address hunger, but it was hunger for a sense of voice and agency, hunger for understanding the world one has taken as inevitable and unchangeable, and hunger to seize the "vocation of humanization" in order to transform the world one lives in.

In 1961, he was asked to initiate a literacy program that would involve teaching five million people previously denied education by institutions of neocolonialism. As in the United States where it was also forbidden to teach slaves how to read and write, such deprivation was used in Northeast Brazil to disempower the masses and make claims of their inferiority easier. Such claims then rationalized abuses of laborers, as they do in the United States. Many were consigned to conditions of poverty, malnutrition, and illness in order that a few with power could profit.

Freire argued that for the disenfranchised, learning to read should involve a process of becoming able to decode not only the words and phrases that are significant to us, but also the cultural and socioeconomic circumstances that shape our day-to-day life and thinking. Once able to decode these conditions, one is more able to participate in their transformation. In Freire's model, an "animator" helps literacy group participants to begin to question how their day-to-day experience, concerns, and suffering is manufactured, rather than accepting it as a given. The animator's role is contrasted with the "tendency of oppressor consciousness to 'inanimate' everything and everyone it encounters, in its eagerness to possess," a tendency common to sadism (Freire, 1989, p. 45). The animator co-creates with the group participants a space in which dialogue becomes possible. The animator does not dominate the group or assume the status of an expert, but rather helps group members pose problems and questions that allow the possibility of insight into the given conditions of everyday life to emerge. In a supportive group that is released from the objectification that its members may have become used to, lived reality becomes freer from the grasp of fatalism. Words begin to open up the realm of "the possible," liberating the everyday. Members are asked to propose generative words or themes that they would like to learn to write and to explore more deeply: words such as water, freedom, and education.

The first step is called "conscientization," an empowering group process that allows one to actively engage with the socioeconomic structures one has previously identified with and been blind to. For instance, an animator might ask questions to open up why a generative word has been proposed: water. A mother might answer that she has been deeply depressed because her child's health is adversely affected by the pollution of the water in their community. "Why is the word 'water' so important? Why is clean water so scarce? What and who controls how much clean water you receive? How was this determined? Was it always this way? What are the other effects of not having enough clean water?" Efforts at change are directed not foremost to the individual level, the depression of a particular mother, but to the wider community and cultural change that will, in the end, affect the well-being of participants.

Studying the chosen situation and generating some common understandings through dialogue, a group can begin to decode an everyday situation, finding its relation to dominant paradigms. At this point, their understanding of how an instance of the everyday is societally constructed enables them to begin to conceive of social arrangements that are more just. This second step in Freirean practice is called "annunciation." Such annunciation of what is desired, as opposed to denunciation of what is undesirable, becomes possible within a community that has begun to feel a sense of solidarity and mutual empowerment. A fatalistic abandonment to things as they are is gradually dislodged by a sense that one in concert with others can move from being objects of an unjust system to being subjects who can act in ways that transform the given reality.

Alschuler (2006), in *The psychopolitics of liberation: Political consciousness from a Jungian perspective*, describes how understanding evolves through the Freirean method. Initially we experience the problems we suffer as inevitable and normal. In this "magical" stage, we sense that things are being caused by factors beyond our control or understanding, and thus our acting for change is futile. We experience ourselves as impotent, without the power to comprehend or to change our circumstances. Next, we begin to see the problems we suffer, but understand them to be caused by single individuals: ourselves or some evil other. There is not yet an understanding of how an unjust and oppressive social system creates oppressors. In the third stage, critical consciousness, "the individual has an integrated understanding of the sociopolitical system, enabling him/her to relate instances of oppression to the *normal* functioning of an unjust and oppressive system" (Alschuler, 1997, p. 290). One can now reject the oppressor's ideology, and seek to transform the system in collaboration with others through the development of utopian imagination and new affective relationships within groups. What was previously seen as "personal" problems are frequently now seen as community problems, and often, as class problems. Only at this point is dialogical collective action used to transform the context.

Why is this process necessary? Freire says that the dominant class attempts "by means of the power of its ideology, to make everyone believe that its ideas are the ideas of the nation" (Freire & Faundez, 1989, p. 74). He understands that the power of an ideology to rule is due to the way it is embedded in the day-to-day activities. A dominant paradigm operates by way of monologue, not dialogue. It requires voicelessness on the part of others to sustain itself.

It is through dialogue that one breaks out of the "bureaucratization" of mind, where there can be a rupture from previously established patterns. "In fact, there is no creativity without *ruptura*, without a break from the old, without conflict in which you have to make a decision" (Freire, in Horton &

Freire, 1990, p. 38). For Freire, true education is not the accumulation of information, deposited in the student by the teacher, through what he calls a "banking" method of education; nor is it the creation of new "master narratives" that articulate fixed realities. True education must encourage rupture through dialogue. Teacher and student must each be able to effect, to communicate with, and to challenge each other, rather than perpetuate domination through monological teaching methods that further disempower. Freire's methodologies create open spaces of deconstruction, dialogue, and imagination, where new alliances and practices can be proposed, tried, and analyzed.

Freire is well aware of the internalization of oppression. Through the animator's questioning, a participant begins to claim what she knows about the situation under discussion. Instead of being a passive recipient of the problematic situation, the generative words encountered in reading, writing, and speaking usher a transformation from experiencing oneself as an object to assuming the role of the questioner. It is such a subject who can then dream a different reality than what is given. The animator, though framed through a specific positionality, is careful not to indoctrinate or to proclaim by himself the problem and the solution. To do so would intensify the oppression the participant is subject to, encouraging inner and outer silence and subservience. Through problem posing, radical listening, and hosting, the animator helps to open a space for voice to occur—both internally and externally. This kind of dialogue leads to critical analysis, the awakening of desire, the hosting of multiple points of view, and the engagement in action to transform the world.

With brilliant clarity Freire (1989) connects such dialogue with love:

> Dialogue cannot exist, however, in the absence of profound love for the world and for women and men. The naming of the world, which is an act of creation and re-creation, is not possible if it is not infused with love. Love is at the same time the foundation of dialogue and dialogue itself. It is thus necessarily the task of responsible subjects and cannot exist in a relation of domination. Domination reveals the pathology of love: sadism in the dominator and masochism in the dominated. Because love is an act of courage, not of fear, love is commitment to others. No matter where the oppressed are found, the act of love is commitment to their cause—the cause of liberation. And this commitment, because it is loving, is dialogical ...
>
> (p. 77)

The dialogical process Freire practiced led to his exile during the years of dictatorship in Brazil. Freire's most famous book, *Pedagogy of the oppressed*, was translated into dozens of languages, while being banned in most Latin American countries as well as the Iberian Peninsula during the years of his exile. His method has affected critical dialogical practice on all continents. After returning to Brazil and before his death in 1997, he became Secretary of Education in São Paulo.

Utopic imagining

Once some measure of critical dialogical practice is established within a community, dreaming the world otherwise becomes possible. Out of attempts to understand our shared brokenness come visions of what is most deeply desired. Following the devastation and horror of World War II, Frances Polak (1973) observed the loss of images for the future of Europe. He began to meet with groups across Europe to help restore an imagination of desired futures. Elise Boulding, a Quaker and a sociologist, translated his work into English. Later as the United States embarked on a nuclear arms race with the Soviet Union, she noted that many American youth and adults faltered in their ability to imagine an ongoing world. Drawing on the work of Polak, Boulding (1983) created workshops called "Imagining a world without weapons." Participants utopically imagine a peaceful world in 30 years, released from the threat of nuclear weapons. Because such images alone can be disheartening due to the gap between reality and vision, she then has participants imagine backwards from their utopic image in five-year increments, asking "What would need to happen by this point, to prepare the way for the utopic reality to come into existence?" Working backwards, one asks what kinds of work in the present are needed to begin to prepare the ground for the more utopic state. In this way, utopic images are partnered with images representing more intermediary states that point toward possible paths from the real to the desired, from the present into the future. This format can be adapted to many concerns other than nuclear holocaust, allowing a small or large group to break out of the present through welcoming images that beckon for incarnation in our shared world.

A basic format can be used in public homeplaces (see Chapter 11) and other group or community gatherings: asking participants to open to utopic images imagined for the future, sharing such images, working backward slowly imagining intermediary stages, and asking oneself and one's group what would need to happen in the present for the desired images to come to fruition. Having art supplies available to enable a variety of modes of expression of the utopic images can be powerful. The format below was adapted by Watkins from Boulding's work. This basic format can be crafted into workshops of several hours or days, depending on the needs of the group. The theme that the group is focusing on can be emphasized in each of the sections.

When we use an enlarged time horizon, such as 30 years, to welcome desires that would otherwise seem impossible or impractical to incarnate, it is not unusual that for a few participants images of catastrophe may also come forward. It is best to warn members that this may happen and may require a tacking back and forth between the feared and the desired.

1. Animator: [Have participants close their eyes and relax, taking some deep breaths.] Imagine being in a favorite place at your home or in your community, a place where you feel relaxed and refreshed.
   Bring all of your senses to bear as you enjoy this place. Notice the smells and fragrances in the air.
   Notice any sounds.
   How does the air feel on your skin?
   What are the colors like?
   What time of day does it seem like?
   Just rest for a few moments in the fullness of this place.
   [This portion is to help awaken imaginal senses so that the subsequent images will be as vivid as possible. It also places participants in a peaceful place, from which they can move into utopic images.]
2. Animator: Close your eyes in this spot. When I ask you to open them up, it will be 30 years from now. Do not let your own mortality deter you. There have been many positive changes in your community, in your nation, and in the larger, global world; transformations that reflect people's deepest desires for their lives. As you begin to travel around your community—visiting schools, places of healing, of government, of spiritual life—notice in as much detail as you can how these desires have manifested. Now open up your imaginal eyes and begin to explore. [Let participants know how much time they will have for each step.]
3. Animator: Now widen your utopic imaginings to explore how things may have changed positively on national and global levels. You might open a newspaper from [state date 30 years hence], or listen to a newscast, and notice how the stories have changed. Or you may find yourself walking in a very different part of the world. If your attention begins to wander, gently bring it back to see how people's deeper desires for their world have been manifested in changes that have taken place. [If there is time, participants can draw their images and tape them to the wall.]
4. Animator: With our eyes closed I invite each of you to share one image of what you imagine your community, nation, or world to be like in your utopic imagining. Describe it in detail, so the rest of us can imagine it clearly. The person on your right will pass a talking piece when he or she has finished so you will know when to begin.
5. Animator: [When each person has had a chance to share, continue with the following instructions.] Chose one of the changes that you feel most deeply about, that you would be willing to honor through

your actions, and hold it in your heart. Ask yourself, "What would need to happen in the next 15 years for this image to have a chance of becoming reality in 30 years?" Give yourself time to reflect on this, allowing yourself to begin to fill in as many of the necessary details as possible.

6. Animator: Now imagine in as much detail as you can, what would need to happen in the next five years for this utopic reality to have the chance of beginning to take root in our world?

7. Animator: What would need to begin to happen in the next year for this utopic image to be set into motion?

8. What part of this can you imagine engaging in? What changes in your current life would such engagement require?

9. Animator: Holding your utopic image in your heart space, ask yourself who within you would most desire your engagement in making this image a reality? If this part of you were a character in a novel, what would this one be like? Where would he or she live? What would he or she be engaged in? Try to get to know this character or figure through a brief active imagination encounter.

10. Animator: Now notice where in your body you feel any resistance to working toward the utopic change you have imagined. If this feeling were a character, what would he or she be like? Again try to engage with this character through active imagination, getting to know him or her as much as you can in a few minutes.

11. Animator: See if these two characters would like time to speak with each other. Allow a dialogue to unfold, if it would like to.

12. Animator: Bring your imagining to a close, and when you are ready please open your eyes. We have time to go around the circle once for you to share the image of the desired change you were working with, how you imagine working toward this in the next year, and anything you noticed about desire and resistance within yourself toward engaging in actions to give this image life in the world.

13. Animator: In closing, I would like you to each briefly ask for anything you might personally or spiritually need to be better able to help manifest into the world around us what you deeply desire.

A group may be convened to work on imagining the future around an area of common concern or to help surface the multiplicity of desires that are present within a group, giving support to each member's calling in relation to their vision.

The Sarvodaya Movement in Sri Lanka has proposed a 500-Year Peace Plan. Understanding that the seeds of current violent conflict, poverty, and injustice have been sown over the last 500 years, it grasps the intensity and duration of efforts that are necessary to create peace. Faced with current ecological and cultural devastation, such utopic imagining is necessary to reverse fatalistic acceptance of the untenable arrangements in which our lives are unfolding (Macy, n.d.).

Appreciative inquiry

Utopic imagining allows us to become temporarily unconfined by the difficulties we face through hosting images that may be far from the realities we currently live. Appreciative inquiry starts at a different dialogical point, bringing into the group an awareness of where in the present what is desired is already rooted. In groups and communities suffering from various forms of difficulties, processes of appreciative inquiry enable the community to name valuable resources and capacities that can be used as they work together toward mutually desired aims. Undoubtedly an ancient practice with many cultural forms, processes of appreciative inquiry were analyzed and developed into a form of action research by David Cooperrider and Suresh Srivastava (1987). They realized that the kinds of questions that are asked radically affect the outcomes we experience in our groups and organizations. Rather than beginning by asking about difficulties and deficiencies, they begin to inquire into what is generative and life-giving, knowing that it is these pieces that should be built on and nurtured. Cooperrider and Srivastava encourage participants to see themselves and their organizations as expressions of beauty and spirit. By focusing in this way, one can avoid contributing to feelings of self-defeat and hopelessness, and instead contribute to feelings of enthusiasm, liveliness, creative competence, pride, and hope. Since its inception, appreciative inquiry has been used in a wide variety of settings in Africa, Europe, Asia, Australia, and the United States. Appreciative inquiry encourages participants to build on past achievements and existing strengths within a community, establishing some consensus around a shared vision of the future, and constructing strategies and partnerships to further achieve that vision.

Appreciative inquiry is designed to generate creative conversations between people. People are encouraged to share through stories, images, and metaphors what has been life enhancing in their work with one another. From this shared knowledge of their collective creative resources, they are encouraged to envision a future toward which they want to work together.

While appreciation is often a part of our approach to other people and to the organizations of which we are members, it is often not practiced in a disciplined and sustained way. Often it is mixed with tendencies to invoke problems and criticisms that undermine what appreciation might be able to occur. Appreciative inquiry gives a group a way of systematically locating and nourishing what is best in the system through taking a stance of genuine curiosity and wonder. Our focus impacts what becomes reality, as we get more of whatever we pay attention to. Appreciative process involves tracking and fanning. Tracking is a state of mind where one is constantly looking for what one wants more of. Fanning is any action that amplifies, encourages, and helps bring this further into being.

Cooperrider (1990) proposes a heliotropic hypothesis (Bushe, 1995). By this he means that a social system evolves toward the most positive images it holds of itself, just as a plant orients toward the sun. These images need not be consciously held. The more these images affirm the group, the more they hold the group to a pattern suggested by the theory/idea/image the group has of itself at its very best. Appreciative inquiry's roots in organizational theory do create limits of its usefulness within public homeplaces and community groups. While helpful in generating an inventory of individual and community resources as well as a shared vision to affect desired changes, it does not address the larger social context that deeply affects the experiences and aspirations of group members, and the relative difficulty of effecting change in inhospitable circumstances.

Without using the term "appreciative inquiry," Martín-Baró (1994) also called for such processes of appreciation in his own words: "Our task is to discover through collective memory, those elements of the past which have proved useful in the defense of the interests of exploited classes and which may be applied to the present struggle" (p. 30). Through his work with Salvadorans, he was able to distill, appreciate, and reflect back the qualities he saw as resources for transformation. "[C]urrent history confirms, day by day, their uncompromising solidarity with the suffering, their ability to deliver and to sacrifice for the collective good, their tremendous faith in the human capacity to change the world, their hope for a tomorrow that keeps being violently denied to them" (p. 31).

It would seem that in actual usage, appreciative inquiry would need to be used in groups along with some kinds of boundary setting regarding undesirable actions. Few groups can survive such things as chaotic acting out or aggressive and threatening behaviors, so of necessity, there must be limits set about acceptable behavior within the group that one is trying to nourish through appreciation. In many cases, these limits may be implicit, but eventually most groups will find some actions that they do not appreciate and need to name as unacceptable. Like all methodologies, appreciative inquiry is useful with a grain of salt and in combination with other dialogical practices.

Bohmian dialogue

The practices of council and appreciative inquiry can be powerful in bringing a group's members together to listen more deeply to one another in ways that are contained, mindful, and generative. Where conversations are developing among people with divergent life experiences, formal processes of dialogue can be helpful in understanding the differing assumptions that construct our lived worlds.

Under the sway of individualism, as individuals are preoccupied with personal survival and well-being, the thought of a community or culture can become fragmented. David Bohm, physicist and colleague of Krishnamurti, proposed a dialogue process in large groups to address this fragmentation. While one is encouraged to give voice to thoughts, one is urged not to over-identify with opinions, but rather to search out the assumptions behind them. One is not to defend or to attack another person's opinion. One sits more to the side and listens to the diversity that is present. Through such careful listening the group can begin to think together, with a foundation in the complexity of the issue at hand as voiced through the many present. The respectful and inquiring manner of presence with each other becomes more important than particular content at any given moment. The relevance of such an intentional stance for the mediation and resolution of deep intergroup and intra-group conflict is clear.

It is through the difference that is present that one can begin to hear one's own assumptions. Bohm asks that once we hear these assumptions, we try to suspend them, rather than engaging in defensive moves of overpowering the other voices and defending our assumptions as *the* one truth. This acknowledgment and suspension of assumptions is done in the service of beginning to see more deeply what it is one means, and what it is the other might mean. It is through the diversity within the group that the partialness of a single perspective can be grasped. The opportunity for this kind of large group dialogue begins to release the self from mindless identification with such partiality, and makes possible a more complex and subtle form of thinking together. De Mare, Piper, and Thompson (1991), colleagues of Bohm's, say that "Dialogue has a tremendous thought potential: it is from dialogue that ideas spring to transform the mindlessness and massification that accompany social oppression, replacing it with higher levels of cultural sensitivity, intelligence, and humanity" (p. 17).

When we defend an assumption, says Bohm (1996), we are at the same time "pushing out whatever is new. ... There is a great deal of violence in the opinions we are defending" (p. 15). The defense of an idea without deep listening into assumptions and the competing ideas of neighbors is a form of oppression, particularly if one has power to impose the idea on others without their agreement.

Through coming to see our own and others' assumptions, we arrive at a place where we can begin to think together, seeing more of the totality that comprises our situation. Social psychologist Edward Sampson (1993b) is careful to remind us that allowing others to speak is not enough, however, if they cannot be "heard in their own way, on their own terms," rather than constrained to "use the voice of those who have constructed them" (pp. 1220, 1223). Here, one is required to take a third-person point of view towards oneself, reflecting on how one's actions, attitudes, and assumptions arise from particular ideologies, and, further, how the ideologies we are identified with have affected others.

Such dialogue helps the participants to approach thought from a cultural level, rather than seeing it as reflective of an individual psyche. To adequately think, we need to invite and witness the multiplicity within the group. Without this reflective conscious practice, thinking remains partial, blinded by the assumptions it has identified with. Such dialogue in a large group requires the suspension of usual egoistic modes of operation: judging, condemning, and deeming oneself superior (or inferior). These interfere with listening deeply and awakening more fully to see where we ourselves are standing.

The art of questions: Dialogue amid divisive conflict

Oh my body, make of me always a man who questions.

(Fanon, 1967, p. 232)

When people are identified with deeply divergent perspectives on an important issue, Bohmian dialogue may prove insufficient to contain the conflict enough to transform it. Borrowing from narrative therapy approaches developed by Michael White and David Epston, Laura Chasin, Sallyanne Roth, and their colleagues at the Public Conversations Project in Massachusetts have developed an approach to dialogue in conflictual situations, which is aimed not at mediation or negotiation but at conflict transformation. The focus is on facilitating relational shifts in participants' understanding of each other's perspectives and commitments and in their ways of expressing conflict (Becker et al., 1995; Chasin et al., 1996).

Both appreciative inquiry and narrative therapy are attempts at disrupting problem-saturated modes of conversation. Narrative therapy does this through questions that encourage the externalizing of problems, disrupting the individual's identification with the problem and setting the stage for dialogue with it. Following Foucault, White grew suspicious of psychotherapy's tendency to individualize suffering, locating problems within persons rather than in the shared social surround. Working initially in the context of family therapy, and later in the areas of violence, trauma, and oppression, White and his colleagues have created "counterpractices" that shift discussions from repetitive conversations by and about persons understood to be suffused with problems, to a languaging of problems as external in order to facilitate a dialogue with them. In the dialogue one is trying to map not only the problem's influence on the individual and those around him, but the individual's and others' effects on the life of the problem. This mapping leads to different stories and knowledge that have been inaccessible given the initial framing of the problem as residing within the individual. These new stories resist the objectification of persons, and open psychic and social spaces for the re-authorship of oneself and one's family or group life.

Questions that promote an externalization of the problem lead to dialogue that can script alternate stories of the situation under exploration. In doing so, they question the dominant stories that are used to shape our lives, stories that are often inadequate, leaving out significant aspects of our experience and our resources. For instance, when a young adult is asked when she has managed not to be overwhelmed by hopeless feelings, a particular incident may emerge. A short story of courage and resistance may come forward that sharply contrasts with her and her family's previous narrative of her as passive in the face of "her" depression. Such new stories about unique outcomes fan feelings of competence and resourcefulness vis-à-vis one's life, rather than feelings of demoralization and futility.

Narrative therapy accomplishes such reframings through the introduction into dialogue of questions that initiate curiosity and encourage collaborative inquiry into new possibilities. Understanding the therapeutic power of this approach, the founders of the Public Conversation Project began a participatory action research project with women leaders on both sides of the abortion debate after the abortion clinic murders in Boston in 1994. They studied the conditions that inhibit productive dialogue among those holding polarized perspectives, as well as those factors that could facilitate it. From narrative therapy they knew that the definition of the problem can shift, where the problem is located can change, and that questions can move people from stuck positions regarding an issue to a more curious and collaborative stance (Roth & Epston, 1996). When we are identified with one side in a conflict, our awareness is often narrowly focused, impeding our listening, and forfeiting the richness available in the ambiguity and paradox of the wider, more complex situation. They invited people to leave behind agendas of winning debates or convincing others, and to engage instead in an opportunity to more deeply listen to both self and others, an opportunity secured through a highly structured use of ground rules, pre- and post-interviews, and willingness to commit to the larger intention of improving the way participants on opposite sides of an issue relate to one another. They struggled to create questions to open the following possibilities: to speak personally, rather than out of an issue; to speak to what is at the heart of the matter for each participant; and to engage with ambiguities that arise as participants listen to self and other. For instance, they might ask: Is there a way in which one value that you have is beginning to bump up against another?

Participants are helped to wonder about the questions they are posing through queries such as these crafted by Roth (1999):

> Is this a genuine question? Is it a question to which I don't know the answer?
>
> What "work" do I want this question to do? That is, what kind of conversation, meanings, and feelings do I imagine this question will invite?
>
> Is this question more likely to call forth a response familiar to the speaker, or to invite fresh thinking/feeling?

Is this question likely to call into question cultural givens that often go unnoticed or ignored, or is the question itself imbedded in these cultural givens?

Is this question likely to generate hope, imagination, creative action, engagement, and a taking-charge-of-future-directions way of being or is it likely to increase hopelessness, blunted imagination, and a sense of being acted-upon by others or circumstance?

Is this question likely to be heard as one that comes from a side-by-side stance with those with whom we work, or an expert stance?

Through exercises in crafting questions, they help participants practice using questions to elicit curiosity and not knowing, instead of rehearsed certainties that exclude others' experiences and beliefs. Rather than reenact polished debates of fixed positions, their questions elicit the personal life stories that are underneath public presentation of positions. It was action research because the members of the group were fully enlisted in the effort to understand the kind of questions and group process that would allow them to engage in conversations that were capable of transforming understandings and behaviors.

The crafting of dialogical situations for those in conflict is difficult, and involves "blocking the usual and facilitating the unusual" (Roth, 1999). Through putting into place restraining structures to avoid painful and unnecessary repetitions of conflictual impasses and inviting structures to facilitate new dialogue, participants are helped to begin to yield their grounds of certainty. Rhetorical questions are avoided, as is name-calling, stereotyping, interruption, and monological recitation of established positions. Responses to questions that invite stories, pertinent personal histories, and heartfelt narratives begin to put human faces on those experienced as "other," as well as surface unexpected commonalities among people formerly locked in polarized positions. The group facilitators of such gatherings practice multipartiality, yielding their personal position on a given issue to a higher goal of bridging the conflictual divide so that each participant can find the humanity in the other. From the early meetings with pro-life and pro-choice advocates, the Public Conversations Project has worked with stakeholders in many divisive conflicts.

Our questions hold the power to open doors or to close them, to challenge us to courageously forge new understanding or to take easy recourse to the already known. The craft of creating questions that invite the complexities of experience and new insight is a fundamental skill in the dialogical processes common to psychologies of liberation. Too often our questions to one another convey opinion, judgment, and unsolicited advice. Understandably they are frequently simple requests for information. In the dialogical work we have explored in this chapter, innovative approaches to questions create psychic and social space to understand and re-imagine situations that lead to suffering. A generative question that evokes curiosity and new understanding is a gift. Like a large tree on a warm day, it provides a cool and protected space under which we can gather and speak together in creative ways. In Part IV, we will return to the importance of the art of questioning in participatory research and cultural work.

Coda

The fabric of human life is woven with relationships. Once we thematize the importance of dialogue, the multiplicity of ongoing and created situations in which dialogical skills can be nurtured abound (Watkins, 1999). As we have seen, this requires us to slow down and turn toward each other, having a clear sense of the relationship between our current footing in dialogue with one another and the future we are trying to create (Gergen, 1998). The nurture of dialogical capacities is essential to human liberation. To encourage it, we need to attend to the organization of child-care contexts where the spontaneous creativity of play can be delighted in, to elementary schools where the leap between self and others in a small group can be rehearsed through activities like council, and to spiritual education and practice where the voices within silence can be discerned and addressed. These educational processes point us toward high schools and learning communities where previously marginalized voices can be admitted to the mosaic, changing the underlying structure of education from the conveyance of dominant paradigms to one of dialogue across differences. They turn us toward the creation of public homeplaces where those sharing similar situations can bring their thoughts into dialogue and art, seeking critical understanding and visions of the deeply desired (Chapters 11 and 12). A commitment to dialogue practices means that we must turn from doing research on others as objects to structuring situations where we can come to understandings with each other, as in practices of critical participatory action research (Chapters 13 and 14). We also need to develop processes of non-violent communication and restoration that might repair old enmities after situations of violence and atrocity. They are critical to creating conditions for peace in the communities—and ultimately the nations—that we are homed in and to protect the environments we have so profoundly damaged (Chapter 15). Part IV of our book surveys and documents methodologies that have been evolved to further these goals.

Part IV   Participatory Practices of Liberation Psychologies

Our personal and communal lives can be bounded by limits that separate us from living how we most deeply desire. Rather than accept these limits as inevitable, Alvaro Vieira Pinto defines a limit-situation not as "the impassable boundaries where possibilities end, but the real boundaries where all possibilities begin; [they are not] the frontier which separates being from nothingness, but the frontier which separates being from being more" (in Freire, 1989, p. 89). Conventional selves defined by official histories accept limit situations as the boundaries of their worlds; those who are marginalized, nomadic, mestiza, or border crossers often feel forced to push at the received limits, especially those that seem foreclosing and frozen. Through the methodologies of liberation psychologies, people may reflect together on how limits came to be, begin to see them as a construction that can be undone, and as a situation that can be rethought and transformed. Through witness, dialogue, mourning, and the re-working of subjectivity, they can re-imagine the diminishing and destructive limits they encounter in order to build a different social reality. But such engagement requires the development of new kinds of liminal spaces and institutions in which to do this work: third spaces or interstitial spaces.

There is a desperate need for the creation of liberatory communities of resistance where subjectivity, dialogue, and innovative ways of being in the world can be explored. These interstitial spaces are like protected coves or small harbors, places to engage with each other in local arenas sheltered from the dangers of open waters. Belenky, Bond, and Weinstock (1997) call these spaces "public homeplaces"; Evans and Boyte (1986) name them "free spaces" for democratic change; Bloom (1997) describes them as sanctuaries. The Zapatistas liken these spaces to the inner sanctums of a snail shell, hidden chambers where the inner workings of a community are protected (DeLeon, 2002). These are intermediate places "between private identities and large-scale institutions" (Evans and Boyte, 1986, p. 190). As we shall see in Chapter 11, public homeplaces are sites where one can become clear about

207

how oppression is internalized, while new forms of liberatory subjectivity can be improvised and rehearsed.

Most liberation psychology projects involve participatory forms of art making to help awaken new symbols for transformation, seeking to liberate underground springs capable of renewing cultural landscapes. Here one can begin to give shape to utopian dreams and re-imagined social arrangements. In Chapter 12, we will present participatory community arts processes and methodologies that have been developed in various projects throughout the world, differentiating them from other forms of art making.

In Chapters 13 and 14 on critical participatory action research, we will explore how research can become an empowering process of searching together for needed liberatory understandings. We will present the basic orientation and ethics of this approach, showing through examples its radical departures from mainstream psychological research practices.

Liberation psychologies are founded on the desire to peacefully work through hostilities with others. In Chapter 11 on communities of resistance, we begin a discussion of reconciliation between individuals, groups, and communities that have been historically alienated from one another. In the cases discussed, the members who join the effort attempt to create supportive relations of understanding. In Chapter 15, we address efforts of reconciliation between communities where there are or have been violent conflicts and abuses of power. We explore the continuum from small group initiatives of restorative justice and reconciliation outside of governmental endorsement to national efforts of reconciliation sponsored by governmental bodies. We address the difficulties that have been encountered in working through hostilities in state-sponsored truth and reconciliation commissions, and discern the conditions that are crucial to addressing historical violence.

In public homeplaces, in liberatory arts and participatory research projects, and in the creation of spaces for reconciliation and restoration, communities of resistance are embodied, renewing imagination and hope. All are part of the participatory methodologies of liberation psychology that contribute to local regeneration as well as to the creation of networks of awakened and committed activist communities emboldened to repair the world.

This work of psychologies of liberation depends on close and ongoing critiques and re-imaginings of psychology's commitments (Part I), readings of psychological symptoms in the context of culture and history (Part II), and the slow and steady building of dialogical spaces in which the ruptures we experience can be understood, embraced, and witnessed (Part III). As these practices evolve in diverse cultural locations, a cornucopia of new methodologies are springing forth that help to restore individuals and communities.

11
Communities of Resistance: Public Homeplaces and Supportive Sites of Reconciliation

> A human community, if it is to last long, must exert a sort of centripetal force, holding local soil and local memory in place. Practically speaking, human society has no work more important than this. Once we have acknowledged this principle, we can only be alarmed at the extent to which it has been ignored.
>
> (Wendell Berry, 1990, p. 155)

Communities of resistance

Amid and in opposition to violence and injustice, it is necessary for people to join together to create communities where justice and peace on a small scale are possible. Such communities resist the dehumanizing forces present in the dominant culture. From maroon communities during slavery in the Americas, to Sarvodaya Movement village gatherings in Sri Lanka, to "niches of resistance" in the Irish women's liberation movement (Moane, 2000), to the Zapatista *caracoles* in Chiapas, Mexico today, such communities of resistance attempt to birth locally more humane ways of being together. From this base it becomes possible to network with others and to slowly address the larger societal structures that create violence and injustice. This work depends on restoring psychological and community well-being.

In a dialogue between Buddhist and Christian peace activists Thich Nhat Hanh and Daniel Berrigan (1975), describes such communities as important in demonstrating to us that life is possible, that a future is possible. By "resistance" he means "opposition to being invaded, occupied, assaulted, and destroyed by the system." The purpose of resistance, here, is to seek the healing of oneself and one's community in order to be able to see clearly. Such local efforts of renewal are crucial to the regeneration of solidarity and the work of transformation.

I think that communities of resistance should be places where people can return to themselves more easily, where the conditions are such that they can heal themselves and recover their wholeness.

(p. 129)

Philosopher Kelly Oliver (2002) defines one aspect of oppression as "the colonization of psychic space that results from a lack of social support" (p. 49). It "flatten[s] psychic space and wage[s] war against the sense of oneself as an active agent" (p. 49). For psychic decolonization to occur we must restore or create several types of communities of resistance. One of the key insights of psychologies of liberation is that liberation of psychic space goes hand in hand with the creation of social spaces that support the development of critical consciousness, the strengthening of dialogue, and the nurturing of imaginative practices of representing history and conceiving the future.

In this chapter, we will take up ideas about the kinds of free and open social spaces that support such personal and community recovery (Oliver, 2002), where protective enclosures can be created in which individual and community regeneration can occur. As individuals become stronger in their abilities to articulate concerns and build solidarities, the communities of which they are a part become more able to resist oppression because they have a firm footing on which to build encounters with oppressive institutions. Sometimes communities of resistance arise through evolving traditions of ritual, performance, or social organization that are already widely shared. At other times, where the social fabric has been devastated, cultural workers, activists, and/or liberation psychologists need to devise together new and original methodologies. This chapter will explore both experiences. At the edges of these communities, we will also look at sites of reconciliation where those divided by histories of oppression can begin to create bridges between their experiences. We will offer several images through which we can imagine such intercommunities of resistance. In Chapter 15, we will address more formal public processes of reconciliation and restoration that attempt to link narratives from communities that have been grievously separated through processes of collective trauma, divisive conflict, and violence.

Community homeplaces

In her book *Yearning*, bell hooks (1990) explores how Black women have traditionally developed homeplaces in their communities that helped create safe and protected spaces for building solidarity.

Historically, African-American people believed that the construction of a homeplace, however fragile and tenuous (the slave hut, the wooden shack), had a radical political dimension. Despite the brutal reality of racial apartheid, of domination, one's homeplace was the one site where one could freely confront the issue of humanization, where one could resist.

(p. 42)

Hooks (1990) describes homeplaces in the African-American community as providing "the warmth and comfort of shelter, the feeding of our bodies, the nurturing of our soul. There we claimed dignity, integrity of being; there we learned to have faith" (pp. 41–2). Patricia Hill Collins (1990) understands such "safe space" as necessary to build a culture of resistance, in order to promote empowerment and resist objectification by dominant ideologies.

According to Belenky et al. (1997) "cultural worker" is a term first used in the United States by African-American women community workers in the Deep South, such as Jane Sapp and others at the Center for Cultural and Community Development. They were dedicated to cultivating the arts and leadership traditions of the African diaspora to strengthen "and draw out the voices of the people and uplift the whole community" (p. 10). Belenky et al. (1997) describe cultural work that turns its attention to the margins of society, listening into voice what has been silenced, attending to the articulation of the knowledge and vision within a community, and fostering the arts as a means to both represent lived reality and to dream past it.

The African American cultural workers build on ancient cultural traditions that place art-making at the center of daily life of ordinary people. They encourage people to participate in the art-making, so the mirror that is constructed will reflect their most passionate statements about themselves and the world in which they live. The art-making also loosens the mind, opens the heart, and leads to dialogue. People begin to imagine that things could be otherwise. They dream of the world as it should be. They realize they share a common vision. Together people begin reaching for goals that everyone agrees are of the utmost importance. ... The cultural workers understand that when a public dialogue is elevated by an art form, a chain of events is likely to be unleashed. The community is apt to broaden its perspective on the world as it is and as it could be, to arrive at a new place of understanding, to find new possibilities for growth and transformation. The improvised and evolving song itself becomes a metaphor for the community dialogue the cultural workers seek. The ability to compose one's own music becomes a metaphor for the ability to compose a life for one's self and one's community.

(p. 256)

Barbara Omolade describes cultural workers as dedicated to drawing out the voices of the silenced. "This form of leadership," she says, "is rooted in an ancient tradition, originating in African tribal societies organized around democratic/consensus-building processes" (in Belenky et al., 1997, p. 11). Omolade says, however, it is a tradition that has no name.

Jane Sapp describes several important functions of cultural work. The first involves processes of appreciation through which people feel affirmed in their capacities to create from their resources:

> To me cultural work is about how you nurture people, how you affirm people, how you help people to know what they know, how you help people to know that they have a culture and a knowledge base to build on, how you help people to know that they are creative and that they have a creative base upon which to build.
>
> (in Belenky et al., 1997, p. 246)

The cultural worker does not aim for homogeneity, but is able to imagine how differences can be brought to work together:

> In a roomful of dissonant voices, a cultural worker takes the sounds and finds a space for them to work in harmony. In a community of many colors, a cultural worker finds a canvas for the colors to work beautifully together. A cultural worker brings cohesiveness to a flurry of movements. She creates a shared drama from the moments of very different lives.
>
> (in Belenky et al., 1997, p. 247)

Cultural workers know the members of a community and can bring people together to work on common projects. They have an eye for locating others can who link members of the community and who are leaders or potential leaders.

> Cultural workers have the skills, imagination, and nature to put people with different shapes, sizes, ideas, and existences together in a way that makes a whole—a whole that creates an inspirational presence.

They are clear about the centrality of the arts to cultural change.

> If there was ever a time in this country for the artists it is now. We know how to take different colors and make them work together. We need to know how to take different textures and make a fabric. That is the instinct of the artist. It is what cultural work is about.
>
> (p. 247)

Sapp is clear that the work of the homeplace embodies a vision that is in conflict with the dominant model that surrounds it. For all its intense efforts at consensus building, making room for other voices, and tentativeness in drafting possible models, when homeplace members come into conversation with those outside, they must powerfully advocate for its vision.

> As a cultural worker I am able to say that I have a model of how to build an institution. I have a model of how you could build communities and schools where people feel included and respected. I have a model of how you respect and love yourself. I have a model of how you can work with and respect children and old people. I have a model of how you can make communities welcoming rather than alienating, discouraging places. I feel strongly committed to that model. I have a model and I have the courage to put my model out here beside your model. You have said to the rest of the world that only your model is important. That only your model can be valued. That only your model can bring true democracy, true happiness, true power, whatever. I dare to put my model of how to live beside your model. I dare to do that.
>
> (p. 249)

Such cultural work does indeed take daring and courage. These kinds of resistance are understood by the dominant culture to be subversive. Their very commitment to peace, as in the peace communities of Colombia, are read as a threat to those involved in sustaining hierarchies of power and the hostilities attendant to them. For this reason, Marcos, subcomandante of the Zapatista movement in Chiapas, Mexico, calls for the linking of such communities of resistance. He imagines archipelagoes of such communities arising that slowly affect the civil societies surrounding them.

Re-building public homeplaces

While there are many locations throughout the world where communities of resistance have sprung up more or less spontaneously through the efforts of local cultural workers building on community traditions, there are other areas where spontaneous forms of public homeplace have been destroyed and new practices for recreating them have begun to emerge. This is so both for those whose lives have been disrupted by various forms of oppression and collective trauma as well as for many of the relatively affluent who have been taught to see themselves within a paradigm of individualism.

Communities need to cultivate practices of deep listening, not only to mindfully conduct business and relationships among themselves, but to ready themselves for the kinds of reconciliatory dialogues with others that are possible at the edges of their communities. In addition, in areas of relative affluence, an individualistic way of looking at oneself and one's difficulties has led many economically privileged people to pursue their personal well-being as though it could be achieved privately, apart from the wider community. Strategies of disconnecting from troubling realities around one have been sought as though one could attain peace, happiness, and fulfillment if only one could win a large enough measure of remove from others' pain and difficulties. Often the groups one is part of mirror this disengagement by enacting processes of exclusion that re-inscribe social divides. Such an individualistic and elitist approach makes it increasingly difficult to understand that one's personal difficulties are often shared by others. Without this knowledge, attempts to gain insight into the causes of these difficulties are directed solely to one's own individual biography, itself seen out of historical and social context. This myopia precludes actions taken together to change the larger context that contributes to personal misery. Without dialogue across different social locations, insight into how one's lifestyle, thoughts, and actions affect others as well as oneself is extremely limited. Once individuals begin to see through or deconstruct individualism, understanding it as a relatively recent way of structuring selfhood that slowly disrupts community, the loneliness, separation, and emptiness that it breeds are thrown into question. This more critical attitude can release yearning for community as well as a sense of inadequacy regarding how to engage in community building that is inclusive of differences and empathically responsive to surrounding groups.

Oppressed communities have had their cultural traditions, values, history, and often even language diminished and assaulted. Processes of exclusion have eroded people's sense of value. Racist, dehumanizing, negative, and disempowering images of their communities and themselves have been internalized, leading to disregard of self and neighbor and a sense of fatalism in the face of daily difficulties and miseries. Experiences of violence have led to an acute fear of lack of safety and understandable distrust. For different but complementary reasons, in both cases—among the economically privileged and the dispossessed—effective community building and dialogue are sometimes in short supply.

When historians look back at the twentieth century in the future, they will perhaps find it odd that an international interest in the redevelopment of practices of public homeplace occurred in the same era as the invention of psychology and psychotherapy. Why this need, at this point in history, in multiple locations all over the world, to make elaborate planned arrangements to sit down and talk with one another, either in a psychotherapy consulting room or in a public homeplace? Unfortunately, this need indicates that families and neighborhoods everywhere have been disrupted by the globalization of corporate capital. Where previously communities were held together by evolving practices of ritual, music making, and food preparation that created the spaces for public dialogue, experiences of social disruption have contracted or destroyed these spaces and scattered the community leaders who knew how to create them. Where people are now socially isolated, public homeplaces need to be consciously rebuilt (Quiñones Rosado, 2007).

Belenky et al. (1997) undertook a study of neighborhood and cultural centers for women that attempt to address the undermining of women's voices. They were trying to discern elements of a common blueprint for birthing public homeplaces. Whereas traditional colleges often cultivate more privileged members of society to excel and to use their achievement to scramble to the top of competitive structures, Belenky et al. were interested in understanding the development and creation of centers where the marginalized could claim and develop knowledge, voice, and leadership for social change. Their chronicling included the Mothers Centers' movements in Germany and the United States, the National Congress of Neighborhood Women, and the Center for Cultural and Community Development. They call the centers they studied "public homeplaces," as they seek to extend the virtues of home—"caring for and raising up the vulnerable members of the community"—to the larger community, as they encourage citizens' commitment to the common good (Belenky, 1996, p. 408).

The intent of these public homeplaces was to nurture the thinking of the community, including as many voices as possible, to evoke the visions and dreams of community participants, and to collaboratively problem solve and create. Their method was to enter into relationship through listening. All of the projects they studied began with interviewing. Belenky et al. (1997) noticed that these founding cultural workers approached with reverence the group they worked with. They trusted that there was knowing in the group that could orient it toward creating a consensually desired future. The leaders asked questions aimed at encouraging people to "think carefully about who they were, where they wanted to go, and what abilities they could cultivate to help them reach their goals" (p. 417). These cultural workers apprenticed themselves to those they listened to. Rather than claim themselves as having all the authority and expertise, they heard authority in those whom they were listening to, seeing them as teachers. "The researchers wanted to hear what the excluded had to say; they would learn from what they had to contribute. And, most importantly, they would bring this voice into a dialogue with the larger society" (p. 417). Their initial questions gave way to others' questions, enabling the research to become fully collaborative, as members worked toward shared understanding of their situation and longed for alternatives. They were clear that it is from a common dream that action flows. For each of the groups they studied, organizations were founded to support the realization of these common dreams. "As each organization reached out to others doing similar work, national and international networks were established, enabling participants to gain the broadest global perspectives without losing touch with the concrete realities of their particular experiences and goals" (p. 426).

Listening, drawing out fledgling thoughts, mirroring and naming strengths, developing an analysis of their situation, evolving problem-solving capacities, and imagining alternative ways to live were all pursued in the context of collaborative dialogue. In such dialogue, hierarchy is laid aside, while those at the margin are encouraged to share their experiences and perspectives. There is a commitment to create a working democratic space, hearing all of the voices present in order to allow a complexity of analysis to evolve that can birth a common vision.

Engaging in such a public homeplace, individuals begin to see that what is being suffered is not only one's own. Through active invitation, the bits and pieces each person knows and remembers about a situation under discussion are placed side by side until a fuller picture emerges. In this more detailed portrait of their shared situation, members begin to understand in what ways their personal problems reflect larger sociocultural arrangements, such as the devaluing and exclusion of women and the poor. Once this process is set in motion, Belenky (1996) says people begin to move from a "paralysis that arose from thinking their difficulties were due to personal inadequacies" (p. 396). The seeming inevitability of the status quo is slowly questioned as together people move from having accepted what they did not fully understand, to critically questioning their lived realities. The numbing of desire and the fading of images for the future so common to disrupted communities are all slowly replaced by the awakening of possibility for things to be otherwise. Such a substitution of possibility for inevitability can only be nurtured through the slow building of trust and an unfolding perception of common aims.

Another ingredient to the success of these public homeplaces is their expectation that members will work toward the common good and while enjoying the support for their own development, they will offer their own support to others. Such a model creates a cascading of empowerment and support. In this work, such as in the Christian Base Communities of the Latin American liberation theology movement, the "*peña*" movement in Chile begun by Violeta Parra, the literacy circles of Paulo Freire, or the "Theater of the Oppressed" organized by Augusto Boal, groups of people form communities to create public homeplaces where new types of dialogue can be heard and new forms of social action can be imagined.

The "Loving Third"

Feminist philosopher Kelly Oliver (2002) works with Julia Kristeva's idea of a "loving third" as she examines what is necessary to create and sustain psychic space in the face of oppressive circumstances. The third she proposes to the mother-child dyad is the social.

> If this third is a loving and supportive third, then we find our own positive meaning through that transference. But if there is no social support or loving third—that is to say, if there is no positive meaning for me

within the social—then I am thrown into narcissistic crisis having to identify with my own meaninglessness of abjection.

(p. 54)

Public homeplaces attempt to provide this "loving third," where experiences can find expression. Here the processes in the dominant culture that have attributed negative meanings to one's very existence are questioned and rejected. In their stead, positive meanings are encouraged that allow members of the community to recover from toxic internalizations and feelings of inferiority, emptiness, and meaninglessness. Only in such processes of restoration can individuals engage as meaning makers who can express needs and desires, knowledge and vision. By providing a "loving third," public homeplaces encourage resistance in the double sense referred to by Gilligan, Rogers, and Tolman (1991) as a health-sustaining process and as a political strategy:

> Thus the word "resistance" takes on new resonances, picking up the notion of healthy resistance, the capacity of the psyche to resist disease processes, and also the concept of political resistance, the willingness to act on one's own knowledge when such action creates trouble.

(p. 2)

When members of a community have suffered greatly, their travail becomes traumatic when it exceeds what can be expressed or represented; when the means for such expression and representation are denied; or when such expression fails to find itself supported and witnessed. Following Kristeva, Oliver (2002) says that it is "through representation, [that] trauma is assimilated into the social order and thereby no longer traumatic, even if still painful or humiliating" (p. 57). For Kristeva, she says, revolt is

> the experience of inclusion through representation, through making language and meaning one's own in order to speak to others. ... Revolt becomes the way that "I" will express my specificity by distorting the nevertheless necessary clichés of the codes of communication and by constantly deconstructing ideas/concepts/ideological philosophies that "I" have inherited. This process of distorting and deconstructing is the way in which "I" make the clichés of culture mine; it is a way of belonging that counteracts alienation from meaning and dominant culture. These distortions can be playful or angry, subversive or conservative, conscious or unconscious, but they must be creative and born from passion. They are ways of finding or creating the living social space that can support and open psychic space.

(p. 57)

"[P]sychic revolt, analytic revolt, artistic revolt," says Kristeva (2002), "refers to a continuous questioning, of transformation, change, an endless probing of appearances" (p. 120). Through participating in activities that aid the movement from affect to representation, through processes of sublimation, psychic space begins to recover from its collapse. Representation can be through language and art. Where literacy has been denied and even access to one's own language thwarted, the recovery of language and the acquisition of reading and writing become primary objectives that are interlaced with liberatory ends.

In discussing pernicious psychic and community effects of colonization, Memmi describes how even positive characteristics of a colonized group are reinterpreted by the colonizing group as negative, stealing ground for respect from individuals and their community. Cultural workers encourage the naming and esteeming of a community's gifts, much as more recent practices of appreciative inquiry have sought to do within organizations (Cooperrider & Srivastava, 1987). The cultural worker carefully mirrors back those gifts so that they can be recognized and claimed, contributing to the strengthening of individual and group identity and self-valuing. They are also careful to mirror back what individuals and groups have come to understand, so that knowledge and the process of constructing knowledge can be claimed as resources.

For instance, in the Listening Partners program in Vermont, Mary Belenky et al. (1997) created groups with mothers of young children, women who had been "silenced" by abuse and neglect in their families of origin and who were experiencing difficulties in their own child rearing. The women's narratives of how they came to understand an aspect of their situation and to act on that understanding were carefully transcribed and read back to the women to help them claim their own capacities for critical thinking and creative problem solving. Within the protective social space of such public homeplaces, those "positive image[s] of oneself as loved and loveable" that are not available in the dominant culture are nurtured, countering the depression that arises from being seen as abject by the dominant culture (Oliver, 2002, p. 50).

Many of the public homeplaces we are describing are active in metabolizing traumatic histories at the levels of individuals, families, and the wider community. In many cultural traditions the sharing of traumatic experiences and stories of survival contributes to the building of resources for resilience in the face of ongoing and future insults. Public homeplaces seek to nurture this kind of sharing through the collection of testimony, the encouraging of artistic expression, and a thoughtful intergenerational connection that provides for community strengths to be passed down to younger members. Landau and Saul (2004) call this a transitional pathway, the "bridge that connects people, creating continuity among past, present, and future, spanning their entire ecosystemic context" (p. 280).

Communal dreaming

> The map to a new world is in the imagination, in what we see in our third
> eyes rather than in the desolation that surrounds us.
>
> (Kelley, 2002b, p. B8)

Public homeplaces allow new visions of the world to take shape (p. 8). As
Homi Bhabha (1994) points out, the Greeks recognized that "the boundary
is not that at which something stops," but "that from which something
begins its presencing" (p. 1). A recuperation of psychic space is necessary to
begin to see the boundaries of the limit situations in our lives as frontiers
instead of fetters. This shift of the perception of a situation from obstacle to
its being an opening is enabled by the kinds of critical insight and sense of
solidarity nurtured in public homeplaces.

Within an individualistic orientation, people turn toward dreams and
images to address personal woes and well-being, and sometimes to nurture
defensive strategies, while often failing to understand sufficiently how inti-
mately these are tied to cultural pathology and community well-being.
Without this critical insight we forget how to practice community dreaming
and visioning, severing ourselves from springs of communal understanding
and regeneration that are sorely needed in our lives with one another. Practices
of community dreaming, imaging, and visioning reconnect individual and
community transformation, creating public spaces to hear the imaginal's
critical and creative commentary on our lives. Whereas ideology usually tends
to conserve status quo arrangements, utopic imagination brings forward the
new, posing a discontinuity (Kearney, 1998a; Ricouer, 1986).

Communities of resistance are fueled by processes of communal dreaming. This visioning contributes to their birth as alternative social spaces and
sustains them through the bonds created by working together toward shared
dreams. Such communal dreaming can be likened to Judaism's utopic
visioning, which is knit into the progression of each week through the celebration of the Sabbath. The Sabbath is thought of as a homecoming to
one's source and to one's destination (Heschel, 1951, p. 30), a time during
which celebrants become attuned to the ways in which paradise is already
embodied, to the ways in which existence is already complete and fulfilled.
During the Sabbath, community members are called upon to create an
atmosphere of peace and joy to awaken their sense of a time when justice,
freedom, and love will flower. Living into a consciousness of the Sabbath
awakens us to the latent possibility of such homecoming in each moment.
Communities need pollination by images that bring one into creative relationship with the limit situations of one's time, that nourish the sense of the
possible, refresh spirits, and renew hope (see Chapter 12).

In contrast, Sloan (1996), following Habermas, describes the underlying
dynamic of globalization: "the state and the market project the existing or

near future reality as the ideal, filling the space in which alternative collective and personal ideals could be formulated through ongoing interaction and debate. The individual's task becomes one of adjustment, of 'fitting in' rather than individuation or self-realization through intersubjective communication" (pp. 62–3). While seemingly offered more and more choices and options, "the frames within which [we] chose are themselves manufactured to a large extent to coincide with market and state imperatives for social reproduction" of the prevailing economic and political system (p. 63). Sloan describes the process of accommodating to these large, invisible powers as entailing the *colonization* of the personality, "replac[ing] symbolic cultural sources of meaning with mere stimulation. Decolonization of this sphere would require that ideological desymbolization be countered by de-ideologizing resymbolization" (p. 131). Our own vital capacities for imagining would need to replace those of the state and the market, reawakening the springs of our visioning together.

Earth democracy: Place and resistance

In the twenty-first century, human-place relations are under siege, and public homeplaces are increasingly orienting their energies to a defense of their rights to steward the places where they reside. The morphing of colonialism into globalization has deprived countless local communities of their economic means of survival, forcing millions to leave their land and families in search of distant employment. A rapacious hunger for profit has led to violent displacement of indigenous groups from land that is rich in coveted natural resources. Many groups trying to build or to sustain homeplaces do so under threat of losing the places they call home or having already sustained this loss (Shiva, 2005).

The psychic damage attendant to the loss of place has been increasingly minimized in America as industrialization and other economic changes have led to migration from the countryside to urban centers, as well as to multiple moves in the course of one's life. Given the sway of individualism, the breaking of human-nature connections have only recently been thematized as injurious to individuals, communities, and to the environment. This injury includes animals that are trapped in ever-decreasing areas, areas often unsuitable for their well-being or even survival (Bradshaw & Watkins, 2006). Waves of migration and urban development have displaced communities, splintering neighborhoods that were once sources of information sharing, social support, and cultural arts (Fullilove, 2005).

Unfortunately, economic injustice tends to force the poor into the most degraded places or uses their neighborhoods as dumping grounds for toxic waste. When poor people are living in areas rich in natural resources, all manner of violence and terror are used to displace them. Such tactics compromise the continuity and stability of literal places, human-place relations, public homeplaces and sites of exchange between communities. De-placing a community can be compared to efforts to destroy access to its language: both are effective in mortally wounding the transmission of culture. When there are multiple understandable claims to single places—as is increasingly the case—strategies of co-existence are critically needed.

For all these reasons, liberation psychologies must also be eco-liberation psychologies that attend to the mutual interdependence of the natural and built environments, animals, and humans. Increasingly, public homeplaces are turning their attention to the environments where their lives unfold. From creating eco-hoods in cities such as Detroit and Washington, D.C., to struggling against their demise by developers as in Los Angeles, many urban communities are attempting to create a relation to place in inhospitable circumstances (Boggs, 1998). Empty lots in dangerous neighborhoods are being reclaimed through mural arts projects as in Philadelphia or community gardens in New York. Indigenous groups, once thought to be isolated, are thrown into struggles around the preservation of place as transnational corporations dispose of toxic waste in remote places such as the Amazon, seize rainforest land for pharmaceutical development, or threaten invaluable community resources such as seed diversity in Mexico and India. Coalitions of indigenous groups have had to organize to take on transnational giants such as ChevronTexaco, Grace Corporation, and Dow Chemical. For instance, in remote areas of the Ecuadorian Amazon, it is alleged that Texaco dumped nearly 20 billion gallons of toxic waste into open pits, estuaries, and rivers between 1964 and 1992, and polluted 2.5 million acres of rainforest along the route of the pipelines and wells (Epstein, 2003). Soaring rates of cancer and birth defects have resulted, as well as displacement of large sectors of the three indigenous groups in the affected region. The survival of indigenous and nonindigenous groups is now clearly seen as linked to the protection of the places on which they depend, although in some cases these places are now unsuitable for human habitation. Of course, this pollution is not limited to the territories of indigenous peoples.

Vandana Shiva, physicist, activist, and a founder of the seed-saving movement, says:

> The way out of this violent cycle is to deepen democracy—to bring decisions that directly affect people's lives as close as possible to where people are and to where they can take responsibility. If a river is flowing through some communities, those communities should have the power and the responsibility to decide how the water is used and whether it is to be polluted. The state has no business giving to Coca-Cola the groundwater of a valley in Kerala, resulting in rich farmland going totally dry. Communities need to take back sovereignty and delegate trusteeship to the state only as appropriate.
>
> (Shiva & van Gelder, 2003)

She describes a meeting of 200 villagers devoted to saving seeds, who together gathered the strength to reclaim this sovereignty.

> These 200 villagers, gathered in a high mountain village near a tributary of the Ganges, said, "We've received our medicinal plants, our seeds, our forests from nature through our ancestors; we owe it to them to conserve it for the future. We pledge we will never allow their erosion or their theft. We pledge we will never accept patenting, genetic modification, or allow our biodiversity to be polluted in any form, and we pledge that we will act as the peoples of this biodiversity"
>
> (Shiva & van Gelder, 2003)

Public homeplaces are essential to the development of this kind of earth democracy. Unfortunately, many public homeplaces are of necessity created in inhospitable environments where strangers are thrown together out of need: refugee camps, brothels, and slums on city margins throughout the world. In such places, one is pushed to extreme challenges of finding what literal and spiritual sustenance is available in the present moment, challenges that are more easily met with the human support that even improvised public homeplaces can nurture.

Grassroots postmodern regeneration

Through the inner workings of public homeplaces as well as their dialogue with supportive others, a new type of identity—a "we-in-solidarity"—can still emerge. In their book *Grassroots postmodernism*, Esteva and Prakash (1998) begin to name this "we" as a community not "constituted by abstract categories: passengers, consumers, owners, members of a club, a church, a party," because history has shown that all such abstract identities can be manipulated by elites through niche marketing, campaign advertising, and demagoguery. The we-in-solidarity formed in public homeplaces begins in the local and unique, creating an atmosphere of nurturing extended family that blurs boundaries between the public and private sphere that often exist in globalized urban spaces. In such spaces, new elements of culture making can begin to emerge, creating local islands of self-reliance and resourcefulness unnoticed by experts and elites who expect to be in charge of any projects of improvement.

Thrown together in postmodern urban neighborhoods, the marginalized may prove to be innovative and practical about regenerating new modes of solidarity that allow them to offer hospitality to others.

> Learning and fighting to stay with their "we's," the post-modern social majorities are still surviving the doom the social engineers of modernity have designed for them. ... They hold joyful celebrations even in the

middle of jungles and urban ghettos. Their "we" knows how to regenerate their traditional arts of living, enabling them to escape from the despair of suburbia.

(p. 180)

Esteva and Prakash (1998) emphasize how the kinds of grassroots postmodern spaces we are describing operate independently of constructs of the nation/ state. Their solidarity is with other local "autonomous zones" across formal national divides. Such a network forms links outside of state-sanctioned affiliations, creating grassroots sources of power that are unexpected. They say: "The only hope of a human existence, of survival and flourishing for the 'social majorities,' therefore, lies in the creation and regeneration of post-modern spaces" (p. 4). Only in these spaces can the cultural homogenization inflicted by the elite "social minorities in both North and South" (p. 16) be resisted. While such postmodern spaces are for the most part decidedly local in their concerns, Esteva and Prakash (1998) describe them as "casting seeds that are flying freely with the wind to faraway places," while "all over the immense earth, others are also striving to grow by escaping national and global 'neoliberal' projects and designs; learning from each others' struggles how to evolve their own cultural notions of 'a good life' lived in thriving local spaces" (p. 466). Esteva and Prakash argue for such communities to orient to a local scale that is "in proportion to the human capacity for knowledge and comprehension" (p. 34).

Los Caracoles/Snail shells

In 1994, on the eve of the North American Free Trade Agreement's (NAFTA) going into effect and in the wake of the Mexican government's repeal of land rights (Article 27 of the Constitution) to those living on and working the land, many indigenous communities in Chiapas joined an armed resistance that had been developing since the early 1980s to draw attention to their plight. Five hundred years of colonization, marginalization, and displacement from their ancestral lands are now being extended due to international trade agreements that are undermining their local economies, displacing them from their homes and communities in order to further exploit the vast natural resources of their region, and contributing to forced migrations due to imposed poverty and state-sanctioned violence.

In 1995 the leading spokesperson of the Zapatistas, Subcomandante Marcos, convened the first National Democratic Convention from a stadium in Aguascalientes. Six months later when the government betrayed the peace negotiations, its military and paramilitary forces destroyed this site. Marcos then called for similar cultural centers of resistance to mobilize and support community self-determination and dignity to be built throughout the world.

The Mexican government was surprised that both Mexican civil society and international organizations were quick to support the indigenous communities who had long lived under the specter of intense and pervasive discriminatory practices. The San Andreas Accords were negotiated, giving indigenous communities a realm of autonomy and rights that were long overdue. Unfortunately, the Mexican government has failed to honor these accords, gutting legislation dealing with indigenous issues.

After ten years of working with the Mexican government to enact the San Andreas Accords, many of the indigenous communities in Chiapas decided to live according to the accords anyway, forming themselves into five autonomous zones called *caracoles*, snail shells. With extremely limited material and financial resources, they took in their own hands the building of schools, health clinics, local and regional systems of representative government, and structures to develop equality for women. These autonomous zones do not overlap with Mexican government zones, but stand apart to create a realm of self-governance.

The Zapatista communities were clear that they were not seceding from Mexico, but attempting to create a form of participatory government that was not corrupt, that was consensually based, and that responded to the needs of the indigenous communities. Unsuccessful in reforming the corruption of the Mexican government, many indigenous peoples in Chiapas creatively leapt ahead to enact in their daily and communal lives what they had requested permission from the government to do. The autonomous areas call themselves rebel zones, where rebellion is affirmed. They invite everyone to create autonomous zones where they live.

Emerging from 500 years of brutal colonization, the communities have recognized the need for three kinds of dialogue. First, they have been careful to create a protected space where their own languages and aspects of their traditional culture can be practiced and strengthened. Within this protected space they are also addressing aspects of traditional culture that they desire to change, such as the unequal treatment of women. Secondly, they welcome others who can act in solidarity with them, who can learn from their communities in order to create autonomous communities elsewhere. In addition to these supportive and educational dialogues between indigenous and nonindigenous, the communities must also be in formal negotiations with the Mexican government and military at whose hands they have suffered profoundly, and with whom they hold deep differences. Sadly, these conversations could not be said to be issuing from either a reciprocal or mutual relationship (see Chapter 15 on public reconciliation work).

They use the metaphor or image of a snail shell, *el caracol*, to differentiate and to link the forms of dialogue. While there is a flexible door-like structure at the mouth of the shell where exchange can happen with civil society, the interior of the shell protects the intimate affairs of the community. They have learned from the intrusions of missionaries, anthropologists, undercover agents of the police and military, and many other "experts" that the interior life of the community must be protected so that its ongoing cultural life can be supported, its languages preserved, and its own processes of education empowered. Negotiations with the Mexican government have taken place away from the communities in formally convened processes of negotiation.

Those from civil society who visit Zapatista communities must request permission for their visit. If an invitation is extended, they are welcomed at the entrance of the community to learn about the community and its struggles. One is asked not to go beyond a clearly delimited area. The careful process of negotiating a visit to these communities attempts to insure that the invasive, nonrespectful, colonizing, and violent modes of interaction that the indigenous have had to suffer are replaced by respectful, knowledgeable, and empathic interest and conduct. Interactions between visitors and the Office of Good Government (*La Oficina de Buen Gobierno*) are thoughtful and formal, moving visitors' attention to their own potential activism in their home communities, activism hopefully inspired by the courageous and creative example of the community that hosts them.

Interstitial spaces for reconciliation

The door-like structure at the mouth of the snail shell (*caracol*) is akin to what Homi Bhabha (1994) calls an "interstitial space," "third space," an "in-between space," which "provide[s] the terrain for elaborating strategies of selfhood—singular or communal—that initiate new signs of identity, and innovative sites of collaboration, and contestation, in the act of defining the idea of society itself" (p. 1). Homi Bhabha is clear that the third space he is noticing and defining is not an "integrative subsumption or sublation. It is a thirdness that is part of an unceasing process or movement that is at once in-between and beside the usual 'polarities' of conflict. ... the third space focuses on the strategic and agential potentialities released in the art of translation" (quoted in Hoeller, 1999).

In the area of the *caracol* delegated for visitors to meet with members of the community, economically privileged, economically exploited, Europeans, Americans, and Mexican indigenous individuals and groups do not appear as binary opposites but as interlocking and overlapping contributors to a common puzzle. In this delimited place, firm lines become blurry, yielding to a yeasty hybridity. Teenage girls walk hand in hand to the school building wearing brightly colored traditional Mayan woven and embroidered clothing, while non-Mexican visitors overhear the Beatles singing out of one of the school's dormitories. The boys play spirited basketball in T-shirts emblazoned with American logos, while next to them a New Yorker teaches Brazilian *capoeira* to a group of American teenagers. Inside the dining hall a group of French dentists discuss their struggle to introduce fair trade coffee into France. This hybridity exists in the midst of continuing struggles for women's equality, dire health-care concerns, plummeting agricultural revenues, and strangulation of the communities from their region by military and paramilitary forces.

A related project in American history, Chicago's Hull House, founded in 1889, was an interstitial space that has spawned many other such public homeplaces in the United States. Middle- and upper-class women and immigrant women suffering poverty and displacement were welcomed together to develop mutual relationships and to better understand the problems facing their city. In a post-college trip to Europe, Jane Addams visited Toynbee Hall in London where affluent students and the poor lived side by side. Inspired by this transgression of usual class boundaries that serve to segregate communities, Addams returned to Chicago to help create a public homeplace where reconciliation between economic classes could develop, and where conversations and initiatives could arise out of the relationships between recent immigrants and those from families already settled for several generations.

> Addams picked one of the most stressed areas in the city of Chicago and built a place she called Hull House. The women moved in and opened the doors of their home to the immigrants living in the neighborhood. Both groups worked together studying the problems facing the community; they made and presented art that reflected on and communicated the condition of their lives. Social science action research, theater, music, and fiction writing all thrived at Hull House. A museum was built to display the immigrants' traditional crafts to honor the arts and industries the people had developed in the Old World.
>
> (Belenky, 1996, pp. 397–8)

Addams opposed a melting pot ideology and instead envisioned the cultural particularities of each immigrant culture as a contribution to the larger American society. For this reason Hull House actively supported the diverse cultural arts of each immigrant group of which it was composed. Understanding that poverty deprived people of social and educational advantages, it sought to make such advantages available in formats that would empower participants in their own critical thinking and understanding.

In reflecting on the Hull House experiment, Addams (1912) said it was important that it stand for no particular political or social propaganda.

> It must, in a sense, give the warm welcome of an inn to all such propaganda, if perchance one of them be found an angel. The only thing to be dreaded in the Settlement is that it lose its flexibility, its power of quick adaptation, its readiness to change its methods as its environment may demand. It must be open to conviction and must have a deep and abiding sense of tolerance. It must be hospitable and ready for experiment.
>
> (p. 126)

For Addams (1912) it was clear that "without the advance and improvement of the whole, no man can hope for any lasting improvement in his own moral or material individual condition" (p. 126).

In 1930 Jane Addams met Myles Horton, who was to become the co-founder of the Highlander Folk School in Tennessee, in 1932. Horton, a union organizer, developed Highlander using the model of Hull House as well as the Danish folk schools. The latter were adult education centers in Denmark that had begun to attract attention in the United States in the late 1800s and early 1900s, as some lamented the absence of adult education in the United States. What interested Horton about both the folk schools and the Hull House model was the potential for education not only to contribute to individual development and advancement, but for it to provide a foundation for citizenship, community action, and broader social and political change.

Horton learned from personal experience that the performance of expertise was antithetical to the kind of empowering education needed to support grass-roots change. He shared an anecdote of meeting with a community group one night and feeling terrible that he did not know the answers people were searching for. In retrospect, he realized that a major turning point in his work was when he realized that he did not have to know the answers in advance, but needed to ask people what *they* knew about the problems the community faced and their potential solutions. He re-imagined his role as providing a community context for members to share their knowledge and to piece together the history of the situation under scrutiny as well as a critical action response to it.

Highlander was critical to the early development of the Citizenship Schools in the South that enabled thousands to learn to read and write, gain citizenship, vote, and begin to understand and be a force within the political process. Early teachers such as Bernice Robinson on John's Island in South Carolina improvised a participatory pedagogy that sought to respectfully partner with adult students rather than to demean them through teaching down to them. Putting aside elementary school primers, Robinson used meaningful materials from her students' daily lives to help them achieve literacy, encouraging them to define the course of their learning (Levine, 2004).

> I started off with things familiar to them. They were working in the fields and I'd have them tell me stories about what they did out and in the fields and what they had in their homes. I'd write these stories out and work with them on the words. I'd say now, "This is your story. We're going to learn how to read your story."
>
> (Robinson, quoted in Levine, 2004, p. 43)

Bernice Robinson, a high school graduate who had never imagined herself a teacher, was convinced that the

> direction and substance of a program must emerge from the people and not brought to them however well intentioned. This is what is called the

"percolator effect" rather than the "drip" technique. If a program is to work the people must have the power of making decisions about what they want to do.

(Robinson, quoted in Levine, 2004, p. 39)

Highlander supported people in their own communities to come forward to be the teachers. These teachers were then brought together in residential workshops at Highlander to reflect on their work and community organizing. People met together across racial lines, which was a rare experience during this period.

Highlander began with a commitment to the establishment of labor unions and to the development of economic democracy. It became apparent that segregation undermined a unified labor movement that needed cross-racial solidarity to succeed. In 1944 a United Auto Workers workshop at Highlander was racially integrated. Economic democracy could not develop in a context of racial segregation and racism. From then on, Highlander served as an interstitial space for Blacks and Whites to nourish relationships across racial lines and to work in solidarity with one another in the midst of a highly segregated and oppressive culture. The interracial bonds of respect that were nurtured strengthened the "loving third" offered by the milieu of the Citizenship School classrooms. Teachers and community organizers created public homeplaces marked by a "radical affirmation of students' dignity," life knowledge, intellectual competence, and capacity for growth (Levine, 2004, pp. 39, 38).

Just as the paramilitary forces in Chiapas, Mexico, have attacked the indigenous communities, burning their meeting places, terrorizing and killing civilians, Highlander and its creators were also attacked. The state of Tennessee revoked its charter, and confiscated its land and buildings. The Ku Klux Klan burned the farm and books of its poet co-founder Don West. Myles Horton was jailed in 1961. The ideas, dreams, and commitments their meeting sites represented, however, could not be destroyed. Highlander reconvened in Knoxville as the Highlander Research and Education Center, later moving to New Market, Tennessee, where it is located today. Under the umbrella of Highlander, Blacks and Whites continued to find a rare meeting place during a time of enforced racial segregation. At Highlander, people such as Rosa Parks discerned their call and devised with others across racial lines their strategies of resistance to segregation and inequality.

Like the Zapatista autonomous communities, Highlander spawned multiple sites for the support of grassroots struggles and the reconciliation of communities that often live side by side largely without authentic communication. An example of such a site is the Pan Valley Institute in Fresno, part of California's Central Valley. Borrowing Highlander's model of popular education, this site places those working on immigrants' rights—refugees, immigrants, and nonimmigrants—into dialogue with one another.

> The Pan Valley Institute organizes intensive educational gatherings where people can work and reside together, away from distractions. ... At the gatherings a facilitator draws out what the participants already know about the problems they face and encourages them to respect their own experience and ideas. Participants listen to each other seriously. The role of specialists is limited and carefully defined. Instead, we encourage group problem solving. At the end of the gathering, participants make commitments for action (next steps) and prepare to carry on the work back home. Organizers follow up with phone calls, visits, and more gatherings. The goal is to create new networks of people who are different from each other, solving common problems. What comes out of these gatherings, trainings, and conversations is up to the participants.
>
> (Pan Valley Institute, n.d.)

Through such a strategy, Pan Valley Institute has built networks of immigrant women and youth from diverse ethnic communities, as well as a consortium of indigenous peoples from Mexico and California. The participants' pictures, stories, and theater pieces have been used to express and communicate their experience related to immigration and the loss of homeland and culture.

As we can see from these examples, not only have people created forms of public homeplace out of the needs of their local culture but also homeplaces from around the world have nourished each other. The Sarvodaya Movement in Sri Lanka borrowed from Quaker process (Macy, 1983), Jane Addams from Toynbee Hall in London, Myles Horton from the Danish Folk Schools, the Zapatista communities from Freire's work in Brazil, and the public homeplaces in the Deep South from African traditions of community building. This hybridization process is strengthening local community homeplaces, while yielding a resilient set of guiding principles to be adapted to local contexts. Public homeplaces can be rehearsal spaces for dealing with hostilities between groups. As we have shown in Chapters 5, 6, and 7, both bystanders to oppression and those bearing the brunt of oppression suffer the shattering and fragmentation of the whole that contains them. Both families and associates of perpetrators also suffer alienation and silencing that cuts them off from others. After violent histories, relations between individuals and groups from different communities may become stunted, and a sense of their overlapping histories may become lost. The distances that increase and are then maintained can lead to spiraling misunderstanding of others, and, thereby, of oneself. Where direct knowledge of others pales, stereotype and projection thrive, contributing to the forces that further distance communities. From Kosovo to Rwanda, one is struck by earlier periods predating recent genocides where people of different ethnic or religious groups lived together peacefully as neighbors. There is no reason not to surmise that communities desiring peace and justice must be in active, respectful communication with others. This is surely true for those communities that are neighboring, but also bespeaks the need to reach out to those at a distance.

To systematically engage in reconciliatory dialogue, one needs to ask what perspectives are being kept apart; what dialogues do not occur, supplanted instead by growing alienation, rage, and grievous and erroneous projections onto one another. Dialogues of reconciliation need to happen where people have grown estranged. This is a practice of the uncomfortable, of difficult conversations where one is pulled up short, surprised by how one is seen by others. Through them one can become aware of the damage caused by neglect and avoidance. This is work that surpasses what individual or family therapy can provide, requiring a larger setting than the consulting room, or even a public homeplace. It requires a setting that draws together those ordinarily not in contact, where dialogue has become impoverished or stereotypic. Here one might ask, "With whom do we feel resistance to being in dialogue?" The practice of reconciliation involves moving toward those who are set apart, to understand the impersonal social dynamics of this division, and to allow intentional dialogue to create resilient threads of interconnectivity that mitigate against hatred, exclusion, violence, and injustice. The skills of dialogue developed in public homeplaces can contribute to readiness to face such encounters.

Freire and Faundez emphasize that the concept of culture should not be linked to the idea of unity, but to ideas of diversity and tolerance. Such a shift invites voices to speak that have been marginalized by the dominant culture and its paradigms; and it allows the humanization of those who have been viewed as so alien that they could not share dialogue. This movement from center to margin requires a process of communication that assumes difference and seeks to articulate it. Truth is not located in a particular perspective, it "is to be found in the 'becoming' of dialogue" (Faundez, in Freire & Faundez, 1989, p. 32).

When people place themselves outside the usual boundaries of their own community and culture by joining in conversations with others whose life experiences have been appreciably different from their own, they forfeit a sense of ease and familiarity that is associated with home. Homi Bhabha describes unhomeliness as a condition of "extraterritorial and cross-cultural initiations" (p. 9). The public homeplace affirms and supports in the absence of wider social affirmation and support. At its edge, where meetings with sympathetic others can occur, these rebel sites hold open an invitation to be deprived of our certainties as we meet challenging aspects of ourselves, others, and the systems of which we are a part. Here the ordinariness of our lives breaks open to reveal the histories we carry, and their overlap with those with whom conversation has been meager or absent. Where streams of possible sociality have been diverted from one another, a commitment to host the unhomely within ourselves allows these streams to carve new meeting points, where social solidarity can be affirmed (Bhabha, 1994, p. 18). The practice of an ethics of discomfort (Foucault, 2003) creates new spaces outside the exercise of territorial powers. These extraterritorial spaces can be seen not only as sites of resistance, but as feeding waters of resilience that will be needed in the future when oppressive powers attempt to consolidate themselves by turning one community against another, championing one history over another, rallying people to violence and injustice by multiple attempts at polarization.

In this tragic period, all the small daily efforts of weathering discomfort to establish relations with others are harvested: to speak falteringly in another's language, to accept an invitation to sit at a neighboring community's table, and to venture into a dialogue where one's ignorance or wrong-headedness is evident. Learning to host the unhomely within oneself while in dialogue with people from other communities is necessary to a way of being in the world that welcomes and seeks dialogues of reconciliation.

Openness to the unhomely is even more needed as we join into dialogues hosted in public conversations that span divisive differences, as well as those in restorative justice initiatives, and in graver processes of reconciliation in postconflict environments. In Chapter 15 on practices of reconciliation and restoration, these more extreme occasions will be looked at, with an eye to the kinds of processes that are being improvised to establish the truth of what has happened, to allow victims to express their suffering to other victims, perpetrators, and bystanders, and to allow perpetrators to ask for amnesty by testifying about their acts of violence. Such processes enable those who hold widely discrepant perspectives to enter into a memorializing and witnessing public space large enough to contain a history of violence too extreme to be held and symbolized in an individual psyche or a public homeplace. Through this public encounter, some individuals may begin to listen to each other in new ways and others may be held accountable for their actions for the first time.

The kinds of public homeplaces we have been looking at in this chapter enact an ethics of deep respect, participatory partnership, joyful collaboration, and engagement in reflective action to further individual and community liberation. In most homeplaces, participatory forms of art making have evolved that foster the development of solidarity and critical self-understanding. In Belenky et al.'s (1997) discussion of public homeplaces, art making is seen as essential to the recovery of community history, to the expression of experience, to the welcoming of marginalized voices, and to the emergence of common dreams (see Chapter 12). Art forms such as murals, plays, photos, poetry, and film can become used for what Aurora Levins Morales (1998) calls medicine history, a radical history that births pride and hope as opposed to imperial or official history, which may be used to further agendas of domination. In the next chapter, we will explore such liberatory arts.

12
Liberation Arts: Amnesia, Counter-Memory, Counter-Memorial

> Encounters with the arts and activities in the domain of art can nurture the growth of persons who will reach out to one another as they seek clearings in their experience and try to be more ardently in the world. If the significance of the arts for growth and inventiveness and problem solving is recognized at last, a desperate stasis may be overcome and hopes may be raised, the hopes of felt possibility. ... Art offers life; it offers hope; it offers the prospect of discovery; it offers light.
>
> (Maxine Greene, 1995, pp. 132–3)

We are in an auditorium in Los Angeles in the spring of 2005 with 700 community activists and cultural workers. Augusto Boal (1985, 1998), now in his seventies, has come from the Center for the Theater of the Oppressed in Rio de Janeiro, Brazil, to explain and demonstrate his latest adaptation of Theater of the Oppressed named Legislative Theater. Boal has been improvising and writing about participatory community theater practices since the 1960s when he was arrested and tortured by the Brazilian military dictatorship and forced into exile, along with many others. In 1992, as part of the electoral campaign of the *Partido dos Trabalhadores* (Workers Party), he was elected to be a member (*vereador*) of the City Council of Rio. He decided to invite groups of people from local neighborhoods to come to the Council to present short theater pieces about the difficulties in their lives that new legislation from the Council could ameliorate. With this public testimony in the form of drama, the *vereadors* then devised new laws that would address the issues raised in order to improve living conditions.

In Los Angeles, the evening opened with a short introduction by Boal and then a local theater presentation by adolescents who had been working with Boal's techniques with assistance from Brent Blair, founder of the Los Angeles Center for Theater of the Oppressed. Twenty-five teenagers gave a supercharged performance about the challenges of living in marginalized neighborhoods with continual police harassment, few city services, inadequate bus service, lack of community centers, and an atmosphere of distrust between youth and business owners. Boal and a local City Council member became the legislators who could begin to imagine new social arrangements in dialogue with the performers and the audience. After the theater piece, the floor was thrown open to public discussion, a town meeting in which members of the audience gave suggestions and comments that the City Council member agreed to take back to the Council. Two hours of public conversation from multiple perspectives about the way Los Angeles neighborhoods function and how they might be imagined differently invigorated everyone present. The adolescent actors felt seen and heard, and their concerns were taken seriously. For many it was the first time they had an experience of public witness. Free workshops in the methodologies of Theater of the Oppressed were offered to all present so that the dialogue of the evening could be extended to other neighborhood organizations searching for ways to extend their cultural work. We cannot say that legislative theater changed the city dramatically; but the event, like its counterparts in Rio, was a part of ongoing efforts at slow and creative grassroots transformation that will someday yield a more livable, democratic, truthful, and peaceful environment.

Most projects that fall within the framework of liberation psychologies at some point introduce community arts into their processes. As we have suggested in earlier chapters, every individual evolves in relationship with a rich local environment of discourse, culture, and custom. Thus subjectivity is layered with expected scripts and official histories, as well as resistant interpretations; threads of dream and fantasy; sediments of forgotten music, ritual, and story; and bits and pieces of iconic memory outside of conventional narratives. Within buried layers of symbolic meaning, there are resources for lives lived otherwise, a compost where energy is building, where seeds of hope and transformation may take root. Because many of these resources will have never been spoken fully, the best access is often through image-making in the arts, a process that allows first for the creation of meaningful symbols and then for dialogues of interpretation.

Liberation arts allow us to create memorials for those aspects of our history and ourselves that have been insufficiently named or honored, and thus the discussion of liberation arts is inseparable from issues of memory and memorial. Most liberation arts projects arise in environments of amnesia where past situations of oppression and violence are silenced in school curricula and public life, yet affect the landscape in myriad ways that are covered over with hypocrisy. Thus the work of liberation arts involves an interruption of dominant narratives, an awakening to silences, an articulation of the modes of forgetfulness that prevent dialogue. Such work has been referred to as counter-memory and counter-memorial and is central to the development of liberation arts. According to Maxine Green (1995), in her book *Releasing the imagination: Essays on education, the arts, and social change*, becoming literate is "a matter of transcending the given, of entering a field of possibles" (p. 111).

> We are moved to do that, however, only when we become aware of rifts, gaps in what we think of as reality. We have to be articulate enough and able to exert ourselves to *name* what we see around us—the hunger, the passivity, the homelessness, the "silences." These may be thought of as deficiencies in need of repair. It requires imagination to be conscious of them, to find our own lived worlds lacking because of them.
>
> (p. 111)

In this chapter, we theorize some of the questions affecting liberation arts projects, especially the issue of having to begin such projects within an atmosphere of amnesia and silence about the past. We list the general qualities of liberation arts and give specific examples of methodologies that have been used.

Erasure, amnesia, and contested memory

Processes involving liberation arts are not engaged primarily for entertainment or experimentation, though they provide spaces for both. The goal of liberation arts projects is to resurrect resources to transform oppressive structures of language and society, and to de-ideologize understandings. They make space for resymbolizing and resignifying the world, enlarging possibilities for restructuring economic, social, and personal realities. Where oppression has succeeded in impeding this process, liberation arts seek to nurture it by restoring capacities for meaning-making. There are other types of community arts projects that do not fall under this rubric. We are using the word "community" to mean any group of participants who have gathered together for transformative action, as we are all potential or actual members of multiple communities.

Most liberation arts projects begin with groups of individuals who have come together to try to understand and intervene in the social and historical context within which their economic possibilities, social location, and subjectivities have been shaped. Unfortunately, such projects do not begin on neutral ground; they begin where there are ongoing struggles over memory about what should be officially understood about the past. Often the experience of violence or exclusion from resources by whole groups of people is being denied by others with more power who refuse to acknowledge what has occurred. Usually one of the first issues that comes to light in arts projects are the effects of silencing and forgetting. In nearly all spiritual traditions around the world, there is a sense that both communities and individuals have obligations to remember and honor those who came before, and if one does not pay them proper respect—if one lives in states of amnesia regarding the past—restless spirits disrupting the present will haunt lives. But whose lives and whose ancestors should be remembered and how?

An example of such a struggle over memory has developed in Selma, Alabama, over the last 40 years where competing public monuments have caused enormous community tensions. The National Voting Rights Museum was founded in Selma in 1992 to memorialize the decades of struggle for the vote by the Black community, because this story was rarely mentioned in the official histories of Alabama. Leading Democratic presidential candidates Hillary Clinton and Barack Obama, both went to Selma on March 4, 2007, to celebrate the 42nd anniversary of the 1965 Voting Rights March that galvanized the Civil Rights Movement and led to the passage of the voting rights act of 1965. This march is often referred to as "Bloody Sunday" because participants were tear-gassed, billy-clubbed, and whipped with cattle prods. In 1965 less than 1 per cent of potential Black voters in Selma were registered to vote—about 250 people; today there are more than 20,000 registered voters and Selma elected its first Black mayor in 2000 after a massive voter registration drive in a highly contested election.

The anniversary events were as much about the present as the past. In 2000, the National Voting Rights Museum was vandalized—pictures were defaced and a Ku Klux Klan robe on display was stolen. At the same time, fund-raising was begun in another part of Selma to erect a major new monument to Nathan Bedford Forrest, a cotton planter and slave trader, who had raised a battalion of rangers in Alabama during the Civil War. Forrest was a leader of the Ku Klux Klan during Reconstruction between 1865 and 1869. The monument was placed on public property in a Black neighborhood in Selma in the fall of 2000. The next year, a group of protestors led by civil rights lawyer Rose Sanders, one of the founders of the National Voting Rights Museum, attempted to pull the statue down. After a series of public protests, the City Council removed the statue to Live Oak Confederate Cemetery at the outskirts of town. The series of lawsuits that were filed cost the city of Selma $100,000. These events in Selma are a clear indication of an unfinished process of coming to terms with the past in Alabama. That these issues of the past are still troubling the present in the United States became painfully obvious in November of 2000, when thousands of Black voters in Florida were illegally disqualified from the voting roles, affecting the outcome of the U.S. national elections.

Wars of memory and memorial are happening all over the world today, often making headline news. The issue of how we honor, forget, or make use of the past—both individual and collective—is the subject of intense and expanding dialogue. The controversy in Selma, Alabama, is being paralleled in Argentina, Guatemala, Chile, El Salvador, Mexico, Rwanda, South Africa, Israel, Japan, and many other countries where there have been histories of brutal violence that one group wants to remember as a heroic gesture or even a national victory, and another wants to remember as an unfinished struggle for justice. We know that such divisions in communities can harden into more violence. This path has unfortunately been well trod, but is it inevitable? What is the alternative?

Silence, suffering, and violence

We are chronicling the link between how we memorialize collective history and how we experience personal history, how silence and suffering in one realm may reproduce silence in the other. Authoritarian structures in the family and individual mirror those in the political world. Amnesia in the political realm can reinforce silencing in personal life. The retrieval of memory and self-expression through the arts can disrupt such a system.

Freudian and Jungian psychology each began with a challenge to Enlightenment notions of human rationality and a presumed sovereignty of consciousness. Freud saw that our words and actions were not entirely of our own choosing, but were embedded in unconscious processes that are at once expressive and obscuring. We forget, bungle, and mis-speak because we are unaware of so much of what we experience and desire. He proposed that suffering be addressed through *Kulturarbeit*, literally, cultural work that involves a long process of recollection, reworking, and mourning the past. We are trapped in our histories, as long as we fail to come to terms with them. For Jung the problem was what he called "the fundamental disso-ciability" of the psyche. He imagined our experiences live in memory like islands in archipelagos not necessarily linked. He added to Freud's ideas about recollection an idea of emergence or rebirth, suggesting that depth psychology and the arts could midwife new visions of how to symbolize and live in the world and how to understand ourselves within it.

Contemporary trauma theory has ratified these insights. Chapters 5, 6, and 7 have presented some of the catastrophic effects that both individual and collective trauma have on psychological life. We have suggested that the symptoms of trauma include the fragmentation of memory, the creation of aporias or "black holes" in the narrative of the self and the world that cannot be filled. With the loss of narrative, time is distorted, and shards of the traumatic event repeat themselves again and again in psychological life as a return of the repressed. These fragments, which might be physical symptoms or tensions, nightmares, hallucinations, or recurring images of events or things, haunt survivors, who live in a state of imperfect amnesia. They may become cut off from others in their inability to speak about what has affected them so deeply. Yet they cannot let go of symptoms because they may be the only memorials to the traumatic event.

Such states of fragmented memory coupled with repression and silence often lead to violence against self or others. Brazilian novelist Paulo Lins has perfectly caught the logic of this transformation in his powerful novel (and, later, film of the same name) *City of God* (2002). He describes the lives of young people living in the poorest *favelas* or shantytowns in São Paulo, surrounded by violence, gang warfare, and police terror. He notes the contradiction of trying to say in words what the youth of the *favelas* say with bullets:

> You see, I risk speech even with bullets piercing phonemes. It is the word – that which is larger than its size—that speaks, does, and happens, here it reels, riddled with bullets. Uttered by toothless mouths in alleyway conspiracies, in deadly decisions. Sands stir on ocean floors. The absence of sunlight really does darken forests. The strawberry liquid of ice cream makes hands sticky. Words are born in thought; leaving lips they acquire soul in the ears, yet sometimes this auditory magic does not make it as far as the mouth because it is swallowed dry. Massacred in the stomach along with rice and beans, these almost-words are excreted rather than spoken. Words balk. Bullets talk.
>
> (Lins, 2005, p. 11)

Living in a society that never acknowledges the extent of the suffering and violence of the marginalized leads to what Caribbean writer Edouard Glissant (1992) calls a history that is "a highly functional fantasy of the West" (p. xxxii). For those omitted from the story such a history retraumatizes each time it is told. Glissant sees the process as pathological:

> Would it be ridiculous to consider our lived history as a steadily advancing neurosis? To see the Slave Trade as a traumatic shock, our relocation (in a new land) as a repressive phase, slavery as a period of latency, "emancipation" in 1848 as reactivation, our everyday fantasies as symptoms, and even our horror of "returning to the things of the past" as a possible manifestation of a neurotic's fear of his past?
>
> (pp. 65–6)

Liberation arts provide alternatives to silence, violence, and historical neuroses for victims of oppression, but not everyone is invested in revisioning the past.

Those whose interests are protected by official histories live in environments where education, family attachments, and normative social milieus reinforce the work of maintaining a heroic tradition that disowns identifications and relationships with what has been degraded and defeated in the past. Writing about post–World War II Germany, Peter Homans (2000) suggests official histories are backed by what Melanie Klein called "manic defense":

> The defense begins with a loss and the refusal to become introspective toward oneself in the face of that loss. Denial of the loss ensues. The denial

shifts into an interest in depersonalized aspects of the external environment, such as technology, and one develops endless energy, always directed outward for the pursuit of such tasks. Successful closure is accompanied by an enormous sense of relief, and the final state of affairs is rightly described as the "inability to mourn" to which we add "the inability to be depressed" as well.

(p. 12)

Homans suggests that after World War II, the Germans were able to make a miraculous economic recovery, but not able to mourn the losses of the war because of manic defenses.

Counter-memory and counter-memorial

Around the world, people involved in trauma work are suggesting that normal processes of education about official national history, and the heroic monuments and museums that are built to memorialize celebrated events, are actually a form of amnesia and deadening, pushing away the real suffering and violence experienced in the past and covering it over with national myths. Such structures create public grave markers that literalize history into dates or victories, but open no space for questioning their psychological and community traces in the present. Yet without such possibilities for dialogue, history hardens and freezes into repetitive patriotic narratives. There are also perpetrators and politicians who are invested in forgetting, retaining their power and impunity through the selective retelling of history. Yosef Yerushalami (1989) speaks of "agents of oblivion, the shredders of documents, the assassins of memory, the revisers of encyclopedias, the conspirators of silence" (p. 116). He writes,

[I]t is no longer merely a question of the decay of public memory ... but of the aggressive rape of whatever memory remains, the deliberate distortion of the historical record, the invention of mythological pasts in the service of the powers of darkness.

(p. 116)

Liberation arts need to create spaces for multiple narratives about national history and overcome the resistances they encounter from those who would prefer not to hear a more complex reinterpretation of the past.

The question then is how to create possibilities for imaginative memorializing and questioning of the past in communities living within a framework of amnesia. We need to develop new forms of recollection, creativity, subjectivity, activism, and freedom. If these spaces are surrounded by active and passive forgetting, part of the work will be creating ways to bring amnesia and forgetting out into the open as gaps in understanding. That is, we need innovative and startling projects that find ways to interrupt amnesia, to question viewers, and to frame memory reflexively so that past forgetting also comes into view. Because human subjectivity emerges within a multi-faceted field of meanings and interpretations, the arts provide an ideal portal for penetrating forgotten, repressed, or only partly formed intuitions about surrounding events. The arts also allow communities to retrieve traditional cultural forms that may have fallen into disuse, and thereby strengthen social networks. These are intermediate steps for both individuals and communities who are involved in processes of moving from silence toward transformative action.

The difficulty of memory within public amnesia has led to the development of work called counter-memory or counter-memorial by activists in community arts. For example, in answer to a 1995 contest by the German government for designs for a "memorial to the murdered Jews of Europe," artist Horst Hoheisel proposed blowing up one of Germany's most beloved monuments, the Brandenburg Gate (Young, 2000, p. 6). He reasoned that this would produce an empty space filled with rubble, a disorienting ruin perfectly representing the outcome of the Holocaust. A new monumental construction would only have created an artificial closure, a new "final solution" that failed to witness the horror of genocide that went unmarked for 50 years. Of course, the artist knew the government would reject his design, but his aim was to open dialogue about memory and forgetting.

What Foucault called "subjugated knowledges" can open out unexpectedly into creative forms of bodily awareness and affective experience through public arts. Hoheisel began his own Holocaust memorial project by visiting classrooms in Kassel where he lives and speaking of the Jewish community that had disappeared during the war. He asked students who knew any Jews in Kassel to raise their hands; no one did, marking the void. He then encouraged each student to research one of Kassel's deported Jews, interviewing their former neighbors, visiting their homes, and writing a short narrative about the person, disturbing the peace of a disowned history. The stories were then wrapped around cobblestones and placed in bins in the railroad station from which the Jews were deported. Now a permanent and ever-growing community art installation, the stone cairns mimic a practice of creating informal rituals of honoring the dead in Jewish cemeteries. Everyone who travels to Kassel by train is now confronted with this puzzling, troubling, unexpected memorial that breaks open new forms of conversation within normalized amnesia.

The work of architect Maya Lin on the Vietnam Veterans Memorial and the Civil Rights Memorial illustrate a similar logic. Each memorial features reflecting surfaces that name the dead while refracting the vision of the viewer toward surrounding viewers, the landscape, and the sky, hinting at the thin veil between the dead and the living. The Civil Rights Memorial has water falling over a waist-high round stone table that lists the dates of important Civil Rights events. Inscribed in the wall behind the table is a phrase from Martin Luther King Jr.'s, "I have a dream" speech that reads: "... until justice rolls down like waters and righteousness like a mighty stream." Those who enter the space usually spontaneously place their hands in the water and rotate around the table to read what is engraved, thus enacting a kind of baptism in the present that engenders a bodily rebirth of solidarity. Spectators become what Augusto Boal has called "spectactors," released from the passivity of spectatorship in order to participate actively.

Community arts of counter-memory are now being practiced all over the world, so that new generations can engage with the diverse perspectives of those who lived through earlier periods. A Los Angeles artist, Kim Abeles, encouraged teens to interview elders in their communities and create sculptures and textual fragments from the themes of the interviews. These were assembled and presented in a large gallery space to which the public was invited, integrating the experiences of diverse communities and creating a living memorial to the multicultural history of Los Angeles. Joyce Kohl worked with artists and AIDS orphans in Zimbabwe during the 1970s to create an AIDS memorial in a park after realizing that there was an official silence on the subject. Each child marked the loss of a parent with a hand-painted tile that was integrated into a wall in the park, creating a powerful reminder of the tragedy and the amnesia surrounding it.

According to art historian Betty Ann Brown (1996), such projects are gifts that generate social cohesion. "They create community by nourishing those parts of our spirit that are not entirely personal" (p. 146). Brown distinguishes between ways of working in the community that are done through "the dynamics of domination" where artists impose their own point of view, and "collaborative community-building," an empowering process through which artists help community members to reflect on and articulate their own self-definitions. Writing to advocate "the re-enchantment of art," to release it from the dictates of the competitive art world in urban America, Suzi Gablik (1991) suggests that such projects are part of a new paradigm that emphasizes our connectedness to a larger whole rather than our isolation and separateness.

New visions of how to mark historical events within the frame of counter-memory and counter-memorial stress the theme of the local, personal, embodied labor of memory in public space through participation and dialogue. Counter-memory explores the way the body in symptom, affect, and dream bears traces of the past that can be given voice when there is an empathic situation of witness. Such witness reverses the original situation of trauma where no one was available to understand and validate experiences of violence so that they were endured in lonely isolation. Tzvetan

Todorov (1998) has proposed that rather than developing literal memory, we need to begin a process he calls "exemplary" memory of past violence and genocide (p. 31). In exemplary memory, the first step is to create protected spaces where recollection can occur, but successfully contain it so that it does not take over one's life completely. Secondly, exemplary memory should be a public process of interpreting the past from multiple perspectives, learning from it, asking what work of reparation and restoration it requires, and building new myths and solidarities for the future. This has been the work of many liberation arts projects.

Liberation philosopher Enrique Dussel (1985) has proposed that liberation is not a problem of social morality based on individual action; instead it requires the creation of ethical communities that live in ways that invite dialogue and action about unjust and silencing arrangements. Dussel argues for what he calls a transmodern perspective, a kind of archeology and autoethnology of silenced narratives, utopian dreams, and indigenous cosmovisions, combined with networks of communities committed to demilitarization, sustainable economies, and the protection of human rights.

Facilitators for liberation arts projects restore the connections between power and freedom, speech and silence. For Gloria Anzaldúa, such people are *"nepantleras"*—those who know how to live in transitional and liminal spaces betwixt and between. In her last work published just before she died, Anzaldúa (2002) wrote this about the work of *nepantleras*, drawing on centuries of Mexican folk tradition of community healers or *curanderas*:

> In gatherings where people feel powerless, *la nepantlera* offers rituals to say goodbye to old ways of relating; prayers to thank life for making us face loss, anger, guilt, fear, and separation; *rezos* to acknowledge our individual wounds; and commitments to not give up on others just because they hurt us. In gatherings where we've forgotten that the aim of conflict is peace, *la nepantlera* proposes spiritual techniques (mindfulness, openness, receptivity) along with activist tactics. Where before we saw only separateness, differences, and polarities, our connectionist sense of spirit recognizes nurturance and reciprocity and encourages alliances among groups working to transform communities. In gatherings where we feel our dreams have been sucked out of us, *la nepantlera* leads us in celebrating *la communidad soñada*, reminding us that spirit connects the irreconcilable warring parts *para que todo el mundo se haga un país*, so that the whole world may become *un pueblo*.
>
> (p. 568)

Cultural workers who help organize community liberation arts projects within the framework of counter-memory and counter-monument, then, are community healers or cultural therapists who help repair the fabric of community life.

Living memory and kinesthetic imagination

There is a range of degrees to which historical memory has been interrupted in various communities. Recent economic and historical disruptions have generally replaced local forms of cultural and bodily memory, what Pierre Nora (1989) calls environments of memory (*milieux de mémoire*). Yet it is local milieux which are home to rich reserves of gestural language, traditional forms of bodily performance, and symbols and images that form a cultural inheritance that can be drawn on to transmit the past and improvise responses to the present. As a result of colonialism, slavery, globalization, migration, and state terror, many of these environments of memory have been fragmented and substituted for by what Nora calls "places of memory" (*lieux de mémoire*) that artificially create official history through museums and monuments. However, "living memory" remains resistant to such a replacement through retention of older forms that can evolve into counter-memory and counter-memorial. People carry with them even into exile strategies of what Joseph Roach (1996) calls kinesthetic imagination, an innovative repertoire of gestural and socially shared meanings that can form a reservoir for expression. According to Roach:

> The kinesthetic imagination, however, inhabits the realm of the virtual. Its truth is the truth of simulation, of fantasy or of daydreams, but its effect on human action may have material consequences of the most tangible sort and the widest scope. This faculty which flourishes in that mental space where imagination and memory converge, is a way of thinking through movements—at once remembered and reinvented— the otherwise unthinkable, just as dance is often said to be a way of expressing the unspeakable.
>
> (p. 27)

Writing about the expressiveness of African diaspora performance in the circum-Atlantic sphere, Roach notices that kinesthetic imagination allows traditional cultural forms to travel and evolve as powerful responses to dislocation.

> Displaced transmission constitutes the adaptation of historic practices to changing conditions, in which popular behaviors are resituated in new locales. Much more happens through transmission by surrogacy than the reproduction of tradition. New traditions may also be invented and others overturned. The paradox of the restoration of behavior resides in the phenomenon of repetition itself: no action or sequence of actions may be performed exactly the same way twice; they must be reinvented or recreated at each appearance. In this improvisatorial behavioral space, memory reveals itself as imagination.
>
> (p. 29)

For the purposes of liberation arts, this means that many communities of marginalized people will already have their own forms of liberation arts in place. They will already be using song, dance, theater, or art in ways that meet all of the general characteristics of liberation arts projects. In other cases, such forms will be present but only valued by older community members and certain activists. Here the problem will be reinstating processes of initiation and mentoring of liberatory processes. Often such forms are being preserved in public homeplaces, although seldom recognized by funding agencies and local governments as important social resources for building community networks. Such inherited forms of living memory need to be deeply honored and respected because they constitute a powerful framework for social solidarity. However, in other communities and in large cities where the population is extremely heterogeneous, older forms may be so shredded, or amnesia so deeply enforced that new restorative practices must be invented.

A survey of liberation arts methodologies

The following sections will present some of the innovative work in the arts that has been done within a framework of participatory communication and liberation psychologies. Sometimes the processes involve a redeployment of traditional art forms in the service of contemporary struggles; at other times, new methodologies have been invented. Many communities evolve these art forms as part of living traditions as they draw on inherited resources to further resistance to oppression; in other places new art forms are introduced by facilitators and community organizers to help groups self-organize for critical consciousness and action. Sometimes both processes are happening simultaneously. The projects have been catalogued into the following categories: music and dance, radio, altars and memorials, storytelling circles, theater, photovoice and other visual arts, video, and happenings and conceptual arts. In reality, many of these categories overlap or are developed simultaneously within social change initiatives. Fortunately, they are far from exhaustive, as new methodologies continue to be born.

Music and dance

For communities with strong and intact musical repertoires, community-building projects will naturally be linked to inherited song forms. It is impossible to overestimate the power of traditional music and dance, learned in childhood and sung in community and congregation, to carry with it iconic meanings embedded in kinesthetic imagination. When these lyrics and melodies are redeployed in the service of liberation, they have enormous capacity to inspire, unite, and empower communities. Perhaps the most archetypal situation to illustrate this is the Civil Rights Movement in the American South generally dated 1954–65, though an argument could be made that it has been going on since slavery began. There was singing everywhere that people met to organize for civil rights in the United States. Bernice Johnson Reagon (n.d.) of the SNCC (Student Non-Violent Coordinating Committee) Freedom Singers and Sweet Honey in the Rock, the great chronicler of music from the Civil Rights Movement, writes:

> If you listen to recordings of mass meetings, you will find, many times, people singing and you need to imagine that everybody in the church is singing. That is congregational singing. It is the kind of singing I grew up with in the Black Church, in school, on the playground. ... The other thing that's important to understand is that the songs that were sung the most were adopted from the repertoire that people already knew.
>
> *(Reflections on an era)*

Just as spirituals had been a source of emancipatory inspiration and a method for the transmission of coded messages during slavery, Civil Rights songs drew from already-known spirituals, gospel, rhythm and blues, calypso, doo-wop, and blues songs to transmit liberatory ideas. By changing a few words to give the songs new meanings, everyone could rapidly catch on to the message and sing along. "Woke up this morning with my mind stayed on Jesus" became "Woke up this morning with my mind stayed on freedom"; "I shall not, I shall not be moved" became "We shall not, we shall not be moved"; and "Go tell it on the mountain that Jesus Christ was born" became "Go tell it on the mountain to let my people go."

Bernice Reagon refers to Civil Rights songs as "singing newspapers." Because African and African diaspora music often has an aesthetic of spontaneous improvisation and a call and response form, events could be commented upon and transmitted as soon as they happened. She gives an example of such an event during the Freedom Rides when integrated busloads of activists rode through the South to end the practice of segregation:

> When the riders finally got to Mississippi, they were arrested and ended up in Parchman Prison. They sang non-stop, pulling songs from all these genres, and refashioning the lyrics. After the first organized loads of bus riders were jailed, people in other parts of the country began to pair up racially, get on the bus and decide they were going to sit differently. They started to do it in small groups, rather than being directed by a larger organization. When the Freedom Riders locked up in Parchman got the news that more riders were on the buses coming south, they started singing "Buses are a'comin, Oh yeah." In one situation, Bernard LaFayette recalled that the prison guards tried to stop the singing. They said to the singing freedom riders, "If you don't shut up, we'll take your mattress," the protesters would sing, "you can take my mattress, you can take my mattress, oh yeah, you can take my mattress, you can take my mattress,

I'll keep my freedom, oh yeah." That song is an arranged concert spiritual, "Chariots a'coming, oh yeah."

(*Reflections on an era*)

Though these forms of music erupted spontaneously, Civil Rights leaders also promoted them. SNCC produced songbooks of protest songs and distributed them throughout the country. Highlander Research and Education Center, discussed in Chapter 11, held music workshops where people shared songs from throughout the South. Both SNCC and CORE (Congress of Racial Equality) had groups of Freedom Singers that traveled the South singing in churches and at rallies, and holding workshops to teach the songs. In 1964 they held a *Sing for Freedom* conference in Atlanta to encourage songwriters and share ongoing work. At the same time, well-known singers such as Mahalia Jackson, Joan Baez, Pete Seeger, Guy Carawan, Bob Dylan, Odetta, Peter, Paul and Mary, Harry Belafonte, and Fannie Lou Hamer toured the country singing the music, helping to popularize it.

The shared repertoire of traditional music meant that small community groups all over the country already had the elements in place to strengthen networks for organizing civil rights actions locally. Power was generated through mass meetings, where singing, testimonies, prayers, and preaching originated and sustained the struggle. Although civil rights actions during this period were dangerous, often leading to incarceration, beatings, home burnings, job loss, or even death, the dominant feeling remembered both at the time and years later, was a palpable feeling of a complete and joyful emancipation. Reagon remembers it this way:

For many people like me, the highest point in our lives was when we gathered in those mass meetings, and when we marched ... we were bonded to each other, not because we went to school together, or were in the same social club. Not because we worked on the same job, but because we had decided that we would put everything on the line to fight racism in our community. Every participant in a local campaign had to decide to take that risk. We had to decide to leave the safety of being obedient to segregation to go to a place where we might lose everything we had. We found in this new place a fellowship that we could not have imagined before we decided to stand. And sometimes in celebration of that coming together you could hear the hymn, "What a fellowship." *"What a fellowship, what a joy divine / Leaning on the everlasting arms / What a blessedness, what a peace is mine / Leaning on the everlasting arms ..."*

(*Reflections on an era*)

Because music is deeply embedded in African-American identity, many wonderful forms of expression have already been elaborated. They have been used to express coded messages about injustice or exclusion and longings for emancipation. Music is like a second language, an ideal form for generating enthusiasm for transformation. Reagon says, "We were young and it was important to us to have songs that named what we saw in our world, and what we wanted to happen with what we saw."

A similar phenomenon of traditional forms of music being both a generator of solidarity as well as a transmitter of resistant messages has been documented in South Africa through the film *Amandla!: A Revolution in Four Part Harmony* (2003). The title of the film refers to a chant that was a call to arms throughout the struggle. One voice in a meeting would call out *"Amandla"* (power) and every one else would respond in unison *"Awethu"* (ours: power to the people). The film documents 40 years of South African anti-apartheid struggle through the song and dance that accompanied and inspired it. Gillian Slovo (2003), reviewing the film for the *Guardian Unlimited*, wrote about the powerful responses called out by music sung by the thousands in mass meetings that spoke to the pain and hopes of the movement:

> [O]ne woman recalls a song to the fallen. "He is gone, the hero of heroes," she sings before grief overwhelms her. And it used to overwhelm me at meetings, I realized, because of this very contradiction: that this lyrical beauty was so full of anguish. That melodic graveyard song, *"Senzeni* – what have we done" that was both a dirge and a call to action; or that maid's song to her employer, "Madam Please" ("before you ask me if your children are fine, ask me when I last saw mine") that was a simultaneous cry of rage.
>
> (p. 1)

The film begins with an exhumation of musician Vuyisile Mini's skull and bones to be reburied in his hometown in the Cape. An African National Congress militant and organizer, he was hanged and secretly given a pauper's grave by the apartheid government in 1964. Mini was well known in the 1960s for writing the threatening song *Beware Verwoerd! / Beware the Black Man!* What is so astounding in the film is that over 30 years later, when one person in a room begins to reminisce about the effects of that song, everyone in the room can sing all the words in four-part harmony as if they had rehearsed it yesterday.

During the 1980s, African National Congress fighters came back from Zimbabwe bringing with them a hybrid of a traditional dance forms called *toyi-toyi*. The dance spread rapidly so that thousands of people would demonstrate against apartheid in cities doing the high-stepping *toyi-toyi* and singing. One of the former police commanders in the film (*Amandla!*, 2003) said,

> I can tell you that most of the riot police and soldiers who had to contain those illegal marches were shit-scared of the chanting Blacks confronting

them. Here was an unarmed mob instilling fear just by their toyi-toyi …
I have guns, I have tanks, I have riot gear, but when they sang it made me
afraid.

When the anti-apartheid movement was in its early stages, many young
people had lost interest in traditional forms of Zulu, Xhosa, and Sutu music
and were listening to rock and roll and disco from abroad. In the heat of
the anti-apartheid struggle, local artists and activists fused international
and traditional music with political messages into hybrid forms that were
sung at churches, mining hostels, bars, and shebeens. As in the Civil Rights
Movement in the United States, people composed songs and also changed
words in already-popular songs so that new meanings emerged. The ANC
Youth Leagues understood the role of culture in social change and promoted
protest songs. Through underground tapes, pirate radio stations, all too
common funeral singing, and mass demonstrations, the new songs and
dances of the anti-apartheid movement were quickly spread. Eventually the
music became synonymous with the struggle. The film *Amandla!* ends
movingly with thousands singing and dancing in a stadium in 1994 where
the newly elected Nelson Mandela joins the *toyi-toyi* to the music of the
ANC Choir.

Music is a powerful and flexible form for resignifying experience in community. Where inherited song traditions are still strong, messages can pass
rapidly from person to person as words change and symbols are created for
new situations.

Radio

Community-owned and controlled radio has been one of the most widespread avenues for the arts to contribute to liberation processes. Often
initially housed in churches, union halls, or community centers, radio
requires only a small initial investment and is an ideal medium to reach
populations that are isolated, marginalized, or illiterate. In many countries,
a whole village may gather to hear programs at the single radio receiver that
is locally available. Radio offers a voice for local practices, traditions, and
cultural forms to be widely shared, and through call-in programs offers
possibility for dialogue that have a very wide reach.

One of the earliest community radio stations in Latin America was created
in Bolivia where a network of miners' stations was established in 1949. At its
peak in the 1970s it linked together 26 independent local stations.
Developed to challenge the monopoly of state-run media, the stations contributed to the resistance to oppressive government and labor practices. This
process has continued up to the present, when Radio Wayna Tambo, playing indigenous hip-hop and hardcore, helped inspire a grassroots youth
movement that contributed to the election of Evo Morales, Bolivia's first
indigenous president in 2005.

According to Alfonso Gumucio Dagron (2001):

> The smallest and most precarious community radio station already makes a difference for a community. The presence of a community radio station, even if it is not highly participatory, has an immediate effect on the population. Small stations usually start airing music for most of the day, thus making an impact on cultural identity and community pride. The next step, closely associated with music programming, is carrying announcements and dedications that contribute to the strengthening of the local social networks. When the station grows in experience and skill, local production of health or education related programs starts. These contribute to share information on important issues that affect the community.
>
> (p. 13)

Dagron (2001) has documented the existence of community radio stations that have multiplied by the hundreds all over the world: Radio Enriquillo in the Dominican Republic, Radio La Voz de la Montana in Mexico, Radio Animus in Bolivia, Radio Qawinakel in Guatemala, Radio Xai-Xai in Mozambique, Radio Tubajon in the Philippines, Radio Sagarmatha in Nepal, Katura Community Radio in Namibia, Kagadi-Kibaale Community Radio in Uganda, Chikaya Community Radio Station in Namibia and so on (p. 13).

In general, community radio plays music and promotes cultural forms that have been silenced or forbidden in mainstream cultural institutions, carrying messages about counter-memory. For example, when Maurice Bishop came to power in a coup in Grenada in 1979, one of the ways people knew that he had been successful was that reggae began to be played on the government radio station. In the Caribbean, this music was loaded with meanings connected to popular resistance to injustice. People danced in the streets when they heard it. When the United States invaded Grenada five years later, one of the first things they did was bomb Radio Free Grenada. When that failed to cut off programming, they sent a team of Navy Seals to cut the feed lines to the antenna to disable the transmitters. Then they set up an alternative radio station, Spice Island Radio, bringing in their own 50-kilowatt transmitter. Now that radio and Internet have begun to merge with many radio stations developing their own Internet sites where their local programs are available internationally, the sky is the limit on what kinds of networks and culture sharing will be built in the future as more people have access.

Altars and memorials

The spontaneous building of community and personal altars and memorials is a long-standing practice both in West African and African diasporic religions in the Americas. Altar creation is also common in Latin American folk arts that have dispersed throughout the United States due to vast migrations from south of the Rio Grande. After a car crash or a shooting, for example, people will spontaneously construct memorials with candles, flowers, and found objects. Particularly in connection with the Day of the Dead on November first of each year, local community centers invite participants to construct altars as memorials to silenced histories, forgotten ancestors, and particularly influential family members. Where this occurs in urban centers such as San Francisco, one may see side by side stories and photographs memorializing the Mexican revolution, the Holocaust, the African diaspora, Japanese internment camps, slavery, indigenous people's histories, labor history, and women's issues, reflecting for the community the diversity of points of view and recollection that need to be integrated. In Day of the Dead processions, participants may carry photographs or iconic objects to place at a common altar at the procession's end. During procession and viewing, diverse neighborhoods have opportunities for dialogue and building alliances or solidarities across local differences in a common commitment to creating networked communities. Even where Day of the Dead memorials are devoted only to Mexican American history, very diverse points of view are expressed that break open fantasies of homogeneity.

This practice is beginning to spread to new locations. For example, in 1999 in Texas, at an international nursing conference focused on ending violence against women, folklorist Mary Margaret Navar helped participants construct a communal altar on the feast day of the Virgin of Guadalupe, December 12. Men and women from around the world highlighted the impact of violence against women in the lives of health-care providers. Together they created a common memorial for multiple experiences of violence that they then used as an orientation point for discussion. Other gatherings devoted to community building are now using this process.

Many neighborhoods in the United States and in Latin America have created murals as a form of altar and memorial as well. In Chicano Park in San Diego, for example, 30-foot high murals were painted under a bridge in the 1970s by various community groups over time illustrating inherited traditions, pre-Columbian arts, historical events, past heroes, and particular struggles such as the Farmworkers Movement in California, indigenous cosmovisions, and hopes for the future. A yearly celebration in April brings the community together. The site has been recognized internationally as an important artistic vision. In Los Angeles, in the 1970s and 1980s, Judy Baca organized a coalition of community groups and graffiti artists to paint *The Great Wall of Los Angeles*, a series of murals that extend for a half a mile along a drainage canal, documenting an alternative history of California that acknowledges the presence of Native Americans, Asian-Americans, African-Americans, Latinos, Chicanos, gays and lesbians, and working-class people. The murals were done in conjunction with symposia and exhibitions organized by local community organizations that invited the public to discuss the history and visions being documented. Later she helped create *The World Wall: A Vision of the Future Without Fear*, a series of ten30-foot portable murals that travel the world in exhibitions paired with similar works from artists in host countries. In San Francisco, many teams of community artists created mural installations in the Mission District on Balmy Alley. Thousands visit these every year on November first, when they are used as the starting point for the Day of the Dead procession. Some of the murals reflect the history of Latin America, particularly the period of the dictatorships, as well as hopes for a more peaceful and fulfilling future. (See cover art of this book.) They provide a permanent memorial for the lives of thousands of people whose experiences of oppression and exile have not yet been understood or integrated into mainstream American histories.

Storytelling circles

Often inherited forms of music and stories about past histories exist below the surface in a community, kept alive in pockets of family and clan, but unknown by others nearby. The most basic form of restoration is a storytelling circle in which people come together to share stories and songs and the social contexts that gave rise to them. Sometimes these offerings are recorded for sharing in radio, video, or in theater projects; at other times they are exchanged and brought to new locations. In indigenous communities where languages are being lost, the goal of such activities is the creation of an archive that can be the basis of a curriculum, as in the PBS project Circle of Stories. The Circle of Stories Web site (n.d.) explains that

> [i]n the basket of Native stories, we find legends and history, maps and poems, the teachings of spirit mentors, instructions for ceremony and ritual, observations of worlds, and storehouses of ethno-ecological knowledge. Stories often live in many dimensions, with meanings that reach from the everyday to the divine. Stories imbue places with the power to teach, heal, and reflect. Stories are possessed with such power that they have survived for generations despite attempts at repression or assimilation.

The archive creates a permanent collection of stories as well as contact information for Native American storytellers who can be addressed through the site. Curriculum instructions help others to become storytellers in their own locations.

Linda Tuhiwai Smith (1999), in her book *Decolonizing methodologies*, has suggested that indigenous peoples need to organize their own projects of remembering and reclaiming the past in story circles. Particularly important to the Maori are approaches that celebrate survival rather than accentuating demise and assimilation:

> The approach is reflected sometimes in story form, sometimes in popular music, and sometimes as an event in which artists and storytellers come

together to celebrate collectively a sense of life and diversity and connectedness. Events and accounts which focus on the positive are
important not just because they speak to our survival, but because they
celebrate our resistances at an ordinary human level and they affirm our
identities as indigenous women and men.

(p. 145)

Smith presents Maori projects that give testimonies about the past, relink
families, represent their own realities, name their own environments, envision future dreams, and reframe discussions about their culture.

Leading African-American educators have formed the Jamestown Project
(2006) at Yale University to help revitalize community democracy in the
United States. They promote local story circles and town meetings in an
attempt to revitalize inclusion in civic democracy:

Storytelling is universal. As a technique it transcends race, class, generations and other differences allowing people to communicate on common ground through a common story. It has its roots in ancient African
societies, and for centuries, people have used stories to entertain and
educate as well as to instill values and inspire people to action. Yet today,
with the advent of complicated electronic media communications
methods, storytelling has become a lost art. And with it, communities
have also lost an important mode of communications that allowed
them to share their knowledge and stories, and to form deep and abiding bonds with one another. The Jamestown Project's storytelling
initiative reclaims this art, and holds story sharing up as a path forward
to reclaim those community bonds and to form a foundation for social
change.

(*Make democracy real*)

In 2006, the Jamestown Project joined forces with Alternate Roots, a
collective of actors, poets, dancers, and musicians from the Gulf Coast to
gather stories about Katrina victims for a performance called *Uprooted: The
Katrina Project*. Alternate Roots then trained story circle facilitators from
the Jamestown Project for a yearlong development of story circles in
New Haven, Connecticut in a project called "Private Narratives for the
Public Good." All participated in the New Haven International Festival of
Arts and Ideas where both groups facilitated story circles in the community.
Graphic recorders accompanied the story circles gathering information for
graphic displays that would capture story themes in pictures and charts
and allow for continuing reflection and response. The Katrina theater piece
was performed at the festival where public intellectuals, educators, and
cultural workers spoke on panels and led workshops on the festival theme,
Crossing Borders.

Theater practices

A prime example of community theater has developed in the United States in Appalachia, one of the poorest regions of the country. Roadside Theater was founded in Whitesburg, Kentucky, in 1975 as a part of Appalshop, a multidisciplinary rural arts and education center whose mission is to celebrate the culture and voice the concerns of the 20 million people living in the 13 state Appalachian region. The theater works "by filling the gaps in the Appalachian historical narrative" through "oral histories, traditional ballads and archetypal stories, the forms of indigenous church services, personal memory" (Roadside Theater, n.d.) Through community-based cultural exchanges, they also aim to tell a national story linking Appalachian history to the stories of other Americans. Because the ensemble is primarily White, they also do intercultural plays with professional ensembles from other communities. For example, in 1981, in response to increasing Ku Klux Klan activity in the South, they began collaboration with JuneBug Productions from New Orleans, a Black theater group, performing for each other's home audiences and later producing the collaborative theater pieces *JuneBug/Jack* and *Roadbug*, which toured nationally for eight years. Between 2000 and 2002, they produced a collaborative play *Promise of a love song* with JuneBug and Paragons Theater, a Puerto Rican ensemble from the Bronx. Roadside Theatre also sponsors multiyear residencies that allow them to work in sustained ways in other communities based on their local aesthetic forms.

The methodology developed by Roadside Theater (n.d.) is a classic example of participatory communication evolved in collaboration with local community organizations interested in social transformation:

> Roadside's community strengthening residencies begin with public performances of plays selected from Roadside's repertoire, complemented by workshops that explore Roadside's history, purpose, and artistic process. In the second phase of a multiyear residency, the community, with Roadside's help, begins to uncover its own stories and music through a specific story and music collecting process (story circles). This second phase culminates with public performances by the community of its stories and music—often in conjunction with big potluck suppers or community cookouts. In the third phase of a residency, a community's stories and music are the natural resource to craft plays, which are produced by a community's artists for the public. The final phase of the residency formally acknowledges the local leaders and artists, seeks to identify infrastructure and resources to establish a place for their work in their community, and introduce their work to other theaters and presenters in the national arts community.

There are projects with similar methodologies in process in many countries around the world. Since 1988 the Aarohan Theater in Nepal has created a network of 30 local theater groups that develop scripts and plays to support local community participation and social change. Wan Smolbag Theater in the Solomon Islands and Awareness Community Theater in Papua, New Guinea have established similar practices in the South Pacific. Street theater in urban settings, often working through youth groups, has been organized by Teatro Trono in Bolivia, Teatro Kerigma in Colombia, and Naladama in India. According to Dagron (2001) summing up these practices in *Making waves: Stories of participatory communication for social change*:

> The tradition of expressing the local history and the dreams of the community through music, dance, and theater are alive and well even in the most isolated places on earth. And that is precisely why the communication projects that aim to build on traditional forms of expression have many chances to succeed.
>
> (p. 19)

A related but very different set of practices in the field of liberation arts has developed through the work of Theater of the Oppressed initiated by Brazilian director Augusto Boal (discussed above) who was influenced by the work of Paulo Freire in community literacy circles. The Theater of the Oppressed refers to a variety of theatrical forms used in community workshop formats without necessarily carrying the expectation of forming a permanent theater company. Local communities invite workshop facilitators to work with them in short-term intensive training sessions through which the techniques are passed on so that they can be repeated in future sessions. Here the goal is the interruption of passivity and the rehearsal of strategies of intervention that in time may be carried over to social change projects outside of the theater. According to Boal (1995):

> The goal of the Theater of the Oppressed is not then to create calm, equilibrium, but rather to create disequilibrium that prepares the way for action. Its goal is to dynamise.
>
> (p. 72)

Theater of the Oppressed begins with theater games and exercises that are fun and that challenge participants to loosen up and try out new postures, developing plasticity in the body and spirit. After a long session of exercises, participants begin the telling of personal stories related to a theme chosen by them, selecting from these stories dramas to work on based on their resonance with the group. After a story has been chosen for dramatization, its protagonist stages the story using participants who may be given lines to speak, or who can be sculpted into expressive body postures demonstrating attitudes and relationships with others in the scene. After this initial staging, Boal has developed a number of techniques for interrupting, elaborating, and reframing the drama. Participants in the group are invited to create alternative scripts and outcomes for the characters, or else they may be invited to enact or speak what was left unspoken in the scene. These processes serve to break down a sense that the situation is fixed and hopeless and to build capacities for dialogue. Gradually the situation moves toward "the first-person plural." Boal (1995) suggests:

> This model will contain the general mechanisms by means of which the oppression is produced, which will allow us to study sympathetically the different possibilities for breaking this oppression. The function of analogical induction is to allow a distanced analysis, to offer several perspectives, to multiply the possible points of view from which one can consider each situation. *We do not interpret, we explain nothing, we only offer multiple points of reference. The oppressed must be helped to reflect on his own action (by looking at alternatives which may be possible, shown to him by other participants who for their part, are thinking about their own singularities). A disjunction of action and reflection on that action must be brought about.*
>
> (p. 45)

Boal's techniques can be quite elaborate and depend on workshop facilitators called "jokers" to organize them. These jokers are trained to be facilitators through joker-training workshops, and everything about the process depends on their cultural competence, their awareness of subtle forms of race and gender oppression, their understanding of local history, oppression, and trauma, and their capacity to lead creatively. An enormous number of elaborations are being developed as this methodology migrates beyond its inception in Brazil and Peru in the 1960s and 1970s (see Schutzman & Cohen-Cruz, 1994: Cruz-Cohen & Schutzman, 2006). Boal's books have been translated into over 25 languages, and Theater of the Oppressed work is being done in at least 70 countries. There are three permanent training centers (in Rio de Janeiro, Paris, and New York) and an international Web site in 22 languages networking practitioners and organizing conferences.

Photovoice and other visual arts

The techniques of photovoice developed during a women's reproductive health project funded by the Ford Foundation in rural Yunnan Province in China. It was led by UCLA faculty member Dr. Virginia Li in 1991. Li took on the project with the agreement that she would involve the women in a bottom-up rather than a top-down approach through which village women themselves would express their needs to policy makers. They began with a health assessment survey of 8000 households. Some of the village women were given cameras and asked to photograph conditions in the villages, which then were discussed and contextualized. Realizing the value of these dialogues, they trained 62 women to take photos and act as discussion leaders for their communities. The photographs were compiled in a book published in 1995 entitled *Visual voices: 100 photographs of village China by the woman of Yunnan China* (Yi et al., 1995), the proceeds of which are returned to Yunnan to support health activities. The process gradually evolved into a research technique systematized by Carolyn Wang of the University of Michigan and Mary Ann Burris of the Ford Foundation.

Photovoice (Wang, 1995) begins with recruiting members of a community who would be willing to participate. A training program is instituted that teaches the techniques of photography, but also raises philosophical issues about ethics and power, critical interpretations of subject matter, and how to dialogue with the community to be pictured in the photographs. After the photographs are taken, the group discusses and selects those they consider the most significant or telling. They then create stories to contextualize the photographs they have selected. Then they codify and document the themes that have emerged from this process. The photographs can be mounted as an exhibit to reflect findings to the community, to engage them in further dialogue, and to show potential funders and policy makers what the community has found to be important in assessing its own needs. These assessments may be very different from what specialists, professionals, and researchers working out of a universalist and positivist paradigm may have identified as needs. For example, thousands of dollars have been spent on radio and television messages telling rural women to "boil their water" to purify it when in fact 80 per cent of rural women in developing countries often walk five or more kilometers a day in deforested environments to find dry sticks to use in cooking food, and do not have the resources to boil all water despite the good intentions of the campaigns (Dagron, 1991). To counter this kind of problem, some programs have begun asking policy makers and funders to also participate in the photovoice process so that they can be in a deeper dialogue about needs and solutions for a particular community.

Similar processes can also be effected in locations where there are no resources to buy cameras and where there are desires for personal and psychological self-expression. In these variations of the methodology that owe debts to the field of art therapy, participants choose a theme to explore and then use paints or drawings, or even collages made from old magazines to express something important to them about the chosen theme. The process of contextualizing, coding, documenting, and exhibiting the work remains similar to that in photovoice. This personal creative work offers the possibility of including not only critical analysis of the past and present but also utopian dreams for the future. Often the work is organized in such a way that participants are asked to create a picture of what currently exists side by side with a picture of what they hope or wish for. The analysis would then decode and create narratives for both, and begin to ask what creative actions would be needed to fill in the gap between reality and desire. This methodology has been used, for example, with homeless children, asking them to draw pictures of what their home lives have been like and what they would like instead; and with gay men to elucidate what were the social environments surrounding their adolescent sexual awareness and what they would have benefited from. When the work is done in groups, awareness quickly develops about oppressive social conditions that need to be transformed while self-recrimination and fears of personal guilt evaporate. This work exports methodologies of art therapy from the clinic to the community.

Video

As the equipment for video production has become less expensive, its ownership has broadened. There has been a shift toward collaborative projects where community members are taught documentary filmmaking skills and then encouraged to create their own work. Community video projects have developed to document testimonies and practices from local groups as storytelling circles do, and to critique problematic conditions in much the same way that photovoice works with photography. Locally produced videos are being used throughout the world to intervene in policy issues at a national and regional level, to seek funding for projects, to document police and paramilitary brutality, and to record other events that are silenced in the national media.

One of the most innovative and elaborate projects for video was developed by a feminist NGO in Nicaragua called *Puntos de Encuentro* (Meeting Points). Founded in 1991, the group began with an analysis of the social conditions that led to women's oppression. They came to believe that "[a]ll forms of oppression are interrelated and are sources of injustice and structural violence." Their analysis focused on authoritarian practices in everyday life, suggesting that

> [T]he progressive, egalitarian agendas of Sandinista ideology clashed with the oppressive, authoritarian everyday practices embodied by the Sandinistas themselves in their interpersonal relations. These women found that one thing was to believe in an abstract utopia, but that the challenge to implement it in the quotidian was a much more difficult task.
>
> (Rodriguez, in Lacayo, 2006, p. 369)

Puntos wanted to accentuate the link between oppressive institutions in the larger society and the kinds of silencing that occur in families and neighborhoods, which prepare individuals to accept repression as normal. They held that:

Authoritarianism in families and society promotes the oppression of women and young people and produces an environment conducive to gender and age-based violence, such as sexual abuse, emotional abuse, domestic violence, and rape.

(*Puntos de Encuentro*, 2006)

The kind of social change they wanted to promote was so deep and far-reaching that they knew it would require work on many different fronts over a long period of time. They created youth camps and workshops for leadership and technical training in media to help strengthen the voices of youth and women. To promote dialogue, they teamed up with service organizations, community groups, and media outlets, put out a newsletter and educational materials, and placed billboard and radio announcements. The center of their efforts was a national television show, *Sexto Sentido* or Sixth Sense, in the form of a *telenovela* (soap opera) of the sort that is very popular all over Latin America. *Sexto Sentido* shows young people struggling with difficult issues in everyday life, and opens discussion about matters that are often silenced in public discourse—domestic violence, rape, unwanted pregnancy, abortion, and homophobia. The goal of the program was not to present public health information or to impose correct answers:

Puntos' purpose is not to create consensus around a topic, but to explore and be exposed to different points of view, in a climate of respect and tolerance. Through the radio and the television show, young people not only claim the right to have an opinion on issues and to make decisions about matters that affect their lives, but also it strengthens and legitimizes the voices of minorities that are not active, or visible, in the mainstream public sphere. ... Puntos believes that people have the right to decide what they want, so rather than presenting some forms of behavior as "good" behavior, or model the behavior "socially desirable" or endorsed by donors and population control organizations, we promote the right for each individual to make informed decisions and take responsibilities for the decisions they make.

(Lacayo, 2006, pp. 29, 34)

The program has consciously chosen to show the point of view of both perpetrators of violence and bystanders who are also struggling with their choices. There are no "bad" characters that do not go through processes of transformation. In one sequence the show followed a "macho" character who infects his wife with HIV by refusing to use a condom, but as the drama continued, he decided to get help and began to act more responsibly.

This way, *Sexto Sentido* shows we all have the capacity to improve ourselves, to reflect, and to change into the kind of person we want to be.

> The "bad" character is not much use in a program where what we are primarily trying to show are the internal processes of reflection and the kind of decisions that lead us to our personal development.
>
> (Weinberg, in Lacayo, 2006, p. 11)

The airing of the program as a weekly series on national television, and rebroadcast by local cable channels, was linked to a weekly national call-in radio show, as well as dialogue tours to local schools and community centers throughout the country where people could confront the cast and discuss the choices that various characters had made. In Nicaragua, a young person may watch the show with friends and family discussing the story, call into the radio show to express opinions, visit a linked service organization to get help with a personal decision, read the national newsletter and billboards, and participate in related workshops and campaigns by local organizations pressuring for policy change. The strength of the social transformation efforts comes from the mix of activities that work to simultaneously change social policy, public opinion, and personal reflexivity and behaviors. In Nicaragua, members of the cast are now celebrities, and the show is wildly successful, currently seen by 70 per cent of the national viewing audience who are talking about the characters as if they were neighbors. It is shown in Costa Rica, El Salvador, Guatemala, Honduras, and the United States.

Few community organizations have the power and resources to produce shows for national broadcast, particularly in countries where the national media are corporate or government controlled. Nevertheless, *Puntos de Encuentro* and *Sexto Sentido* have raised the bar on the kinds of collaborative work that may be possible in the future.

Performances, happenings, conceptual arts

To create a larger arena for entering into dialogue with others, some social change organizations have created special forms of public conceptual and performance arts. These either question social arrangements by parodying or undermining hierarchies or else propose utopian solutions for changes that are already underway. Performative projects highlight relationships and connections that exist in the world without being publicly acknowledged. One way to think about these forms is through the notion of "happenings" developed in the art world during the 1960s.

During that period, Allen Kaprow (1968) at the California Institute of the Arts began to critique dominant forms of art being promoted in the art world. He complained that art was being made

> in a rectangular studio, to be shown in a rectangular gallery, reproduced in a rectangular magazine, in rectangular photographs, all aligned according

to rectangular axes, for rectangular reading movements and rectangular thought patterns.

(p. 33)

He began to promote the development by artists of innovative environments or installations, or, when moved outdoors, "happenings" that attempted to maximize participation and to minimize direction.

[The supervisor of] the happening would provide the basic performance directives and materials but people would be free to improvise as their mood dictated. Happenings merged drama, painting, music—and whatever else fit. In the happening, the boundary between life and art closed. The happening's problem, that of life itself, was its fragility. The experience stayed with the individual participant: the happening disappeared.

(Pelfrey & Pelfrey, 1985, p. 320)

Outside the art world, various types of creative hybrid performances were innovated by community groups all over the world that merged conceptual arts with campaigns for social transformation. We have extended the concept of happenings to include community-building efforts that are not primarily seen as art projects but as vehicles for dialogue and protest.

In Argentina and Chile, *Los Hijos de Los Desaparecidos* (the Children of the Disappeared) and the Funa Commission have been doing conceptual performances. Because many of the perpetrators who kidnapped and tortured during the dictatorship have never been named or held accountable, the group carries out research to find them, comparing themselves to the Nazi hunters of a previous generation. When they locate one of the torturers, they plan events in his neighborhood or workplace. These events are called *escraches* in Argentina and *funas* in Chile. On the sidewalk they may paint signs saying "300 meters to a torturer's house," "100 meters to a torturer's house," and finally "a torturer lives here." By this means, as well as through hanging posters, they begin to enter into dialogue with people in the neighborhood about the past and the silence that surrounds it. Thus they recreate the situation of the dictatorships where people have to decide once again whether to be bystanders hiding in their houses or participate in a call for justice. *The Hijos* create visibility in place of brutal repression that was done with invisibility, silence, and impunity.

Eventually the group stages a demonstration confronting the torturer, in his home, workplace, or another public space. These stagings can be very dramatic, often with hundreds of neighborhood people participating. A demonstration may feature drums, usually in the *batucada* style of Afro-Brazilian music or *murga*. *Murga* is a musical style that evolved in southern Spain and is practiced in Uruguay and Argentina, where costumed groups organized for carnival parades and other outdoor events perform satirical singing, chanting, and street theater. Like samba schools in Brazil and *krewes* in New Orleans, they spend all year working out themes and creating songs, skits, dances, and costumes. The demonstrations and *murga* may bring the neighborhood into a discussion of the dictatorship and its effects on contemporary issues, and the torturer face to face with the children of those he murdered. *Escraches* and *funas* have been compared to Greek tragedies in the children's insistence on public justice and mourning.

On May 25th of 2006, the Funa Commission in Chile organized a massive *funa* outside the building of the Department of Labor in Santiago, Chile to denounce the presence of Edwin Dimter Bianchi, an ex-military officer and School of the Americas graduate who has been identified as the officer directly responsible for the death of legendary Chilean folk singer Victor Jara. A group of 15 demonstrators, including Victor Jara's daughter, Amanda Jara, went up to the 14th floor office to confront the ex-military officer and hand out informational flyers to his co-workers denouncing his crimes against Victor Jara and other political prisoners who were held at the Estadio Chile. Bianchi has never been prosecuted for his crimes. While this confrontation did not result in the arrest of Bianchi, it opened a potential space for restorative justice through which perpetrator and victim can confront each other directly (see Chapter 15).

Another example of critical performative art has been developed in the United States by a group called "Billionaires for Bush", which currently has over 65 chapters and hundreds of members. In each local area, the group presents itself as spokespeople for billionaire corporate leaders who have earned millions from war and have no sense of social responsibility. They may dress up in tuxedos and evening gowns and arrive at the locations of their performances in limousines, chanting and carrying placards that express the program of these interests: "Small Government, Big Wars! Blood for Oil! Hands off Halliburton! Widen the Income Gap! Give War a Chance! Privatize Everything!" People occasionally believe they in fact are joining Republican gatherings; on one occasion the Billionaires leading an audience chanting "Four more years" gradually changed the slogan to "Four more wars." The audience then stopped in confusion when they realized something was wrong. Primarily though, the group uses the performances to enter into dialogue with others about whose interests are served by the billions of dollars the United States has spent on warfare. There are many other groups doing similar satirical performances in the United States, including, for example, Reverend Billy and his Church of Stop Shopping Gospel Choir, the Clandestine Insurgent Rebel Clown Army, the Missile Dick Chicks, Greene Dragon, and Yes Men.

At the other end of the spectrum of performative projects are those that try to build toward a utopian future that is wished for by participants. Artist Betsy Damon (1996) has pioneered "Keepers of the Waters" projects that deal with issues of water pollution and environmental responsibility. Summing up her work in Minnesota, she wrote:

> The project built relationships among artists, scientists, community organizations, educational institutions and government agencies to form alliances that structured projects to create a language and a vision of living water in the world. It connected people, inspired initiative and hope, and created new imagery and language about water quality, and facilitated change in the treatment of water.
>
> (1990, p. 196)

In 1995 she received a grant to work on a Keepers of the Waters project for the Yangzi River in Chengdu, China. Working with the mantra "relationships are everything," she again brought together artists, educators, government officials and community groups to work on the project. Teachers began to help students monitor water quality. White cloths were placed over every discharge pipe into the river and later displayed with the brown stains they collected. Traditional art forms became the basis for performances and displays. A ritual storytelling session was held and prayers collected for the river. A Tibetan artist produced 70 prayer flags that were hung along the riverfront. People blessed lotus flowers that were placed in baskets with candles and sent floating down the river as a flotilla of light. Martial artists performed at river's edge. Long pieces of white silk were floated in the river gradually turning gray and brown in a stunning display that touched people deeply. A public official spoke, and a closing ceremony was held that brought together everyone who had participated. Every event was televised and a video was made that was shown nationally.

Some conceptual performance pieces aim to articulate and bring to consciousness changes that are already underway. In Joensuu, Finland, American artist Suzanne Lacy helped to bring together 18 artists and performers who organized a four-day event called "The Road of Poems and Borders." The work highlighted the many ways that people were emigrating across borders constantly. During the four-day festival, six hundred letters about crossing borders were read out loud by pairs of women in business meetings, homes, parks, and stores. After each reading, they outlined their feet in yellow chalk, leaving a trail throughout the city of the festival sites. Public radio featured women leaders who had crossed borders discussing the realities of their lives. On another day, pairs and groups of women staged meetings lying on the ground at Joensuu's public market and then traced their bodies on the asphalt, leaving a portrait of the community. All of these activities were surrounded by community dialogue on the experiences and meanings of border crossing.

Sometimes happenings are a form of direct action, aiming to prevent specific events. The Chipko movement in Northern India that began in the

1970s organized large groups of village women to protect the rights of local people to utilize local forest produce and prevent commercial exploitation of trees. They went into the forests, sometimes playing drums, to prevent the cutting of trees by hugging them and placing traditional sacred threads around them as a token of their vow of protection. Religious texts were read and often the women fasted. Songs and poems were composed supporting their project, which were then recited to the laborers who were supposed to cut the trees. In February of 1979 when two truckloads of police arrived at the Adwani forest that had been auctioned off to commercial interests, women from fifteen villages were committed to its protection and each tree was being guarded by three volunteers. The movement has had many successes in staving off threats to regional forests. Vandana Shiva (1989) traces the history of the Chipko movement back 300 years to the Bishnoi community in Rajasthan, where over 300 women led by Amrita Devi sacrificed their lives to save khejri trees. The Chipko women were doing direct action to save their forests, but they were also doing symbolic actions that reshaped meanings, reclaimed autonomy and empowerment, built community strength, and revindicated centuries old cultural forms. Today in the Narmada Valley, many thousands of people, including Arundhati Roy, are continuing this environmental tradition in protesting the Sardar Sarovar Dam.

Qualities of liberation arts

While many of the arts projects of counter-memory and counter-monument are individual, unique, and spontaneous, developing in the heat of community struggles, there are also some systematized methodologies that have been so successful that they are widely practiced, reinterpreted, and debated. There is beginning to be a wider appreciation of the efficacy of such projects in multiplying the impact of social change initiatives. According to Denise Gray-Felder of the Rockefeller Foundation (Dagron, 2001), writing an introduction to a survey of community arts projects,

> We have found—through this project and the other work of the Foundation's Communication for Social Change Grantmaking effort— overwhelming evidence of development and aid agencies increasing support for projects that return to traditional forms of communication: drama, dance, music, puppets, storytelling, and dialogue circles. We have come to appreciate the true power of face-to-face and voice-to-voice communication. Every meaningful lesson or belief I've garnered in life came from someone I value explaining the issue to me and involving me in a process of figuring out the solution.
>
> (p. 4)

Throughout this text, we have given examples of successful liberation psychology projects incorporating arts methodologies. Though these methodologies have developed in completely different locations, each has similar characteristics, though always inflected by local conditions, history, and culture. Here we will list some general characteristics of liberation arts projects not in order to prescribe them, but to summarize tendencies that have been developed in multiple arenas. Various projects emphasize some of the elements more powerfully than others.

1. **Participatory:** These projects share an emphasis on collaboration and participation in both production and spectatorship. They are anti-hierarchical and value process over product, working in contrast to arts scenarios where a conductor, composer, author, producer, or director has final say over the end product.

2. **Unpredictable:** They create events in which the outcome is unknown and contingent, aleatory, depending on a feedback loop among spectators, dialogue partners, and performers.

3. **Proactive:** The purpose of the work is not a retrieval of painful memories for their own sake, which can be retraumatizing, but the building of a shared understanding of history and social context in a community environment that will witness past events in order to prevent future violence and exclusion and build up possibilities for constructive social change.

4. **Sheltered:** The work is envisioned in a protected space with responsible facilitators guaranteeing that each individual participating be free to enter a transformative process at his or her own pace.

5. **Egalitarian:** Each person who joins the process is considered to be in a unique way a victim of violence and amnesia about the past, who can recuperate lost symptoms, memories, and feelings that will contribute to a more awakened and lively response to suffering and joy. The binary of "helpers" and "helped" is dissolved.

6. **Creative:** Arts media are made available, revived, promoted, or sometimes taught, in order to resurrect and develop symbolic resources that have the potentiality of helping individuals rethink possibilities and solidarities, to awaken imagination, and to uncover hidden feelings that have not yet been owned.

7. **Rupturing:** The work is innovative and interruptive of commonly held narratives, breaking open taken-for-granted unities, and questioning old understandings, silences, and assumptions for the purpose of challenging and naming forms of amnesia.

8. **Dialogical:** The core of the project is active forms of participatory communication that invite members of the community to enter long-term sustainable processes of local critical dialogue about the past, present, and future.

9. **Transformative:** The project has as a goal of creating a better life for the community, attempting to discern together what kinds of local initiatives can be developed that will create change.

10. **Consciousness-Raising:** The project helps create a new and sometimes dramatic symbolic language to bring to consciousness previously unnamed problematics and solutions.

11. **De-Centering:** The creative process functions to slowly expand the capacity of the individual participant subjectivity to hold in dialogue multiple interpretations, feelings, and points of view within self and between self and others for the purpose of expanding dialogical capabilities, enhancing self-understanding, and enlarging responsiveness to otherness and unexpectedness.

12. **Performative:** Theater and arts presentations or performances are offered to the public, encouraging and supporting new conversations.

13. **Communicative:** The outcome of the project is communicated to others at a regional, national, or international level through Web sites, film or video, public speaking, public forums, public actions, or printed materials, for purposes of entering into dialogue about important issues uncovered.

14. **Evaluative:** Because these projects can have surprising and unpredictable outcomes, when they are evaluated for funding purposes, processes of participatory evaluation at the local level are used to assess successes and failures. Rather than trying to decide in advance what the goals of the project should be and then proving that known-in-advance goals have been met, community members meet to critically assess the benefits and shortcomings of their own activities. This self-correcting process leaves room for the transformation of initial anticipations, and its collaborative and reflective praxis already constitute a performance of a successful outcome to the project. A pre-project survey of attitudes and awareness can later be used to reflect on what has shifted through the collaborative arts process.

Liberation arts methodologies are rehearsals for democratic processes that in many cases are still utopian dreams. By breaking down the wall between arts creators and arts spectators, liberation arts begin processes of dialogue and imagination that strengthen individuals and communities to engage their past, present, and future.

Conclusion

The arts have played a crucial role in assisting communities to resignify and resymbolize their experiences and environments. Cultural activists have been brilliantly inventive in adapting art forms to local conditions to awaken new sensibilities and develop collaborative methodologies that allow people with no arts training to participate. These experiences can be life changing. According to bell hooks (1989):

Moving from silence into speech is for the oppressed, the colonized, the exploited, and those who stand and struggle side by side a gesture of defiance that heals, that makes new life and new growth possible. It is that act of speech, of "talking back," that is no mere gesture of empty words, that is the expression of moving from object to subject—the liberated voice.

(p. 9)

Liberation arts excel at this process of transformation. The right symbol or name in the right place can break silences, provide new insights, and reframe hierarchies in an instant. The conversations that follow can bring down barriers and transcend borders that seemed immoveable. In the next two chapters, we will explore participatory action research methodologies that build on the work of public homeplaces and liberation arts already taken up in Part IV. This form of research also aims at creating or joining local, collaborative processes that build energies for social transformation.

13
Critical Participatory Action Research

> ... speaking nearby or together with certainly differs from
> speaking for and about.
>
> (Trinh Minh-ha, 1989, p. 101)

Re-orienting psychological research: Principles of critical participatory action research

A small group of women factory workers in Tijuana, Mexico, have been collaborating with a filmmaker, an artist, a human rights group, a women's group, and a transborder environmental health coalition in a dynamic testimonial practice. These community activists, *promotoras*, are members of *Grupo Factor X*, a women's group that helps women factory workers learn about improving working conditions and human rights. The *promotoras* began an innovative form of autoethnography, a portrayal and exploration of their experience in order to understand their situation better. They are trying to improve factory working conditions and environmentally toxic conditions in their neighborhood that have worsened as the greed of transnational corporations has strengthened its hold on this region. Over 4000 giant industrial factories that produce the goods Americans enjoy plague the Mexico border with the United States. Around Tijuana a million workers, primarily young women, work long hours, often amid environmental toxins and without adequate workplace safety precautions, barely making subsistence wages. They live in neighborhoods, *colonias*, that have little infrastructure, such as reliable provision of electricity, clean water, sewage, passable roads, and adequate health care and education. Factor X sought to expose the devastating health effects of factories that allow manufacturing toxins, including heavy metals, to run freely into communities, and, ultimately, into the ground water.

In their documentary film project, *Maquilapolis: City of Factories*, the workers were centrally involved in every stage of the process, from planning to shooting, from scripting to outreach, using consensus to reach decisions.

The *promotoras* were tutored in the basics of telling stories through documentary film, and in the use of video and sound recording equipment. Working in pairs they filmed intimate portraits of their daily lives, the conditions in the factories where they labor, their neighborhoods, and their work educating fellow factory workers about issues of human rights and environmental justice. The project merged reflection with action, and art making with community development, making sure that the film's voice was that of the women (Funari, 2006).

This research project was not simply about the daily life of several factory workers. As in other testimonial situations, these women are aware that their experience expresses some part of the experience of other Mexicans who work in *maquiladores*, as well as that of workers in distant countries caught in similar globalized rushes to corporate profit taking. They were not only trying to illumine their personal experiences, but to put these experiences in their larger historical, political, social, economic, and gender context. This research into the effects of globalization on the daily lives of women factory workers at the Mexico/U.S. border was not conducted by psychologists or any other academic experts, though professionals did consult and support the women in their research and subsequent litigation against several environmental polluters, as well as and to secure severance pay when factories moved to Asia for cheaper labor. The collaborative team understood the workers themselves as experts who could educate both workers in the South and consumers in the North about the human and environmental costs of corporate globalization. The study did not make its first and final appearance in a scholarly journal. It was created not only for understanding but to be a source of catalytic change. This documentary has been shown from Norway to Korea. It is being used at the border as a tool of education about workers' rights, community organizing, and environmental health hazards.

Some of the women who grew up in Chilpancingo remember families picnicking and camping by the river. Now as you enter the shantytowns along the river, you see children playing in a stream that is polluted with heavy metals from manufacturing and *E. coli* bacteria due to inadequate infrastructure. When there is even five minutes of rain the nearby factories release their wastewater, flooding the neighborhoods with toxic runoff. The women from *Colectivo Chilpancingo* are often present as workers return to their humble accommodations built from wooden pallets and other cast-off items. They hand out flyers educating about public health concerns and environmental pollution that has caused respiratory problems, skin sores, and serious birth defects, including anencephaly, babies born without brains who die at birth.

It is clear that the process of research contributed not only to community education but also to successful litigation and resulting toxic cleanup. At their bustling community center, *Colectivo Chilpancingo Pro Justicia Ambiental*, a visitor quickly picks up the authority and pride with which the leaders speak, the growing environmental awareness that is being built at the neighborhood and community level, and the empowerment of the children as they help their mothers make signs for a rally or hand out leaflets. Here women students become teachers, passing on their knowledge. There is a therapeutic aspect of such participatory action research, therapeutic in the original sense of the care or attending of the soul. Indeed, in a setting in which workers become commodities, and factory owners and the government fail to provide adequate and safe housing and working conditions, one can easily suffer a kind of soul loss from one's life energies being used up for the gain of others. To articulate one's own experience and insights, to learn about and then begin to defend her rights, to make a space to invite others' testimonials, and then to act to redress the injustices one has witnessed are acts of psychological restoration. Through the process of such research and collective action, those who have found themselves objectified regain or strengthen a subject position, their own position of authority and knowledge.

The collaborative process has proved restorative not only to the women caught in oppressive and unjust circumstances. The one who taught them filmmaking skills, Vicky Funari, is frank in admitting that the process has been healing for her as well. When she confronted the living conditions of these women for the first time, she also encountered their capacity to create insight into their situations and to offer their energy to organizing workers to transform the present nearly impossible situation for mothers and children.

> Yet, there they were, living their lives. And at the same time, they were not just living their lives and taking care of themselves and their kids; on top of those things they were choosing to become activists, choosing to try to work for a solution and work for change. I couldn't help but be inspired by seeing the fact that someone who's putting up with more than I could ever imagine myself putting up with is doing it, and then doing more. Seeing that gives me hope and makes me feel that there might be a way through this. So that's why I feel like I'm less cynical—despite all the cruddy things that are happening in the world right now—as a result of this film. It makes me think that if Vianey can do it and Carmen can do it and Lourdes can do it, then maybe we'll find our way.
>
> (Funari, 2006)

The work of the *Colectivo Chilpancingo* has created a public homeplace such as the ones studied in Chapter 11. Their partnership with the filmmakers, *Grupo Factor X*, the transborder Environmental Health Coalition (a nonprofit environmental and social justice organization), and CITTAC (The *Maquiladora* Workers' Information Center) is an example of a site of reconciliation and collaboration, where relationships are forged to help bring about needed liberatory changes, and where the psychological suffering of all those involved is helped by the very process of collaborating across customary social separations. Each of the women involved has gone through a powerful process of developing voice, life direction, leadership capacities, and social and psychological insight into her situation and the power dynamics surrounding it. Their work exemplifies new ways of doing "research" that are breaking out across the globe.

In this chapter, we describe the dynamic shifts that need to happen in the way psychologists ordinarily think about psychological research in order to revision research to assist in human liberation. The work of liberation psychology inevitably involves us—formally or informally—in critical participatory action research as we struggle to understand and transform oppressive situations. Liberatory research efforts can help open or hold open a social space where psychological experience can be understood in social and historical context, where critical understandings can be built, differences and their impacts explored, and emancipatory action initiated and reflected upon. This chapter will outline the principles that guide critical participatory action research, distinguishing it from other research approaches in psychology.

Research is "critical" when it leaves behind a naive approach to issues of power, and engages in careful self-reflection regarding the possible shadows of its research presence and processes. This reflexivity involves researchers in a critical stance toward the processes and uses of research in the history of their discipline(s), and asks them to be willing to dis-identify with aspects of their training and practice that reinforce the divides a critical participatory action approach questions and works to heal. From a critical perspective, researchers cannot rest in the idea that they are increasing knowledge through their work. Knowledge is used for purposes that must be clearly and ethically discerned. A critical approach involves researchers in reflecting on and clarifying their own motives and commitments, and then to question the effect of these on those they are partnering with to do research. Within a research situation a critical approach looks deeply into how both the research context and the issue(s) it studies have become structured, attempting to understand the social, economic, and political pressures that are playing out in the research situation.

Our efforts are "participatory" because we work to develop critical knowledge *with* our fellow community members or, if we are not from the community in question, we seek to work alongside community members as invited guests. This working alongside destabilizes notions of expertise such that the role of researcher transforms into that of a co-researcher and collaborator. Such liberatory research is spoken of as "action" research because reflection and the action that flows from it are not dissociated. We work to understand in order to act differently in the world. As we enact new ways of being in the world, we need to step back and evaluate whether our actions are facilitating the emancipatory outcomes we desire, creating a spiraling dynamic as we move back and forth between reflection and action. Critical participatory action research holds the vision of a more just and peaceful world. It engages in research as both a possible means to this end and as a process that embodies in the present respectful, collaborative relations that host critical insight and emancipatory change.

Principles help us to clarify our aspirations. The principles we describe involve shifts away from more mainstream practices of research, shifts that enable us to describe continuums along which a given project can be assessed. For instance, a project may succeed in being highly participatory, but lack any plan for the insights of the project to effect change in the systems that negatively impact the well-being of the participants. Research may effectively posit and achieve some liberatory changes, while pursuing the research in a manner that re-inscribes power differentials among professionals and co-participants. Rare projects will succeed in being wholly critical, participatory, and action oriented. Nevertheless, these are aspirations we can use as we plan, pursue, communicate, and critique our research efforts. The next chapter will help the reader apply these principles as he or she moves through each stage of a research effort, using queries to stimulate reflection and dialogue. We have been developing these guiding principles and practices over a decade of working with graduate students who pursue fieldwork and research in a wide range of community and convened group situations.

In contradistinction from much of mainstream psychological research that is conducted by "experts" *on* research subjects, participatory research seeks to democratize the generation of understanding. It trusts community members' capacities to generate significant questions for research, to gather relevant "data," to work together toward understandings, and to embody these in action, creatively transforming their situations. Liberation psychologists are committed to co-creating *with* others contexts for inquiry that are dialogical and emancipatory, trying to ensure that both the process of the research, as well as its fruits, are liberatory. Whether situated within an ongoing community or a group convened to explore a particular topic, participants seek to critically understand the past, fueled by the emerging and embodying of alternative visions for the future.

Rajesh Tandon (1984, 1988) made an odyssey from the top-down research practices of the university to partnering with villagers in India to do research that mattered to them. He says that participatory research has an ancient history, a history of ordinary people working together to understand their world. This has most often been accomplished through oral traditions and art, rather than writing and formalized research. Such efforts have been largely unrecognized and delegitimized by those producing knowledge at the dominant centers of societies. Such neglect of indigenous research has functioned to disempower marginalized peoples (Tandon, 1988).

For a century, psychological research fashioned after the natural sciences has dominated mainstream research in American universities and their satellites throughout many parts of the world. At the edges of this formidable center, multiple alternatives have struggled to take root. Critical participatory action research has roots in community research in India, Africa, and Latin and Central America; in critical theory and action research in Europe and the United States; and in feminist research from many different geographical locations. The research efforts growing from these multiple roots disrupt disciplinary boundaries, allowing debates and research in disciplines such as anthropology, education, performance studies, cultural studies, art, religion, sociology, and philosophy to enrich the theorizing about and the practice of research in psychology. These research efforts have arisen both as a critique of mainstream social science research and a delineation of a visionary set of principles and practices that re-orient psychological research toward emancipatory ends.

To differentiate participatory research from positivistic psychological research, we can speak of it as "post-empirical," as "work toward the development of an alternative to scientific methods for studying the social and cultural world" (Nielsen, 1990, p. 32). This is not because quantitative studies would never be used in liberatory research. Such studies can often be of great use at particular historical moments. For instance, in El Salvador in the 1980s when it was too dangerous for single individuals to speak out against repressive government policies, a social science poll of experiences and attitudes was able to represent the deeper sentiments of a community while offering anonymity to its contributors (Martín-Baró, 1994). "Post-empirical" implies that the whole framework of relations, practices, and goals that surrounds both quantitative and qualitative work need to be in striking contrast to many of the assumptions and practices common to the mainstream of psychology. It is these shifts in assumptions in liberatory approaches to psychological research—as they affect relationships, practices, and goals—that we hope to share in this chapter and the next.

The fuel of these shifts is a vision of research as a way of transforming human relationships that in turn transform daily life. Here individual change, interpersonal change, and social transformation are linked, as the development of critical understanding at the individual and small group level is the prelude to emancipatory action. In Martín-Baró's (1994) words: "... conscientization supposes that persons change in the process of changing their relations with the surrounding environment and, above all, with other people. No knowledge can be true if it has not attached itself to the task of transforming reality, but the transformative process requires an involvement in the process of transforming human relationships" (p. 41). From the articulation of guiding principles and their embodiment in examples of research, we sketch what this transformative process looks like.

From center to margin

According to bell hooks (1990), there are implications of a move from center to margin:

> This is an intervention. I am writing you. I am speaking from a place in the margins where I am different, where I see things differently. I am talking about what I see. ... This is an intervention. A message from that space in the margin that is a site of creativity and power, that inclusive space where we recover ourselves, where we move in solidarity to erase the category colonized/colonizer. Marginality as site of resistance. Enter that space. Let us meet there. Enter that space. We greet you as liberators.
>
> (p. 152)

In speaking of her graduate school apprenticeship in mainstream psychological research at the University of Chicago, feminist psychologist Mary Belenky (1998) shared that a senior professor impressed by her graduate work took her aside to confide one of the rules for successful psychological research in the American academy: "When you are forming your sample of subjects, don't include women and African-Americans. They screw up your results." In other words, successful research that will be rewarded should not include marginalized groups because they will introduce too much variation into statistical results. Fortunately, such advice served paradoxically as a directive to Belenky to conduct her research at the margins. She dedicated herself to studying women's ways of knowing, focusing largely on economically disadvantaged women's use of community contexts for developing understanding, as opposed to formal educational settings.

Much of psychological research has not questioned how the values of the mainstream status quo are reproduced and fostered in research (Prilleltensky, 1994). Psychological research that is "critical" questions how the "status quo" has been constructed and who and what these constructions serve (Prilleltensky & Nelson, 2002). It looks and listens carefully to see who and what has been marginalized by constructions that have been made to seem normal, natural, inevitable, and preferable.

White feminist psychological researchers in the 1980s became critical regarding the relative absence of psychological research on and by women. Their own overgeneralization of their understandings from one group of girls or women to others whose experiences were different was critiqued, influencing not only the focus and content of subsequent research, but the research processes themselves. The research path of Carol Gilligan and her community of research colleagues exemplifies research that dedicates itself to inviting into dialogue what has been marginalized or excluded, moving from center to margin. The evolution of their research methodology displays the use of critical feedback about what the research itself has marginalized, even while it specifically set out to critically challenge the marginalization of girls' and women's experiences in psychological research.

Gilligan, a student of the then foremost moral development theoretician Kohlberg, noted that when his schema of moral development was applied to girls and women, they consistently scored lower than men. Since she did not believe girls and women were inferior moral reasoners, Gilligan (1982) began to inquire into the reasons they received poorer scores than boys and men. In looking more closely at Kohlberg, Erikson, and Perry's theories of development, it became clear that they were predominantly constructed from studies of boys and men. When Gilligan began to listen into how women actually made moral decisions, she heard what she called "a different voice," one that was less oriented to issues of abstract justice and more to an ethics of care in embodied situations. They called into dialogue those left at the margins of Kohlberg, Erikson, and Perry's theories of development: girls and women.

Asking how this "different voice" might have come into being, Gilligan and her colleagues turned to study the psychological development of pre-adolescent and adolescent girls in America. Rather than fit girls and women into a developmental theory derived from studying boys and men, she asked if talking to girls and women would reveal dynamics that could not be seen through the eyes of male-derived theories. The first groups of girls studied were predominantly White, American, and affluent due to the private school settings that hosted Gilligan's research group that was itself largely White and economically privileged.

Through extensive interviews with these girls, Gilligan and her colleagues began to describe a process whereby self-assured, latency-aged girls, able to announce their opinions and disagreements, became increasingly unable to voice their differences. In order not to "rock the boat" of their relationships, they allowed others to make decisions, openly disagreed less, and in some cases became vague not only in what they expressed, but in how they privately thought, backing off from points of view that were liable to create disagreement and conflict.

No research is without its own processes of marginalization, however. In liberatory research, one is encouraged to ask what and who is being marginalized by the assumptions, focus, and approach one is taking, and to listen carefully to critics who point out the borders of one's conception and the applicability of one's work to others. Brown and Gilligan were criticized for essentializing gender and for overgeneralizing individualistic notions of self (Lykes, 1994). They came to realize that their work at the margin had created it own margins: namely, girls of color who were growing up under the weight of poverty and racism in urban America. In *Between voice and silence: Women and girls, race and relationship*, Gilligan, Taylor, and Sullivan (1995) shift from the primarily White, upper-middle class, private-schooled world of adolescence to begin to examine how race and class might impact the theories they have been developing. We stress the word "begin" here, because this work is both groundbreaking and tentative. The economically privileged girls of their earlier research "assumed others were interested in who they were and what they had to say," they worried about jeopardizing "these relationships by revealing what seemed like unacceptable parts of themselves." "[T] hey will modulate their voices to blend in or harmonize with the prevailing key" (p. 3).

Listening to girls challenged by racism and the inequities of class in America revealed some distinct differences from listening to the daughters of the elite. For the latter, "fitting in" and abandoning voice held out the prospect of rewards up ahead, the privileges granted to those who are White, who have economic resources, and who are skillful at accommodation. For the at-risk girls they studied, there were few payoffs for conforming and waiting. Many of the girls were highly vocal regarding what was wrong all around them. In using their voices, they often ended up feeling isolated and alone. They had not lost voice, but was there anyone to listen to what they were saying? Without that listening support, many withdrew into a brittle independence, their adolescent dreams of who they could be meeting with disillusionment, and at times, embitterment. The at-risk group now attended to "could speak, but for the most part felt that few cared or listened" (Taylor, Gilligan, & Sullivan, 1993, p. 3).

Martín-Baró wanted psychology to be a force to listen and care about those caught in poverty, such as these girls. He argued that liberation theology's giving of priority to the poor rather than to the privileged needs to be heeded in psychology. Community psychology in the United States, Canada, and Australia, and much community work in India, Latin America, and Africa does heed this call to re-orient the resources of psychology toward oppressed communities. While some may claim that such a shift injects values and politics into psychological research, psychologies of liberation argue that research has always reflected the underlying values and commitments of its researchers. The task is to make these values explicit and to inquire into the kind of world that is being created and sustained by them.

Many advocates for boys' emotional and academic education claim that the increased focus on girls and their needs in the 1980s shifted attention and resources away from boys whom they see as suffering in feminized schools. Furthermore, boys, they say, are less likely to enjoy the healing of psychotherapy because their suffering is expressed more by externalizing behaviors and addictions than by the internalizing disorders common to women and girls in the United States. The latter often bring girls and women to psychotherapy, and the former bring men and boys to detention centers and jails modeled on retributive justice models (see Kipnis, 2002, 2004). The Harvard Center on Gender and Education was structured to help gender-focused study to be accomplished while minimizing the pitting of the needs of girls against those of boys, or vice versa.

The paths from center to margin have involved odysseys away from research being centered in the university. In moving research from center to margin, further care is taken to select participants who live within the "margin" as it is constituted by the research project. Bat-Ami Bar On (1993) argues that it is not simply a case that all knowledge is perspectival, but that some perspectives are more revealing than others, namely, that of those who have been socially marginalized (p. 83). The movement from center to margin has encouraged research to privilege "outsider" voices normally marginalized in academic settings (Hill Collins, 1991). Hill Collins argues that this outsider status gifts feminist researchers of color with a critical vantage point on self, family, and society that is sorely needed. She stresses that the "outsider within" is more likely to see and challenge the knowledge claims of insiders. They have greater objectivity, and an ability to articulate patterns that insiders are too immersed in to see. Speaking of African-American women's experience, bell hooks (1984) says, "Living as we did—on the edge—we developed a particular way of seeing reality. We looked both from the outside in and from the inside out" (p. ii). In contrast to a dominant center that is unaware of itself, the "outsider" sees the center from another vantage point, encouraging critique and reflection on what would otherwise be unreflectively taken as normal.

From colonizing research to indigenous research

Liberation psychologies seek to nurture research within marginalized communities by community members themselves, "insiders." They question the importation of dominant models of psychology into oppressed communities, being mindful of the harm inflicted by both cultural invasion and a concomitant neglect of knowledge from within indigenous and other marginalized communities. In *From colonial to liberation psychology: The Philippine experience*, Enriquez (1992) shares the Philippine's odyssey from hosting psychology as a colonized discipline. In many places abroad, psychology departments accepted with little question the dominant models of American psychology, rather than recognize and engage with their country's own indigenous psychologies. Many Philippine professors had studied in the United States and imported to their homeland American behavioral and cognitive psychology, along with natural science methodologies. Despite wide cultural differences, American psychology was the lens used in the Philippine academy. Enriquez and others began to ask what were the psychologies indigenous to Philippine cultural communities? They studied these with the hope of empowering them through formal articulation and recognition and substituting them for the foreign psychologies adopted from the West. Enriquez differentiates indigenous research from participatory research. In the former the subjects, called "culture bearers," define the problem and collect the data. The research is for the sake of the culture bearers, and is only shared beyond the group if not at the expense of the culture bearers. Such a clarification became necessary to counter historical abuses of and unconsciousness about power differences in research situations, even in many instances of participatory research. When we reflect on proposals for research, we need to ask ourselves who through the process of research is likely to gain in power, knowledge, and the capacity to transform the world. Enriquez's category of indigenous research guides us toward a clearer discernment of whether the proposed research re-inscribes patterns of power and privilege or disrupts them.

Arundhati Roy (2004), Indian writer and activist, stresses that it is not so much that communities and their members are voiceless, but that others have intentionally turned a deaf ear to their well-being and concerns. Linda Tuhiwai Smith (1999), director of the International Research Institute for Indigenous Education at the University of Auckland and a Maori, concurs: "How can research ever address our needs as indigenous people if our questions are never taken seriously. It was as if the community's questions were never heard, simply passed over, silenced" (p. 198). Writing on "de-colonizing" methods, she has delineated some of the methods of and purposes for research in indigenous communities: research to assist in claiming resources; *testimonios*, storytelling, and remembering to claim and speak about extremely painful events and histories; and research that celebrates survival and resilience and that revitalizes language, arts, and cultural practices. Communities beset by various forms of oppression, whose members have suffered from diminished senses of themselves by virtue of racism and classism, can use research to not only nurture community understanding, but to help preserve community and cultural practices.

Such moves from center to margin, from colonizing to indigenous research, demand and contribute to the democratization of knowledge. Researchers schooled in the academy step down from the role of detached expert that has been dictated by the natural science paradigm and either accompany a group or community that has invited them to be a part of a research effort, convene a group around a particular research topic that is explored together, or work within their own community, often "studying up," reversing the trend of making those of lower socioeconomic classes the object of research for academics (Hale, 1991).

Can participatory research also be useful for work with groups not at the margins of society? As we have shown in Chapter 5, there are many in every environment who live alongside violence and suffering as bystanders without being aware of or being able to articulate its effects on their own psychological life. Many such people are cut off from their own feelings of empathy and vulnerability and are beset with inexplicable symptoms and longings. Thus though socially and economically they may be nearer the center of power than the economically marginalized, psychologically they may suffer dissociation from their own multiple and even unconscious understandings of the interrelatedness of suffering. When participatory research begins with privileged groups, it is very quickly possible, at least in the United States, to establish a widespread discomfort with consumerism, violence, alienation, addictions, sexism, and workaholism, among other issues. Participatory research is very useful in helping people break out of closed systems of symptom and isolation. The group, whether privileged or marginalized, begins to ask new types of questions about the social context. An exploratory process begins where multiple interpretations of the situation can be articulated. The role of the research facilitator in this case can be to open the group to lenses from different social locations in order to increase the dialogical possibilities for interpretation and action. The research facilitator does not give a correct and expert interpretation as in other forms of research, but accompanies the group in its discernment and struggle to reinterpret its experience. This process unfolds through time, as participants begin to mull over their situation, and that of others. Changes in point of view may occur suddenly or gradually as multiple interpretations begin to rupture previous beliefs and certainties.

When in situations of accompaniment, the traditional distance between the researcher and the researched narrows as participants are involved together in the generation of research questions, design, analysis, and implementation of action strategies. Through deepened dialogue, researchers can often become more aware of not only common ground but also differences. Paulo Freire shared that as he first started out as an educator, his wife, Elza, took him aside to correct his pedagogy. One night after working with a group of adults, Elza said to him: "'Look, Paulo, it does not work like this.' And I asked her: 'what did I do? I spoke serious about serious things.' She said, 'Yes, of course. All you said is right, but did you ask them whether they were interested in listening to you speak about that? You gave the answers and the questions'" (Horton & Freire, 1990, p. 65).

Those who are identified with assuming the role of the expert unwittingly can usurp the group members' process of articulating their own knowledge, unintentionally mitigating against community change by disempowering those who join them in conversation. This can happen with the best intentions held, as the performance of one's own adequacy that many experts are schooled in can silence others who have been socialized to feel inferior and "foreign" in formal academic settings, such as in many research meetings. Too often researchers have used those involved in the research for their own purposes, rather than assisting participants in the achievement of their own aims. This can happen when social scientists engage research participants and communities to answer questions posed solely by the researcher, questions often irrelevant to the participants. Even when relevant, too often researchers have not returned the results to the participants or their community so that they could be challenged or amended, or the understandings utilized. Researchers who have "harvested" knowledge from communities to advance their own careers have justifiably heightened people's suspicion regarding the ethics and motives of psychological research.

Psychologies of liberation take pains to avoid cultural invasion and usurping of participants' full participation in the research. Liberatory research consciously intends to respect, validate, and help legitimize local knowledge, and to listen attentively to how community members themselves understand the relevant dimensions of their experience. A researcher may have alternative ideas about that experience, or know of other points of view, which she also has a right to put forward as one member of an analytic team. Only through thorough collaboration can the ownership of the production of knowledge be adequately shared, including participation in the use of research findings. A deepening of dialogue is at the heart of the movement from expertism toward participatory research. In Chapter 14, we will outline some considerations for how research can be conducted from a more dialogical stance at each stage of the research process.

From claims of universality to appreciation of social location

Much of psychological research has been conducted with little or no awareness of the social locations of the researcher and the impact of this on the research participants and their community. Liberatory research requires a process of becoming aware of and critiquing one's own subjectivity, described by Ngugi wa Thiong'o (1986) as "decolonizing the mind." This process requires that we "become archaeologists of the site of [our] own social formation ... [This] contemplation of the condition of our lives represents a freedom, or at least an attempt to achieve freedom" (JanMohamed, quoted in McLaren & Lankshear, 1994, p. 207). It asks that we study and reflect on how aspects of our identity such as gender, nationality, ethnicity, class membership, sexual orientation, and religious affiliation influence the way we see and participate within the research situation, particularly vis-à-vis issues of power. For instance, how do a person's identifications and experiences affect the questions posed, the way they are pursued, the interpretation of the data, and the dissemination of the findings?

This reflection needs to be an ongoing process and requires dialogue with others whose experiences are different from our own. Those schooled in research within the academy have often absorbed an approach to their research that naturalizes their own cultural point of view, taking it for granted as universal and/or preferable. Only in dialogical exchanges with others from different social locations can one begin to effectively confront the bias and assumptions of one's perspective. As feminist research has developed, such conversations have clarified how early feminist research unwittingly spoke for "women's experience" generally, when those researched and those doing the research were largely White, middle class, and American. For instance, studies of "women" entering the workforce at midlife often failed to acknowledge that it was White women being researched by White women. Many African-American women had been in the workforce since their youth, as their foremothers had been dating back to slavery. Their experiences were unintentionally unacknowledged.

As Taylor, Sullivan, and Gilligan (1995) listened carefully to the transcripts of their meetings with Latino and African-American girls struggling with poverty and racism, they learned that what a girl speaks about is affected by whom she is speaking with. The girls were attuned to whether their interviewers had shared experiences of class and race. In addition, when White and economically privileged women researchers worked with transcripts of conversations with girls of color from economically disadvantaged families, they often failed to hear many of the nuances of the girls' experiences. Within such feminist psychological research the notion of social location and its impact on the generation of knowledge has been further refined, as conversations between women of different races, cultures, classes, and sexual preferences have led to a more differentiated notion of context (hooks & Mesa-Bains, 2006).

Taylor et al. (1995) found that a more complex understanding was possible with a broader range of participants in the dialogue. It became important to include women with whom the girls could comfortably share. It was crucial that the interpretive community be widened to be inclusive of more social locations. This move toward interpreting the girls' interviews through a diverse interpretive community, composed of women of different ethnic, racial, and class backgrounds, helped each researcher to learn where she was deaf to particular girls' experiences because of her own different life situation. Through such an interpretive community each researcher could delve more deeply into understanding her own cultural identifications, what they allowed and denied access to in listening to the girls' experiences.

In a study on compassion, Judith Thompson (2002) describes coming to the same conclusion:

> If it had been just me engaging in individual conversations with all these different people, I would have been the hub of the wheel of possibility and the meaning would have been interpreted through me because qualitative research is interpretive research. I would have used their narratives but I would have translated those narratives through my own lens. By bringing everyone together, what I hoped would happen—and I think did—is it becomes what you would call an interpretive community or a discourse community, which is another way to describe "participatory knowing." Exploring something like this within a community

makes a lot more sense to me. I also am convinced that one gets to unwind things a bit more when you bring people from other cultures together—face-to-face—so that you really are enriching the field of knowing. Someone from South Africa might see it in one way and someone from Thailand is going to see it in a different way. Then you are going to find out what are the commonalities and particularities in the way that we see and experience things. That not only engages us together in the process of knowing, but in the process of interpreting, too. Because as people respond to each other, a thread of interpretation is occurring there.

(para. 18)

When these identifications are not articulated and the effects of them go unquestioned, often the results of research are falsely generalized to other contexts where experiences are quite different. The widening of one's interpretive community makes it more difficult to engage in overgeneralizations of one's findings to communities that do not share critical aspects of cultural experiences. A wide interpretive community can overcome the Eurocentric, universalist, and, more or less, mainstream middle class bias traditional in academic research. At the same time, it overcomes the limitation of the individualism that is taken for granted within these traditions.

Such shifts have enabled feminist research to become more critical, articulating and dislodging dominant ideologies. This kind of participatory research attempts not only to listen to marginalized voices but to move from the implications of what is heard for social policy in order to generate greater justice and opportunity for women and girls. It has been careful to differentiate research *about* women, research *for* women, and research *with* women. While research about women can read like a "doleful catalogue of the facts of patriarchy," research for and with women stands as an "opposition to the very facts it discovers" (Westkott, 1990, p. 64). It does so by refusing to be resigned to the present, and working with an "imaginative alternative that stands in opposition to the present conditions" (Westkott, 1990, p. 64). Whereas the natural science approach emphasizes the search for repeatable, simple, universal laws, a post-empirical approach in psychology seeks complex, contextualized understandings. Universality is replaced by location, grand theories by often-vulnerable perceptions. Listening into how something is experienced from different points of view allows the challenging of a tendency to universalize what is actually a dominant class point of view. Post-empirical research presupposes that where the researcher is located—historically, culturally—gives access to the situation in certain ways, obscuring it in others.

Rather than resting in a dominant class perspective that takes its assumptions for granted as true and universalizable, liberatory research embodies a vision of knowledge as polycentric, as generated in multiple situations. Speaking of feminist research, Ruth Behar (1996) imagines "a vision of utopia—where objectivity will be so completely revised that situated knowledges will be tough enough to resist the coups of dictatorial forms of thought" (p. 29). Dialogue with others from different contexts provides a primary pathway to assess the scope of relevance of one's research.

From pure knowledge to the synthesis of critical reflection and action

> [T]rue dialogue cannot exist unless the dialoguers engage in critical thinking—thinking which discerns an indivisible solidarity between the world and men and admits of no dichotomy between them—thinking which perceives reality as process, as transformation, rather than as a static entity—thinking which does not separate itself from action, but constantly immerses itself in temporality without fear of the risks involved.
>
> (Freire, 1989, p. 81)

Post-empirical liberatory approaches to research do not conceive of researchers as discovering facts about a pre-existent and static reality. Rather research is imagined as attempts to open psychological and social spaces where understanding can be developed that helps in creatively transforming daily lived realities and the structures that determine them. In critical participatory action research, investigation reaches toward creating a more just and peaceful world through the linking of cultural understanding and transformative action.

For instance, German feminist Maria Mies (1978, 1983, 1991), uniting a critically minded participatory action project with feminist research, joined the forces of feminist activists and a group of women who suffered physical abuse in their intimate relationships. Using taped interviews, group discussions, and role-playing, they sought not only to document the experiences of individual women suffering domestic violence, but to create a shared understanding of domestic violence that could lead to community education and change that would mitigate against intimate violence against women (Klein, in Bowles & Klein, 1983). Utilizing a Freirean approach to consciousness raising, individual interviews yielded to group discussion. This allowed each woman's story of domestic abuse to quicken the insight of the other women, and to relieve the guilt and shame that make it difficult to gain insight into the structural dynamics of physical abuse against women. The women's stories showed the critical need for a safe house within their community. They decided to craft their stories into dramatic form in order to educate the wider community and to raise funds for the creation of a safe house refuge for women. Here understanding flowed into

changing the status quo arrangements by which women are isolated in situations of domestic abuse and unsupported by the larger community in their
desires for safe shelter. Research was linked to the development of critical
understanding that flowed directly into efforts to transform social relations.

Participatory action research has roots in a number of approaches that
have argued for a research cycle that moves fluidly between the development of critical understanding, the use of such understanding to inform
action to transform a situation, reflection on whether such action achieved
its goals, and then refinement of action or involvement in subsequent cycles
of reflection and action. Its success depends on a collaborative partnership
between researchers—sometimes from a variety of disciplines—and community members. In some situations, community members conduct the
research wholly independently. Without a process of inclusion, interventions by researchers are often experienced as intrusions. Once researchers
from the outside leave such a site, the previous system often reasserts itself
in resistance to changes that were imposed from the outside rather than
desired and owned by the stakeholders.

The traditional separation between knowledge and action in research was
challenged by John Dewey who described the process of inquiry as beginning with the delineating of a problematic situation, where our ordinary
responses are inadequate for fulfilling our needs and desires (Field, 2006).
It is then necessary to understand how this situation is constructed and to
understand the critical aspects that would need to be changed for a desirable
shift to occur. Hypothetical solutions are reflected on, and then embodied
in action to see if in fact a movement toward a more desired state of affairs
is achieved. Following in Dewey's footsteps, Frankfurt School member Kurt
Lewin, first used the term "action research." Lewin was committed to creating an action science that could improve social actions by studying their
condition and effects through partnerships with community members.
Lewin (1951) studied a process through initial fact-finding, planning of an
intervention, execution of the change, and then watching the effects, studying the new dynamics that arose. Planned intervention in a social system
with a process of reflection became the seed for what is called action science.
In order to create a systemic change, re-education is necessary to change
well-established patterns of thinking and acting in individuals and groups.
The intended change is typically at the level of norms and values expressed
in action. Participants need to be involved in the original location of the
problem, in fact-finding, and in choosing to engage in new actions (Argyris,
Putnam, & Smith, 1985). Examples of Lewin's action research include his
studies on authoritarian, democratic, and leaderless groups, and on efforts
to reduce prejudice and discrimination against minority groups in communities. "The practice of action research involves working with a community to
create conditions in which members can engage in public reflection on
substantial matters of concern to them and also on the rules and norms of

inquiry they customarily enact" (Argyris, Putnam, & Smith, 1985, p. 35). As it is presently practiced, action research may or may not be truly participatory, just as its values may or may not be liberatory. Habermas (1987) and other critical theorists argued for an emancipatory approach to research in which knowledge and action, theory and practice, could be joined to create change.

Projects often start small and develop through a "self-reflective spiral: a spiral of cycles of planning, acting (implementing plans), observing (systematically), reflecting, and then replanning, further implementation, observing and reflecting again" (McTaggart, 1997, p. 34). McTaggart says that projects usually start in one of two ways: (1) to collect some data in an area of general interest, to reflect on it, and then make a plan for changed action; (2) or to "make an exploratory change, collect data on what happens, reflect, and then build more refined plans for action" (p. 35). In the early phase of research, the methods of phenomenology, ethnography, and case study may be helpful to gain an understanding of the context the research is taking place in. Later phases of research may involve widening the community of researchers, and expanding the scope of understanding and action to the larger social and institutional context.

Dialogue throughout the stages of research maximizes the possible links between knowledge generation, theory building, and social intervention. "Dialogue becomes the vehicle for critical consciousness and praxis ... [It] acts as a method to integrate inquiry and intervention" (Tandon, 1981, p. 299). As discussed in Chapter 10, Belenky et al. (1986) studied women's ways of knowing through intensive individual interviews. Belenky found herself most moved by those whom they saw as "silenced knowers." These women experienced themselves as mindless and voiceless. They were dependent on external authorities, and passive in relation to them. They did not report having dialogues with themselves, nor did they have a sense of an inner voice. Their childhoods had been characterized by an absence of dialogue and play, and a presence of gross neglect and physical and/or sexual abuse. Belenky kept worrying about these women who did not think they could think, who felt voiceless, and who lived at the margins of their communities. Often having grown up in poverty, they were stigmatized as deficient and different. Belenky (1997) wondered if it was possible to support such women to become active thinkers, to help cultivate their ability to confront and solve problems, personal, familial, and community. She began to work with isolated, rural, low-income mothers of preschool children, all of whom were silenced or received knowers. Many lived in households where they were treated as the objects of authoritarian power over relationships. They often passed this experience on to their children in their modes of punishment, and in the absence of dialogue with their children.

Belenky, Bond, and Weinstock (1997) wondered whether inviting these women into reciprocal and mutual dialogue with each other, engaging them in reflective dialogue, practicing their problem-solving abilities together might help them to claim, develop, and voice their thoughts. Her hope was that this would also help them in supporting the articulation of their children's thoughts, paving a path for a more dialogical practice of mother-child relationship.

As the women engaged in dialogue they came to see that the difficulties they had thought were due to personal inadequacy were shared, and that "many of their problems were a function of the social arrangements that devalued and excluded women (especially mothers) and the poor" (Belenky, 1996, p. 396). The facilitators were careful to support collaborative thinking, to take a long-term perspective on the difficult problems the women were addressing, and to caringly mirror back to the women their words. Through comparisons with a control group they found that the participants increased in their capacities for self-reflection, dialogue, making friends, and in encouraging their children through dialogue to actively reflect. Belenky and her colleagues' research moved from reflection to action, using earlier insights to help create a context in which changes in knowing were linked with changes in a sense of agency and in dialogical parenting skills.

From expert to vulnerable co-participant and advocate

Those involved in helping to create participatory research situations find themselves without the usual defenses deployed in traditional academic research. Their subjectivity, life experiences, bias, and predispositions are thrown into relief rather than quietly taken for granted. For instance, Brown and Gilligan's (1992) research team members found that they could not listen to and understand the girls in their research without opening themselves to painful, repressed experiences of their own adolescent development as girls. The words of the girls began to sound familiar to them, though that painful period in their own adolescent lives seemed locked away from their easily accessible memories. Their vulnerability to their own unfolding memories allowed them deeper access into the meanings the girls were conveying, often as much through the girls' hesitations and pauses as through their words. As the research process allowed space for the girls' mothers and teachers to also become aware of their histories of distancing from their own needs and thought in the service of continuity of relationships, albeit often inauthentic relationships, the women were able to pause and reflect before intervening to encourage girls to take such steps of disassociation. To gain access to their own memory, they listened closely to the girls who were in the early stages of self-silencing and who were still able to articulate their decision making. These younger girls' self-awareness fostered growing awareness in the researchers who were then able to listen more keenly to the often hidden and ambiguous messages of the older adolescent girls.

The vulnerability of the participatory researcher is increased when the formal interview process of question and response is loosened. Ann Oakley (1981) suggests respondents be allowed to "talk back," viewing the interview as a relational exchange. The respondent, if fully informed about the purposes of the research, may be able to address the kinds of questions asked, introducing greater complexity into the research process. This may challenge the protective space for the researcher, created by the usual formalities of research. One of our students embarked on a series of interviews of individuals who were "homeless." One man stepped aside from the questions she was asking him, and asked her what her life experience was that led her to this interest in homelessness. Bursting into tears, a stream of repressed and painful memories flowed into her awareness, memories of leaving Argentina as a young girl during the Dirty Wars, arriving in the United States, far from her home. The interview form yielded to a deeper conversation, where both commonalities and differences in their experiences of homelessness could be explored.

In a critical hermeneutic approach, Ellen Herda (1999) drops the term "interview," replacing it with "research conversation" to indicate the mutuality, reciprocity, free-ranging, and spontaneous aspects of the research encounter. Brown and Gilligan (1992) describe a transition in their research from formal interviewing to such conversation. They brought questions to the girls at the Laurel School, but over time these questions yielded.

We became more conscious and less directive, more interested in following the girls' lead; they in turn became more invested in teaching us what they know, more disruptive, more outspoken, and also more playful, warmer, more genuinely in relationship.

(Brown & Gilligan, 1992, p. 26)

Dialogue supplanted one-sided question and response. Relationship grew around and through the initially more formal researcher-research participant dichotomy. Dialogue is foundational to such research and requires those involved to engage at a deeper level. The members of the collaboration in dialogue stretch from their native locations toward the experience of the other. This stretching requires empathic imagination, the capacity to identify with another, and an effort to try to see and feel the questions that are essential to the other's being vis-à-vis the situation being studied. It also requires an awareness of the gaps between self and other, a knowledge that the other's experience does not completely overlap with my own, that to be in dialogue I must wait for difference to become articulate, learning to bend my being toward it with a desire to understand, rather than to erase it with rejection or false identification.

Liberatory research has everything to do with opening a space where this difference that the other's being poses to me can come forward. At the same time we are attentive to those places where beneath that which separates us, we find slender threads of common experience, yielding a place to stand together. From this perspective on research, we can speak of liberatory aims characterizing both the process and the goals of research. Gadamer (1976) likens the kind of dialogue we are describing to play, where through unanticipated and unintended turns, participants find themselves displaced from their initial horizons. Gadamer describes the "buoyancy" of such play.

"Buoyancy," however, does not capture the vulnerability of the researcher involved in such dialogue. For when we actually open to the difficult narratives that are shared with us, we find ourselves and our view of the world changed. Taylor, Gilligan, and Sullivan (1995), reflecting on their relationships with the at-risk girls in their research interviews, say,

> Listening to these girls is to invite disruption, disturbance, or dissolution of the status quo. To support the strengths, intelligence, resilience, and knowledge of girls whose culture or class is marginalized by society is to support political, social, educational, and economic change. It may be easier to sacrifice girls than to support their development, and when girls sense this, it may be hard for them, with the best of intentions, not to give up on themselves and sacrifice their own hopes.
>
> (pp. 202–3)

Taylor, Gilligan, and Sullivan (1995) address two key concerns that were prevalent in their interviews with inner-city girls: teenage sexuality and pregnancy. The girls in the study were at risk for teenage pregnancy. Some of them had been the result of their mothers' teenage pregnancies. Yet all of those who did become pregnant had clearly earlier stated their desire not to become pregnant before finishing school. They wanted to establish a place for themselves in the work world before motherhood, if they wanted to be a mother at all. When one listens to their stories of how they became pregnant and reviews some of the recent research on teenage pregnancy, an alarming story emerges that challenges many stereotypes about teenage pregnancy.

> "Teen pregnancy" and "teen motherhood" can readily become euphemisms for statutory rape and the sexual abuse of adolescent girls by adult men.
>
> A California survey in which teenage girls were interviewed found that, of 47,000 births to teenage mothers in 1993, "two-thirds of the babies were fathered by men who were of post-high-school age." ... "Among California mothers ages 11–15, only 9 percent of their partners were other junior high school boys. Forty percent of the fathers were high school boys, and 51 percent were adults" (Steinhauer, 1995).
>
> (Taylor, Gilligan, Sullivan, 1995, pp. 201–2)

In two large studies of teenage mothers, from 61 to 68 per cent said they had been sexually abused, beginning at an average age of 11. The average age of the fathers was 24.

The stories that girls tell about their schools are also difficult to hear. One of the girls talked about how difficult it was to go from elementary school where she was caringly watched over to secondary school where she felt so unwanted. In the world of the large urban public high school, the girls often felt completely on their own. They felt they had no continuity of relationship with teachers and counselors. Their youthful aspirations for their futures were not matched by adults who could help them avail themselves of opportunities, help them make connections, and gather information needed to turn their dreams into reality. They experienced their teachers as unwilling to engage with them around the controversial issues they wondered and thought about the most.

The action and emancipatory components of the research project are evident in trying to establish situations for girls that encourage the emergence and sustenance of voice. They foster conditions that mitigate against feeling that to enjoy connection, one needs to mute one's thoughts and feelings. Being listened to and having faith in the importance of voicing one's thoughts and feelings are crucially interlinked. Gilligan and her colleagues created clubs for girls that encouraged inner and outer dialogue through journals and poetry writing, voice and dramatic work, and attention to relational impasses within the group. Many schools and groups concerned with girls' development have used the insights from this body of research to create classroom and public homeplaces that invite girls into authentic dialogue with themselves and others, and which hope to establish solidarity with girls by acting with them to address the issues that deeply affect their well-being.

From manifest to latent: Listening for gaps, silences, and polyvocality

Careful listening to narratives is particularly important when research efforts intersect with issues of collective and individual trauma, as much of liberatory psychological research does. It is necessary to listen for what is on the edge of coming into words, for what cannot yet be clearly stated, for the ellipses between assumed certainties, and for iconic meanings that stand in for experiences that were overwhelming. Much psychological research begins with provisional understandings of the researcher that are stated through hypotheses. The researcher uses these to generate structured questions to which a research subject responds. There is often little or no space for participants to frame their own questions and perspectives on the research endeavor. Some qualitative approaches to research, including phenomenological ones, have sought to use open-ended questions that invite participants' narratives and perspectives on understanding. As is always the case in languaging experience, we convey more than we consciously intend or understand. Researchers working with narratives have sought ways to work with significant gaps between what is consciously known and conveyed on the manifest level by the interviewee and subtexts or alternate voicings of which the interviewee may be unaware. These gaps and subtexts multiply when one's experience involves trauma. This has given rise to a variety of methods of tracking alternate voicings and of inviting expression through nonverbal media.

Chanfrault-Duchet (1991) suggests three readings of narratives to listen for key phrases and patterns and narrative modes. These listenings help one to understand how the individual places herself in relation to dominant models. For instance, is the relationship between self and aspects of societal expectation one of harmony, indifference, ambiguity, or conflict? Where does the narrative share an identification with and acceptance or compromise with dominant norms, and where are defiance, refusal, and resistance evident? Discernment of the narrative model reveals the person's underlying orientation to dominant values: identification (epic style), a quest for "authentic values in a degraded world" (romanesque), or an "ironic and satirical position in relation to hegemonic values" (p. 80).

To analyze the polyphony of voices in narratives, Gilligan and her colleagues developed a method of tracking different voices through an interview transcript. Feminist voice-centered methods embody sensitivity to the multiplicity of imaginal voices of psychic life, to their relations with one another, and to processes of the marginalizing and retrieving of psychic voices. Voice-centered methods are attuned to the interpenetration of psyche and culture, arguing that the "words of individuals cannot be separated from the cultural and societal context in which these words are embedded. The cultures in which people live are always already a part of their words" (Way, 1997, p. 707). These methods are based on a relational model, suffused with metaphors of voice and hearing. In addition, they offer a way to listen to the dissociative processes attendant to living through traumas of various kinds. They give a systematic set of ways to attend to changes in voice and to how the speaker is situated among multiple psychic voices.

In voice-centered research, we are seen as each internalizing dominant cultural discourses through processes of socialization, formal and informal. Thought is understood as retaining its roots in speech, preserving its dialogical structure. This dialogical structure is sometimes hard to recognize because as speech travels inward it becomes more elliptical, as though we are speaking to someone whom we are close to, who knows our references without our needing to spell them out (Vygotsky, 1962). In voice-centered research, there is a working assumption that we have the capacity to become conscious of our identification with internalized dominant perspectives, to resist them, and to improvise new possibilities. Voice-centered relational analyses of language and discourse attempt to capture the polyvocality, the shifting between perspectives, that accompanies a complex multiple self. Within conversation we can hear processes of marginalization and resistance going on. The changes in voice and relationships between voices that a depth and imaginally oriented psychotherapist would be attuned to in a therapeutic context are tracked formally in this method of research.

Valerie Walkerdine (1990) states: "We never quite fit the 'positions' provided for us in these regulatory practices [of socialization]. ... That failure is ... both the point of pain and the point of struggle" (p. 198). Within conversational discourse, as within thought itself, we encounter what Freire called "limit-situations": where we are met both as though with an impassable limitation and at the same time given the possibility of finding a new voice, understanding, and way of being-in-the-world. This new voice may itself echo bits and pieces of people and conversation in the world to which we have been exposed, although it is not a matter of simple parroting, but of working at an improvisational edge that is sometimes uncomfortable and even frightening.

Such voice work involves us in what Ricouer (1970) called a hermeneutics of suspicion—looking behind or beneath the surface of the text, a surface that often conceals the political interests of the text. It requires us to track the dynamics of oppression and liberation through the polyvocality of narratives. Gilligan and her colleagues' voice-centered methods understand thought as comprised of a polyphony of voices, and a variety of dynamics that operate between them, as in a conversation (Brown, 1998).

The Listening Guide used in Brown and Gilligan's (1992) research with adolescent girls focuses on four slow and systematic listenings to an interview transcript or a transcript of a group session:

(1) *Listening for plot: The who, what, where, why of the narrative.* They attend to "recurring words and images, central metaphors, emotional resonances, contradictions or inconsistencies in style, revisions and absences in the story" (Brown & Gilligan, 1992, p. 27). They locate the speaker in the narrative by listening for "shifts in the sound of the voice and narrative position: the use of first-, second-, or third-person narration" (Brown & Gilligan, 1992, p. 27). The delicacy of listening into another's experience at this level is acknowledged: "[T]his first listening requires that we reflect on ourselves as people in the privileged position of interpreting the life events of another and consider the implications of this act. An awareness of the power to name and control meaning is critical; and to avoid abuses of this power, we name and think about the meanings of our own feelings and thoughts about the narrator and about her story" (p. 27). During these readings, Brown and Gilligan suggest that we look for how we identify or distance ourselves from the interviewee. How are our experiences similar and different? How do our own thoughts and feelings affect our understanding, our interpretation, and the ways we write about the person? They ask us to write out where we are

"upset or delighted by the story, amused or pleased, disturbed or angered" (p. 27). This kind of slow and careful listening and self-inquiry "brings us into relationship with that person, in part by ensuring that the sound of her voice enters our psyche" (p. 27).

(2) *Listening for the voice of the self, the I, how the person speaks of herself.* Allowing the other's voice to enter our psyche and to deepen into a relationship with it is crucial for this kind of research. "[B]y taking in the voice of another, we gain the sense of an entry, an opening, a connection with another person's psychic life. In this relational reframing of psychology, relationship or connection is key to psychological inquiry" (p. 28). These two listenings bring us into "responsive relationship with the person speaking and thus are key to what we mean by calling our approach a relational method" (p. 28). In this listening, by tracking the use of "I" and self-references, the reader draws close to how the speaker looks at and speaks about herself and her world. One listens carefully to what characterizes the places she stands in relation to self, others, and what is important to her.

The researchers describe themselves as "resisting listeners" because they are listening for and against conventions of relationship that contribute to inauthenticity and inequality. In the next two listenings, the researchers listen closely to how people talk about relationship and how they experience themselves in relationships.

(3) *Listening for the voice of relationship, for evidence of struggles for authentic and resonant relationships.* How does the speaker experience herself amid the relational landscape of her life? Brown and Gilligan (1992) define authentic relationship as those in which each member can speak his/her thoughts and feelings, risk being heard, and extend such listening to the other(s). In this reading one attends to the desire and struggle for this manner of resonant relationality.

(4) *Listening "to the ways in which institutionalized restraints and cultural norms and values become moral voices that silence voices, constrain the expression of feelings and thoughts, and consequently narrow relationships, carrying implicit or explicit threats of exclusion, violation, and, at the extreme, violence"* (p. 29).

The resisting listener tracks

> signs of self-silencing or capitulation to debilitating cultural norms and values—times when a person buries her feelings and thoughts and manifests confusion, uncertainty, and dissociation, which are the marks of a psychological resistance. We also listen for signs of political resistance, times when people struggle against abusive relationships and fight for relationships in which it is possible for them to disagree openly with others, to feel and speak a full range of emotions.
>
> (p. 30)

Brown and Gilligan (1992) tutor us to become resisting listeners, making efforts to see where relationships are narrowed and distorted by gender stereotypes and where they are sites that generate suffering from marginalization, abuse, subordination, and invalidation. Their telos is relationships that are "healthy, joyous, encouraging, freeing and empowering" (p. 29). To facilitate this aim, they nurture awareness of how psychological violation, physical violence, and oppression leave their marks on psyche, on the structure of its language, the staccato of its gaps and silences, and the forms of its images.

Niobe Way (1997) differentiates "theory driven data" from "theory generating data" (p. 707). In the former, the researcher proceeds first with the theory being developed, as when Brown and Gilligan (1992) listen for the voice of authentic relationship in dialogues with adolescent girls, or when Brown (1997) listens to the voices that represent cultural norms of femininity in the conversation of working-class girls from rural Maine. In theory-generating voice-centered work we listen to a narrative for the voices it brings forward or to surprising relationships between voices. For instance, Annie Rogers (1994) in "Exiled voices: Dissociation and the 'return of the repressed' in women's narratives" set out to listen for how women remembered traumatic experiences. As she listened deeply to the emergent narratives, she found an unexpected dialectical relationship between voices of dissociation and those of recognition and between voices of disavowal and those of self-preservation. This approach looks for voices locked within a main narrative, sometimes indicated by only several words and then a silent pause. These smaller voices unable to control the narrative can be seen as the forces working against the hegemony and safety of accepted narratives.

Niobe Way (1997) argues that it is important that we "generate theories from the stories and lives" of those we are speaking with, particularly those "who have been excluded from theory-building research. Aiming to generate theories leads me, as an interviewer and data analyst, to listen with both ears: one familiar with existing theories and the other attentive to something new and different" (p. 707). For this reason, a research project may include both theory-driven and theory-generating work. For instance, when Gilligan explored women's narratives of moral decision making, she listened in a theory-generating manner, discerning two main voices orienting moral thought and action: the voice of care and the voice of justice. Then driven by theory, she and her colleagues tracked these voices through many narratives to find out more about how they operated.

To mitigate against the potential disempowerment that can result when others determine that there are meanings to our words of which we have been unaware, researchers need to work collaboratively with the co-participants. Annie Rogers' work on listening to the voices present in the narratives of women who were sexually abused exemplifies this. While Rogers spent hours pouring over transcripts of the women she interviewed, the emergent understandings were fully discussed with the interviewees, creating a research process akin to psychotherapy's "working through." Such close analysis of voices within thought and narrative can contribute to insights that lead to an empowering de-ideologization of dominant discourses that have been internalized. This de-ideologization creates a space for processes of re-symbolization (Sloan, 1996).

How is the researcher who has spent long hours on the research to respond when her interpretations are rejected? Borland (1991) and others have made sure the people whose narratives have been interpreted have the chance to read and discuss the narrative and the interpretations offered, and to make their own amendments and sometimes contrapuntal analysis. When Borland presented to her grandmother an analysis of a set of conversations they had, her grandmother rejected as false and biased her granddaughter's feminist interpretation. Borland decided to present both interpretations, allowing them to stand side by side in their difference. The attempt to understand their divergence became a focal interest.

Freire criticized teachers who use educational settings to speak publicly what they have learned in private, failing to invite students to think together with them. Most researchers take what is shared with them back into their own private and professional worlds, withholding or restricting the possibility of making meaning together with the research participants. Participatory research tries to stem the leave-taking so that the processes of understanding can enrich and empower the individuals and group or community involved in the research.

In critical, participatory hermeneutic research on women and caretaking, Melinda Harthcock (2005) brought the transcripts of each group session to the next group for the women to review themselves, listening into gaps, defensive backing away from dangerous insights, and ambivalent relations to mainstream expectations and derogations of them as caretakers. This kind of group effort at becoming aware of the psychological effects of soci-ocultural and economic structures on their narratives is crucial to a working through process that can help participants forge more active and conscious relationships to traumatic or oppressive situations. Such work exemplifies some of the goals of participatory hermeneutic field inquiry as described by Herda (1999). In this approach, research is a "reflective and communal act" that allows for collaborative creating of texts (p. 86). Working together to articulate the themes in these texts helps us to reflect on and critique our understandings, allowing us to "see where we have been, where we are, and what future we might envision and project" (pp. 88–9).

As we discussed in Chapters 11 and 12, dialogical situations that help one to understand the deeper meanings of experiences and visions need to open to a range of artistic expressions: poetry, film, psychodrama, painting, movement, *testimonio*, and song. Brown, Debold, Tappan, and Gilligan (1991) describe their own process of dropping standardized questions and moving to encourage their interviewees to become storytellers, re-enacting their conflict in the interview setting, recounting actual dialogue at times (pp. 163–4). There is a noticeable openness toward and encouragement of creative and expressive means of communication in critical participatory action research. Photovoice documenting everyday life, theatre, visual imagery, songs, cartoons, community self-portraits, and poetry are all invited into the research process (Sohng, 1995, p. 6). Nonverbal means of expression are particularly important in situations of trauma where experiences surpass what words cannot fully convey, and images are pregnant with meanings that can be communicated as trust and safety are established. Lykes's (1997) use of photovoice with Guatemalan women survivors of genocide exemplifies this.

From speaking "for" to speaking "with" to testimonial practices

As psychological research turned to study marginalized groups who were often denied means of self-representation, many researchers spoke of a telos of their work being "to give voice" to the people with whom they were working. Unfortunately, despite the best of intentions, this manner of conceptualizing research carries a colonial shadow where those with privilege imagine themselves as "giving" voice to the "voiceless". While it is true that some individuals and groups ask for help in creating safe spaces in which they can deepen the process of listening to themselves and expressing their experiences and insights, the voice they develop is not given by another though it may be nurtured by the experience of being listened to carefully.

For instance, Suzan Still (1998, 1999), in the context of a community fieldwork externship, conducted a creative writing class in a maximum-security prison. This setting encouraged deep listening to self and others. The men availed themselves of her help in disseminating their poetry outside the prison walls. Their voice was not hers to give, though her presence was critical to bringing the men together to write and listen to one another's experiences and writing. The use of her freedom was crucial in getting their writing beyond the prison wall. With this kind of awareness there is emerging a new breed of researchers whose role is much more akin to that of a cultural worker, than to a mainstream psychological researcher. They are concerned with helping marginalized groups and communities have the means and media to represent themselves. These testimonial practices have multiple and, sometimes, overlapping aims such as

- the creation of *testimonios*, "an indigenous literary genre motivated by the narrator's goals of representing a collective experience" (Brabeck, 2003, p. 2522).
- the collection of oral history in a situation where dominant public discourse about the past or present does not represent some people's experiences that have been neglected.

- the bringing forward of experiences that have been silenced.
- the provision of testimony to truth and reconciliation and human rights commissions.

For instance, the Chiapas Media Project contributed cameras and training to Zapatista communities. When army tanks make incursions into their autonomous communities, filming and targeting those in resistance, indigenous filmmakers are filming back and distributing their news to civil society across the Internet and through documentary films.

The people involved in this kind of work are not only psychologists, but come from a variety of professions. They are aware of the healing functions of self-expression, communal processes of creation, the documentation of experience and history that is systematically distorted or denied, and the way in which art can be a fuel to resistance and vision. Their relations to the people in the group they are working with often leads to their own professional work, be it photographs, documentaries, and professional monographs. These are not thought of as standing in for the voice of others. Ethical issues of appropriation and of professional and financial gain are brought forward to be discerned and discussed.

Brabeck (2001, 2003) describes *testimonios* as a form of narrating life history so that it represents more than the life experience of a single individual. It attempts to give words and shape to experiences that many within a community have suffered. It is defined by resistance to oppression (Brabeck, 2003). *I ... Rigoberto Menchu*, a *testimonio* of Mayan women's experiences during the Civil War in Guatemala, is often given as a classic example. In studying the features of *testimonios*, Brabeck differentiates it from autobiography. In the latter, a specific person is relating her experiences and calls upon the reader to make an identification with her. In *testimonios* the "I" explicitly stands in for a sense of "we," of what those like the narrator have gone through. The reader or listener is not asked to identify—since their experience is not the same— but to form a relationship to the teller of the narrative that admits difference and requires respect (Brabeck, 2003). "[T] *estimonios* produce knowledge based on subjective experience, not as empirical historical facts, but as strategy of cultural survival and resistance" (Brabeck, 2001).

These testimonial practices allow the literary presentation of an individual's experience of a traumatic past to be placed within a mosaic of community voices. The chorus of corroborating narratives assumes a testimonial power that psychologically benefits the individual contributors and the larger group, and advocates for changes in the structures that caused the oppression. What may be less evident is the healing offered to the researcher or cultural worker assisting in such testimonial practices. For instance, the Liberian Truth and Reconciliation Commission decided to include the testimony of Liberians forced into exile by the long armed conflict suffered in that nation. Many Liberians settled in Minneapolis.

It became the site of training people to take testimonies. Seventeen hundred people volunteered for 400 positions that would take considerable time and emotional forbearance. Many volunteers were White Americans who have never set foot on African soil. What psychological healing might the taking of such testimony provide White middle- to upper-class Americans? Here we see the potential of moving from bystanding to active engagement, of countering a national history of division between American Whites and American people-of-color and between Americans and Africans. While listening carefully to the intimate descriptions of torture, rape, maiming, and murder that happened in Liberia could be said to include aspects of voyeurism, it seems more likely that it is an experience of reconciliation for which selves that have been severed from the larger fabric of the human community of which they are a part thirsts. In our work with several hundred psychology graduate students crossing such divides in community fieldwork experiences, it is notable that even amid extremely difficult experiences—in prisons, with the homeless, with people who have suffered torture—when authentic communication broke through hierarchical roles and privileges, when relationship began to develop where there had been no history of interrelatedness, a notable joy was experienced. This joy seems to mark the experience of being knit into a human community one has been separated from by virtue of the distance and remove offered by normative late capitalist culture.

Toward contextual, interpretive, catalytic, and psychopolitical validity

As research shifts from quantitative to qualitative approaches, from an expert model to a collaborative and participatory one, and from collusive to critical research, we need to rework what validity can mean in this different context. Brydon-Miller and Tolman (1997, p. 805) argue that the definition of validity in positivistic research as "correspondence with 'reality,' assessed by specific techniques" needs to be changed in the "context of a practice of research in which multiple, contradictory realities are recognized" (p. 805). The overall validity of a research process can be considered as a dynamic that emerges from each phase of the research. In the next section, we will propose queries for researchers that can provoke the kinds of reflection that lead to research processes that have integrity. Here we will propose some of the understandings of validity that have emerged within of critical hermeneutic research.

Contextual validity concerns the fruitfulness of how the research effort and its questions are framed (Sung, 1995). It also includes the relevancy of the data-collection process to those involved in the research (Tandon, 1981). *Interpersonal validity* is increased as conditions of interpersonal openness and trust are established (Sung, 1995). This openness, as we shall see, will affect the outcome of all phases of the research: from the framing of basic questions to the ability to dispute interpretations to the representations of the research to the wider community.

Interpretive validity increases as people in a research community experience themselves as free to discuss possible meanings of narratives and to propose alternate interpretations to one another. A researcher is encouraged to articulate carefully where (s)he is standing in order to see what she perceives in the analysis of the transcript. Others should be able to take her perspective and understand what she saw, or dispute its limitations. In such a dialogical approach, researchers try on each others' interpretations, allowing a collaborative portrait of the experience to emerge that is less riddled by idiosyncratic interpretations, while at the same time having discussed these to the point that valuable insight is not lost. We agree with McTaggart (1997) that validation involves an explicit process of dialogue and "can only be achieved if there are appropriate communicative structures in place throughout the research and action" (p. 13). Interpretive validity increases as the interpretive community is composed of people from varying social locations to create a more complex and nuanced reading of the narratives and images that have emerged from research conversations. Including the authors of the collected narratives helps to avoid projections of bias by other members of the interpretive community.

Catalytic validity is key to critical action research. It asks whether the research has and will lead to creative transformation in the individuals who have participated, their community, and the larger world (Sung, 1995). Hopefully, the research not only describes the psychological dynamics of a situation in context, but points toward how the oppressive aspects of a given situation can begin to be envisioned otherwise. Following Freire (1989), we search for the actions that correspond to our understandings. Prilleltensky and Fox (1997) ask us to discern whether our research *ameliorates* the effects of oppressive realities or seeks to *transform* those realities that give rise to suffering.

Aware of the gap between our knowledge of oppression and liberation and our research and action, Prilleltensky (2003) proposes the concepts of *epistemic psychopolitical validity* and *transformative psychopolitical validity*. The former addresses our understanding of the psychopolitical dynamics of oppression in the issue at hand, and the latter our interventions toward liberation. To work toward epistemic psychopolitical validity, he asks that in each research effort we seek an understanding of the impact of global, political, and economic forces on the issue, as well as the relevant actors and their communities. In transformative psychopolitical validity, Prilleltensky (2003) suggests we ask the following questions:

(1) Do interventions promote psychopolitical literacy?
(2) Do interventions educate participants on the timing, components, targets, and dynamics of best strategic actions to overcome oppression?

(3) Do interventions empower participants to take action to address political inequities and social injustice within their relationships, settings, communities, states, and at the international levels?

(4) Do interventions promote solidarity and strategic alliances and coalitions with groups facing similar issues?

(5) Do interventions account for the subjectivity and psychological limitations of the agents for change (p. 200)?

As research becomes a more collaborative process, Wertz (Personal communication, 2006) emphasizes the importance of delineating distinctive contributions psychologists may be able to make. Those trained in psychologies of liberation are aware that oppressed communities may sadly replicate the dynamics of oppression they are caught in through horizontal violations and violence. The co-creation and sustaining of collaborative spaces for inquiry is the first and most necessary contribution psychologists can support. This requires an understanding of the dynamics of oppression and liberation. Those trained in modes of narrative analysis are needed to work with participants to share how to hear and articulate the themes within the stories people offer. This is extremely time-consuming work that goes well beyond what most community members can afford. At times a group may prefer the researcher to accomplish a thematic analysis, and, then present it to the group for discussion and processes of supplementation, revision, critique, and validation. Critical psychologists sensitive to the internalized dynamics of oppressive and traumatic conditions are able to recognize unmetabolized dominant discourses in the structure and content of narratives. When part of a process of building critical consciousness, such close analysis can help participants dis-identify with destructive and disempowering thoughts, feelings, and assumptions. Psychologists can provide bridges between formal psychological knowledge and the research areas embraced by the individuals, small groups, or communities they work with. This allows the collaborating team access to the understandings reached by associated projects. Finally, psychologists provide a way for the research findings to enrich the body of psychological knowledge through publication in formal journals and academic books, in addition to the modes of communication used within the community or group involved in the research.

Liberatory research is provisional. Its results do not seek to be overly generalized or to make the kind of universal truth claims that natural science has accustomed us to. It actively acknowledges the local context of most of its efforts. In some ways, it is a humble enterprise, self-conscious, self-correcting, and confessing of limitation. We place to the side what we already know so that we can learn from what comes forward as new, surprising, and contradicting of our assumptions and biases. The vulnerable researcher is available to being proven wrong, brought up short, to find her life changed as she is moved to action in thoughtful and heartfelt response to what she has been privileged to understand alongside others.

In other ways, critical participatory action research is a bold enterprise, its practitioners not only dreamers of a world "otherwise," but people trying to birth such a world in their research relationships, paying attention to misuses of power and to the kinds of respect and mutuality we would like to see more of in this world. It boldly tracks the dynamics of oppression and liberation, crossing disciplinary and professional boundaries as well as levels of organization from the individual, to the community, and the collective. Academic reports make room for documentary films, theatrical presentations, and visual art. Professional psychologists understand the need for interdisciplinarity and seek mentorship from cultural workers who have many of the skills and much of the critical insight so badly needed within psychology.

Such critical inquiry is an act of restoration, replacing paradigms of research that have re-inscribed social divides and failed to address the transformation of situations that cause unnecessary human suffering. Dialogue, empathic listening, and compassionate and insightful analysis and action are threads that can begin to re-member experiences that have gone unheeded. Psychological research centered in emancipatory and dialogical ethics (Sampson, 1993a) can be a restorative process, as we shall describe in the next chapter.

14
Placing Dialogical Ethics at the Center of Psychological Research

The ethical dilemmas that often surface in qualitative research are not put to rest by scrupulous adherence to the standard procedures for informed consent, anonymity, and confidentiality. "Who owns the data?" is an ethical question that participants in laboratory studies do not think to ask. Whose interpretation counts? Who has veto power? What will happen to the relationships that were formed in the field? What are the researcher's obligations after the data are collected? Can the data be used against the participants? Will the data be used on their behalf? Do researchers have an obligation to protect the communities and social groups they study or just to guard the rights of individuals? These kinds of questions reveal how much ethical terrain is uncharted by official guidelines, such as those of the American Psychological Association or of IRB reviews.

(Maracek, Fine, & Kidder, 1997, p. 641)

Any qualitative researcher who is not asleep ponders moral and ethical questions: Is my project really worth doing? Do people really understand what they are getting into? Am I exploiting people with my "innocent" questions? What about their privacy? Do respondents have a right to see my report? What good is anonymity if people and their colleagues can easily recognize themselves in a case study? When they do, might it hurt or damage them in some way? What do I do if I observe harmful cases? Who will benefit and who will lose as a result of my study? Who owns the data, and who owns the report? The qualitative literature is full of rueful testimony on such questions, peppered with sentences beginning with "I never expected ..." and "If only I had known that ..." and "I only belatedly realized

that. ..." We need to attend more to the ethics of what we
are planning and doing.
(Miles and Huberman, 1994, p. 288)

When an ethics of liberation motivates psychological research, those
schooled in psychological research must involve themselves in a process of
re-orientation toward collaboration and dialogue at each stage of research.
This requires a concerted shift in one's own role vis-à-vis the research
situation. In most qualitative studies the researcher is at the center of power
in the situation: formulating the research area, choosing the research
approach and methodology, crafting the research questions, conducting or
directing the interview process, interpreting the data, and formulating and
distributing the findings. To be part of facilitating research as a liberatory
process, this powerfully controlling role often needs to be abandoned for a
more dialogical and collaborative one at each stage of the research process.
This involves re-thinking research approaches and methodologies, reflecting
on where they may consciously or unconsciously foreclose the possibilities
of collaborative dialogue throughout the research process, thereby limiting
the development of self-understanding and empowerment for all of the
research co-participants.

Ethical guidelines for research in psychology were first developed for
positivistic methodologies modeled on the natural sciences. These methodologies involved an intentional hierarchical distance between researcher
and "subject." In addition, they broke apart the "subject" from his/her context, in an effort to narrow the study to variables that could be controlled in
a laboratory. The meanings of the research were controlled by the researcher
(see Lincoln, 1990; Mishler, 1986). The issue of a power differential between
the researcher and the researched, and between the community of the
academy conducting the research and the community being researched
were rarely thematized or understood to be ethically problematic. Doing
fieldwork and research from the perspective of psychologies of liberation
requires sustained reflection on issues of power, raising important ethical
concerns that need to be anticipated in the planning of the work and navi-
gated with integrity during each stage of engagement.

Research inspired by psychologies of liberation is less akin to mainstream
psychological research than it is to the kind of postmodern anthropological
fieldwork that focuses on collaboration, witnessing, and accompaniment
(Scheper-Hughes, 1995b). Reflection on the colonial aspects of academic
research and a purposeful shift away from colonizing research occurred in
anthropology before psychology. Anthropological fieldwork often began
with an attempt to join the context being studied, encouraging participation and relationship rather than distance between fieldworker and those
in the context being entered. As has been amply documented in anthropology, work that grounds itself in relationship presents ethical dilemmas that

are often not covered in more positivistic research. For instance, feelings of having been betrayed or deserted may arise when the researcher withdraws from the community and/or is seen to use the research primarily for his/her own academic advancement, rather than for the benefit of those with whom the research was conducted. Anthropologists often did not share their interpretations of events with the communities they studied, sometimes producing reports that enraged local communities when they read them after they had been published.

Anthropology initially flourished in and profited from an unequal power encounter between the West and the "Third World" (Asad, 1973). In a colonial context, anthropology gave "the West access to cultural and historical information about the societies it has progressively dominated" (Asad, 1973, p. 16). Much of the research it generated flowed back not to the individuals and societies studied but to the funding sources of these studies, to the academy, and in some cases to counterinsurgency campaigns organized by colonial powers. This limited the extent to which anthropology could produce subversive forms of understanding (Asad, 1973, p. 17). Postmodern anthropology has attempted to look at this shadow of fieldwork and research and to tentatively explore a more participatory form of research that is grounded in a stance that seeks to be increasingly self-reflective and aware of power issues (see American Anthropological Association, 1998). It has been critical of earlier research where the researcher could be likened to a voyeuristic spectator to what is construed as "exotic", an uninvited guest unaware of his/her tendencies toward cultural invasion. Scheper-Hughes (1995b) has been critical of anthropologists' attempt to remain politically neutral, taking refuge in cultural relativism. Her critique has its seeds in a moment where the mothers she was studying in Northeast Brazil confronted her remove and neutrality in the face of their suffering, and urged her to enter their political struggles. Through this encounter and her work in a South African township, she "want[s] to ask what anthropology might become if it existed on two fronts: as a field of knowledge (as a 'discipline') and as a field of action, a force field, or a site of struggle" (pp. 419–20).

Caught in a natural science model, psychology has been even slower and more divided in turning toward the integration of knowledge and action that would require a more radical self-assessment of its ethics. The clinical arm of psychology that has focused on individual healing has been the primary "action" orientation of the field. It has often been split off from and diminished by the natural scientific approach to psychological research conducted within academic psychology. Research from the perspective of liberation psychologies attempts to bridge the split between knowledge and action, seeking knowledge that is necessary for transformative efforts and taking pains to carry research through an action phase. It tries to assure that both the process and product of research are restorative at the individual and community levels. It often strives to provide research findings that can inform policy decisions, hoping that the larger structures that generate injustice and suffering can be changed.

The following sections are oriented around a set of queries that will help research groups to discern and work through possible ethical problems, when pursuing fieldwork or research from a critical participatory action approach. They were developed in the course of ten years of advising community and ecological fieldwork and research in a graduate program with foci on bridging depth and liberation psychologies, and on understanding individuals and groups in their social and historical context. We are explicitly taking up qualitative research, as it is usually more conducive than quantitative approaches to the kinds of questions that come forward at this interface. It is also more accessible to non-professional participants. Nevertheless, many of the ethical concerns we will be outlining occur in quantitative studies as well. Rather than state an abstract set of principles, we have tried to capture the dynamic questioning and response that characterizes an ethical approach to liberatory fieldwork and research. Such questioning is best accomplished in the company of others, to allow the work to be viewed from different perspectives. We encourage discussion using these queries with all the members of a research community. As research work is designed, dialogue is needed that thematizes and systematically addresses the ethical issues that unfold at various stages of the work. As the research process develops, unanticipated ethical dilemmas will arise that should be addressed collaboratively.

Early stages of formulating research

Most liberatory psychological fieldwork and research begins with a desire to learn something about a psychological issue within a particular community. The ethical principle of beneficence immediately appears. Paulo Freire (1989) asks us to reflect on whether the work we do mirrors *our* dream for a community or *the community's* dream for itself.

Research questions can be located on a continuum from those that are centrally important to the researcher and minimally to others to those questions which have shared importance to the researcher, other co-participants, to the community in question, and to many outside of the community. If the research question has arisen from your own personal experience, it is necessary to dialogue with others to see how their experience may or may not overlap with yours, and to find the terms of inquiry that are general enough to capture experience beyond, yet alongside of your own. The researcher needs to confront whether or not the topic is idiosyncratic to him, and whether he has failed to frame it in terms that go beyond his own specific circumstance.

One way to avoid these dilemmas from the beginning is to allow research questions to arise through dialogue with others. This is a formal part of participatory research, but can be implemented in various forms of research, both quantitative and qualitative. What are the questions that a group or community itself has and would like to explore through research? Is the research project of possible benefit to the co-researchers and their community or does the benefit go entirely to the academic researchers and others? Such considerations move us from needing to attain "informed consent" to a study conceived privately to engaging in a collaborative process of generating the questions and procedures to be used in the research with others in a community.

Most research is extremely time consuming. Given that it is a possible resource for understanding, it should be carefully discerned with others whether and how it might contribute needed understanding and assist in individuals' and community's creative restoration. Has the formulation of the work you want to do with members of a group or community been informed by dialogue and participation with its members? Have you determined in advance what you think the community needs or wants and are you entering to deliver your understanding? If so, slow down and step back to consider what a more dialogical approach might look like. Are you able to take the necessary time to apprentice yourself to the context and allow your own pre-understandings to be challenged, negated, corroborated, or made more complex by your dialogue with others and your witnessing of the situation? Are you present to others with an openness and flexibility that allows your early definitions to shift as your participation evolves in concert with others in your setting? Ideally "outsiders" would spend time with those open to their research concerns before formulating specific research ideas. Each of us has life experience that draws us to particular communities and questions. They are a potential bridge to greater understanding, but only if held lightly as we engage with others. Others may or may not be interested in pursuing the questions we have formulated. The kind of research we are describing here comes out of spending time together, coming to know one another, and the often slow process of finding common ground and purpose.

Does one have the competence to pursue the work one is outlining, or are there steps one needs to take (i.e., supervision, training in research skills, foreign language study, adequate time in the particular field site) to increase one's competence to adequately take on the work that is being proposed (Miles & Huberman, 1994)?

Invitation to work with community participants

Both "insiders" (members of a community) and "outsiders" must negotiate with those they hope will be involved in the process of research. In both cases, a request from the researcher(s) must be met with an invitation from the individuals or group. Unfortunately, "outsiders" have gained a reputation for using communities for their own professional gain. Some would say "outsiders" should simply stay away from communities that are not their own. While not taking this position, we wish to articulate the kind of self-reflection that is needed to avoid past abuses and misuses of research privileges.

"Outsiders" have a responsibility to hold their own agenda lightly, seeking first to listen to what questions people have that research resources could be used to address. They have an ethical obligation to fully inform those they are talking with about their aims and commitments, including their institutional affiliations and funding sources.

Often "insiders" in communities also have a struggle when they try to do research in their own communities. Internalized racism, class issues, and differences in educational background can divide the "insider" coming back from the academy to do research with her home community.

In both cases we need to ask ourselves the following questions. Does our participation have the possibility of benefiting only ourselves or also the co-participants and the group or community we are approaching? Does our intrusion into a community carry possibilities of harm? How are we attending to these possibilities? Are we being clear about our purpose(s) with members of the community, i.e., have we fully informed them about the purposes of our research and what we are seeking from them? Have they extended an invitation to us with full knowledge of how we understand our participation?

It is necessary to be clear about the limits of your participation in terms of time spent there, duration of stay, and duties being taken on. Are you mindful of potential dependency on you that may arise and be difficult to responsibly handle when you exit the community? Some researchers have implicitly entered into seemingly close relationships with respondents in order to obtain "better" data, confusing respondents about the nature of the relationship. Can you be mindful of any ways you are subtly or overtly misrepresenting the nature of your relationship with your respondents, perhaps even unintentionally or intentionally misleading them?

If this is your own community and your role is shifting to that of a researcher, are the people you are speaking with clear that your conversations with them are part of a research effort? Being a member of the community involves you with others in a variety of relationships. Are any of these conflicting in a way that makes it difficult for individuals to chose not to be part of your research effort?

Gathering of co-participants

Unfortunately, sometimes a researcher unwittingly gathers co-participants who mirror his/her own experience, rather than gathering individuals who are likely to have different experiences, challenging and extending one's pre-understandings of a situation. For this reason, it is important to ask whether care has been taken to engage participants who live within the margin as it is constituted by the research project. To successfully answer this question necessitates increasing clarity about your own social location and its effects on the research situation. A straightforward way to assess this is to ask yourself and your research community who they would feel most discomfort with in speaking about the research topic. Inquire into why this is so. Ask yourself if you are stretching your comfort zone to speak with those who are most likely to disagree with your pre-assumptions and understandings. Try to sketch out the multiplicity of possible perspectives on your topic, asking yourself if you are willing to engage the variety of these standpoints (Maracek, Fine, & Kidder, 1987).

Transparency and informed consent

Have you explained face to face and in written format the process and goals of the research in a way that can be easily understood by the co-participants? Have you provided a forum for people to enter into dialogue about these?

People need to be able to anticipate where their words and perspectives are likely to show up before consenting to participation. If you are unsure of potential audiences, share this and explore with your participants whether they have concerns about the research being used adversely in particular contexts. Have you been clear about all the potential audiences of your work? Have you carefully thought through with others the possible harm that could come from this work, and have you discussed this clearly with your respondents?

Are you obtaining informed consent for your own safeguarding and fulfilling of academic requirements or are you also entering the full spirit of "informed consent," discussing the work with your respondents so that they will be able to choose freely whether or not to participate, and to what extent? If, during the course of the study, your agenda regarding the research or fieldwork diverges from what you originally told your participants, have you taken steps to update them and gain their consent for your new direction, its procedures, goals, and any changes in the intended audience? Such renegotiation is usually necessary in ongoing fieldwork and research.

In what ways might your respondent(s) not be free to choose nonparticipation? For instance, does he/she fear (perhaps rightly so!) a change in the nature of the relationship with you if the decision is not to participate? Have you been clear about whether or not respondents have veto power over aspects pertaining to them in your final report? If they have not been included in analyzing the "data," can they submit a different interpretation of data relating to themselves, if they disagree with yours?

Confidentiality

Most participants want to know that their anonymity will be safeguarded. For some, however, the offer of anonymity re-inscribes the asymmetry of power in the research relationship, where authorship goes to the researcher and anonymity to the research participants. Let your respondents know that they have a choice in this matter, thinking through with them any potential downsides regarding the disclosure or nondisclosure of identity. Individuals may wish to claim their words and perspectives as their own.

When you are working with a small community that is to be named or easily identified in your writing, be mindful that personal identities will be easily deduced, sometimes even if extreme care has been taken to disguise them. Embarrassment as well as serious kinds of harm can come to respondents when their privacy is dismantled by others being able to attribute to them thoughts and actions they preferred or needed to have remain private. One safeguard against such harm is to allow your respondents to read and approve any writing you may do that characterizes them.

At times researchers have found themselves in the unsavory position of choosing between the harm caused by revealing something unfavorable about a person or a community and the potential "good" to be gained by doing so. Such a dilemma should be addressed with others, not alone. The way we characterize communities and their participants in our writing, even when anonymity has been preserved, can be a source of hurt and anger. Read your research report as though you were each of the participants and feel your way in to how it would impact them were they to read it and were they to know others had read it. Many times researchers have made the unfortunate, and initially self-serving, miscalculation that their respondents would never read the writings about them. There may be research topics you pursue where you consciously chose to publish your findings knowing that the people you spoke with will not approve of your characterizations of them and their actions. Lifton's (1983) interview work with Nazi doctors and Ezekiel's (1995) study of neo-Nazi skinheads are examples. All the participants were informed of the research and consented to be part of it, but they were not consulted in the final analysis and presentation of the data.

Selection of interviewers

Has consideration been given to whom research participants are most likely to feel comfortable with in communicating about the issue under discussion? Is there provision for follow-up regarding a participant's assessment of the effect of the identity of the interviewer on the content of the interview? How does the social location and life experience of both interviewer and interviewee affect the particular interviewing situation?

Is the interviewer ready to be moved and changed by the conversation with the co-researcher or does she retreat into a position of pseudo-objectivity and detachment? Is she a vulnerable observer (Behar, 1996) and participant? Is the interviewer capable of partial identification? Has she placed herself alongside those she wishes to understand sufficiently to make such a partial identification, as well as to be capable of witnessing and learning from the differences between her own experiences and those of the person with whom she is speaking? The validity of a study is increased when one ensures that participants feel free to share deeply about their experience and understandings. Attention should be given to where the interviews and discussions take place with the aim of putting participants at ease, while freeing them from unnecessary distractions.

Collection of data

How are participants engaged in the research conversations? Are they only able to respond to how the researcher has cast the experience within her questions (as in responding to a highly structured questionnaire), or is the conversation open enough for the participants' experience to emerge? Mishler (1986) asks if the interviewer allows the lived context of the respondent to come fully into the interview situation. Or is the experience of the interview more akin to a "degradation ceremony" (Garfinkel, 1956) or an "identity-stripping process" (Goffman, 1961)?

If participants are fully informed about the purposes of the research, creating a conversational space where respondents can "talk back," Oakley (1981) encourages them to be able to comment on the kinds of questions asked and the research process. This has been called a "counter-interview." The honest and frank answering of questions posed to the researcher puts co-participants on more of an equal footing, and begins to shift a formal interview to a "research conversation" (Herda, 1999). Jourard (1971) showed how self-disclosure can elicit further disclosure: "dialogue is like mutual unveiling, where each seeks to be experienced and confirmed by the other. ... Such dialogue is likely to occur when the two people believe each is trustworthy and of good will" (p. 21). Self-disclosure, of course, should not be used as a manipulation to disarm the other, but as part of a mutual process of searching together for understanding. Buber (1965) says:

> But where the dialogue is fulfilled in its being, between partners who have turned to one another in truth, who express themselves without reserve and are free of the desire for semblance, there is brought into being a memorable common fruitfulness which is to be found nowhere else. At such times, at each such time, the word arises in a substantial way between men who have been seized in their depths and opened out by the dynamic of an elemental togetherness. The interhuman opens out what otherwise remains unopened.

> (p. 86)

Those involved in liberatory research are gifted when fed by this opening that extends their mutual understanding.

It is important that you have not placed your respondents in a situation where there is a conflict of interest. If the respondent depends on the relationship with you for any reason, is he/she free to share things that may displease you or disconfirm your hunches or theories? Interview situations may be positive experiences for interviewees, places where space is made for them to share experiences and points of view, and to be listened to carefully. It also has the potential to be misleading, confusing, seductive, and possibly dangerous (Kvale, 1996; Patai, 1987, 1991). At times the intimacy of the interview situation may encourage the interviewee to share things he/she later regrets. The privacy of the interview situation is different from the stark public light of presentation and publication of research. To the extent the interviewee has misconstrued the interview as a friendship situation, he/she may be sharing things for the benefit of the researcher, hoping that friendship will in turn be quickened. Allowing the interviewee to read the transcript and to veto things that may have been said is an ethical safeguard against some of the harm that can result from misconstruals about or misrepresentations of the interview situation.

Addressing the validity of a different ways of obtaining data, Tandon (1981) argues, "*the data-collection process that is most relevant to both parties determines its validity.* When the data-collection process is disjointed from the context and the content of the dialogues, it becomes invalid" (p. 299). Pilot conversations that are open to honest and critical feedback can be a powerful tool to assess whether interview questions and format foreclose the very world of understanding they had hoped to open. Co-participants are asked, "What do you wish I had asked you? What did we fail to talk about that you think is important to the situation we are discussing?" "Is our approach to this topic 'off' in any way? What do you think might help?" These kinds of questions enlist co-participants in evaluating the kind of data being collected.

Analysis of data

Data analysis is too often a largely unconscious interplay of the participants' meanings with the values and experiences of the data analyst. Working toward "good" interpretations involves becoming increasingly aware of how one's pre-understandings are preempting the emergence of new understanding from the data. To accomplish this the recording of reflections and inner dialogue during the analysis phase is often helpful. A researcher has specific questions that he or she wants to pose to the text, interrogating it for what it can yield regarding the topic(s) of research. Yet as we slow down and begin to listen to a text, a world is becoming disclosed and unfolded (Ricouer, 1982). This world tells a lot about the author of a text, but it also goes beyond what he/she can articulate directly. As we work with a text and begin to relax our questioning of it, we often begin to hear it as an answer.

Sometimes we are surprised to find that it answers something we had not yet been able to pose.

Gadamer (1988) says that in the deciphering and the interpreting of a text "a miracle takes place: the transformation of something strange and dead into a total simultaneity and familiarity. This is like nothing else that has come down to us from the past" (p. 145). When we begin with a text, we are situated in a horizon that is familiar to us. As "we make our own that which is said in conversation or in a text, our horizon has changed; the present (that which is alien to us) has fused with the past (what is familiar to us)" (Herda, 1999, p. 123). This is what Gadamer (1988) called a fusion of horizons.

A key path to increase consciousness about new understandings that a text offers is to work data in a group, to try out one's interpretations and subject them to feedback and criticism. This approach is maximized when the group analyzing the data is comprised of a variety of people from different contexts. Such a group can work together to clarify what questions of a narrative transcript facilitate "better" (i.e., more valid) interpretations (Brown, Debold, Tappan, & Gilligan, 1991). We each come to a narrative with our own experiences and values. Our perspectives are the edges at which we encounter the other (Gadamer, 1976). The point where these overlap with those of the narrative's author provides a beginning place to listen into the meanings of the narrative. It is from this initial place that others who are also listening can begin to help us hear what we ourselves cannot.

The inclusion of co-participants in the understanding of the data can be done in all stages of data analysis or in the final stage, giving the participants a chance to read and comment on the analysis. Carefully ask yourself and your co-participants: What might you gain from this inclusion? What might you be afraid of losing? In some cases, this questioning will lead to a fruitful interrogation of the assumptions of the data analysis process you are employing.

Not all of the research that contributes to liberatory aims is critical participatory action research, which is our focus in these two chapters. A special case to consider in the working through of ethical issues in research is that of investigations into communities that foment violence. For example, in recent years researchers have approached the Ku Klux Klan (Blee, 2002), Brazilian torturers (Huggins, Haritos-Fatouros & Zimbardo, 2002), and former South African death squad leaders in the military (Gobodo-Madikizela, 2003) for interviews. In such cases, researchers may chose not to share their results with participants in the same way they would in doing research with victims of violence. Some may argue that researchers have a right to lie to their subjects about who they are and what they plan to do with their research, that it is acceptable to pretend to be doing empathetic participatory research or participant observation while planning to expose confidences and publicize secrets. These breaches of relational ethics should be discussed with others. Because research with violence workers has the potential to prevent harm, to forestall attacks, and to expose secret terror to public scrutiny such choices must be carefully considered. The ethical responsibilities of academic or journalistic research cannot be assessed in isolation from social context; and the researcher is always undertaking an action that will influence that context even when that is not intended. Liberation psychology rejects the notion of the neutral researcher who is only increasing knowledge in the abstract, who feels that academic publishing is sufficient action. Since the research will affect outcomes in the world, we are asked to sort through as consciously as possible, with input from an interpretive community, what values we represent and what ethical responsibility we bear in each research setting.

Discussion and communication of findings

Ordinarily discussion and communication of psychological findings happens within the professional group(s) of the researcher. Too often, results of research have been whisked away from co-participants and their community. In liberatory approaches discussion and communication with the participants and the community from which they come is a critical component of the research. When a researcher involves a group of participants in research without attention to how the knowledge derived can be of some use to them, one can characterize such research as cultural invasion, where the ends of the researcher are satisfied without regard to those of the participants. The research community needs to ask what the implications of the research are for the group being studied. Obviously, such questions are best answered through dialogue.

Sometimes an overly academic presentation of a final report is not helpful to the community the research has come from. Sharing the results with those who have participated in an accessible manner allows the knowledge gained to be demystified (Smith, 1999). Through such sharing the participants are more empowered to use the understandings derived from the research to further their goals. Make sure that there are forums and feedback opportunities provided for where the study can be discussed, criticized, and its implications reflected on. At times, the wider dissemination of particular research may serve to harm the community one has studied. A researcher may be faced with foregoing a wider audience, in order to keep faith with the people on whom she has depended for that work.

Implementation of findings

Educational research has amply shown that when teachers are asked to implement changes suggested by outsiders' research, little long-term change takes place. The researcher—even if bringing ideas congruent to the teachers'—is experienced as an alien force, attempting to override the teachers with expert knowledge. If teachers are involved from the beginning with the research, the potential for long-term change is enhanced.

To implement findings within a social context, the participants need to be the main catalysts for change. Ideally, the research has felt as though it has arisen from their own experiences and queries, addresses their areas of concern, and can then lead to changes that will positively affect their well-being. Such collaborative involvement maximizes the potential that the research findings will actually lead to positive social change.

Conflicts of interest

Additional ethical issues arise when funding is obtained for one's study from outside of the community one is working with. In such cases, the researcher must attempt to clarify to whom loyalty is owed, and to be clear about this with all parties concerned. For instance, after painful experience, most anthropologists refuse governmental contracts with a secrecy clause. Such a clause requires that the funder receive a report of the research, but not the community being studied (Rynkiewich & Spradley, 1976). Carefully think through how contractual and informal obligations with your funding source may lead to betrayal of those you are partnering with in your research.

When publication of research becomes financially profitable, who should profit? In what ways might the community from which the research came be helped to profit? The ethics of this issue becomes more pressing if one has "studied down" in one's research, so that the economic need of the research participants is marked in contrast to the researcher (Patai, 1987). Even if publication does not incur profit, it is likely that the researcher will incur indirect benefits from the research (career building, status) (Patai, 1987). What steps can be taken to insure that all the parties to the research incur benefit commensurable to their efforts?

Chrisman (1976) describes how he became embroiled in a conflict of interest between the secret society he had joined for the purpose of a study and the possible publication of his findings that included material the society did not want to be public knowledge. Such a conflict might well have been anticipated at the outset. With full disclosure of the researcher's intentions, respondents may chose not to share information they do not want circulated. While this may compromise the extent of knowledge gathered, it does not involve deception and betrayal.

Social responsibility

At times researchers seek entrance into a community without deliberation regarding whether they can adequately honor the relations they develop. Liberatory research can often end up asking more of us than we at first have anticipated. Phenomenology speaks of fidelity to the phenomenon being studied. Liberation psychology must include some ethical measure of fidelity and commitment to the people one has partnered with and to the issues that have come forward.

Daphne Patai (1987), an anthropologist who interviewed Brazilian women suffering poverty, argues that we should not deceive ourselves that we have satisfied our moral obligations by "furnishing opportunities for otherwise silenced people" to share their voices, when "our obligations must extend beyond the immediate situation to the structure that allows that situation to be perpetually reproduced" (p. 21). It may well be that a psychologist's economic and status privileges permit them easier access than some of their research participants to policy-level changes beyond the local context of the research. At its most participatory reach, however, critical research plans for the clear inclusion of participants who would like to assist in structural changes. In Chapter 12, for example, we presented the work of Augusto Boal in Brazil with Legislative Theater. Here a process of local community theater work helped citizens to share their dilemmas and desires for change. Through Theater of the Oppressed techniques, participants rehearsed transformative approaches to their difficulties. These were then offered to legislative bodies in order to effect legislative changes that would improve their daily lives.

In the course of liberatory research, you may witness suffering, violence, extreme poverty, or degradation of status. One of the deepest discernments for a researcher in this tradition is determining what our witness requires from us. What responsibilities toward the community emerge vis-à-vis addressing these conditions? Even if you have done no harm, and have treated members of the community with respectful consideration, is your engagement with a particular community or issue terminated when you have collected all of your fieldwork or research data? In what ways might what you learned through your research implicate you morally to further engagement with a community or the issues it suffers?

Many contemporary researchers are finding that they struggle with these questions even if they have few clear answers. This discernment is part of an ethical approach to fieldwork and research. It is necessary but insufficient to determine if any of your research could be used to oppress or undermine the community you write about, as happened to many communities that anthropologists studied. In critical participatory action research, the researcher is asked to look at the structural causes of the situation being studied and to address how these could be transformed.

McTaggart describes validation as "an explicit process of dialogue" that "can only be achieved if there are appropriate communicative structures in place throughout the research and action" (1997, p. 13). We hope that the queries above will open and sustain dialogues that will lead to research that has validity through integrity. The concerns are intended to be suggestive, rather than exhaustive. Our intent has been to engage you in a process of reflecting on the ethical issues embedded in your fieldwork and research that will hopefully become an organic part of your way of thinking about and practicing inquiry.

15
Dreams of Reconciliation and Restoration

Through all the sorrow of the Sorrow Songs there breathes a hope—a faith in the ultimate justice of things. The minor cadences of despair change often to triumph and calm confidence. Sometimes it is faith in life, sometimes faith in death, sometimes assurance of boundless justice in some fair world beyond. But whichever it is, the meaning is always clear: that sometime, somewhere, men will judge men by their souls and not by their skins. Is such a hope justified? Do the Sorrow Songs sing true?

(Du Bois, 1903/1989, p. 214)

"[A] hope—a faith in the ultimate justice of things" feeds dreams of reconciliation and restoration in the midst of oppression and in the aftermath of violence. Today more and more people live in situations where there has been a recent history of community or family violence. When they live within differing national or regional boundaries, victim and perpetrator can retreat to separate spaces and build up border fortifications; but those who continue to live together in the same territory after such events are often forced to renegotiate their relationships in an atmosphere of anger, mistrust, and misunderstanding. Young people who come of age in periods of catastrophe are more likely to be educated in warfare, revenge, and suffering rather than peacemaking. Without the thoughtful building of alternative nondestructive paths to livelihood, pride, empowerment, and a sense of community, hatred will flourish, giving rise to further cycles of violence. The economic chaos that frequently follows periods of violence will mean that many will be forced to migrate or turn to crime in order to survive. Those privileged to remain sheltered outside such scenarios often feel helpless in the face of so much devastation. Yet if no effort of reconciliation is taken after collective or personal violence, wounds may fester for generations causing repeated cycles of aggression. The past will haunt the present, and it will be subject to ideological manipulation.

313

Lederach (1999) differentiates efforts at reconciliation based on whether they are grounded in a focus on the past, the present, or the future. Truth commissions bend back toward the past to establish an official record of what transpired, so that it will be possible to forge a future in common. In some postconflict situations, it can be too soon to renegotiate the past, and yet common needs call forth joint efforts across historical divides. The past is bracketed until a later moment. In other situations it proves impossible to establish new solidarities regarding the past and even about the present. Parties may be so traumatized and exhausted that the only thing that can be agreed on is a hope for the future, a common hope that their children and grandchildren will be spared the loss and violence that has maimed their parents' lives.

In this chapter, we are going to discuss both reconciliation and restoration in situations where there has been violent conflict and abuse of power. By exploring examples of reconciliation and restoration from varied local contexts, psychologies of liberation are capable of acting as forces for cross-fertilization, cross-hybridizing needed approaches for individual, community, national, and international healing. We will use the term "reconciliation" to refer to the still distant dream about whole countries with a violent past coming to an honest national consensus about facts and causes of historical wrongs and agreeing on a program of healing, reparations, peace, and hope. National reconciliation of this scope has to be led by governments because it involves everyone and affects national policy. Many argue that such reconciliation has not been accomplished anywhere, though there have been important efforts to engender it. Following Arendt, Scheper-Hughes (2004) proposes the ironic term "un-doing" to address the nearly impossible task of re-conciling what was never conciled in the first place.

We are defining restoration as efforts to heal fragmented social networks that fall short of formal national and international processes. These occur during a transitional period between epochs of hatred and mistrust caused by violence and an eventual period of reconciliation that could extend many years into the future. They may happen at the family, group, community, and intercultural levels of organization. Restoration does not imply a return to a golden age in the past, but a compassionate proactive awareness of ruptured flows of relationship and communication in the present that may be reopened in the future. They do not have to wait for government efforts, and in fact they have an important role in bringing about and hastening such efforts. Such grassroots initiatives till and enrich the soil out of which the desire for broader reconciliation may grow.

Efforts of restoration are central to liberation psychologies, because people cannot thrive outside of social networks. Research has repeatedly shown that people living in isolation or with few social ties, or in environments where there is an extreme inequity in wealth and/or little social trust, have a much greater incidence of illness, stress, and heart attacks. According to Kawachi, Kennedy, and Lochner (1997):

> The notion that social cohesion is related to the health of the population is hardly new. One hundred years ago, Emile Durkheim demonstrated that suicide rates were higher among populations that were less cohesive. In 1979, after a nine-year study of 6,928 adults living in Alameda, California, epidemiologists Lisa Burkman and S. Leonard Symes reported that people with few social ties were two or three times more likely to die of all causes. ... The lower the trust between citizens ... the higher is the average mortality rate.
>
> (p. 57)

Liberation psychologies are focused on the long-term well-being of individuals, communities, and environments. Essential to this concern is the rebuilding of relationships of trust, care, and neighborliness where they have been broken, or establishing them for the first time when they have been absent.

Prerequisites for reconciliation

Efforts of formal reconciliation often begin when trust, care, and neighborliness have been so breached that informal efforts of repair are insufficient to allow people to begin to move forward again toward a common future. Generally what victims of violence, torture, marginalization, or apartheid want (along with their families and allies) during a period of postconflict transition has been virtually impossible to achieve. Once safety has been guaranteed, most victims want a full public accounting of what has happened, complete with material and forensic evidence and testimony. They deserve open discussion in the press and government institutions. They want perpetrator's identities and structural issues such as racism and economic exclusion openly named and acknowledged. They desire public apologies, hopefully accompanied by a sense of remorse and contrition, and safeguards that human rights violations will not be allowed in the future. They hope for an examination and analysis of the conditions and ways of thinking that allowed violence to occur. They want the education system to present an honest and complete accounting of historical injustice as part of school curriculum. Particularly those who lost family members wish to prosecute publicly those responsible through the legal system with sentences to include imprisonment and/or capital punishment. They may want compensation, redress, or reparations for lost livelihood and life possibilities. Finally, they want a commitment to new opportunities in the future. This will involve a movement away from repeating cycles of vengeance and warfare. For some, it will entail a movement toward forgiveness, allowing wrongs to be placed in the past, freeing the present and the future from vengeful anger and the use of energies for exclusion. For others, the notion of forgiveness will remain unthinkable.

In general, perpetrators and their families and supporters want a general amnesty absolving everyone who participated in crimes of violence. When questioned publicly about their role, many lie outright or claim to have been ignorant of what was happening. Others will state that they were simply following orders and doing their patriotic duty to secure their country from threats. They often idealize the former government or period of time as a golden age, mourning its passing and claiming hero status for militants, generals, and politicians who led the fight for order and progress in the face of threat from antigovernment insurgents. They are not usually interested in commissions that attempt to discern details and facts about past history. In many cases, such people or their friends are still in power during transitional periods and can still control most of what happens. When this is the case, the desires of victims and their families go largely unrealized and a sense of further insecurity and fear pervade the atmosphere.

It is very difficult to negotiate these differences that leave communities divided into factions with little communication and empathy. The future of reconciliation projects depends partly on shifts within bystanders that enable them to become witnesses, achieving a critical mass of witnesses who are willing to take a stand for a more peaceful future. Crucial to the effort are former bystanders who begin to grasp that their own well-being and that of their neighbors depends on the opening of their hearts and minds to the suffering and complexity they have defended against. This may involve listening to victims' testimonies in order to confront one's denial and awaken benumbed pathways to connection and action. The bystander's journey during processes of reconciliation must also involve a critical analysis of the societal pressures and ideologies that were foundational to the eruptions of violence and injustice. The moral challenge of confronting whether or not one's own social location contributed to the suffering and violence will need to be embraced, requiring fantasies of one's own neutrality to be surrendered. When internal and external bystanders unite in efforts to increase awareness and support needed transformation, even such defended structures as the Berlin Wall can be torn down. Public opinion altered the course of the Vietnam War, slavery, and women's suffrage in American history. The first steps toward reconciliation projects may be opening spaces where bystanders are called to painfully witness what has not yet been understood.

For perpetrators and their associates to ethically re-enter postconflict society and participate in efforts of reconciliation, they must also begin to experience the pain their actions have caused others, sometimes achieved through listening to the testimony of victims or their families. There will need to be a rupture in their previous understandings and commitments that encouraged and justified their actions. A deep level of analysis will need to be set in motion, so that they can begin to grasp the social and economic forces that they were engulfed by and which predisposed them to violence (Staub, 2001). Such an analysis is not embarked on to excuse their actions but to encourage their understanding and acknowledgment of their wrongdoing.

In teaching about his training work to create situations for reconciliation and restoration in postconflict Rwanda, social and peace psychologist Ervin Staub (2001) stresses the importance of critically understanding the local history shared by all members of the conflict. This includes an articulation of the instigating conditions for violence that may include poverty and severe economic instability, political and social chaos, and scapegoating ideologies promulgated by those in authority to deflect attention from their governmental mismanagement and corruption. As Freire warned from his experience in the Brazilian context, analysis needs to move beyond the blaming of single figures to understanding the socioeconomic and political system that generates corrupt leadership. Staub found that in situations where victims and perpetrators can discover they were suffering at the hand of the same system, new solidarities can be found to change the underlying societal structures that predisposed the situation to violence and injustice.

Government projects of reconciliation

We cannot be naïve about settling such intractable historical arguments at a national level during the period following violent events. Many transitional governments have set up official government commissions to hear testimony about incidents of violence during a previous regime. In the 25 cases where government truth commissions (List of Truth Commissions, n.d.) have played a role in the last 25 years—such as those in South Africa, Chile, Argentina, Peru, Liberia, and East Timor—the legal and political frameworks of the transitional governments that convened them necessitated tradeoffs. In order to avoid military coups or a new upsurge in violence, caution seemed prudent in prosecuting military officers who were still in power. Blanket amnesty was often deemed necessary. Usually a new collaboration of elites used the concept of national reconciliation to create legitimacy for a reconfiguration of government that would ensure rule of law and governability without significantly transforming underlying economic relationships. In some cases, as in Peru, proceedings were denied wide media attention, allowing those in power to claim a reckoning had occurred, protecting those responsible for the losses, without it touching many of those who had bourne them. In some cases, as in South Africa, the truth and reconciliation process is imagined as focused and short term, encouraging people "to remember in order to forget" (Hamber, 1998, p. 2). Official processes of reconciliation will need to be supplemented with restorative initiatives for generations to come.

Some official truth commissions have made important gains in bringing to light information about human rights abuses and opening spaces for public dialogue about the past. In many cases they have allowed a fragile truce to remain intact, avoiding further civil war. Yet, often they have fallen far short of the goals of healing and reconciliation. Mahmood Mamdani (in Castillejo-Cuéllar, 2007) is one of the many dissatisfied with the outcome of the South African Truth and Reconciliation Commission (TRC).

> Injustice is no longer the injustice of apartheid: forced removals, pass laws, broken families. Instead the definition of injustice has come to be limited to abuses within the legal framework of apartheid: detention, torture, murder. *Victims of apartheid are now narrowly defined as those militants victimized as they struggled against apartheid, not those whose lives were mutilated in the day-to-day web of regulations that was apartheid.* We arrive at a world in which reparations are for militants, those who suffered jail or exile, but not those who suffered only forced labor and broken homes.
>
> (p. 32)

Government truth commissions framed within a legal structure concerned with human rights abuses have tended to focus on testimonies of individuals who were wronged, presenting them as passive and innocent victims. In many cases, these choices silenced other important narratives about the creative work these individuals were doing as active participants in transforming their societies. Many "victims" were labor or youth organizers, cultural workers, educators, or members of political and military organizations struggling for social and economic justice over many years. According to Elizabeth Oglesby (2007) writing on Guatemala, "It is not just that people suffered atrocities, but that they were targeted in the majority of cases because they were members of social organizations, such as peasant leagues, progressive church groups, unions, student groups, and so on" (p. 81). Many people have been hesitant to talk about their activist work because "social organizing was stigmatized through years of repression and the manipulation of language (even unarmed activists were often called 'subversives'), producing both fear and 'clandestine habits'" (p. 80).

In situations where victimhood and perpetration were traded back and forth, individuals are sometimes reluctant to publicly voice their suffering for fear of being denounced for their own violence. The heavy silence that hangs over such communities follows them as refugees from both sides settle side by side into neighborhoods far from home.

In most cases, government truth commissions are short-term projects lasting only a few years. Afterward, the multivolume reports are easily

buried and ignored or denounced by former or current military and government leaders as lies and distortions. However, for popular organizations,
they have sometimes been important milestones vindicating years of work
and linking many local experiences to a larger national picture. Most victims
end up wanting more than they got: more prosecutions, information,
response, and commitment to reparations and future structural changes.
It is difficult to create and define working methodologies for reconciliation,
despite an ever-increasing need for them. While most people want peace, it
has been hard to create methods to implement national reconciliation in
such a way that they are acceptable to both perpetrators and victims.

Hizkias Assefa (n.d.), founder of the African Peacebuilding and
Reconciliation Network in Nairobi, Kenya, says, there is little understanding
of what reconciliation means among social scientists. While theologically
minded people may be better equipped to discuss the concept, they have little experience putting conceptual understandings into practice (Assefa,
n.d.). Despite a rhetoric of reconciliation, even methods that have been
granted some success, such as some of those of the South African TRC, are
judged in starkly different terms depending on the social location of the
speaker. What to some may seem like inspiring movement toward societal
reconciliation, may to others appear as "reconciliation propaganda" that
artificially manipulates decontextualized histories into "scenarios of forgiveness" (Castillejo-Cuéllar, 2007, p. 13).

In Rwanda traditional ceremonies called *gacaca* were promoted by the
government to international donors as a process of local truth and reconciliation. Waldorf, researching the government's use of reconciliation rhetoric
to secure international aid, raised a red flag.

> [*Gacaca* narratives] point up the problematic nature of humanitarian and
> reconciliation discourses, which often insist on simple dichotomies
> between victims and perpetrators. Finally, they show how well-meaning,
> post-genocide interventions (such as international donor funding for
> gacaca) may become complicit in an authoritarian regime's legitimation
> strategies.
>
> (Waldorf, 2006, p. 18)

In Guatemala, USAID (United States Agency for International
Development) introduced a multimillion dollar human rights and reconciliation program to fund human rights groups around the country. Each project had to display the same USAID logo with a stars-and-stripes pattern
many Guatemalans associate with the USAID model villages program of
the 1980s that funded the Guatemalan genocide, obviously undermining
the credibility of such projects. Now the USAID, acknowledging the failure
of the reconciliation rhetoric, is funding education projects that attempt
to impose "a culture of peace" to replace what they say was the cause of

genocide: "a culture of violence" (Oglesby, 2007, p. 90) carried out by individuals who have been improperly educated. According to Oglesby (2007), this redefinition of the conflict "precludes any discussion of the broad social forces aligned on both sides, the deep social and political cleavages, and the diverse forms of social mobilization around particular political-economic visions" (p. 91).

In Chile, Elizabeth Lira has defined many obstacles to any project of reconciliation after participating in the 1999 *Mesa de Dialogo* (Round Table on Human Rights) with representatives of the military, human rights lawyers, religious organizations, and selected academics. The opening event was repudiated by human rights organizations and the Association of the Relatives of the Disappeared who refused to participate and demonstrated outside. Afterward Lira (2001) wrote:

> The victimizers do not characterize themselves as such but rather as saviors and heroes. This view is reminiscent of the claim by the Spanish Inquisition that they did not victimize but purified and restored social health. Memory of "the past" conveys different moral meanings; without remorse or at least understanding the possibility of remorse, the process of reconciliation can hardly begin.
>
> (p. 118)

For Lira, and many others, it seems impossible to agree even on what reconciliation might mean in the Chilean context:

> [T]he greatest obstacle to building a culture of social peace is that negotiating the terms of "reconciliation" takes place under the cloud of the residual social fear created by the dictatorship and its institutional legacy. Calls for prudence and moderation, juxtaposed with insistence on "truth and justice," reconfirm for victims and their families the enduring effects of the military regime in the present and the transformation of Utopian dreams into an insistence on seeking "the possible" as defined by the victors in September 1973.
>
> (p. 118)

The work of reconciliation cannot be accomplished all at once. A society will need to return to it as conditions for fuller disclosures and accountability are created. Even when a unified narrative has been forged and is officially validated, it will be assaulted from the sides by a multiplicity of conflicting accounts. There is an "inescapable inadequacy of each possible response to collective atrocities" (Minow, 1998, p. 5). Reconciliation at a national level requires support from civil society initiatives before, during, and after formal national efforts. Understanding restorative justice is essential to the work needed at the individual, community, intercommunity, and national levels.

Retributive versus restorative justice

Bishop Tutu, who led the South African TRC, has been a powerful advocate for the concept of restorative justice:

> We contend that there is another kind of justice, restorative justice, which was characteristic of African jurisprudence. Here the central concern is not retribution or punishment. In the spirit of ubuntu, the central concern is the healing of breaches, the redressing of imbalances, the restoration of broken relationships, a seeking to rehabilitate both the victim and the perpetrator, who should be given the opportunity to be reintegrated in the community he has injured by his offense.
>
> (Tutu, 1999, p. 5)

Promoting the idea of restorative justice necessarily leads to a reflection on the limits of a democracy framed within the logic of retributive justice. Governmental attempts at shoring up transitional coalitions have failed to mark the ways in which long-standing institutions of supposedly democratic countries have always silenced those set aside by society. In its early incarnations, democracy was based on the notion of two stations of humanity: the upright citizen who votes and follows rules, or at least who can break the law with impunity (male, racially/ethnically privileged), versus the "other" who has few, if any, rights and cannot vote or participate in legislative and judicial bodies (the "criminal," the "alien," the colonized, the slave, the immigrant, prisoners, detainees, women, the mentally ill, and children). Historically, those protected within the system of law have obligations to each other that they do not have to members of excluded classes who are seen as having lesser value and capacities. Over time the others may be thought of as less than fully human and as incapable of proper decision making. There is a general agreement that environments of genocide and human rights abuse begin with such discourses of dehumanization and exclusion. These types of discourses have been embedded within the constitutional law of democracies since their inception.

Retributive justice seeks to establish guilt and exact punishment, and to separate the guilty from the innocent. There is no attempt to knit the victims' and perpetrators' families and communities into the process. The Western legal approach is adversarial, and discourages the accepting of responsibility for one's wrongdoings (Lanek, 1999).

While denouncing grievous acts as wrong, restorative justice does not collapse the personhood of the wrongdoer with the acts. There is a critical gap between the deed and the doer that is held open. A space is theorized and believed in from which recognition, remorse, guilt, desire for forgiveness, and efforts of reconciliation may some day arise. To hold this space open requires an act of faith. In Fanon's (1967a) words: "I want the world to recognize with me, the open door of every consciousness" (p. 123). This makes it possible to imagine conditions under which the wrongdoer can be re-knit into a family or group.

There are multiple roots of restorative justice in various traditions, such as the family group conferences of the Maori, family and interfamily restorative practices of the Kanaka Maoli (Native Hawaiians), sentencing and community holistic circles of the aboriginal peoples in Canada, the peace circles of the Navajo, and Meetings for Reconciliation within Quaker communities (Brown & Bye-Brown, 2001). Comparing retributive to indigenous restorative approaches in Africa, Bob-Manuel (2000) describes the latter's attempt to see a conflict or wrongdoing within a larger context. Elders attempt to help the participants move "away from scenarios of accusation and counter-accusation, to soothe hurt feelings and to reach a compromise that may help to improve future relationships" (Brock-Utne, 2001, p. 8).

When we talk about projects of restoration and reconciliation in their historic local contexts, we are necessarily drawn into discussions of restorative justice that go far beyond democracy and constitutional law, asking us to include everyone in communities as equals, capable of learning and transformation. Moana Jackson (1988) of New Zealand has suggested that traditional Maori values promote a different sort of thinking about justice than a focus on guilt and punishment: "A Maori system would endeavor to seek a realignment of those (*Pakeha*) goals (of retribution, revenge, deterrence and isolation of the offender) to ensure restitution and compensation rather than retribution; to mediate the case to everyone's satisfaction rather than simply punish" (p. 4).

Aitken (2001) describes the process of Ho'oponopono problem solving and reconciliation in the Kanaka Maoli of Hawaii. This family spiritual practice opens a space, traditionally at the New Year, where transgressions, disagreements, and misunderstandings can come forward. This is done with the understanding that what is not right in one part of the system will affect all other parts. Following initial prayer, a family elder or respected outsider introduces the process, explores participants' resistance to it, and appeals for full participation. The elder identifies the transgression or disagreement that is understood to be a knot of difficulties (*hihia*) with a series of misunderstandings and offenses that have come before and after the specific instance of transgression.

> The elder chooses one of the difficulties, and works through it with discussion among the participants. Under firm leadership, each speaker is given latitude, and interruption is not countenanced. The speakers address the elder and do not confront others. Each person who has been affected, directly or indirectly, is asked to share his or her feelings. It is understood by all that outbursts of emotion tend to escalate and this hampers problem-resolution. ... As one level of the *hihia* is resolved, the

discussion is led to the next level, and painstakingly and thoroughly, one layer at a time, the entire knot is disentangled and its many factors are clarified.

(Aitken, 2001, p. 14)

By patiently waiting for all to be content with the resolution, the ground is prepared for confession of wrongdoing, forgiveness, and discussion of restitution. Both wrongdoers and victims acknowledge a "loosening of negative entanglements." These are then "cut off" and "buried in the ocean." The elder reviews what has transpired, declares the problem closed, offers a prayer of completion and thanks for heavenly guidance. The assembled group then eats a meal together to which each has contributed, moving back to daily life with one another.

Because restorative justice focuses on the web of relationships in community, rather than on the guilt of an individual, it does not have to wait for a crime to be committed to come into action. Because it is based on compassion and caring, one can notice early when there has been a breach or when someone is isolated and marginalized. For example, Virginia Tech killer Seung-Hui Cho had no friends at all on a campus of 25,000 students and had been bullied and made fun of throughout his education. He went through each day talking with almost no one. Teachers, counselors, and police living within structures of retributive justice felt they could not help him because he had not committed a crime. Yet here was a young person, in a wealthy institution dedicated to caring for youth, whose behavior was a long cry for help. If restorative justice had been a component of their education, students and teachers might have sought ways to incorporate him into the life of the campus or get him help rather than shunning or ignoring him. His isolation could have been marked as a wound to the collective body rather than labeling him as "weird" or "crazy". In his suicide note, he wrote, "You had a hundred billion chances to have avoided today ..." ("Massacre in Virginia", 2007, p. 1). Unfortunately, such isolation of the marginalized is well embedded in American culture, and many do not feel any obligation to turn towards others deemed unwanted.

Restoration through civil society

While the reconciliation work of official commissions of transitional governments can be extremely important in publicly addressing past wrongs and aligning the national government with hopes for a future of greater justice and peace, it is generally insufficient as a means to address the restoration of torn social networks. Psychologies of liberation hold out hope for a deeper rebuilding of society. They can play an important ongoing role in forming the spaces for public discussion and memory, in keeping alive practices for recollecting the past, and in preventing the covering over of events with lies and silence. Projects of liberation psychology can offer those who were neither perpetrators or victims, and those who were both, those who were active and those who were silent bystanders, the opportunity to witness the histories they have lived through and become participants in shaping a consensus of public interpretations of these events. From small personal exchanges to more systematic and formal frameworks for interaction, creative work can invent new ways to repair ruptured communication and relationship.

Many people have stressed the importance of civil society in carrying forward the work of truth and reconciliation through restoration projects. These projects can consist of building grassroots archives of testimony and evidence, creating sites of memory that the public can visit, developing activities such as memory tours or anniversary visits, creating curricula for teaching young people about what happened in the past, and building institutions that begin reparations through wealth sharing. In Guatemala, the 36-year internal war caused 580 massacres, the destruction of 440 villages, 150,000 deaths and 50,000 abductions or missing people (Cabrera, 1998a). Such an accounting was accomplished not by a governmental commission but by efforts of the Catholic Church and 800 volunteers who collected 5180 testimonies, documenting 55,021 victims of human rights violations. Begun in 1995 the Recovery of Historical Memory Project (REMHI) was necessary to confront governmental failure to take account of the human rights abuses against civilians, "the patterns of violence, its effects, the socio-political context of the war and the list of victims" (Cabrera, 1998a, p. 3). Cabrera (1998a) argues that the collection of testimony needs to be linked to wider societal efforts of constructing a common history and promoting deeper awareness of "the causes, effects, and consequences of state terrorism," as well as efforts "to dream new life projects" (p. 5).

Victoria Baxter (2005) has documented the work of human rights groups in Chile to create a site of memory at Villa Grimaldi, a notorious torture center during the Pinochet dictatorship. Working with and pressuring the government, the groups succeeded in putting aside land for a Peace Park, preserving remaining buildings of the torture centers with plaques, and building a wall of names for the 226 victims of torture who died at the center. The human rights groups did not invite government officials to attend the dedication of the Wall of Names because the government had refused to allow Pinochet to be tried in Spain for crimes against humanity. Baxter calls this a form of transitional justice that may take many years to complete:

> The metaphor often used to describe the process of reconciliation is one of a long road or a journey. This notion carries the sense that reconciliation as well as justice, is a process—not a single event with a clear conclusion. Transitional justice is a period of articulating a new common future for the government and for the society. This vision of the future includes one that is based on democracy, the entrenchment of the rule of

law, greater respect for human rights, and some degree of reconciliation with the past. Given the enormity of the challenge, many actors must take part in this process of building a new future, including many civil society actors, such as human rights activists, academics, and social justice organizations.

(p. 134)

During a period of transitional justice, civic organizations can attempt many creative projects to work on parts of the puzzle of how to effect reconciliation.

In Australia we can see the way in which grassroots restorative efforts might work to gradually undermine governmental resistance to efforts of reconciliation. Australians of British descent bear a 200-year history of genocidal assaults on the Aboriginal population. For over a century, mixed-race children with Aboriginal mothers and English fathers were kidnapped from their Aboriginal homes and communities and sent to punitive and deprivatory boarding schools. In 1967 a national referendum led to the first inclusion of Aborigines into the national census. According to Michael Henderson (2001), in the 1970s some Australian citizens began to address Australia's history of genocide and the continuation of cultural assault. In 1997 a governmental report was issued called "Bringing Them Home," referring to the displaced children of Aboriginal mothers and communities. It called for a national apology and the institution of a National Sorry Day. While the report led to the government's provision of 63 million dollars over four years for counseling and family reunion, it decided together with its Prime Minister John Howard to ignore the possibility of a national apology and an annual day of acknowledgment (Hoffman, 2002). A grassroots movement to hold a Sorry Day developed that included both Aborigines and non-Aborigines. With the help of churches and schools, it successfully conducted a day of acknowledgment without governmental support. More than 400,000 people participated in creating Sorry Books for the event. These Sorry Books carried personal messages of acknowledgment of and apology for "The Stolen Generations." In ceremonies throughout Australia these were given to Aboriginal elders.

Former Prime Minister Malcolm Fraser wrote a plea for apology in 2000:

Facing the truth about our past, when it is contrary to that which we have been taught for generations, is difficult. Unless non-Aboriginal Australians are prepared to look at the past honestly, there will be no real reconciliation with the Aborigines. It also involves matters of spirit. This is where an apology for past wrongs is relevant. An apology does not say "I am guilty"; it is a recognition that our society perpetuated a wrong and that we are sorry it happened. ... An apology says that by today's standards these things should never have happened.

(Hoffman, 2002, p. 1)

Members of the Stolen Generations offered a Journey of Healing to work with remaining wounds among peoples of all races.

Two years after the call for a national apology, as a result of massive and innovative grassroots efforts of restoration, Prime Minister Howard reversed his stance and offered a formal, government-sponsored apology: "The greatest blemish and stain on the Australian national story is our treatment of the indigenous people. It is important that we recognize that, we confront it and acknowledge it" (quoted in Hoffman, 2002). Such a narrative of restoration and reconciliation must exist side by side with a fuller awareness of the continuing devastation of many Aboriginal communities that suffer the psychic and social symptoms outlined in Chapter 7, and where alcoholism and petrol sniffing among the young contribute to a continuingly tragic near future. There is a 17-year difference in the life expectancy of Aboriginal versus non-Aboriginal Australians, a gap Reconciliation Australia (n.d.) is trying to eliminate. Apology alone cannot put a tragic past in order or solve the ongoing devastation that is accruing from it. It does provide a new symbolic starting point from which efforts of healing can be renewed with greater consensus.

To address the sequelae of trauma, many societies need integrated approaches to reconciliation, restoration, and healing. Liz Murphy (2005) outlines this in her work on the aftermath of abuse and neglect of children in Catholic-run child welfare institutions in Ireland. Side by side with the victims' and families' needs for individual and family therapy, there were needs for formal acknowledgment of abuse and subsequent apology, not only from the Catholic orders involved, but by the national government. The latter had annually inspected the orphanages and schools and turned a blind eye to the abuses they could have noted. In her own restorative small group work, she addressed the need for dialogical processes within the Catholic orders involved. Some perpetrators are in prison; others not. Some members were passive bystanders to perpetration. Some were present but were not aware of the abuse. All have been affected by the stories of victims, national attention, and feelings of shame. Healing within religious orders is foundational to the wider work of apology and repair. The work of repair depends not only on the relational work of testimony, acknowledgment, apology, and potential forgiveness. It depends on a critical look at the institutional structures of life for the religious that provided the soil for abuses, as well as the structures of relation between of the state, civic society, and the church. Murphy's work also highlights the way in which art provides a yeast to efforts of individual and collective insight and healing.

Most restoration projects consciously attempt to rebuild relationships of participatory communication in order to heal historical wounds through commemorative work, education, policy initiatives, and sharing of resources. In restoration projects, everyone can play a role as witness and participant, no matter what their history has been. The goal here is beyond confrontation, protest, interruption, or testimony related to past wrongs; restoration projects attempt to imagine and enact in the here and now the kind of meditative commemoration of the past, repair of relationships, and dialogue about the future we hope for in peaceful communities and balanced environments. The work is frankly utopian, offering up models that awaken us to new possibilities for living with a troubled past. These projects are exemplary, creating oases of restoration in a desert of embattled histories where nothing new can grow. The hope is that over time, the transformed microclimates will affect the larger environment around them.

A visionary commemorative project with a goal of restoration has been developing in recent years in relationship to the bicentennial of the Lewis and Clark expedition of 1804–6. The bicentennial might have produced just another scattering of heroic monuments and official history, but a number of visionaries, Native American leaders, and environmental activists in the region had other ideas. Many of them had heard of the work of Maya Lin on the Vietnam and civil rights memorials and they wanted her to come and work with them. They spent several years calling and visiting her, sending along a box of rock, sand, shells, and feathers from the Columbia River Basin, before she agreed.

From the beginning, the commemoration that came to be called the Confluence Project was conceived as an attempt at restoration of the river, wetlands, and salmon and bird habitat, as well as the social webs that had been broken through imperial conquest. Lin's subtly spiritual approach to her work builds bridges among realms: honoring ancestors, inviting contemporaries to reflection, and awakening desires to protect future generations. In the Confluence Project, Lin has worked closely in an unprecedented way with the Umatilla Confederated Tribes, the Nez Perce Tribe, civic groups, and official Lewis and Clark bicentennial committees.

At each significant meeting site of Native Americans with members of the Lewis and Clark expedition, Lin will design landscape and memorial sculptures with excerpts of Native American stories and Lewis and Clark's diaries. These sites will mark the beauty and diversity of the environment that existed 200 years ago, providing reflective sites where dialogue and rethinking might occur as this abundance is compared to the social and ecological devastation that exists today. The project is linked to local school curricula, involving large numbers of students and teachers in the study of local history and environmental restoration. Local organizations and foundations are in the process of raising 22 million dollars to complete the project. The Confluence Project (n.d.) aims at dialogue and healing:

Looking to the future, the Confluence Project can raise questions, heighten awareness and offer hope. What has happened to the abundance of life that teemed within, above and around the Columbia 200 years ago? Despite the environmental damage the river has sustained, the sites of the Confluence Project can mark important turnabouts in the health of the river and in the life of the land's native people. The Confluence Project—like Lewis and Clark's journey—is an exploration of our potential to make the future better than the past.

(The Confluence Project)

A similar project in Los Angeles is attempting to restore the Los Angeles River. Hundreds of schools, community organizations, and governmental agencies are participating in a review of the history of the river and its environment and planning for dozens of small parks, bike paths, and riverside recreation areas that will incorporate the river once again into the life of the city. The project has a strong focus on environmental justice, as the river runs through some of the poorest neighborhoods, which will now have new parks and recreation facilities. Of course, some fear that developers and bankers will derail the project for their own benefit, using it to replace ever more low-cost housing along the river with luxury condos that few can afford. Nevertheless, the project is visionary at this stage, inviting everyone to participate in envisioning the Los Angeles of the future, with community meetings and school workshops built into the process to create a master plan for restoring the social and ecological environment.

Because the outcome of generations of violence and marginalization has led to profound income gaps and impoverishment, many innovative restoration projects at the grassroots level are attempting to focus on wealth transfer as a form of repair. These projects are different from impersonal missionary collections or charity, focusing instead on direct dialogue among all participants. For example, the Women for Women International project, begun by Zainab Salbi with $2000 in wedding gifts when she was 23 years old, has blossomed into an organization in nine countries and a network of 166,000 sponsors and donors. With projects in Bosnia, Afghanistan, Nigeria, Congo, Kosovo, Colombia, Sudan, and Rwanda, they have transformed the lives of 30,000 women and affected 160,000 community and family members. They direct their energies to refugee camps containing women who have been raped and made homeless by violence. In the camps, the work focuses on emotional support, dialogue, and the fulfilling of basic rights and necessities. The women use forms of participatory research to assess their strengths and needs, deciding on skills to acquire and types of work that could be developed locally. Many form cooperatives that can market goods together. In Rwanda, this evolved into a project where Hutu, Tutsi, and Twa women sat side by side weaving baskets for market, and beginning to think about reconciliation in new ways. The money they earn allows them to send children to school, feed their families, provide jobs for others, and bring resources such as water to their villages.

On the side of the sponsors, who are linked to individual women for a year, the effect is often life changing. Sponsors provide a small stipend to support—as little as $30 a month—and are in regular contact through letters and photographs with the women they sponsor. They provide witness to and support for previously unimaginable situations. The sponsor is opened to a new form of friendship across borders that break paradigms of insularity and noninvolvement. Women for Women International sponsors conferences and tours where sponsors can gather together to meet and discuss issues with each other and hear from recipients about what has altered in their lives. This changes the lives of sponsors as they begin to discuss international human rights issues in public contexts, which may energize their own vision and leadership capacities. As the organization grows, it creates a huge network of repair of relationships within families and communities, and across borders. While these efforts cannot provide reparations to victims of violence, they can help to rebuild neighborhoods after catastrophe, transform bystanders to witnesses, and begin a transitional process leading toward truth and justice.

Kiva.org in San Francisco, which has linked microcredit with the Internet, began a similar project with a new twist. Kiva means unity or agreement in Swahili. Kiva.org is built on the pioneering work of Nobel Prize winner Muhammad Yunus and the Grameen Bank, which has given seven million dollars in small loans to women in poverty, but moves the locus of lending from banks to private individuals. Joining forces with local agencies in dozens of countries, Kiva.org relies on the agencies on the ground to organize, screen, mentor, and monitor potential enterprises that can help the poorest to begin earning money to support and educate their families. Many of these agencies involve potential recipients in analysis of local conditions and discussions of planning, as well as providing skills training. As projects are developed, profiles are listed on the Kiva.org Internet site, giving information about the situations of the individuals involved, their plans, and financial needs. Potential donors log onto the site and make loans that they assign to specific projects that agree to begin repayment within the year. After Kiva.org was featured on the PBS documentary program *Frontline* in 2006, the site crashed for days because so many people wanted to be involved. Once a loan has been made, sponsors stay in regular e-mail contact with recipients learning about the development of their project and often forging personal bonds. In the process, they learn about conditions of unimaginable suffering created by the globalization that pretends to create progress, development, and wealth. So far millions have been loaned with a payback rate of 99.83 per cent. People all over the world who are distressed by the expansion of world poverty can now participate directly in its amelioration without waiting for governments or the World Bank to change global economic policy.

Civic groups have also developed policy initiatives that outpace what most governments have been able to consider. In 2005 the People's Health Assembly held its second international meeting in Cuenca, Ecuador, with 1200 people from 77 countries. The meeting included 500 children through the Global Children's Forum and the launch of the first Global Health

Watch Report. The Assembly is essentially a world participatory action research program, with participants analyzing the conditions of health in their own countries and setting a grassroots agenda for health initiatives separate from those of governments, corporations, and insurance companies. Rather than stressing medicine and illness, the Assembly wanted to focus on health and community. Dr. Julio Monsalvo (2005) of Argentina, a leader of the Assembly who has worked for the last 30 years with the Toba indigenous communities in Northern Argentina, has argued that there are local visions of health that are more perceptive than the Western medical model:

> That vision has a series of consequences that in our days have become scandalous: the suicidal exploitation of nature ... and the destruction of the values of native peoples. ... Health cannot exist in the absence of true life in community and with other people and with nature ...
>
> (People's Health Assembly)

The Assembly has focused on six elements that make health possible: love, water, air, shelter, happiness, and art. Monsalvo has defined the goal of life as "alegremia," a word he coined to talk about a philosophy of being happy; "the bubbling, fizzing joy in our blood, helping us leap over mountains of doubt and fear, dissolving pride and racing past petty disagreements" (People's Health Assembly, 2005).

The goals of the Assembly are to create a grassroots vision of desired states of health and medical practice and then measure that against the actual situations that exist in local environments. In the process they hope to create a confluence of multiple cultural expressions of health, appreciating contributions from diverse locations and forming a worldwide network of democratic institutions that can advance a vision of the goals of community restoration. They see their work as part of a revolution taking place throughout the world in which many individuals and organizations are learning to reframe and revalue the conservation and restoration work they do at a local level as part of a visionary and global environmental agenda. Small acts of saving seeds, promoting biodiversity, retaining knowledge of herbal medicines, and convening community healing rituals will be built upon to imagine sustainable environments of health that in the long run, it is hoped, will transform public policy.

Another hopeful project of restoration was developed in Baghdad, Iraq, in 2004 by a group of both Sunni and Shiite men and women who created Radio Dijla. Their idea was to create a public dialogue space where every point of view could be represented, in contrast to other radio, print, and Internet sources that were reporting events through a single perspective. They never expressed their own points of view, and listeners were always trying unsuccessfully to find out who was Sunni and who was Shiite. The idea was to create a space where people could begin to experience civil dialogue in an environment where it was being rapidly destroyed. According to station founder Ahmed Rikabi:

> At first ... callers were often rude and even cursed one another. Slowly and gradually, we noticed the dialogue becoming more intellectual, more developed. After a while, people got used to listening to different opinions.
>
> (Susman, 2007, p. A3)

The station managed to stay on the air during three years of the war until it was attacked and burned by Al Qaeda on World Press Freedom Day in May 2007. "We're a symbol of unity. What we were doing is absolutely against their thinking," said Rikabi. Radio Dijla continues on a Web site for now.

All of these projects are intended to help create the scaffolding for future possibilities of reconciliation. Each is designed to build up the critical mass of witnesses who will fight for a public accounting of policies that silence dialogue about the past and continue structures of oppression in the future. For those of us who live in the United States, it is noteworthy how much we have to learn from other societies about reconciliation, how thin our own traditions and history of reconciliation and restoration are, while our need is so great and, sadly, continues to increase. The work of reconciliation and restorative justice is critical to the building of majorities that are committed to processes that promote truth and justice. During the last several decades, many groups in the United States have begun to build local memorial and restoration projects (see Chapter 12). The first truth and reconciliation process in the United States was the Greensboro TRC in 2004. More recently, Kenneth Brady has called for a TRC to examine human rights abuses that have resulted from U.S. foreign policy over the last 40 years. Joshua Micah Marshall has called for a TRC about U.S.-sponsored torture in Iraq.

Remorse, apology, and forgiveness

> Only in a spirit of generosity can the injured one let go the wrong, resist the instinct to settle accounts, and forgive the other in the name of their shared life. Beyond the moral code and legal code, the act of forgiveness can reconcile the parties and restore the sociality that sustains each one ...
>
> (Rawlinson, 2006, p. 141)

When filmmakers Frances Reid and Deborah Hoffman (2000) went to South Africa to create a documentary under the auspices of the TRC, they hoped to interview many perpetrators of violence who had taken the path of remorse. They were given just one name. In national processes of reconciliation, remorse and acknowledgment are often in short supply, limiting the healing that is available. Likewise, forgiveness is far from certain, and not always even deemed desirable. True forgiveness, Derrida (2001) argues, is always forgiveness of the unforgivable. It cannot be dictated, extracted, or manufactured. It cannot be given by governments, but only by individuals who have suffered directly. When it occurs, it graces those responsible for wrongdoing with an invitation back into the fold of humanity, giving them a chance to begin again and to act more humanely. Forgiveness is also a gift to those who find themselves able to offer it, relaxing the hold of anger, resentment, and vengeful fantasies. It rests on a living sense of our interdependence with others, between their sorrows and our own.

Engaged Buddhist Sister Chau Nghiem (2002), in the aftermath of 9/11, says,

> Forgiveness means coming back to ourselves when we are hurt or angry to take care of our pain. It is only when we are calm and lucid that we can see clearly and respond skillfully to someone who has wronged us. When we look deeply, we can see the roots of other person's actions and know that they do not have a separate self. They did not create themselves like that; innumerable conditions came together to make them who they are. With this understanding, we can begin to forgive. Forgiveness is understanding our interdependence with those who cause us to suffer and with all of life.
>
> (p. 13)

When people have suffered great losses, their capacity to forgive can help others to see the situation more clearly. In the United States, this is happening through the September Eleventh Families for Peaceful Tomorrows who have steadfastly turned away from supporting the revenge of war as a means to protest the loss of their loved ones. Instead they are working to promote nonviolent responses to terrorism and more open discussions about peaceful and just responses. In South Africa, Amy Biehl's family's forgiveness of their daughter's murderers and their search for an understanding of the conditions for that violence have inspired others to not let their losses deter them from building a more just post-apartheid South Africa. Amy Biehl was a young American who committed herself to a vision of justice in South Africa. She was murdered by a group of young men who did not know her or her work. According to Scheper-Hughes (2000), one of Biehl's murderers said:

> [H]e decided to "confess" because he was not doing well. He could not sleep. He could not have a girlfriend. He could not take up work. He could not study. His days were very dark. He hid from people. Above all, he was full of "shame."
>
> (p. 33)

He shared that he thought that if he could get Amy Biehl's father to listen to him "that would be as good as bread" (quoted in Scheper-Hughes, 2004, p. 33). Linda and Peter Biehl's forgiveness served as an act of blessing and breaking bread for the young man who confessed and his family.

The act of compassionate listening that may lead to remorse or forgiveness can be initiated from either side. Being listened to carefully by perpetrators, along with acts of apology, signal to victims that one is no longer being seen in a dehumanized way, and that thereby the threat of future violence is decreased. In some instances, it allows for spontaneous acts of forgiveness that surprise the victim herself. For instance, during processes of reconciliation in South Africa, when a policeman met with the mother of a young man he had murdered, he succeeded in carefully listening to her experience and anger. By his doing so, the mother was able to see his humanity and was moved unexpectedly to forgive him (Reid, in Payne, 2001). This acknowledgment is one of the most potent healing salves for victims and their friends and families, helping to bring some measure of closure and a renewed sense of agency.

Building families, groups, communities, cultures, and nations that are capable of offering and accepting apology for wrongs committed is lengthy and arduous work (Lee, 2007). In part, it depends on individuals coming together who have explored this dialogical path in their own lives and who see its necessity for healing on a larger scale. It requires a gathering practice of what Lederach (1999) has called "vulnerable transparency" (p. 127). Here one has come to understand the importance of trading in feelings of superiority to and difference from the other for an openness to knowing about ways in which we may find ourselves also accountable for causing pain, and sustaining unnecessary distance and animosity. One works to find a language to convey one's own concerns, fears, and hopes, and cultivates a deep listening that establishes relational and emotional contact. These skills are unfortunately still rare, and the hope for widespread remorse, apology, reparation, and forgiveness leading to reconciliation remains for the most part an important but unfulfilled dream. We can only imagine that sometime far in the future more awakened people in the United States will meditatively visit innovative shrines and monuments honoring those we have perpetrated violence against in our national history—including the Vietnamese murdered in the Vietnam War, the Africans abused and killed during slavery, the Native Americans and Mexicans exterminated during the colonial landgrab, the Caribbean and Latin American populations who perished in multiple covert interventions and military excursions, the Japanese who died at Hiroshima and Nagasaki, and the multiple generations of immigrants from all over the world who have had their dreams of a new life met with racism, xenophobia, and social exclusion. To honor together the divinity in these people would help the healing for which we thirst.

Afterword—*Tikkun Olam*: The Restoration and Repair of the World

As we entered into our collaboration ten years ago we were moved to discover that each of us was imagining our work in psychologies of liberation through the creation story crafted by kabbalist Isaac Luria, who wrote in the century following the Inquisition and the devastating expulsion of the Jews from Spain in 1492. Luria, whose exiled family settled in Safed, Palestine, developed a creation myth to express the brokenness of the world and its restoration (Scholem, 1941). In it we find elements borrowed from Heraclitus, Plato, Stoic philosophy, Gnosticism, Meister Eckhart, Yoruba myth, and Sufism. In the thirteenth century through Avraham Maimonides, who lived in Egypt, African and Arabic mysticism streamed into Jewish thought, contributing to the imagery that later blossomed in Jewish Hasidic mysticism (Block, 2001–2).

The myth imagines an incomplete creation: in the beginning, God was everywhere. In order to create, the divine had to contract and concentrate its being, to inhale, so that a space could arise. Just as a garden holds the smell of jasmine even when the plant is removed, this space held the light of the divine presence suffused in it (Ponce, 1978). Creation began with a series of inhalations and exhalations. The initial exhalation of the divine being created the first human, Adam Kadmon. From then on the divine light was channeled through Adam's eyes, mouth, nostrils, and ears. This streaming created vessels of light in order that more light could be differentiated and contained. Initially this process went well. But as the light came through Adam's eyes, it suddenly surged forward with great intensity. The fourth and earlier vessels intended to carry the energy broke under its radiance, spreading bits and pieces of divine sparks throughout the world. Sparks entered into the organic and the inorganic, into each and every being. Like seeds, each divine spark was hidden by husks, *kelipoth*, with good and evil intertwined.

In this creation story, human beings do not find themselves in a paradisiacal garden, soon to be exiled from a perfection that God has already provided. Instead, human beings find themselves in a world that is not

334

finished. Indeed, they find themselves unfinished: flawed, broken, and incomplete. There is no possible return to a paradise because it does not yet exist. Each human has a role in the work of ongoing creation, a creation that is necessarily also one of restoration—not to a former past but to potentials in the future for peace and justice. According to this creation story, this work is comprised of two interrelated aspects of restoration: *tikkun nefesh*, repair of our souls, and *tikkun olam*, repair of the world through our relations with others and nature. Our task as humans is to recognize and acknowledge the divine spark in each and every being and thing and to assist in releasing it from the restrictive shell around it. Human beings are created so that they can go through the world gathering up sparks of goodness to restore the healing wholeness of the divine. We encounter sparks of the divine in every human individual and community. Buried in the dross of conventional habits and blindness, we discover divine potentials for kindness, wisdom, love, compassion, and forgiveness. We find them also in the natural world, animals, and spiritual presences. Luria himself was known to be an expert in conversing with trees, birds, and angels (Kaplan, 1982). The work of *tikkun olam*, or repair of the world, is to release these sparks and to help them connect and strengthen in fragmented environments. The gathering of them is understood to assist in the coming of messianic time, where longings for peace, justice, and love are fulfilled (Watkins, 2004).

The commitment to restoration is prevalent in many spiritual traditions. In the engaged Buddhism that Thich Nhat Hanh (1993) has helped to create, we grow peaceful and just communities through practicing the Five Precepts of Buddhism. These orienting principles are meditated on and discussed in community. They arise from an awareness of the roots of suffering, suffering caused by the destruction and exploitation of life, social injustice, stealing, oppression, sexual misconduct, unmindful speech, the inability to listen to others, and unmindful consumption. The first precept encourages the cultivation of compassion and the learning of ways to protect the lives of people, animals, plants, and minerals. We vow "not to kill, not to let others kill, and not to condone any act of killing in the world." In the second precept, we vow to cultivate loving kindness and learn ways to work for well-being through the generous sharing of time, energy, and material resources with those in need. While respecting the property of others, we vow to prevent profiting from human or animal suffering. We vow "not to steal and not to possess anything that should belong to others." The third precept urges us to "cultivate responsibility and learn ways to protect the safety and integrity of individuals, couples, families, and societies." We promise "not to engage in sexual relations without love and a long-term commitment" and to respect the commitment of others. In the fourth precept, we vow to cultivate loving and truthful speech and "deep listening in order to bring joy and happiness" and to inspire hope and self-confidence, relieving others of their suffering. We commit to "efforts to reconcile and resolve all conflicts." In the fifth and final precept, we vow to "cultivate good health, both physical and mental ... by practicing mindful eating, drinking, and consuming ... ingest[ing] only items that preserve peace, well-being, and joy" in our body, in our consciousness, and in the collective body and consciousness of our family and society," avoiding toxins in both physical and cultural environments (Thich Nhat Hanh, 1993, pp. 3–4).

Reflecting on and practicing these precepts eventually cause an "awakening" to the world, helping us to see others—human and animal—with loving compassion and as interconnected with our own destinies (Thich Nhat Hanh, 1993). The practice of the precepts allows the veil between us and the divine to become thinner.

Because we live in an era of failed states, fragmenting cities, unprecedented violence, and assaulted ecosystems, the work of repair has never been more urgent. We are convinced that millions of people throughout the world are conscious of some part of the issues we have raised in these chapters, and have entered into processes of restoration through participatory dialogue and creative action. One can feel it in parts of Los Angeles where a vibrant mix of origins, advocacies cultures, skin tones, and arts has gone so far beyond the staid efforts of tolerance and multiculturalism that those concepts are virtually irrelevant. Standing on Grand Avenue outside California Plaza with several thousand people rapturously dancing and singing the lyrics of hybrid homegrown bands, one feels a sense of linking with others determined to live out liberatory scripts different from the imperial offerings in the mainstream media: Dengue Fever playing Cambodian rock and roll, and the Yohimbe brothers combining hip-hop and rhythm and blues. Ozomatli, merging Latin American, Chicano, and Middle Eastern genres in Spanish and English, sings out: "Now can you imagine a world without oppression / and no need to dabble in greed and transgression / ... emergency, emergency, evacuate the premises." Children and adults of all ages sing and move to these sounds with joy and radiance, interacting with others around them energized by their recognition of the vision of a just and peaceful world that is being born among them this very moment. When our gaze meets, and a brief gesture is exchanged, it is clear that we are sharing in one of the sweet ecstasies available to us as humans. There is a magnificence to this gathering that is matched by its vulnerability; that our daily life, as well as our fate and future are bound up with one another is tacitly clear. As we move together in the rhythm of this interdependence, we are aware that the world also has need of us. Here in this moment, the veil of the divine is sheer indeed.

Once one enters the participatory spaces we have been describing throughout this book, one begins to be able to recognize their distinctive effervescent feel, as various as they are: one might be among a cooperative of Kenyan women newly learning to plant and nurture trees, or a small group of mothers in Boston looking at the cultural stereotypes of mothering that have crept into their relations with their children; it might be amid a group of Dominican-American teens planning a mural about their neighborhood's history in East Harlem; or it might be a council gathering of former prisoners and their advocates in East Los Angeles trying to create community on the heels of their release from prison; or in any part of the world one might join a public conversation full of hope, where one has challenged oneself to hear past one's own position into the deeply held commitments of others.

Here too one enters a space that is framed and hallowed with vulnerability and joy, energy and common intent. It is protected from the intrusive and disruptive demands of daily life. A sheltering circle has been drawn that makes it more possible to move deeply into one's own experience and to be more fully open to other people's experiences. There is a respect given to each person present, known and unknown, an acknowledgment of the divine spark within each. There is a sense of pilgrimage toward what is longed for, while there is an excitement about learning what each other has to share through his or her different life experiences. What becomes possible will emerge because each person has participated in the ways that are given by his or her history and creativity. There is a commitment to the local, and to an unfolding sense of how this particular gathering is resonant with many others in diverse places throughout the world. Here the husk around the heart can soften and break open (Penington, 1987).

The possible work of repair is all around us and within us. It awaits us and is dependent upon us. Attention to the psychological dimensions of restoration is urgently needed, but, as we have labored to show, this attention must be grounded within the larger sociocultural context that bends back to histories that are still upon us and forward in ways that open us to engagement with visionary images and hope for a restored world. As Luria's creation story teaches us, the longing for home that suffuses us is a longing not for a past to which we cannot return or to a past that never was, but for a different way of being with each other, and a better home with one another and the natural world in the present and the future. To this longing and hope, shared by so many, we dedicate the spark of our words.

Acknowledgments

> I wrote four books under dictatorship, and social space is what I recovered for myself during that period. But never for an instant did that make up for the wrongs, the humiliations, the fear, the suffering or the powerlessness of the system's victims. Writing in that space was something passional and personal. My secret political resistance. When one lives in a world that is collapsing, constructing a book perhaps may be one of the few survival tactics.
>
> (Diamela Eltit, 1997, p. 5)

Our learning and writing about the tributary springs of psychological and community regeneration throughout the world has helped us to survive. It is these sites of restoration that nurture our hope. From their visions of liberation, we are heartened to imagine a re-orientation of psychology. We are deeply grateful to the many cultural workers and critical theorists we have written about for their transgressive ideas, creative practices, and inspiring commitments to live and work today in the manner that they ardently desire to see born more widely in the world.

We are extremely fortunate in having the opportunity to work with our editor Tod Sloan, a founder of critical psychology, whose invitation to publish, ongoing encouragement, profound grasp of the issues we address, and insightful commentary on our many drafts guided us deftly toward a more articulate book. We thank Miranda Bergman and O'Brien Thiele, the mural artists whose work graces the cover of this book. For over a decade, the images they painted on a garage door have served as a beacon for our imaginations through their juxtaposition of the suffering of oppression, injustice, and violence with the prophetic vision of vibrant, sustainable, and empowered individuals and communities, mindful of their history and joyful in their practice of community arts. We appreciate the thoughtful and careful work of the editorial and production teams at Palgrave Macmillan and Macmillan India Limited.

During our eight years of teaching together at Pacifica Graduate Institute, we struggled to create a space where the ideas of liberation psychology could be explored in relation to depth psychology, qualitative research, pedagogical practice, and community and ecological fieldwork. Our conversations were enriched by our colleagues Kathleen Jenks, Randi Kristensen, Jim Peal, Marina Roseman, and Jennifer Selig. Early in this period, our discussions with Dan Hocoy and Aaron Kipnis helped us begin to distill the orientations of psychologies of liberation (Hocoy, Kipnis, Lorenz, & Watkins, 2003). Mark Kelly, gifted reference librarian at Pacifica, generously supported us in our research efforts. For several years, our graduate program resided at La Casa de Maria, where the vision of the women and men of the Immaculate Heart Community inspired us. During this time, Cathie Walker and Diane Huerta graced us with their friendship and support. We were fortunate to be able to invite visiting faculty whose work we greatly respected, and had the pleasure of joining their classes and lectures: Gloria Anzaldúa, Mary Belenky, Raphael Ezekiel, Susan Griffin, Ellen Herda, Robin Kelley, Aurora Levins Morales, Bill Meyers, Kelly Oliver, Isaac Prilleltensky, Sallyann Roth, Edward Sampson, Chela Sandoval, Mady Schutzman, Tod Sloan, and Maurice Stevens. Years of discussion and analysis with our students and their often groundbreaking research, questions, and analyses contributed so much to our work that we cannot imagine having written this book without our immersion in this cauldron of shared intellectual life.

During our writing, we were fortunate to have many read and give feedback on portions of the manuscript, including Ed Casey, Shanna Lorenz, Ellen Moore, Jorge Osuna, Dennis Rivers, Evelyn Serranno, Kathleen Vickery, and Fred Wertz.

Mary Watkins: A work such as this unfolds over decades, bearing the fruit of so many different periods in one's life and the relationships that have blessed them. I begin in gratitude to my early mentors, James Hillman and Bernard Kaplan, who taught me how to break the vessels of the psychologies I received, to reach for understandings that are more adequate to the teloi of love, justice, and peace. I would like to thank the women of the Global Psychotherapy Group in Boston who met together in the early 1990s: Sarah Conn, Miriam Greenspan, Janet Surrey, and Anne Yeomans. Together we learned how to hear the intrapsychic and interpersonal effects of culture in ourselves, and those we were gifted to work with in psychotherapy. I continue to be inspired by Janet Surrey's clear vision of the value of creating community to shelter the unfolding of mindful relational practices, as I am by Sarah Conn's deep sensibility about the interdependence of psyche and nature. In transitioning from individual and family therapy to group and community work, I have been nourished by ideas about dialogue, council, and public conversation, and wish to thank the Ojai Foundation and the Public Conversations Project for their dialogical vision and trainings. Participating in human rights delegations through

Global Exchange and BorderLinks deepened my understanding of the effects of transnational globalization on local communities. I am grateful to Steve Aizenstat, who invited me to join the table at Pacifica Graduate Institute, and who held open my place while I developed and explored these ideas in the classroom, in the creation of a community and ecological fieldwork and research portion of a doctoral psychology program, and in my writing.

Through his own example of devotion to scholarship and writing, as well as his generous encouragement, Ed Casey has lovingly held open the door each day to the intense and sustained work that has been necessary for the completion of this endeavor. To Rachel, Ani, Danielle, and Lily, I thank you for your love, liveliness, and good company that are my sweet daily bread. It is a deep sadness for elders to pass along a world in such need of repair. In the end, this book is for you and your generation.

Helene Shulman: I am grateful to all the friends and visionaries who have helped me to discern the logic of coherence connecting our multiple utopian dreams, especially the inspiration and mentorship of Gloria Anzaldúa, who passed away during the writing of this book and is much missed. During this time, I have enjoyed the challenge and innovative thinking of the folks at the Center for the Theater of the Oppressed in Los Angeles (CTO/ATA/LA), particularly Mady Schutzman, Brent Blair, Norma Bowles, B.J. Dodge, Corky Dominguez, and honorary member Chela Sandoval, and the constant grounding in community life and political activism over decades from the women of the Berkeley/Oakland *Tertulia* and the *compañeros* and *familia* of Casa Chile and La Peña. Another source of strength was the C.G. Jung Institute in Küsnacht, Switzerland, which nurtured my capacity to respect the rich, contradictory, and evolving nature of imaginal life while enduring the emergence of surprising new insights and ideas that break from conventional discourses. I thank my son Aaron, daughter Shanna, granddaughter Ema-Luz, and her dad, Josh, for their love and constant support, and note the good fortune of endless ongoing family discussions and enactments of cultural studies, psychology, music, dance, and critical race theory that make being in a family and circle of friends who are both teachers and activists so much fun. They have all helped me to understand that like Emma Goldman, "I want freedom, the right to self-expression, and everybody's right to beautiful, radiant things." (To discuss issues raised in this book, Helene Shulman can be contacted through e-mail at: liberationpsych@ yahoo.com).

References

Abraham, N. & Torok, M. (1994). *The shell and the kernel: Renewals of psychoanalysis, Volume 1*. Chicago: University of Chicago Press.

Addams, J. (1912). *Twenty years at Hull House with autobiographical notes*. New York: Macmillan.

Aitken, R. (1998, Summer). "Buddhadasa and the BASE community ideal." *Turning Wheel*, 28–30.

Aitken, R. (2001, Fall). "Restorative justice: Polynesian style." *Turning Wheel*, 13–15.

Ajami, F. (2001, October 7). "Nowhere man." *New York Times Magazine*, 19.

Alcoff, L.M. & Mendieta, E. (eds). (2000). *Thinking from the underside of history: Enrique Dussel's philosophy of liberation*. New York: Rowman and Littlefield.

Alschuler, L. (1997). "Jung and politics." In P. Young-Eisendrath & T. Dawson (eds), *The Cambridge companion to Jung*. New York: Cambridge University Press.

Alschuler, L. (2006). *The psychopolitics of liberation: Political consciousness from a Jungian perspective*. New York: Palgrave Macmillan.

Altman, N. (1995). *The analyst in the inner city: Race, class, and culture through a psycho-analytic lens*. Hillsdale, NJ: Analytic Press.

Altman, N. (2004). History repeats itself in transference and countertransference. *Psychoanalytic Dialogues*, 14, 6, 807–15.

Amandla! A Revolution in Four Part Harmony (2003). Simpson, S. (Producer), Hirsch, L. & Markgraaff, D. (Directors). USA: Artisan Entertainment.

American Anthropological Association (1998). *Code of ethics of the American Anthropological Association*. Arlington, VA: American Anthropological Association.

Anzaldúa, G. (1987/1999). *Borderlands/La frontera: The new mestiza*. Second Edition. San Francisco: Aunt Lute Press.

Anzaldúa, G. (2002). "Now let us shift ... the path of conocimiento ... inner work, public acts." In G. Anzaldúa & A. Keating (eds.), *This bridge we call home: Radical visions for transformation*. New York: Routledge.

Anzaldúa, G. & Keating, A. (eds). (2002). *This bridge we call home: Radical visions for transformation*. New York: Routledge.

Argyris, C., Putnam, R., & Smith, D.M. (1985). *Action science*. San Francisco: Jossey-Bass.

Asad, T. (1973). *Anthropology and the colonial encounter*. New York: Humanities Press.

Assefa, H. (n.d.). "The meaning of reconciliation." *European Platform for Conflict Prevention and Transformation*. Retrieved March 11, 2007 from http://www.gppac.net/documents/pbp/part1/2_reconc.htm.

Avelar, I. (1999). *The untimely present: Postdictatorial Latin American fiction and the task of mourning*. Durham: Duke University Press.

Baldwin, C. (1998). *Calling the circle: The first and future culture*. New York: Random House.

Baldwin, J. (1961). *Nobody knows my name*. New York: Dell.

Bar On, B. (1993). "Marginality and epistemic privilege." In L. Alcoff & E. Potter (eds), *Feminist epistemologies*. New York: Routledge.

Baxter, V. (2005). "Civil society promotion of truth, justice, and reconciliation." *Peace & Change*, 30 (1), 120–36.

Bearak, B. (1998, August 27). "Trying to wreck India's romance with the bomb." *New York Times*, p. 2.

Becker, C., Chasin, L., Chasin, R., Herzig, M., & Roth, S. (1995). "From stuck debate to new conversation on controversial issues: A report from the public conversations project." *Journal of Feminist Family Therapy*, 7 (1–2), 143–63.

Behar, R. (1996). *The vulnerable observer: Anthropology that breaks your heart*. Boston: Beacon Press.

Belenky, M. (1996). "Public homeplaces: Nurturing the development of people, families, and communities." In N. Goldberger, J. Tarule, & B. Clinchy (eds), *Knowledge, difference, and power: Essays inspired by Women's Ways of Knowing* (pp. 393–430). New York: Basic Books.

Belenky. M. (1998). Lectures on participatory research. Depth Psychology Doctoral Program, Pacifica Graduate Institute, Carpinteria, CA.

Belenky, M., Bond, L.A., & Weinstock, J.S. (1997). *A tradition that has no name: Nurturing the development of people, families, and communities*. New York: Basic Books.

Belenky, M., Clinchy, B., Goldberger, N., & Tarule, J. (1986). *Women's ways of knowing: The development of self, voice, and mind*. New York: Basic Books.

Berry, W. (1990). *What are people for?* San Francisco: North Point Press.

Berryman, P. (1987). *Liberation theology: Essential facts about the revolutionary movement in Latin America and beyond*. Philadelphia: Temple University Press.

Bhabha, H. (1990). *Nation and narration*. New York: Routledge.

Bhabha, H. (1994). *The location of culture*. New York: Routledge.

Bhabha, H. (2004). Lectures, Literature and Interdisciplinary Humanities Departments. University of California, Santa Barbara.

Bhatia, S. (2003). "Is 'integration' the developmental end goal for all immigrants? Redefining 'acculturation strategies' from a genetic-dramatistic perspective." In I. Josephs (ed.), *Dialogicality in development* (pp. 197–216). Westport, CT: Praeger.

Black is ... Black Ain't (1994). Atkinson, N., Dellal, J. (Producers), Riggs, M. & Bedgely, C. (Directors). USA: Newsreel.

Blee, K.M. (2002). *Inside organized racism: Women in the hate movement*. Berkeley: University of California Press.

Block, T. (2001–2). "Abraham Maimonides: A Jewish Sufi." *Sufi*, 52, 10–13.

Bloom, S. (1997). *Creating sanctuary: Toward the evolution of sane societies*. New York: Routledge.

Boal, A. (1985). *Theater of the oppressed*. New York: Theater Communications Group.

Boal, A. (1995). *The rainbow of desire: The Boal method of theater and therapy*. London: Routledge.

Boal, A. (1998). *Legislative theater*. London: Routledge.

Bob-Manuel, I. (2000). "A cultural approach to conflict transformation: An African traditional experience." Paper for course at European Peace University, Stadtschlaining, Austria.

Boggs, G.L. (1998). *Living for change*. Minneapolis: University of Minnesota Press.

Bohm, D. (1996). *On dialogue*. London: Routledge.

Borland, K. (1991)."'That's not what I said': Interpretive conflict in oral narrative research." In S. Gluck & D. Patai (eds), *Women's words: The feminist practice of oral history* (pp. 63–76). New York: Routledge.

Boulding, E. (1983). "The social imagination and the crisis of human futures: A North American perspective." *Forum for correspondence and contact*, 13 (2), 43–56.

Bowles, G. & Klein, R.D. (eds) (1983). *Theories of women's studies*. Boston: Routledge and Kegan Paul.

Brabeck, K. (2001). "Testimonio: Bridging feminist ethics with activist research to create new spaces of collectivity." Bridging the Gap: Feminism and Participatory Action Research Conference Papers, Boston College, June 22–24. Htpp://ggsc.wamu.edu/gap/brabeck.htm.

Brabeck, K. (2003). Testimonio: A strategy for collective resistance, cultural survival and building solidarity. *Feminism and psychology*, 13 (2), 252–58.

Bradshaw, G. & Watkins, M. (2006). "Transpecies psychology: Theory and praxis." Spring 75, *Psyche and Nature, Part I, A Journal of Archetype and Culture*, 69–94.

Braidotti, R. (1994). *Nomadic subjects: Embodiment and sexual difference in contemporary feminist theory*. New York: Columbia University Press.

Braidotti, R. (2002). "Difference, diversity and nomadic subjectivity." htpp://women. ped.kun.nl.cbt/rosilecture.html.

Briggs, J. (2005). *Innocents lost: When child soldiers go to war*. New York: Basic Books.

Brock-Utne, B. (2001). "Indigenous conflict resolution in Africa." Paper presented to the weekend seminar on indigenous solutions to conflicts, University of Oslo, Institute for Educational Research.

Brown, B.A. (1996). *Expanding circles: Women, art, and community*. New York: Midmarch Arts Press.

Brown, L.M. (ed.) (1988). *A guide to reading narratives of conflict and choice for self and moral choice*. Cambridge, MA: Center for the Study of Gender, Education and Human Development, Harvard University.

Brown, L. M. (1997). Performing femininities: Listening to white working class girls in rural Maine. *Journal of social issues*, 53 (4), 683–702.

Brown, L.M., Debold, E., Tappan, M., & Gilligan, C. (1991). "Reading narratives of conflict and choice for self and moral voice: A relational method." In W. Kurtines & J. Gewirtz (eds), *Handbook of moral behavior and development: Theory, research, and application*. Hillsdale, NJ: Lawrence Erlbaum.

Brown, T. & Bye-Brown, F. (2001, June). "Restorative justice: An overview." *Friends Bulletin*, pp. 8–9.

Brown, L. & Gilligan, C. (1992). *Meeting at the crossroads*. New York: Ballantine Books.

Brown University's Debt to Slavery. (2006, October 23). *New York Times*, p. 10.

Buber, M. (1958). *I and Thou*. New York: Scribner's.

Buber, M. (1970). *The way of man*. New York: Citadel Press.

Buber, M. (1965). *The knowledge of man: A philosophy of the interhuman*. New York: Harper.

Bushe, G.R. (1995, Fall). "Advances in appreciative inquiry as an organization development intervention." *Organization Development Journal*, 13, 14–22.

Cabrera, R. (1998a). "Dealing with the past: Reconciliation processes and peace building." Belfast, Northern Ireland. Retrieved June 6, 2006. http://www.incore.ulst.ac.uk/research/projects/thepast/roberto.html.

Cabrera, R. (1998b). *Should we remember?* Retrieved June 6, 2004.http://lugh.incore. ulst.ac.uk/home/publication/conference/thepast/roberto.html.

Caruth, C. (ed.) (1995). *Trauma: Explorations in memory*. Baltimore: Johns Hopkins University Press.

Casey, E. (1992). "Forgetting remembered." *Man and World*, 25, 281–311.

Castillejo-Cuéllar, A. (2007, Winter). "Knowledge, experience, and South Africa's scenarios of forgiveness." *Radical History Review*, 97, 11–42.

Césaire, A. (1972/2000). *A Discourse on colonialism*. New York: Monthly Review Press.

Chambers, I. (1994). "Leaky habits and broken grammar." In G. Robertson, M. Mash, L. Tickner, J. Bird, B. Curtis, & T. Putnam (eds), *Travellers' tales: Narratives of home and displacement*. London: Routledge.

Chanfrault-Duchet (1991). "Narrative structures, social models and symbolic representation in the life story." In S.B. Gluck & D. Patai (eds), *Women's words: The feminist practice of oral history* (pp. 77–92). New York: Routledge.

Chasin, R., Herzig, M., Roth, S., Chasin, L., Becker, C., & Stains, R. (1996). "From diatribe to dialogue on divisive public issues: Approaches drawn from family therapy." *Mediation Quarterly*, 13, 4, 323–44.

Chitty, B. (1998). *Indian wars and the Vietnam experience*. Retrieved August 28, 2007 from http://www.vvaw.org/commentary/?id=3&hilite=Ben+Chitty.

Chrisman, N.J. (1976). "Secret societies and the ethics of urban fieldwork." In M. Rynkiewich & J. Spradley, J. (eds), *Ethics and anthropology: Dilemmas in fieldwork*. New York: Wiley.

Circle of Stories (n.d.). *Many voices*. Retrieved on April 20, 2007 from http://www.pbs.org/circleofstories/voices/index.html.

City of God (2002). A. Ribiero, M. Ramos, E. Tolomelli (Producers) and F. Meirelles, K. Lund (Directors). USA: Miramax.

Cohen-Cruz, J. & Schutzman, M. (2006). *A Boal companion: Theater, therapy, and activism*. New York: Routledge.

Combatants for Peace (2006). *On Democracy now*. Retrieved June 14, 2007 from http://www.democracynow.org/article.pl?sid=06/07/24/1439247.

Communication for Development Group & Coldevin, G. (2001). "Participatory communication and adult learning for rural development." *Journal of International Communication*, 7 (2). Retrieved March 10, 2007 from http://www.fao.org/sd/2001/kn1104a2_en.htm.

Community/Ecological Fieldwork and Research (n.d.). Pacifica Graduate Institute. Retrieved January 11, 2008 from http://www.online.pacifica.edu/depthfieldwork.

Cone, J.H. (1972). *The spirituals and the blues: An interpretation*. New York: The Seabury Press.

Cone, J. (1990). *A Black theology of liberation*. Turlock, CA: Orbis Press.

Confluence Project (n.d.). *Confluence project grassroots vision features many firsts*. Retrieved May 4, 2007, http://www.confluenceproject.org/.

Cooperrider, D.L. (1990). "Positive image, positive action: The affirmative basis of organizing." In S. Srivastava & D.L. Cooperrider (eds), *Appreciative management and leadership* (pp. 91–125). San Francisco: Jossey-Bass.

Cooperrider, D.L. & Srivastava, S. (1987). "Appreciative Inquiry in Organizational Life." *Research in Organizational Change and Development*, 1, 129–69.

Courage to Refuse (n.d.). Retrieved June 5, 2006 from http://www.seruv.org/english.

Cross, W.E. (1991). *Shades of black: Diversity in African-American identity*. Philadelphia: Temple University Press.

Cushman, P. (1995). *Constructing the self, constructing America: A cultural history of psychotherapy*. Reading, MA: Addison-Wesley.

Cyclo (1995). Rossignon, C., Lecallier, A., Rocca, A. (Producers), & Trahn Anh Hung (Director). USA: New Yorker Films.

Dagron, A.G. (2001). *Making waves: Stories of participatory communication for social change*. New York: Rockefeller Foundation. Retrieved April 5, 2007 from http://www.communicationforsocialchange.org/pdf/making_waves.pdf.

Damon, B. (1996). "The keepers of the waters." In B. Brown (ed.) *Expanding circles: Women, art, and community*. New York: Midmarch Press.

Danto, E. (2005). *Freud's free clinics: Psychoanalysis and social justice, 1918–1938*. New York: Columbia University Press.

Daughters of the Dust (1991). Geechee Girls Productions. Dash, J. (Director). USA: Kino International.

DeLeon, J. (2002). *Our word is our weapon: Selected writings of Subcomandante Insurgente Marcos*. New York: Seven Stories Press.

Deleuze, G. & Guattari, F. (1986). *Nomadology and the war machine*. New York: Semiotext(e).

Deleuze, G. & Guattari, F. (1987). *A thousand plateaus* (B. Massumi, trans.). London: Athlone Press.

de Mare, P., Piper, R., & Thompson, S. (1991). *Koinonia: From hate, through dialogue, to culture in the large group*. London: Karnac Books.

Derrida, J. (2001). *On cosmopolitanism and forgiveness* (M. Dooley & M. Hughes, trans.). New York: Routledge.

Derrida, J. (2003, Oct. 23). "Vivre 'ensemble'—Living together." Keynote address, Conference, "Irreconcilable Differences: Jacques Derrida and the Question of Religion," University of California at Santa Barbara.

Diagnostic and statistical manual of mental disorders. (1994). Fourth Edition. Washington: American Psychiatric Association.

Dorfman, A. (1978). "The invisible Chile: Three years of cultural resistance." *Praxis*, 4, 191–7.

Du Bois, W.E.B. (1903/1989). *The soul of Black folks*. New York: Penguin.

Dussel, E. (2003). *Philosophy of liberation*. Eugene: Wipf & Stock Publishers.

Edkins, J. (2003). *Trauma and the memory of politics*. Cambridge: Cambridge University Press.

Ellis, M.H. (1987). *Toward a Jewish theology of liberation*. New York: Maryknoll.

Eltit, D. (1997). *E Luminata*. Santa Fe: Lumen, Inc.

Enriquez, V. (1992). *From colonial to liberation psychology: The Philippine experience*. Quezon City, Philippines: University of the Philippines Press.

Epstein, H. (1979). *Children of the holocaust: Conversations with sons and daughters of survivors*. New York: Penguin Books.

Epstein, J. (2003, July). "Nowhere to hide: Global corporates, when sued, used to walk away. Not for much longer—Latin American lawsuits." *Latin Trade*.

Erikson, K. (1976). *Everything in its path: Destruction of community in the Buffalo Creek flood*. New York: Simon and Schuster.

Erikson, K. (1994). *A new species of trouble: The human experience of modern disasters*. New York: W.W. Norton.

Esteva, G. (1992). "Development." In W. Sachs (ed.), *The Development Dictionary. A Guide to Knowledge as Power* (pp. 6–25). London: Zed Books.

Esteva, G. (4/8/2006a). "The revolution of the new commons, Part IV." *In Motion Magazine*. Retrieved December 15, 2006 from www.inmotionmagazine.com/global/gest_int_4.html – 81k.

Esteva, G. (4/8/2006b). "The society of the different." *In Motion Magazine*. Retrieved December 15, 2006 from http://www.inmotionmagazine.com/global/gest_int_1.html.

Esteva, G. & Prakash, S. (1998). *Grassroots postmodernism: Remaking the soil of cultures*. London: Zed Books.

Evans, S. & Boyte, H. (1986). *Free spaces: The sources of democratic change in America*. New York: Harper and Row.

Ezekiel, R. (1995). *The racist mind: Portraits of American neo-Nazis and klansmen*. New York: Viking Press.

Fals-Borda (1988). *Knowledge and people's power: Lessons with peasants in Nicaragua, Mexico, and Colombia*. New Delhi, India: Social Institute.

Fanon, F. (1963). *The wretched of the earth*. New York: Grove Press.

Fanon, F. (1965). *A dying colonialism* (H. Chevalier, trans.). New York: Grove Press.

Fanon, F. (1967a). *Black skin, white masks* (C.L. Markmann, trans.). New York: Grove Press.

Fanon, F. (1967b). *Toward the African revolution*. New York: Grove Press.

Felman, S. (1992). "The return of the voice: Claude Lanzmann's *Shoah*." In S. Felman, & D. Laub (eds), *Testimony: Crises of witnessing in literature, psychoanalysis, and history*. New York: Routledge.

Field, R. (2006). "John Dewey." *Internet encyclopedia of philosophy*. http://www. iep.utm.edu/d/dewey.htm#H2.

Flinders, C.L. (1998). *At the root of this longing: Reconciling a spiritual hunger with a feminist thirst*. San Francisco: HarperCollins.

Foucault, M. (2003). "For an ethics of discomfort." In *Essential works, 1954–1984: Power*. J. Faubian (ed.) (R. Hurley, trans.). London: Penguin.

Freire, P. (1970/1989). *Pedagogy of the oppressed*. New York: Seabury.

Freire, P. & Faundez, A. (1989). *Learning to question: A pedagogy of liberation*. New York: Continuum.

Fromm, E. (1960). "Psychoanalysis and Zen Buddhism." In D.T. Suzuki, E. Fromm, & R. De Martino (eds), *Zen Buddhism and psychoanalysis*. New York: Harper.

Fromm, E. (1976). *To have or to be*. New York: Harper & Row.

Fullilove, M. (2005). *Root shock: How tearing up city neighborhoods hurts America, and what to do about it*. New York: Oneworld.

Funari, V. (2006). "Interview with filmmaker." P.O.V. Retrieved September 5, 2006 from www.pbs.org/pov/.

Gablik, S. (1991). *The Reenchantment of art*. London: Thames and Hudson.

Gadamer, H.-G. (1976). *Philosophical hermeneutics*. Berkeley: University of California Press.

Gadamer, H.-G. (1988). *Truth and method*. New York: Crossroads Publishing.

Garfinkel, H. (1956). "Conditions of successful degradation ceremonies." *American Journal of Sociology*, 61, 420–4.

Gebara, I. (1999). *Longing for running water: Ecofeminism and liberation*. Minneapolis: Fortress Press.

Gergen, K. (1998). *Resources for sustainable dialogue*. Thousand Oaks, CA: Sage.

Gandhi, M. (1972). *An autobiography: The story of my experiments with truth*. Boston: Beacon Press.

Gilligan, C. (1982). *In a different voice: Psychological theory and women's development*. Cambridge: Harvard University Press.

Gilligan, C., Rogers, A., & Tolman, D. (eds) (1991). *Women, girls & psychotherapy: Reframing resistance*. New York: Harrington Park Press.

Gilman, S. (1993). *Freud, race, and gender*. Princeton: Princeton University Press.

Gilroy, P. (1993). *The Black Atlantic: Modernity and double consciousness*. London: Routledge.

Glissant, E. (1992). *Caribbean discourse: Selected essays*. Charlottesville: University Press of Virginia.

Gobodo-Madikizela, P. (2003). *A human being died that night: A South African woman confronts the legacy of apartheid*. New York: Houghton Mifflin.

Godoy, S. (1999). "Probing the membrane between horror and hope: Artist Claudia Bernardi." *Clas Newsletter*. Retrieved June 3, 2005 from http://socrates. berkeley.edu:7001/Gallery/bernardi/angelina.html.

Goffman, E. (1961). *Asylums*. New York: Anchor Books.

Goizueta, R.S. (1988). *Liberation, method, and dialogue: Enrique Dussel and North American theological discourse*. Atlanta: Scholars Press.

Griffin, S. (1992). *A chorus of stones: The private life of war*. New York: Anchor Books.

Griffin, S. (1995). *The eros of everyday life*. NY: Anchor Books.

Greene, M. (1995). *Releasing the imagination: Essays on education, the arts, and social change*. San Francisco: Jossey-Bass.

Gruen, A. (1987/2007). *The insanity of normality: Toward understanding human destructiveness*. Berkeley: Human Development Books.

Gutiérrez, G. (1988). *A theology of liberation*. Maryknoll, New York: Orbis.

Habermas, J. (1987). *Theory of communicative action, Vol. 2: Lifeworld and systems: A Critique of functionalist reason.* (T. Mc Carthy, trans.). Boston: Beacon.

Hale, S. (1991). "Feminist methods, process, and self-criticism." In S. Gluck & D. Patai (eds), *Women's words: The feminist practice of oral history.* NY: Routledge.

Hall, S. (1996). "When was the postcolonial: Thinking about the limit." In I. Chambers & L. Curtis (eds), *The post-colonial question* (pp. 242–60). London: Routledge.

Hamber, B. (ed.) (1998). "The past imperfect: Exploring Northern Ireland, South Africa, and Guatemala." Retrieved January 15, 2008 from http://www.csvr.org.za/wits/pubstrc2.htm.

Hanh, T.N. (1988). *The sutra on the full awareness of breathing.* Berkeley: Parallax Press.

Hanh, T.N. (1993). *For a future to be possible.* Berkeley: Parallax Press.

Hanh, T.N. & Berrigan, P. (1975). *The raft is not the shore: Conversations toward a Buddhist-Christian awareness.* Maryknoll, New York: Orbis Books.

Harris, E. (1999). "Alleged suicide note." Retrieved June 6, 2007. http://www.zmag.org/ZMag/articles/july99bronski.htm.

Harthcock, M. (2005). "Caring as a subversive activity: A study in liberation pedagogy." Doctoral dissertation, Pacifica Graduate Institute, Carpinteria, CA.

Henderson, M. (2001). *Forgiveness: Breaking the chain of hate.* Kent, WA: Amica Publishing.

Herda, E. (1999). "Research conversations and narrative: A critical hermeneutic orientation to participatory inquiry." Westport, CT: Praeger.

Hermans, J.M. & Kempen, H.J. (1998). "Moving cultures: The perilous problems of cultural dichotomies in a globalizing society." *American Psychologist*, 53, 1111–20.

Heschel, A. (1951). *The sabbath: Its meaning for modern man.* New York: Farrar, Straus and Giroux.

Hill Collins, P. (1990). "Learning from the outsider within." In M. Fonow & J. Cook (eds), *Beyond methodology: Feminist scholarship as lived research.* Bloomington, IN: Indiana University Press.

Hillman, J. (1975). *Re-visioning psychology.* New York: Harper & Row.

Hillman, J. (1992). *The thought of the heart and the soul of the world.* Woodstock, CT: Spring Publications.

Hirsch, M. (1997). *Family frames: Photography, narrative, and postmemory.* Cambridge: Harvard University Press.

Hocoy, D., Kipnis, A., Lorenz, H., & Watkins, M. (2003). "Liberation psychologies: An invitation to dialogue." Retrieved August 29, 2007 from http://www.online.pacifica.edu/depthfieldwork/libpsych.

Hoeller, C. (1999). "Don't mess with mister in-between: Interview with Homi K. Bhabha." Retrieved September 21, 2006, from http://www.translocation.at/d/bhabha.htm.

Hoffman, G. K. (2002). "On beginning where you are: Michael Henderson's *Forgiveness: Breaking the chain of hate.*" *Journal of Cooperative Communication Skills*, 11, 3–7. http://www.newconversations.net/gkh_essay08.htm.

Hollander, N.C. (1997). *Love in a time of hate: Liberation psychology in Latin America.* New Brunswick: Rutgers University Press.

Homans, P. (ed.) (2000). *Symbolic loss: The ambiguity of mourning and memory at century's end.* Charlottesville: University Press of Virginia.

hooks, b. (1990). *Yearning: Race, gender, and cultural politics.* Boston: South End Press.

hooks, b. (1992). *Black looks: Race and representation.* Boston: South End Press.

hooks, b. (1994). *Outlaw culture: Resisting representations.* New York: Routledge.

hooks, b. & Mesa-Bains, A. (2006). *Homegrown: Engaged cultural criticism.* Cambridge: South End Press.

Horney, K. (1950). *Neurosis and human growth: The struggle toward self-realization.* New York: Norton.

Horton, M. & Freire, P. (1990). *We make the road by walking: Conversations on education and social change.* Philadelphia: Temple University Press.

Huggins, M.K., Haritos-Fatouros, M., & Zimbardo, P.G. (2002). *Violence workers: Police torturers and murderers reconstruct Brazilian atrocities.* Berkeley: University of California Press.

Hyde, L. (1983). *The gift: Imagination and the erotic life of property.* New York: Vintage Books.

Jackson, M. (1988). "The Maori and the criminal justice system: A new perspective: He Whaipanga Hou." *Department of Justice Study Series 18.* Wellington: Department of Justice.

Jacoby, R. (1975). *Social amnesia: A critique of contemporary psychology from Adler to Laing.* Boston: Beacon Press.

Jacoby, R. (1983). *The repression of psychoanalysis: Otto Fenichel and the political Freudians.* Chicago: University of Chicago Press.

The Jamestown Project (2006). *Make democracy real.* Retrieved March 4, 2007 from http://www.jamestownproject.org/.

JanMohamed, A.R. (1993). "Some implications of Paulo Freire's border pedagogy." *Cultural Studies,* 7, 107–17.

Jelin, E. (2003). *State repression and the labors of memory.* Minneapolis: University of Minnesota Press.

Jourard, S. (1971). *Self-disclosure: An experimental analysis of the transparent self.* New York: Wiley Interscience.

Jung, C.G. (1969). *The structure and dynamics of the psyche. Collected Works of C. G. Jung, V. 8.* G. Adler & R.F.C. Hull (eds & trans.). Princeton: Bollingen Series, Princeton University Press.

Jurgensmayer, M. (2000). *Terror in the mind of God: The global rise of religious violence.* Berkeley: University of California Press.

Kalff, D. (2003). *Sandplay: A psychotherapeutic approach to the psyche.* Cloverdale, CA: Temenos Press.

Kaplan, B. (1983a). "A trio of trials." In R.M. Lerner (ed.), *Developmental psychology: Historical and philosophical perspectives.* Hillsdale, NJ: Lawrence Erlbaum Associates.

Kaplan, B. (1983b). "Genetic-dramatism: Old wine in new bottles." In S. Wapner & B. Kaplan (eds), *Toward a holistic developmental psychology.* Hillsdale, NJ: Lawrence Erlbaum Associates.

Kaplan, A. (1982). *Meditation and kabbalah.* York Beach, MA: Samuel Weiser.

Kaprow, A. (1968, Summer). "The shape of the art environment." *Artforum,* 10, 32–3.

Kawachi, I., Kennedy, B.P., & Lochner, K. (1997, November/December). "Long live community: Social capital as public health." *The American Prospect,* 35, 56–9.

Kearney, R. (1998a). *Poetics of imagining: Modern to post-modern.* Edinburgh: Edinburgh University Press.

Kearney, R. (1998b). "Towards a British-Irish council." *Céide accent on e* 2 (2), 11–13.

Kelley, R. (2002a). *Freedom dreams: The black radical imagination.* Boston: Beacon Press.

Kelley, R. (6/7/2002b). "Finding the strength to love and dream." *Chronicle of Higher Education,* pp. B7–B10.

Kipnis, A. (2002). *Angry young men: How parents, teachers, and counselors can help "bad boys."* San Francisco: Jossey-Bass.

Kipnis, A. (2004). *Knights without armor: A guide to the inner lives of men.* Santa Barbara: Indigo Phoenix Books.

Kiva.org (n.d.). *Kiva: Loans that change lives*. Retrieved June 6, 2007 from http://www.kiva.org/app.php.

Kleinman, A. (1988). *Re-thinking psychiatry*. New York: Free Press.

Kolvenbach, P.H., Father (2000, Oct.). "The service of faith and the promotion of justice in American Jesuit higher education." Commitment to Justice in Jesuit Higher Education conference, Santa Clara University. http://www.loyola.edu/yotc/father_kolvenbach.html.

Kozol, J. (1991). *Savage inequalities: Children in America's schools*. New York: Harper.

Kristeva, J. (1982). *Powers of horror*. New York: Columbia University Press.

Kristeva, J. (2002). *Revolt, she said*. New York: Semiotext(e).

Krystal, H. (1995). "Trauma and aging: A thirty-year follow up." In C. Caruth (ed.) (pp. 76–99). *Trauma: Explorations in memory*. Baltimore: Johns Hopkins Press.

Kvale, S. (1996). *InterViews: An introduction to qualitative research interviewing*. Thousand Oaks: Sage Publications.

Lacayo, V. (2006). *Approaching social change as a complex problem in a world that treats it as a complicated one: The case of Puntos de Encuentro in Nicaragua*. Retrieved March 3, 2007 from http://www.ohio.edu/commdev/upload/Approaching_social_change_as_a_complex_problem.pdf.

Landau, J. & Saul, J. (2004). "Family and community resilience in response to major disaster." In F. Walsh & M. McGoldrick (eds), *Living beyond loss: Death in the family*, Second Edition (pp. 285–309). New York: Norton.

Lanek, R. (1999). "Integrating indigenous approaches with national and international mechanisms for conflict resolution and reconciliation." Paper presented to All-Africa Conference on African Principles of Conflict Resolution and Reconciliation, Addis Ababa, Ethiopia.

Langer, M. (1992). *From Vienna to Managua: Journey of a psychoanalyst* (M. Hooks, trans.). London: Free Association Books.

Lanzmann, C. (1995). "The obscenity of understanding: An evening with Claude Lanzmann." In C. Caruth (ed.), *Trauma: Explorations in memory* (pp. 200–20). Baltimore: Johns Hopkins Press.

Laub, D. (1992). "An event without a witness: Truth, testimony and survival." In S. Felman & D. Laub (eds), *Testimony: Crises of witnessing in literature, psychoanalysis, and history* (pp. 75–92). New York: Routledge.

Lavie, S. & Swendenburg, T. (eds) (1996). *Displacement, diaspora, and geographies of identity*. Durham, NC: Duke University Press.

Lederach, J.P. (1999). *The journey toward reconciliation*. Scottsdale, PA: Herald Press.

Lee, G. (2007). Doctoral dissertation. Depth Psychology Doctoral Program. Pacifica Graduate Institute, Carpinteria, CA.

Levine, D.P. (2004). "The birth of the citizenship schools: Entwining the struggles for literacy and freedom," *History of Education Quarterly*. Retrieved September 28, 2006 from http://www.historycooperative.org/journals/heq/44.3/levine.html.

Lewin, K. (1951). *Field theory in social science; selected theoretical papers*. D. Cartwright (ed.). New York: Harper & Row.

Lifton, R.J. (1967). *Death in life: Survivors of Hiroshima*. NY: Random House.

Lifton, R.J. (1986). *The Nazi doctors: Medical killing and the psychology of genocide*. New York: Basic Books.

Lifton, R.J. (1993). *The protean self: Human resilience in an age of fragmentation*. New York: Basic Books.

Lifton, R.J. (2007). "Lectures on trauma." International Trauma Studies Program, Columbia University.

Lincoln, Y.S. (1990). "Toward a categorical imperative for qualitative research." In E.W. Eisner & A. Peshkin (eds), *Qualitative inquiry in education: The continuing debate*. New York: Teachers College Press.

Linklater, K. (1976). *Freeing the natural voice*. Los Angeles: Drama Publishers.

Lins, P. (2002). *City of God*. New York: Black Cat.

Lipsitz, G. (1998). *The possessive investment in whiteness: How white people profit from identity politics*. Philadelphia: Temple University Press.

Lira, E. (2001). "Violence, fear, and impunity: Reflections on subjective and political obstacles for peace." *Peace and conflict: Journal of peace psychology*, 7 (2), 109–18.

Lispector, C. (1967). *The apple in the dark*. New York: Alfred A. Knopf.

List of Truth Commissions. Retrieved July, 1, 2007 from www.usip.org/library/truth.html#tc.

Lives of Others, The. (2007). Berg, Q. & Wiedermann, M. (Producers). Henkel von Donnersmarck, F. (Director). USA: Sony Pictures Classics.

Long Night's Journey into Day. (2000). Reid, F. (Producer). Reid, F. & Hoffman, D. (Directors). U.S.A.: California Newsreel.

Lorde, A. (1984). *Sister outsider: Essays and speeches by Audre Lorde*. Berkeley: The Crossing Press.

Loveman, B. & Lira, E. (2007). "Truth, justice, reconciliation and impunity as historical themes: Chile, 1814–2006." *Radical History Review*, 97, 43–76.

Lykes, M.B. (1994). "Whose meeting at which crossroads?: A response to Brown and Gilligan." *Feminism and psychology*, 4 (3), 345–9.

Lykes, M.B. (1997). Participatory research among the Maya of Guatemala: Constructed meanings from situated knowledge. *Journal of Social Issues*, 53 (4), 725–46.

Lykes, M.B., Blanche, M.T., & Hamber, B. (2003). "Narrating survival and change in Guatemala and South Africa: The politics of representation and a liberatory community psychology." *American Journal of Community Psychology*, 31 (1/2), 79–90.

Maalouf, A. (2000). *In the name of identity: Violence and the need to belong*. New York: Arcade Publishing.

Maathai, W. (2003). *The Green Belt movement: Sharing the approach and the experience*. New York: Lantern Books.

Maathai, W. (2004). Nobel prize acceptance speech. Retrieved December 1, 2006, from http://nobelprize.org/nobel_prizes/peace/laureates/2004/maathai-lecture.html.

Macy, J. (1983). *Dharma and development: Religion as a resource in the Sarvodaya self-help movement*. West Hartford: Kumarian Press.

Macy, J. (n.d.). "The great turning." Retrieved October 9, 2007, from http://joannamacy.net/html/great.html.

Mama, A. (2002). "Gender, power, and identity in African contexts." *The Wellesley Centers for Women, Research and Action Report*, 23 (2), 1–3.

Mann, S.J. (2003). "The enigma of hypertension and psychosomatic illness: Lesson for psychoneuroimmunology from beyond the conscious mind." In J.M. Wilce (ed.), *Social and cultural lives of immune systems*. New York: Routledge Press.

Maquilapolis: City of Factories. (2006). Funari, V. & de la Torre, S. (Producers and Directors). USA: Newsreel.

Marable, M. (2004). Lecture, Multicultural Center, University of Santa Barbara, Santa Barbara, CA.

Maracek, J., Fine, M., & Kidder, L. (1997). "Working between worlds: Qualitative methods and social psychology." *Journal of Social Issues*, 53 (4), 631–44.

Marcos, Subcomandante (2002). *The word is our weapon*. New York: Seven Stories Press.

Marks, L.U. (2000). *The skin of the film: Intercultural cinema, embodiment, and the senses.* Durham: Duke University Press.

Martín-Baró, I. (1994). *Writings for a liberation psychology.* Cambridge: Harvard University Press.

"Massacre in Virginia" (2007, April 19). *New York Times* (p. 1).

Mc Laren, P. & Lankshear, C. (eds) (1994). *Politics of liberation: Paths from Freire.* New York: Routledge.

McTaggart, R. (ed.) (1997). *Participatory action research: International contexts and consequences.* Albany: State University of New York.

Mead, G.H. (1934). *Mind, self, and society.* C.W. Morris (ed.). Chicago: University of Chicago Press.

Memmi, A. (1965). *The colonizer and the colonized.* Boston: Beacon Press.

Memmi, A. (2006). *Decolonization and the decolonized* (R. Bononno, trans.). Minneapolis: University of Minneapolis Press.

Mies, M. (1978). "Methodische Postulate zur Frauenforschung—dargestellt am Beispiel der Gewalt gegen Frauen: Beitrage zur Feministischen." *Theorie und Praxis,* I (1), 41–63.

Mies, M. (1983). "Towards a methodology for feminist research." In G. Bowles & R. Klein (eds), *Theories of women's studies* (pp. 117–39). London: Routledge & Kegan Paul.

Mies, M. (1991). "Women's Research or Feminist Research? The debate surrounding feminist science and methodology." In M. Fonow & J. Cook (eds), *Beyond methodology: Feminist scholarship as lived research* (pp. 60–84). Bloomington, IN: Indiana University Press.

Miles, M. & Huberman, A. (1994). *Qualitative analysis* (Second Edition). Thousand Oaks, CA: Sage.

Minh-ha, T. (1989). *Woman, native, other: Writing, postcoloniality and feminism.* Bloomington, IN: Indiana University Press.

Minow, M. (1998). *Between vengeance and forgiveness: Facing history after genocide and mass violence.* Boston: Beacon.

Mishler, E.G. (1986). *Research interviewing: Context and narrative.* Cambridge: Harvard University Press.

Mitscherlich, A. & Mitscherlich, M. (1975). *The inability to mourn. Principles of collective behavior* (B. Placzek, trans.). New York: Grove Press.

Moane, G. (2000). "Making connections: Systems of resistance." *Irish Journal of Feminist Studies,* 6, 221–6.

Montero, M. (1996). Parallel lives: Community psychology in Latin America and the United States. *American Journal of Community Psychology,* 24, 589–606.

Morales, A.L. (1998). *Medicine stories: History, culture, and the politics of integrity.* Cambridge: South End Press.

Morrison, T. (2004). *Beloved.* New York: Vintage Press.

Moulton, P. (ed.) (1989). *Journal and major essays of John Woolman.* Richmond, IN: Friends United Press.

Moyers, B. (2004, Dec. 1). Acceptance Remarks by Bill Moyers for the Global Environmental Citizen Award at Harvard University Center for Health and the Global Environment. Retrieved July 20, 2007 from http://chge.med.harvard.edu/events/documents/Moyerstranscript.pdf.

Muñoz, J.E. (1999). *Disidentifications: Queers of color and the performance of politics.* Minneapolis: University of Minnesota Press.

Murphy, E. (2005). "The power of paradox: An institutional psychoanalysis of Catholic religious congregations." Doctoral dissertation, Depth Psychology Doctoral Program, Pacifica Graduate Institute, Carpinteria, CA.

Nandy, A. (1983). *The intimate enemy: Loss and recovery of the self under colonialism.* Delhi: Oxford University Press.

Nghiem, C. (2002, Spring). Deer park monastery. *Deer Park Breeze*, p. 13.

Nielsen, J. (ed.) (1990). *Feminist research methods: Exemplary readings in the social sciences.* Boulder, CO: Westview Press.

Nora, P. (1989). "Between memory and history: Les lieux de memoire." *Representations* 26, 7–25.

Norberg-Hodge, H. (1991). *Ancient futures: Learning from Ladakh.* San Francisco: Sierra Club Books.

Nussbaum, M. (2/2001). "The end of orthodoxy: Review of Edward Said's *Reflections on exile and other essays.*" *New York Times Book Review*, 18.

Oakley, A. (1981). "Interviewing women: A contradiction in terms." In H. Roberts (ed.), *Doing feminist research.* New York: Routledge & Kegan Paul.

Oglesby, E. (2007). "Educating citizens in postwar Guatemala: Historical memory, genocide, and the culture of peace." *Radical History Review*, 97, 77–97.

Oliver, K. (1998). *Subjectivity without subjects: From abject fathers to desiring mothers.* New York: Rowman and Littlefield.

Oliver, K. (2001). *Witnessing: Beyond recognition.* Minneapolis: University of Minnesota Press.

Oliver, K. (2002). "Psychic space and social melancholy." In K. Oliver & S. Edwin (eds), *Between the psyche and the social: Psychoanalytic social theory.* Lanham, MD: Rowman and Littlefield.

Oliver, M. (1986). *Dream work.* New York: Atlantic Monthly Press.

Pan Valley Institute (n.d). Retrieved September 20, 2006 http://www.afsc.org/pacificmtn/fresno.htm.

Patai, D. (1987). "Ethical problems of personal narratives, or, Who should eat the last piece of cake?" *International Journal of Oral History*, 8 (1), 5–27.

Patai, D. (1991). "U.S. academics and third world women: Is ethical research possible?" In S. Gluck & D. Patai (eds), *Women's words: The feminist practice of oral history* (pp. 137–54). New York: Routledge.

Payne, K. (Fall, 2001). "Long day's journey into night: an interview with the filmmakers." *Turning Wheel*, 32–5.

Pelfrey, R. & Pelfrey, M.H. (1985). *Art and mass media.* New York: Harper and Row.

Penington, I. (1987). *The Inward Journey of Isaac Penington. Quaker Classics in Brief: William Penn, Robert Barclay, and Isaac Penington.* Wallingford, PA: Pendle Hill Publications.

People's Health Assembly (2005). Retrieved March 11, 2007 from http://www.phmovement.org/files/phm-newsbrief16–17_0.pdf.

Perluss, E. (1998). "Stories in the land." Community/ecological fieldwork paper. Depth Psychology Doctoral Program, Pacifica Graduate Institute, Carpinteria, CA.

Peters, L.G. (1998). "Culture and personality disorders." In R.J. Castillo (ed.), *Meanings of madness.* Pacific Grove, CA: Brooks/Cole Publishing Company.

Polak, F L. (1973). *The image of the future* (E. Boulding, trans.). New York: Elsevier.

Ponce, C. (1978). *Kabbalah.* Wheaton, IL: Quest Books.

Pratt, M.L. (1992). *Under imperial eyes: Travel writing and transculturation.* New York: Routledge Press.

Prilleltensky, I. (1994). *The morals and politics of psychology: Psychological discourse and the status quo.* Albany: State University of New York Press.

Prilleltensky, I. (2003). "Understanding, resisting, and overcoming oppression: Toward psychopolitical validity." *American Journal of Community Psychology*, 31 (1/2), 195–201.

Prilleltensky, I. & Fox, D. (1997). *Critical psychology: An introduction.* Thousand Oaks, CA: Sage.

Prilleltensky, I. & Nelson, G. (2002). *Doing psychology critically: Making a difference in diverse settings.* New York: Palgrave Macmillan.

Prilleltensky, I. & Nelson, G. (2005). *Community psychology: In pursuit of liberation and well-being.* New York: Palgrave Macmillan.

Puntarigvivat, T. (1994). *Bikkhu Buddhadasa's dhammic socialism in dialogue with Latin American liberation theology.* Dissertation, Temple University, Philadelphia, PA.

Puleo, M. (1994). *The struggle is one: Voices and visions of liberation.* Albany, New York: SUNY Press.

Puntos de Encuentro (2006). Retrieved March 10, 2007 from http://www.puntos.org.ni/english/about.php.

Queen, C. & King, S. (eds) (1996). *Engaged Buddhism.* Albany: State University of New York.

Quiñones Rosado, R. (2007). *Consciousness-in-action: Toward an integral psychology of liberation and transformation.* Caguas, Puerto Rico: Ilé Publications.

Rahnema, M. & Bawtree, V. (eds) (1997). *The post-development reader.* London: Zed Books.

Rawlinson, M. (2006). "Beyond virtue and the law: On the moral significance of the act of forgiveness in Hegel's. *Phenomenology of the Spirit.*" In N. Potter (ed.), *Trauma, truth and reconciliation: Healing damaged relationships.* New York: Oxford University Press.

Reagon, B.J. (n.d.). *Reflections on an era: Music in the civil rights movement.* Retrieved April 5, 2007 from http://www.pbs.org/wgbh/amex/eyesontheprize/reflect/r03_music.html.

Reconciliation Australia (n.d.). Retrieved March 4, 2007 from http://www.reconciliation.org.au/i-cms.isp.

Ricoeur, P. (1970). *Freud and philosophy.* New Haven: Yale University Press.

Ricouer, P. (1982). *Hermeneutics and the human sciences.* New York: Cambridge University Press.

Ricoeur, P. (1986). *Lectures on ideology and utopia.* G.H. Taylor (ed.). New York: Columbia University Press.

Rivers, D. (n.d.). *The seven challenges—A free workbook and reader on cooperative communication.* www.newconversations.net.

Rivers, D. (2005). www.liberationtheology.org.

Rivers, D. (2006). NoNukes. Org, http://www.nonukes.org/.

Roach, J. (1996). *Cities of the dead: Circum-Atlantic performance.* New York: Columbia University Press.

Roadside Theater (n.d.). *About us.* Retrieved March 16, 2007 from http://www.roadsidetheater.com.

Robinson, B. (1984). "Reaching out: "Empowerment of the estranged, the powerless," Box 4, Bernice Robinson Collection, Avery Center Of Afro-American History and Culture.

Roediger, D. (1999). *Wages of whiteness: Race and the making of the American working class.* New York: Verso.

Roediger, D. (2005). *Working toward whiteness: How America's immigrants become white. The strange journey from Ellis Island to the suburbs.* New York: Basic Books.

Rogers, A. (1994). "Exiled voices: Dissociation and the 'return of the repressed' in women's narratives." Wellesley Centers for Women, Wellesley, MA.

Roth, S. (1999). "The uncertain path to dialogue: A meditation." In S. McNamee and K. Gergen (eds), *Relational responsibility: Resources for sustainable dialogue* (pp. 93–7). Thousand Oaks, CA: Sage Publications.

Roth, S. & Epston, D. (1996). "Consulting the problem about the problematic relationship: An exercise for experiencing a relationship with an externalized problem." In M. Hoyt (ed.), *Constructive therapies, Volume 2*. New York: Guilford Publications.

Roy, A. (1998). *The end of imagination*. Washington: D.C. Books.

Roy, A. (8/27/2004). "Peace and the new corporate liberation theology." City of Sydney Peace Prize Lecture. Retrieved Feb 6, 2006 from http://www.abc.net.au/rn/bigidea/stories/s1232956.htm.

Rynkiewich, M. & Spradley, J. (eds) (1976). *Ethics and anthropology: Dilemmas in fieldwork*. New York: John Wiley & Sons.

Sachs, H. (1992). *The development dictionary: A guide to knowledge as power*. Atlantic Highlands, NJ: Zed Books.

Said, E. (2004). *Freud and the non-European*. New York: Verso.

Sampson, E. (1988). "The debate on individualism: Indigenous psychologies of the individual and their role in personal and societal functioning." *American Psychologist*, 43 (1), 15–22.

Sampson, E. (1989). "The challenge of social change for psychology: Globalization and psychology's theory of the person." *American Psychologist*, 44, 914–21.

Sampson, E. (1993a). *Celebrating the other: A dialogic account of human nature*. Boulder, CO: Westview.

Sampson, E. (1993b). "Identity politics: Challenges to psychology's understanding." *American Psychologist*, 48, 1219–30.

Sandoval, C. (2000). *The methodology of the oppressed*. Minneapolis: University of Minneapolis Press.

Santner, E. (1990). *Stranded objects: Mourning, memory, and film in postwar Germany*. Ithaca: Cornell University Press.

Santner, E. (2001). *On the psychotheology of everyday life: Reflections on Freud and Rosenzweig*. Chicago: University of Chicago Press.

Scent of Green Papaya, The. (1994). Rossignon, C., Lecallier, A., Rocca, A. (Producers), & Tranh Anh Hung (Director). USA: First Look Pictures.

Scheper-Hughes, N. (1995a). *Death without weeping: The violence of everyday life in Brazil*. Berkeley: University of California Press.

Scheper-Hughes, N. (1995b). "The primacy of the ethical: Propositions for a militant anthropology." *Current Anthropology*, 36, 3, 409–40.

Scheper-Hughes, N. (2004). "Undoing: Social suffering and the politics of remorse in the new South Africa." In N. Scheper-Hughes & P. Bourgois (eds), *Violence in war and peace* (pp. 459–67). Malden, MA: Blackwell.

Scholem, G. (1941). *Major trends in Jewish mysticism*. New York: Schocken.

Schumacher, E.F. (1973). *Small is beautiful: Economics as if people mattered*. London: Blond and Briggs.

Schutzman, M. & Cohen-Cruz, J. (1994). *Playing Boal: Theater, therapy, activism*. New York: Routledge.

Schwartz, R. (1997). *The curse of Cain: The violent legacy of monotheism*. Chicago: University of Chicago.

Seed, J. (2001). "The Bradley method of bush regeneration." Retrieved May 10, 2005 from http://www.rainforestinfo.org.au/deep-eco/bradley.htm.

Selig, J. (2003). *Martin Luther King, Jr.: Depth psychologist of the cultural soul*. Doctoral dissertation, Pacifica Graduate Institute, Carpinteria, CA.

Selman, R. & Schultz, L. (1990). *Making a friend in youth*. Chicago: University of Chicago Press.

Seshadri-Crooks, K. (2002). "The ethics of travel." In K. Oliver & S. Edwin (eds), *Between the psyche and the social: Psychoanalysis and social theory* (pp. 67–83). Lanham, MD: Rowman and Littlefield.

Shabad, P. (2000). "The most intimate of creations: Symptoms as memorials to one's lonely suffering." In P. Homans (ed.), *Symbolic loss: The Ambiguity of mourning at century's end.* Charlottesville: University Press of Virginia.

Shine, A. (2001). *Ancestral echoes and modern voices: The family story of Thomas Jefferson and Sally Hemings.* Dissertation, Depth Psychology Doctoral Program, Pacifica Graduate Institute, Carpinteria, CA.

Shiva, V. (1989). *Staying alive: Women, ecology, and development.* London: Zed Books.

Shiva, V. (2005). *Earth democracy: Justice, sustainability, and peace.* Boston: South End Press.

Shiva, V. & van Gelder, R. (2003, winter). "Earth Democracy—An interview with Vandana Shiva." Retrieved February 17, 2007 from www.yesmagazine.org/article.asp?ID=570 — 101k.

Shoah (1985). Lanzmann, C. (Producer and Director). USA: New Yorker Films.

Shulman-Lorenz, H. (1997a). *Living at the edge of chaos: Complex systems in culture and psyche.* Einsiedeln, SW: Daimon Verlag.

Shulman-Lorenz, H. (1997b). "The shattered lens: Revisioning the end of monocultures." In American Association of University Women (eds), *Gender and race on the campus and in school: Beyond affirmative action,* Symposium Proceedings featuring current research and model programs presented at the June 19–21, 1997, College/University Symposium.

Shulman-Lorenz, H. & Watkins, M. (2002a). "Depth psychology and colonialism: Individuation, seeing-through, and liberation." In D. Slattery & L. Corbett (eds), *Psychology at the threshold.* Carpinteria, CA: Pacifica Graduate Institute Publications. Illustrated online version http://www.mythinglinks.org/LorenzWatkins.html.

Shulman-Lorenz, H. & Watkins, M. (2002b). "Silenced knowings, forgotten springs: Paths to healing in the wake of colonialism." *Radical Psychology: A Journal of Psychology, Politics, and Radicalism* (online journal). http://www.radpsy.york.ca. Also see illustrated online version at http://www.mythinglinks.org/LorenzWatkins2A.html.

Shulman-Lorenz, H. & Watkins, M. (2003). Individuation, seeing-through, and liberation: Depth psychology and culture, *Quadrant,* 33, 11–32.

Sivaraksa, S. (1992). *Seeds of peace: A Buddhist vision for renewing society.* Berkeley: Parallax Press.

Sivaraksa, S. (ed.) (1994). *The quest for a just society: The legacy and challenge of Buddhadasa Bikkhu.* Bangkok: Thai Inter-Religion Committee for Development.

Sloan, T. (1996). *Damaged life: The crisis of the modern psyche.* New York: Routledge.

Sloan, T. (1999). "The colonization of the lifeworld and the destruction of meaning." *Radical Psychology,* 1 (2). http://www.radpsynet.org/journal/vol1-2/Sloan.html.

Slovo, G. (2003). "Mandela did his part. But songs saved South Africa." *Guardian Unlimited (UK).* Retrieved March 5, 2007 from http://film.guardian.co.uk/features/featurepages/0,1106612,00.html.

Smith, L.T. (1999). *Decolonizing methodologies: Research and indigenous peoples.* New York: Zed Books.

Sohng, S.S.L. (1995). "Participatory research and community organizing." Paper presented at The New Social Movement and Community Organizing Conference, University of Washington, Seattle, WA, Nov. 1–3.

Staub, E. (1993). "The psychology of bystanders, perpetrators, and heroic helpers." *International Journal of Intercultural Relations,* 17 (3), 315–41.

Staub, E. (2001, February 23–24). "After trauma: The impact of trauma, the hope of reconciliation." Headington Institute, Fuller Theological Seminary, Pasadena, CA.

Staub, E. (2003). *The psychology of good and evil: Why children, adults, and groups help and harm others.* London: Cambridge University Press.

Still, S. (1998). "The hero's journey: Breaking depth psychology *into* prison." Unpublished paper, Pacifica Graduate Institute, Carpinteria, CA.

Still, S. (1999). "We wish we could write this in fire: Writings of marginalized men." Unpublished paper, Pacifica Graduate Institute, Carpinteria, CA.

Susman, T. (2007, May 8). Baghdad radio station burns. *Los Angeles Times.* p. A3.

Swearer, D. (1994). "Three legacies of Bhikkhu Buddadasa." In S. Sivaraksa (ed.), *The quest for a just society: The legacy and challenge of Buddhadasa Bhikkhu.* Bangkok: Thai Inter-Religion Committee for Development.

Tandon, R. (1981). "Dialogue as inquiry and intervention." In P. Reason & J. Rowan (eds), *Human inquiry: A sourcebook of new paradigm research* (pp. 293–302). New York: Wiley.

Tandon, R. (1984). *With people's wisdom.* Video by Ruth Pelham. Highlander Center.

Tandon, R. (1988). "Social transformation and participatory research." *Convergence,* 21 (2/3), 5–14.

Taylor, J. M., Gilligan, C. & A. M. Sullivan (1995). *Between voice and silence: Women and girls, race and relationship.* Cambridge: Harvard University Press.

Thomas, A. (2006, April 6) "Enemy soldiers gather—to strive for peace." *Christian science Monitor,* Retrieved February 10, 2007 from http://www.csmonitor.com/2006/0406/p13s02-wome.html.

Thompson, J. (2002). "Reflections on compassion and social healing: An interview with Judith Thompson." http://www.brc21.org/resources/thompson/thompson.html retrieved 11/11/06.

Todorov, T. (1998). *Les abus de la memoire.* Paris: Arlea.

Tolman, D. & Brydon-Miller, M. (eds) (1997). "Transforming psychology: Interpretive and participatory research methods." *Journal of Social Issues,* 53 (4), 597–604.

Turner, V. (1977). *The ritual process: Structure and antistructure.* Ithaca, New York: Cornell University Press.

Tutu, D. (1999). *No future without forgiveness.* NY: Random House.

Verhelst, T. (1987). *No life without roots: Culture and development.* London: Zed Books.

Vertical Ray of the Sun, The (2001). Rossignon, C., Lecallier, A., Rocca, A., Faiver, B. (Producers), & Tranh Anh Hung (Director). USA: Sony.

Villareal, S. (2004). "Reshaping cultural identities: A phenomenological study of eight borderland Latinas." Doctoral dissertation, Pacifica Graduate Institute, Carpinteria, CA.

Virginia Faces Role in Slavery. (2007, February 3). *Los Angeles Times,* p. A17.

Vygotsky, L.S. (1962). *Thought and language.* Cambridge, MA: MIT Press.

wa Thiong'o, N. (1986). *Decolonizing the mind: The politics of language in African literature.* London: James Currey.

Waldorf, L. (2006). "Don't ask me for forgiveness: Narratives from Rwanda's community genocide trials." The Human Rights Institute, University of Connecticut, http://humanrights.uconn.edu/conf_2006.htm, p. 18.

Walkerdine, V. (1990). *Schoolgirl fictions.* NY: Verso.

Wang, C. (2005). "Photovoice: Social change through photography." Retrieved August 10, 2007, from http://www.photovoice.com.

Watada, E. (2006). "Lt. Ehren Watada's speech at the veterans for peace national convention." Retrieved February 4, 2007 from http://www.antoniajuhasz.org/article.php?id=249.

Watkins, M. (1986). *Invisible guests: The development of imaginal dialogues.* Hillsdale, NJ: Analytic Press.

Watkins, M. (1992). "From individualism to interdependence: Changing paradigms in psychotherapy." *Psychological Perspectives*, 27, 52–69.

Watkins, M. (1999). "Pathways between the multiplicities of psyche and culture: The development of dialogical capacities." In J. Rowan & M. Cooper (eds), *The plural self: Multiplicity in everyday life.* Thousand Oaks, CA: Sage Publications.

Watkins, M. (2000a). "Depth psychology and the liberation of being." In R. Brooke (ed.), *Pathways into the Jungian world.* London: Routledge.

Watkins, M. (2000b). "Seeding liberation: A dialogue between depth psychology and liberation psychology." In D. Slattery & L. Corbett (eds), *Depth psychology: Meditations in the field.* Einsiedeln, SW: Daimon Verlag.

Watkins, M . (2004). "Liberating soul sparks: Psyche, classroom, and community." In A. Dalke & B. Dixson (eds), *Minding the light: A collection of Quaker pedagogies.* New York: Peter Lang.

Watkins, M. (2005). "Adoption and identity: Nomadic possibilities for reconceiving the self." In K. Wegar (ed.), *Adoptive families in a diverse society.* Brunswick, NJ: Rutgers University Press.

Way, N. (1997). "Using feminist research methods to understand the friendships of adolescent boys." *Journal for Social Issues*, 53 (4), 703–4.

Weingarten, K. (2003). *Common shock: Witnessing violence every day. How we are harmed, how we can heal.* New York: Dutton.

Werner, H. (1940). *Comparative psychology of mental development.* E.B. Garside (trans.). New York: Harper & Brothers.

Wertz, F. (2006). Personal communication.

Westkott, M. (1990). "Feminist criticism of the social sciences." In. J.M. Nielsen (ed.), *Feminist research methods: Exemplary readings in the social sciences* (pp. 58–68), Boulder CO: Westview Press.

Wilce, J.M. Jr. (ed.) (2003). *Social and cultural lives of immune systems.* New York: Routledge Press.

Wilkinson, T. (Nov. 2003). "In two worlds: Bereaved Israeli and Palestinian parents unite for peace." *Peaceworks*, p. 10.

Winnicott, D.W. (1971). *Playing and reality.* New York: Penguin Books.

Winnicott, D.W. (1989). *Psychoanalytic explorations.* Cambridge: Cambridge University Press.

Wolf, C. (1980). *A model childhood.* New York: Farrar, Straus, and Giroux.

Women for Women, International (n.d.). Retrieved August 27, 2007 from http://www.womenforwomeninternational.org.

Yerushalami, Y.H. (1989). *Zakhor: Jewish history and Jewish memory.* Seattle: University of Washington Press.

Yi, W.K., Li, V.C., Tao, Z.W., Lim, Y.K., Burris, M.A., Ming, W.Y., Yun, X.Y., & Wang, C. (eds) (1995). *Visual voices: 100 photographs of village China by the women of Yunnan province.* New York: The Ford Foundation.

Young, J.E. (2000). *At memory's edge: After-images of the holocaust in contemporary art and architecture.* New Haven & London: Yale University Press.

Zerubavel, E. (2003). *Time maps: Collective memory and the social shape of the past.* Chicago: University of Chicago Press.

Zimmerman, J. & Coyle, V. (1996). *The way of council.* Las Vegas, NV: Bramble Books.

Author Index

Abeles, K., 240
Abraham, K., 59
Abraham, N., 121–122, 341
Adam, K., 334
Addams, J., 226–227, 229, 341
Adler, G., 348
Aitken, R., 37, 39, 322–323, 341
Ajami, F., 139, 341
Alcoff, L., 341
Alschuler, L., 194, 341
Altman, N., 56–57, 341
Anzaldúa, G., 135–136, 158, 171, 241, 340–341
Aramim, B., 97
Argyris, C., 282–283, 341
Asad, T., 301, 341
Assefa, H., 319, 341
Atkinson, N., 342
Atta, M., 139
Avelar, I., 105, 111, 119–120, 124, 341

Baca, J., 249
Bachelet, M., 121
Baez, J., 245
Baldwin, C., 191, 341
Baldwin, J., 64, 341
Bar On, B., 275, 341
Bartov, O., 100
Bawtree, V., 40, 353
Baxter, V., 324, 341
Bearak, B., 148, 341
Becker, C., 202, 342, 344
Behar, R., 31, 281, 307, 342
Belafonte, H., 245
Belenky, M., 3, 144, 187–189, 207, 211–212, 215–216, 218, 226, 231, 272, 283–284, 342
Benjamin, W., 127
Berrigan, P., 209, 347
Berry, W., 209, 342
Berryman, P., 35, 342
Bhabha, H., 3, 166–167, 170, 208, 219, 225, 230–231, 342
Bhatia, S., 169, 342
Bianchi, E. D., 260

Biehl, A., 333
Biehl, L., 333
Biehl, P., 333
Bird, J., 343
Bishop, M., 248
Blanche, M. T., 17, 350
Blee, K. M., 309, 342
Block, T., 334, 342
Bloom, S., 207, 342
Boal, A., 216, 232–233, 253–254, 342
Bob-Manuel, I., 322, 342
Boggs, G. L., 221, 342
Bohm, D., 201, 342
Bond, L. A., 3, 144, 187, 207, 283–284, 342
Borland, K., 292, 342
Boulding, E., 196, 342, 352
Bowles, G., 281, 342, 351
Boyte, H., 207, 345
Brabeck, K., 293–294, 342–343
Bradshaw, G., 220, 343
Braidotti, R., 159, 165–167, 169, 171, 343
Briggs, J., 82, 343
Brock-Utne, B., 322, 343
Brooke, R., 357
Brown, B. A., 240, 343–344
Brown, L.M., 184–185, 284–285, 289–290, 292, 309, 343
Brown, T., 322, 343
Brydon-Miller, M., 295, 356
Buber, M., 176, 208, 307, 343
Buddhadhasa, Bikkhu, 37–39
Burris, M. A., 255, 357
Bushe, G. R., 200, 343
Bye-Brown, F., 322, 343

Cabrera, R., 22, 324, 343
Carawan, G., 245
Cartwright, D., 349
Caruth, C., 123, 343, 349
Casey, E., 70, 343
Castillejo-Cuéllar, A., 318–319, 343
Castillo, R. J., 352
Césaire, A., 74, 95, 343

Chambers, I., 148, 343, 347
Chanfrault-Duchet, M.-F., 288, 343
Chasin, L., 202, 342, 344
Chasin, R., 202, 343–344
Cheney, R., 93
Chitty, B., 98–99, 344
Chrisman, N. J., 311, 344
Clinchy, B., 187, 342
Clinton, H., 232
Coldevin, G., 344
Cone, J. H., 34, 344
Cook, J., 347, 351
Cooper, M., 357
Cooperrider, D. L., 199–200, 218, 344
Corbett, L., 355, 357
Coyle, V., 191, 357
Cross, W. E., 171, 344
Curtis, B., 343
Cushman, P., 58–60, 70–71, 344

Dagron, A. G., 248, 253, 255, 262, 344
Dalke, A., 357
Damon, B., 260–261, 344
Danto, E., 55–56, 344
Dash, J., 124, 127, 344
Dawson, T., 341
de Kock, E., 89
de Mare, P., 201, 345
De Martino, R., 346
Debold, E., 292, 309, 343
DeLeon, J., 207, 344
Deleuze, G., 127, 161, 173, 344, 345
Dellal, J., 342
Derrida, J., 150, 332, 345
Dewey, J., 282
Dixson, B., 357
Dorfman, A., 116, 345
Du Bois, W. E. B., 166, 313, 345
Durkheim, E., 315
Dussel, E., 36, 99, 155, 241, 345
Dylan, B., 245

Eckhart, M., 334
Edkins, J., 111, 345
Edwin, S., 352, 355
Eisner, E. W., 350
Ellis, M. H., 35, 345
Eltit, D., 338, 345
Enriquez, V., 275, 345
Epstein, H., 122, 345
Epstein, J., 221, 345

Epston, D., 203, 354
Erikson, K., 106–107, 118, 345
Esteva, G., 32–34, 43, 46, 48, 158, 222–223, 345
Evans, S., 207, 345
Ezekiel, R., 306, 345

Fals-Borda, O., 27, 345
Fanon, F., 49, 90, 113–114, 163, 168, 202, 321, 345
Faubian, J., 346
Faundez, A., 194, 230, 346
Felman, S., 50–51, 79, 90, 115, 123, 346, 349
Fenichel, O., 58
Field, R., 282, 346
Fine, M., 299, 305, 351
Flinders, C. L., 69, 161, 346
Fonow, M., 347, 351
Forrest, N. B., 235
Foucault, M., 202, 231, 239, 346
Fox, D., 11, 296, 353
Freire, P., 27, 71, 193–195, 207, 230, 277, 281, 296, 303, 346, 348
Freud, S., 5, 16, 55–56, 159, 167, 236
Fromm, E., 71, 75, 346
Fullilove, M., 220, 346
Funari, V., 267–269, 346

Gablik, S., 240, 346
Gadamer, H.-G., 286, 309, 346
Galeano, E., 76
Gandhi, M., 20, 81, 346
Garfinkel, H., 307, 346
Garside, E. B., 357
Gebara, I., 152, 153, 346
Gergen, K., 205, 346, 354
Gilligan, C., 66, 184–186, 191, 217, 273–274, 279, 284–286, 289–292, 309, 343, 346, 356
Gilman, S., 56, 346
Gilroy, P., 171, 346
Glissant, E., 237, 346
Gluck, S., 342–343, 347
Gobodo-Madikizela, P., 89, 309, 346
Godoy, S., 122, 346
Goffman, E., 307, 346
Goizueta, R. S., 35–37, 178, 346
Goldberger, N., 187, 342
Gray-Felder, D., 262
Greene, M., 232, 347

Griffin, S., 76, 105, 127, 167, 347
Gruen, A., 64, 347
Guattari, F., 161, 173, 344, 345
Gutiérrez, G., 32, 34, 347

Habermas, J., 283, 347
Hale, S., 276, 347
Hall, S., 171, 347
Hamber, B., 17, 317, 347, 350
Hamer, F. L., 245
Hanh, T. N., 37, 209, 335–336, 347
Harash, A., 61
Haritos-Fatouros, M., 91–93, 309, 348
Harris, E., 140, 347
Harthcock, M., 292, 347
Henderson, M., 325, 347
Heraclitus, 334
Herda, E., 285, 292, 307, 309, 347
Hermans, J. M., 172, 347
Herzig, M., 342, 344
Heschel, A., 219, 347
Hill Collins, P., 211, 275, 347
Hillman, J., 53, 62, 73, 76, 347
Hirsch, L., 341
Hirsch, M., 125, 347
Hitler, A., 140
Hocoy, D., 339, 347
Hoeller, C., 225, 347
Hoffman, G. K., 325–326, 347
Hoheisel, H., 239
Hollander, N., 8, 23, 58, 347
Homans, P., 2, 237, 348, 355
hooks, b., 133, 170, 210, 265, 272, 275,
    279, 348
Horney, K., 68, 348
Horton, M., 99, 194, 227– 229, 348
Howard, J., 325
Hoyt, M., 354
Huggins, M. K., 91–93, 309, 348
Hull, R. F. C., 348
Hurley, R., 346
Hyde, L., 35, 71, 79, 348

Jackson, J., 106
Jackson, M., 245, 322, 348
Jacoby, R., 54–58, 63, 348
JanMohamed, A. R., 169, 278, 348
Jara, V., 260
Jelin, E., 94, 111, 348
Jesus Christ, 145

Josephs, I., 342
Jourard, S., 307, 348
Joyce, K., 240
Jung, C. G., 138, 177, 236, 348
Jurgensmayer, M., 115, 348

Kalff, D., 156, 348
Kaplan, A., 335, 348
Kaplan, B., 9, 32, 348
Kaprow, A., 258, 348
Kawachi, I., 315, 348
Kearney, R., 170, 219, 348
Keating, A., 171, 341
Kelley, R., 13, 219, 349
Kempen, H. J., 172, 347
Kennedy, B. P., 315, 348
Kidder, L., 299, 305, 351
King, Jr, M. L., 106
King, S., 40, 353
Kipnis, A., 274, 339, 347, 349
Klebold, D., 140
Klein, M., 59, 138, 237
Klein, R., 281, 342, 351
Klein, R. D., 281, 342, 351
Kleinman, A., 62–63, 107, 349
Kohlberg, L., 273
Kolvenbach, P. H., 48, 349
Kozol, J., 349
Krishnamurti, J., 201
Kristeva, J., 70, 174, 217–218, 349
Krystal, H., 109–110, 349
Kvale, S., 308, 349

Lacan, J., 128
Lacayo, V., 256, 257–258, 349
Lacy, S., 261
LaFayette, B., 244
Landau, J., 218, 349
Lanek, R., 321, 349
Langer, M., 59, 349
Lankshear, C., 24, 278, 351
Lanzmann, C., 123, 349
Laub, D., 115, 346, 349
Lavie, S., 172, 349
Lecallier, A., 344, 354, 356
Lederach, J. P., 314, 333, 349
Lee, G., 333, 349
Lerner, R. M., 348
Levine, D. P., 227–228, 333, 349
Lewin, K., 282, 349

Li, V. C., 254–255, 357
Lifton, R. J., 73, 81, 84–86, 98, 171, 350
Lim, Y. K., 255, 357
Lin, M., 327
Lincoln, Y. S., 300, 350
Linklater, K., 350
Lins, P., 237, 350
Lipsitz, G., 170, 350
Lira, E., 118, 320, 350
Lispector, C., 159, 350
Littleton, C., 140, 142
Lochner, K., 315, 348
Lorde, A., 82, 350
Lorenz, H., 339, 347
Loveman, B., 350
Lund, K., 344
Luria, I., 334, 335
Lykes, M. B., 17, 273, 293, 350

Maalouf, A., 114–115, 163, 172–173, 350
Maathai, W., 18–19, 350
Macy, J., 37, 199, 229, 350
Mahalia, J., 245
Maimonides, A., 334
Mama, A., 165, 350
Mann, S. J., 143, 350
Marable, M., 170, 351
Maracek, J., 299, 305, 351
Marcos, S., 79, 223, 351
Markgraaff, D., 341
Marks, L. U., 111, 126–127, 351
Marshall, J. M., 331
Martín-Baró, I., 8, 24, 26–27, 69, 111, 175, 200, 271, 351
Mash, M., 343
McEachin, A. D., 101
McGoldrick, M., 349
McLaren, P., 24, 278, 351
McTaggart, R., 283, 296, 351
Mead, G. H., 180, 351
Meirelles, F., 344
Memmi, A., 69, 115, 351
Menchú, R., 294
Mendieta, E., 341
Mengele, J., 86
Mesa-Bains, A., 279, 348
Mies, M., 281, 351
Ming, W. Y., 255, 357

Minh-ha, T., 266, 351
Mini, V., 246
Minow, M., 320, 351
Mishler, E. G., 300, 307, 351
Mitscherlich, A., 86, 351
Mitscherlich, M., 351
Moane, G., 209, 351
Monsalvo, J., 330
Montero, M., 8, 351
Morackis, A., 80
Morales, A. L., 76, 161, 231, 351
Morales, E., 247
Morris, C. W., 351
Morrison, T., 126, 351
Moses, 36
Moulton, P., 72, 351
Moyers, B., 145–146, 351
Muñoz, J. E., 164, 352
Murphy, E., 326, 352

Nandy, A., 81, 352
Nelson, G., 4, 272, 353
Nghiem, C., 332, 352
Nielsen, J., M., 271, 352, 357
Nora, P., 242, 352
Norberg-Hodge, H., 43–45, 352
Nussbaum, M., 165, 352

Oakley, A., 285, 307, 352
Obama, B., 106, 235
Odetta, 245
Oglesby, E., 318, 320, 352
Oliver, K., 162, 210, 216–218, 352, 355
Oliver, M., 109, 352

Parra, V., 216
Patai, D., 308, 311–312, 342–343, 347, 352
Payne, K., 333, 352
Pelfrey, M. H., 259, 352
Pelfrey, R., 259, 352
Penington, I., 337, 352
Perluss, E., 77, 352
Peshkin, A., 350
Peter, Paul and Mary, 245
Peters, L. G., 75, 352
Pinochet, A., 116, 119–120, 324
Piper, R., 201, 345
Polak, F L., 196, 352
Ponce, C., 334, 352

Potter, E., 341
Potter, N., 353
Prakash, S., 43, 158, 222–223, 345
Pratt, M. L., 168, 352
Prilleltensky, I., 4, 11, 272, 296, 353
Puleo, M., 34, 36, 353
Puntarigvivat, T., 37–38, 353
Putnam, R., 282, 283, 341
Putnam, T., 343

Queen, C., 40, 353
Quiñones Rosado, R., 241, 353

Rahnema, M., 40, 353
Ramos, M., 344
Rantisi, A., 129
Rawlinson, M., 331, 353
Reagon, B. J., 244, 353
Reason, P., 356
Ribiero, A., 344
Ricoeur, P., 353
Riggs, M., 124, 342
Rivers, D., 34, 78, 176, 353
Roach, J., 242, 353
Roberts, H., 352
Robertson, G., 343
Robinson, B., 227–228, 353
Rocca, A., 344, 354, 356
Roediger, D., 170, 353
Rogers, A., 41, 217, 291, 346, 354
Rosenzweig, F., 151
Rossignon, C., 344, 354, 356
Roth, S., 203–204, 342, 344, 354
Rowan, J., 356, 357
Roy, A., 148, 276, 354
Rynkiewich, M., 311, 344, 354

Sachs, H., 46, 345, 354
Said, E., 159, 173, 354
Salbi, Z., 328
Sampson, E., 171, 201, 298, 354
Sandoval, C., 2, 29, 50, 96, 167, 354
Santner, E., 86–89, 128–129, 151–152,
    171, 173, 354
Saul, J., 218, 349
Scheper-Hughes, N., 61, 300–301, 314,
    332–333, 354
Scholem, G., 334, 354
Schultz, L., 178–179, 181, 355
Schumacher, E. F., 38

Schwartz, R., 163, 354
Seed, J., 15, 354
Seeger, P., 245
Selig, J., 62, 354
Selman, R., 178–179, 181, 355
Serrano, G., 80
Seshadri-Crooks, K., 160, 167, 355
Seung-hui, Cho, 323
Shabad, P., 54, 355
Shapira, Y., 97
Shine, A., 77, 355
Shiva, V., 220–222, 262, 355
Shulman-Lorenz, H., 2, 60, 62–63, 168,
    355
Sichrovsky, P., 86
Simmons, R., 100
Simpson, S., 341
Sivaraksa, S., 37, 39, 355–356
Slattery, D., 355, 357
Sloan, T., 71, 163, 176, 219, 292, 355
Slovo, G., 246, 355
Smith, D. M., 282–283, 341
Smith, L. T., 250, 276, 310, 355
Sohng, S. S. L., 293, 356
Spradley, J., 311, 344, 354
Srivastava, S., 199, 218, 344
Stains, R., 344
Staub, E., 52, 65, 317, 355, 356
Still, S., 77, 293, 356
Sullivan, A. M., 66, 186, 273–274, 279,
    286, 356
Sullivan, H. S., 57
Susman, T., 331, 356
Suzuki, D. T., 346
Swearer, D., 38–39, 356
Swedenburg, T., 172, 349

Tandon, R., 270, 283, 295, 308, 356
Tao, Z. W., 255, 357
Tappan, M., 292, 309, 343
Tarule, J., 187, 342
Taylor, J. M., 66, 186, 273–274, 279,
    286, 356
Thomas, A., 97, 356
Thompson, J., 279, 356
Thompson, S., 201, 345
Tickner, L., 343
Todorov, T., 341, 356
Tolman, D., 217, 295, 346, 356
Tolomelli, E., 344

Torok, M., 121–122, 341
Trahn Anh Hung, 124, 344, 354, 356
Turner, V., 136–137, 356
Tutu, D., 153, 321, 356

van Gelder, R., 221–222, 355
van Gennep, A., 136
Verhelst, T., 40, 356
Villareal, S., 77, 356
Vygotsky, L. S., 179, 288, 356

wa Thiong'o, N., 278, 356
Waldorf, L., 319, 356
Walkerdine, V., 289, 356
Walsh, F., 349
Wang, C., 255, 356–357
Wapner, S., 348
Watada, E., 103, 357
Watkins, M., 2, 6, 52, 55, 61–63, 66,
    158, 188, 205, 220, 339, 343, 347,
    355, 357
Watt, J., 146
Way, N., 288, 291, 357

Wegar, K., 357
Weingarten, K., 76, 357
Weinstock, J. S., 3, 144, 187, 207,
    283–284, 342
Werner, H., 33, 357
Wertz, F., 297, 357
Westkott, M., 280, 357
Wilce, J. M. Jr., 143, 350, 357
Wilkinson, T., 166, 357
Winnicott, D. W., 66, 135, 357
Wolf, C., 357

Yerushalami, Y. H., 238, 357
Yi, W. K., 255, 357
Young, J. E., 239, 357
Young-Eisendrath, P., 341
Yun, X. Y., 255, 357
Yunus, M., 329

Zerubavel, E., 357
Zimbardo, P. G., 91–93, 309, 348
Zimmerman, J., 191, 357
Žižek, S., 128

Subject Index

abject, 28, 69–70, 175
absolute empiricism, 151
Abu Ghraib prison, 83, 93
accompaniment, 277
action research, 204, 271, 282, 296
  definition of, 269
adolescent girls, 273, 284
  teenage pregnancy, 286
adoptive parents, 26, 173
advertising, 72
Afghanistan, 118
Africa, 12, 41, 105, 164, 271, 274, 322
African American(s), 99, 186
  community, 211
  cultural workers, 210–213
  educators, 251
  girls, 66
  identity, 245
  migration of, 77
  women, 210–213, 275, 279
African diaspora, 211, 242
  religions, 248
African National Congress, 246
African Peacebuilding and
    Reconciliation Network, 319
agency, 25
Aguascalientes, 223
AIDS memorial, 240
Al Qaeda, 331
Alabama, 235
alegremia, 330
alexithymia, 109, 143
Algeria, 24, 49, 90, 172
Algerian revolution, 83
alienation, 28, 174
aliveness, 149, 152
Allah, 146
allegory, 120, 124
altars, 248–250
*Amandla! A Revolution in Four-Part
    Harmony*, 246
Amazon, 221
America, 19, 63, 66, 71, 169
  histories, 98, 100, 250, 316

American Anthropological Association,
    301
American Psychological Association,
    299
Americanization, 29
Americans, 105, 225, 273, 279
Americas, 209, 248
amnesia, 14, 129, 238, 239, 240, 243,
    263, 334–336
  social, 54–55, 57
amnesty, 316
anaesthetized heart, 73
anamnesis, 88–89
anarchism, 39
anasemic effects, 121
ANC Youth Leagues, 247
ancestors, 235
  and difference, 285
  and social change, 234
anhedonia, 109
animator, 193, 195
annunciation, 194
anomie, 2
anthropologists, 148, 301, 311–312
anthropology
  and colonial encounters, 301
  postmodern, 301
  that breaks your heart, 31
antiapartheid struggle, 118
antihierarchical, 263
anurak, 39
anxiety, 60
apartheid, 89, 318
apology, 81, 331, 333
aporias, 236
Appalachian region, 252
Appalshop, 252
appreciative inquiry, 218
archetypal dominants, 54
Argentina, 35, 106, 118, 120, 235, 259,
    285, 330
Argentine Psychoanalytic Association,
    59
Armageddon, 145

arts
  and healing, 122
  and memory, 122
  liberation, 232–265
Asia, 27, 44
assisted regeneration, 15–16, 48
Association of Maya Ixil Women, 16
Atlanta, 245
atrocity, 320
  producing environments, 92–94, 109,
    116
  technologies, 93
auras, 127
Auschwitz self, 85–86
Auschwitz, 86, 123
Australia, 15, 274, 325
authoritarian
  approaches, 28
  structures, 236
authoritarianism, 257, 283
autoethnography, 17–18, 168, 266
autoethnology, 241
automaticity, 128, 236
autonomous zones, 22, 170, 223–224
Aztecs, 135

Baghdad, 330
Balmy Alley, 250
base communities, 39, 112, 216
Belgium, 40
beneficence, 302
Berlin, 57
Berlin Wall, 316
biblical prophecy, 146
Billionaires for Bush, 260
binary oppositions, 8, 11, 162, 175
biodiversity, 222
bioregionalism, 45
Black is, Black Ain't, 124
Bohmian dialogue, 200–202
Bolivia, 247, 248, 253
Book of Revelations, 145–146
border crosser, 23, 28, 171, 174, 207
Border Dynamics, 80
Bosnia, 328
Boston, 203, 337
bourgeois conventionality, 55
Bradley Method, 15
Brazil, 1, 60, 61, 91, 93, 153, 159, 195–196,
  229, 232, 260, 301, 309, 312, 317

Brazilian military dictatorship, 232
Brown University, 100
Buddhism, 37, 209
  dependent co-arising, 38
  five precepts of, 335
Buddhist economics, 38
Buddhist Peace Foundation, 39
bullying, 13, 142–143, 165, 180
Burma, 106, 121
burn out, 91–93
bystanders, 61, 65, 125, 130, 229, 276,
  316, 329
  collusion with perpetrators, 80
  communities of, 93
  silence of, 80
bystanding, 50, 51, 64–66, 73, 76
  amputation of seeing, 51
  and privilege, 65
  habitual, 65
  injustice, 50
  pathologies of, 64, 66
  symptoms of, 65–74

Calcutta, 30
California, 229, 249
California Plaza, 336
California's Central Valley, 228
caliphate, 146
Canada, 274, 322
caracoles, 224–225
cargo cults, 145
Caribbean, 248, 333
Catalina Island, 77
Catholic Church, 34, 324
  abuses, 326
Catholic Worker movement, 39
Center for Cultural and Community
    Development, 211, 215
centrifugal forces, 149, 154, 155,
  209
character disorders, 62
Chernobyl, 61
Chevron Texaco, 221
Chiapas, 22, 39, 79, 170, 209, 213, 224,
  228
Chiapas Media Project, 294
Chicago, 226
Chicago's Hull House, 226
Chicano Park, 249
Chicanos, 99

Chikaya Community Radio Station, 248
Chile, 82, 84, 116–121, 130, 216, 235, 259–260, 320, 324
Chilpancingo Colectivo, 267–268
China, 61, 254, 261
Chipko movement, 44, 261–262
CHRICA, 24
Christian Base Communities, 39, 112, 216
CIA, 118
circle of learners, 144
Circle of Stories Web, 250
circle, 26
circum-Atlantic, 242
Citizenship Schools, 227–228
CITTAC, 268
Civil Rights Memorial, 239–240
Civil Rights Movement, 7, 235, 243, 247
civil wars, 82, 235
Cochabamba, 30
Colectivo Chilpancingo Pro Justicia Ambiental, 267–268
collaborative
    community-building, 240
    inquiry, 203
    projects, 256
collection of data, 307–308
collective memory, 94–96
collective trauma, 14
Colombia, 34, 213, 328
colonial
    conquest, 21, 68, 116
    dynamics, 49
    thinking, 31
colonialism, 1, 4, 10, 28, 30–31, 33, 64, 75, 114–115, 129–130, 160, 242
    assimilation, 114
    construction of otherness, 69
    definition of, 2
    effects on unconscious of, 51
    longterm effects of brutality, 95
    morph into globalization, 220
    normalization of injustice, 115
    psychic wounds of, 1
colonias, 266
colonization, 224
    appropriation of ancestral lands, 223
    internal, 113–114

of psychic space, 210
of the personality, 220
psychic costs of, 114–115
colonized, 113–114
colonizer, 114
color blindness
    naive, 20, 170
comfort zone, 305
Committee for Health Rights in Central America, 24
communal dreaming, 219–220
Communication for Social Change, 262
communication, 220
    collaborative, 42
communitas, 137–138, 156
communities of liberation, 36
communities of resistance, 207, 210, 213, 219
communal dreaming, 219–220
community
    arts, 233
    ethical, 126
    fieldwork, 270
    healers, 241
    homeplaces, 210–213
    identifications within, 152
    imagined, 21, 170
    of memory, 130
    of revelation, 151–152
    psychology, 1, 274
    radio, 247–248
    research, 271
    theater, 232
    video, 256–258
comparative neurosis, 67
compass points, 3, 6
compassion, 279, 323, 335
compassionate engagement, 176
compassionate listening, 333
complexes, 113
concentration camps, 51, 116, 141
    survivors, 109
confidentiality, 306
conflicts of interest, 311
Confluence Project, 327–328
Congo, 328
conquest, 30
conscientization, 48, 193, 271
consciousness raising, 22
    through group research, 281

constructed knowing, 190
consumerism, 71, 72
  and war, 72
contested memory, 234–236
conventional narratives, 233
conversion, 48
CORE, 245
council, 190–192
counter-development, 11, 30, 43–45
  psychological, 45
counter-interview, 307
countermemorial, 238–242
countermemory, 232–233, 238–242, 248
countermonument, 241, 262
counterpractices, 202
creative arts, 150
creolization, 23, 171
critical
  consciousness, 18, 25, 131
  hermeneutics, 285
  psychology, 1, 34
  race theory, 18, 168
  reflection, 281–284
  research
    definition of, 269
  theorists, 283
  theory, 271
  thinking, 81
cross burnings, 84
cross-cultural alliances, 21, 170
Crusades, 147
Cuba, 99
cultural
  amnesia, 9, 163
  discourse, 133
  identity, 41
  ideologies, 79
  invasion, 278, 301
  memory, 76
  pathology, 62
  resistance, 116
  therapists, 241
  unconscious, 75
  work, 236
  workers, 117, 211–215, 241, 318
culture bearers, 275
culture of resistance, 211
culture of silence, 86
culture wars, 7
culture
  and idea of diversity, 230

culture-bound reactive syndromes, 75
cultures of peace, 191
cultures of violence, 71
curanderas, 241
Cyclo, 124

Danish folk schools, 227, 229
data analysis, 308–310
  in group, 309
  including interviewees, 309
data collection, 308
Daughters of the Dust, 124, 127
Day of the Dead, 249, 250
decolonization, 21, 31, 170
  psychic, 115
de-colonizing methods, 276
deculturation, 41
defensive strategies, 143
dehumanization, 68, 86, 118, 321
de-ideologization, 98, 292
demilitarization, 241
democractic practices, 131
democracy, 220–222
Dengue Fever, 336
denial, 31, 106, 131, 143
Denmark, 227
depersonalization, 118
de-placing, 221
depression, 134
deprofessionalized intellectual, 32
depth psychology, 7, 49, 52–53, 75
  as countercultural discipline, 58
  unclaimed theorists, 58
derealization, 84–86, 118
desymbolization, 220
deterritorialization, 7, 22, 161, 170
Detroit, 221
development, 34, 39, 44
  and culture, 40
  austerity and, 43
  dependent relationships in, 35
  dismantling mental structure of, 46
  engaged Buddhist critiques of, 37–40
  failure, 27
  genuine, 34
  history of term, 34
  hoax of, 45
  individual, 32, 38
  international, 16

development (*Contd.*)
  large-scale, 40, 43
  liberation psychology's critique of, 34
  material, 32
  psychological, 33
  planning, 30, 31
  projects, 27
  rejection of term, 35
  rhethoric, 30, 44
  small-scale, 40
  top-down planning, 41
  TOT model, 41
developmental psychology
  cultural values, 32
dhammic socialism, 37–38
Diagnostic and Statistical Manual of
    Mental Disorders, 62, 68, 108, 110
dialogical
  capacities, 176–178, 205
  encounters, 142
  spaces, 25, 173, 176
dialogue, 8, 9, 27, 165, 173, 176,
    182–184, 187–188, 195, 201–202,
    207, 224, 230, 277, 281, 283, 285
  across differences, 20
  across lifespan, 176
  and play, 180
  and subjectivity, 157
  Bohmian, 200–202
  child-rearing and, 188
  in polarized environments, 98
  inner, 177
  intrapsychic, 187
  participatory, 28
  practices, 130
dialogues of reconciliation, 230
diasporic identities, 23, 148, 171
dictatorship, 117–118, 122
dirty wars, 35, 58
disappearances, 84
disavowal, 84–86, 185
discipliary boundaries, 14–15, 271
  transgression of, 62
disidentification, 11, 17, 147, 164,
    168
dissociation, 53, 69, 74–75, 131, 141
  dissociated states, 109
  doubling, 84–86
  mending, 75–79
dissociative
  complex, 76

response, 128
  strategies, 125
dissociative processes, 288
diversity training, 130
divine light, 334
divine spark, 176, 334, 337
domestic abuse, 281
dominant
  ideas, 133
  ideologies, 280
domination
  dynamics of, 240
Dominican Republic, 99, 248
Dominican-American teens,
    337
double consciousness, 15, 166
double oblivion, 70
Dow Chemical, 221
dreaming
  communal, 219–220
dreams, 231
drive theories, 54
dualistic thinking, 8, 162, 190

earth democracy, 220–222
East Germany, 101
ecocide, 44
ecofeminism, 152
eco-liberation psychologies, 221
ecosystems, 31
  assaulted, 336
Ecuador, 30
  Amazon, 221
education
  banking method of, 195
educational system
  abandonment by, 187
ego-defense, 46
Egypt, 139
Eichmann trial, 109
El Salvador, 10, 23–24, 122, 235,
    258, 271
elders, 322
elite, 28, 35
emancipatory change, 270
Emory University, 100
emotional stress, 143
engaged Buddhism, 37–40, 332,
    335
  Four Abodes, 38
  mindfulness meditation, 38

ensembled self, 23, 171
environmental justice, 328
escraches, 259–260
Eshu, 136
ethical communities, 241
ethics
    breaches of relational, 309
    contracts of the same, 150
    dialogical, 300
    of hospitality, 150–151
    of liberation psychology, 152
    psychological research, 300
ethics of otherness, 8, 162
Ethiopia, 122
ethnic identity, 20, 169
ethnography, 16, 283
Eurocentric psychologies
    critique of, 24–25
Eurocentrism, 7, 15, 148, 280
Europe, 96, 271
European culture, 135
Europeans, 105, 225
    feeling of superiority, 113
euthanasia, 86
evaluation, 264
exile, 117
exiled consciousness, 154–155
existential homelessness, 28, 174
Exodus, 34–36
expertism, 27
experts, 35, 270, 284

faculdad, 135
failure
    personalistic understanding of, 23,
        67
false entitlement, 72
false unity, 29
Familiares de Los Desaparecidos, 120
fantasy, 180
FAO, 41, 42
farmers, 42
Farmworkers Movement, 249
fascism, 74, 88
Fatah party, 97
fatalism, 2, 15, 25, 31, 111–113, 139,
        144–145
    symptoms of, 112
feelings of superiority, 68
    colonial ideologies and , 64, 69
feminist research, 271, 278–281

fieldwork, 300–305, 312
    community and ecological, 6, 77
Finland, 261
fixed identifications, 148
food production, 42
forced migration, 14
forgetfulness, 120
forgetting
    passive, 105
forgiveness, 81, 319, 331–333
France, 24, 96, 172
Franco-Maghrebis, 24, 172
Frankfurt School, 282
Freedom Riders, 244
freedom
    interconnected levels of, 37
Fresno, 228
frontier dwellers, 25, 172
frozen identities, 128–129
Funa Commission, 260
fundamentalism, 115
funding agencies, 42, 243
fusion of horizons, 309

gacaca rituals, 319
Ganges, 222
Gaza, 97
gender roles, **42**
    heteronormative, 4
gender
    essentializing, 273
    generative words, 195
generosity, 335
genocide, 9, 85, 138, 239, 320
    Guatemala, 16
    Native American, 14, 57
Germans, 238
Germany, 60, 84, 87, 109, 215, 238–239
globalization, 1, 10, 28–30, 50, 52, 119,
        140, 145, 242
Gnosticism, 334
God, 146, 334
Grace Corporation, 221
Grameen Bank, 329
grassroots
    democracy, 59
    postmodernism, 222–223
greed, 72–73
Green Belt Movement, the, 17–19
Greensboro Truth and Reconciliation
        Commission, 331

Grenada, 248
Grupo Factor X, 266–268
Guantanamo, 93
Guatemala, 16, 21–22, 82, 84, 106, 118, 122, 235, 248, 258, 293–294, 318–319, 324

habitats
  decreasing, 220
habitual thinking, 133–134
Haiti, 99
Hamas, 97, 129
happenings, 258–262
harambee spirit, 18
Harvard Center on Gender and Education, 274
Hawaii, 322
heliotropic hypothesis, 200
hermeneutics
  critical, 285
  of love, 96
  of suspicion, 289
heterogeneity, 147, 153
heterogeneous histories, 148
hierarchical principles, 28
high blood pressure, 143
Highlander Folk School, 227–228
Highlander Research and Education Center, 99, 227–228, 245
Hijos do Los Desaparecidos, 120, 259
Himalayan foothills, 44
Hiroshima, 73, 333
Hispanic, 186
historical memory, 14
history, 5, 50, 238
  as neurosis, 237
  denied, 5
  medicine, 231
  official, 50, 95, 100, 105, 119, 237
  weakening of official, 96
Ho'oponopono problem solving, 322
Hoheisel, Horst, 239
holocaust, 50, 58, 68, 78, 79, 84, 109, 111, 115, 122–123, 239 *See also* genocide
  memorial, 239
homeplaces
  and artistic expression, 218
  displacing of, 220
homophobia, 135
hospitality, 133, 222
  ethics of, 5, 150–151, 159–160

Hull House, 226–227
human rights, 241, 324
  abuse, 321
Human Rights Office of the Archdiocese of Guatemala, 22
humanization, 211
Hungary, 60
Hutus, 328
hybrid identity, 164, 171
hybridity, 8, 15, 23, 27–28, 162, 166, 171, 173–174, 225
hyperarousal, 108
hypervigilance, 108
hypocrisy, 233

I and Thou, 137
iconic memory, 233
identifications, 280
identity, 12, 13, 149, 162, 164
  and nationalism, 21
  Chicano, 77
  decentered, 13, 165
  hybrid, 11, 23
  migratory, 23
  national, 170
  nomadic, 20, 149
  Western model of, 9, 162
ideology, 219
  of dominant culture, 131
images
  transgressive, 133
imaginal dialogue, 188
imagination, 3, 6, 138, 150
  kinesthetic, 242–243
  utopic, 219
immune system, 143
impunity, 259
inbetween spaces, 208
India, 20, 63, 253, 261, 271, 274
indigenous, 224
  cosmovisions, 241, 249
  groups, 22, 170
  knowledge, 42
  people, 16, 33
individualism, 9, 24, 33, 163, 201, 214
individualistic paradigm, 62
individuation, 149
inferiority
  feelings, 68
  epidermalized, 113
informed consent, 305

injustice, 34
Inquisition, 147, 320
interconnectivity, 30
interdependence, 30, 36, 152–154
internalized racism, 304
interruption
  aesthetics of, 129–130
interstitial space, 125, 207, 225–231
interview, 308
intrapsychic wounds, 64
introjection, 12, 165
invulnerability, 135
Iraq, 83, 103, 118, 146, 330
IRB reviews, 299
Ireland, 326
  women's liberation movement,
    209
isolation, 143, 240, 314
Israel, 14, 97, 129–130, 145–146, 166,
    235
Israeli Defense Force, 102

Jamestown Project, 251
Jamestown, 101
Japan, 235, 333
Jews, 7, 145, 239
jokers, 254
Journey of Healing, 326
Judaism, 219
Junebug Productions, 252
Jungian psychology, 149, 236
Jungians, 54

kabbalist, 334
Kagadi-Kibaale Community Radio,
    248
Kanaka Maoli, 322–323
Kassel, 239
Katrina, 251
Katura Community Radio, 248
Keepers of the Waters, 260–261
kelipoth, 334
Kenya, 17, 19, 21, 319, 335
  National Council of Women, 17
Kerala, 39, 221
kherjri trees, 262
Kiva.org, 329
knowledge
  situated, 281
Korea, 99
Kosovo, 229, 328

Ku Klux Klan, 146, 228, 235, 252
Kulturarbeit, 236

labor unions, 228
Ladakh, 43, 44
Latin America, 8, 29–30, 34–36, 58,
    105, 111, 118, 216, 247, 250,
    271, 274, 333
Latin American folk arts, 248
Latino girls, 279
legistlative theater, 232
lesbian, 135
Lewis and Clark, 327
liberation arts projects
  qualities of, 21
liberation arts, 233–234, 237–238, 241,
    243, 262–264
  dance, 243–247
  happenings, 258–262
  music, 243–247
  performances, 258–262
  qualities of, 262–264
  radio, 247–248
  storytelling circles, 250–251
  theater practices, 252–254
  video, 256–258
  visual arts, 254–256
liberation psychologies, 2, 3, 5,
    8–9, 12–13, 19, 22, 25–26,
    27–29, 34, 37, 41–42, 45–51,
    55, 62, 63, 77, 80, 108,
    130, 133, 149, 154, 156,
    162, 164, 207, 208, 233,
    269, 274–275, 302,
    310, 315
  compass points of, 3, 6
  emerging, 4
  geneology of, 22, 27
  imagination and, 29
  prophetic vision of, 131
liberation, 10, 30–31, 36–38, 40, 46, 48,
    113, 155
  and dialogue, 178, 205
  as jailbreak, 47–48
  Buddhist goals of, 37
  Buddhist thought and, 40
  contested history, 46–47
  defined, 46
  ethics of, 300
  interdependence and, 36
  new commons and, 48

liberation theology, 34–38
  Black, 34
  preferential option for the poor, 63
liberatory work
  dynamics of, 19–20
Liberia, 78, 295
Liberian Truth and Reconciliation
      Commission, 78, 294
liminal spaces, 5, 132, 135–137, 147,
      150, 155–156, 160
  cultivation of, 155–157
  loss of, 137–138
  reconstruction of, 156
liminal states
  betwixt and between, 4
liminality, 7–10, 26, 34
      See also liminal space
limit situation, 207
listening environments, 106
Listening Guide, 289
Listening Partners Program, 144, 218
listening
  resistant, 43
  to oneself, 185
literacy education, 193, 227
local regeneration, 41
London, 120, 226
loneliness, 68
Los Angeles, 30, 221, 232, 240, 249,
      328, 336
love, 8, 49, 162
loving kindness, 335
loving speech, 335
loving third, 216–218
lynchings, 84

Madagascar, 96
Madam Please, 246
Madres de Los Desaparecidos, 120
manic defense, 29, 125, 129, 138,
      237
Maori, 250–251, 276, 322
maquiladores, 72, 267
Marcos, Subcomandante, 79, 223
marginality
  and resistance, 272
marginalization, 273, 289
marginalized dependency, 26
matoput rituals, 82
Mayans, 16, 225

meaning making, 234
  capacities for, 234
Medellín Conference, 23, 34
Meetings for Reconciliation, 322
melancholia
  psychoanalytic theory of, 124
memorials, 233, 248–250
  metonymic, 120
memory, 33–34, 115, 119
  and mourning, 119
  belated, 115–116
  environments of, 242
  exemplary, 241
  fragmented, 236
  iconic, 127–128, 156
  labor of, 94
  living, 242–243
  narrative, 127
  places of, 242
  recovered, 128
  synaesthetic, 124
  wars of, 235
  work of, 128
mental health, 62
Mesa de Dialogo, 320
messianic narrative, 145–146
mestiza consciousness, 23, 136,
      171
mestiza, 24, 28, 136, 171, 174, 207
metaethical self, 151
metonymy, 127
Mexican-American history, 249
Mexican government, 170
Mexico, 22, 59, 79, 99, 106, 170, 235,
      266, 348
  Chilpancingo, 267
  government, 22, 223–225
  indigenous in, 225
Mexico/U.S. border, 266–267
microcredit, 329
Middle East, 2, 96
middle-class bias, 280
migration, 242
migratory identities, 171
military dictatorships, 106
military service
  refusing, 103
Minnesota, 261
"missionary" work, 46
Mississippi, 82, 244

model villages program, 319
modernity
    other side of, 148
monotheism, 10, 163
Monticello Association, 77
monuments, heroic, 238
moral
    courage, 65
    reasoning, 273
moral reorientation, 28
Mothers Centers, 215
mourning, 26–27, 36, 43, 105, 207
    belated, 124
    non-redemptive, 122–123, 124–126, 129
    resolution of, 124
    without understanding, 123–124
Mozambique, 248
multiculturalism, 334
multiculturalist inclusive identity, 23, 171
multipartiality, 204
Murga, 259–260
museums, 238
music
    Civil Rights songs, 244
    singing newspapers, 244
mysticism
    Arabic, 334
    Jewish Hasidic, 334

naming of a tradition, 3
narcissism, 68
    social, 139
narrative frameworks, 141–142, 155
narrative therapy, 202–204
narratives
    of dissociation, 142–144
    of fatalism, 144–145
    of messianic transformations,
        145–147
    of participation, 147–149
national identities, 170
Native American, 18–19, 128, 168–169
    genocide, 98
Nazis
    children and grandchildren of, 87
    doctors, 84–86
    ideology, 86
Nazism, 74
negative possession states, 72
Negritude Movement, 74

neocolonialism, 1, 4, 28, 158
nepantla, 135–136
New Jerusalem, 36
New Orleans, 125
Nicaragua, 59, 99
nightflying, 6–7, 161
Nobel Prize, 18
nomad, 14, 26, 148, 166, 173
nomadic consciousness, 1, 4–5, 13–14,
        16, 26, 159, 161, 165–166, 169,
        173, 207
nomadic identity, 20, 132, 169
nomadic self, 28, 174
nonsubject, 1, 3, 6, 27, 158, 160–161,
        174–175
nonsubjecthood, 7, 28, 162, 174
nuclear weapons, 78

object relations, 54, 59
Office of the Good Government, 225
Ojai Foundation, 191
Old Testament, 34
operative thinking, 110
oppositional consciousness, 29
oppression
    dynamics of, 297
    internalization of, 195
organic farming, 45
ostracism, 65
other, the, 178
outsiders, 303–304
Ozomatli, 336

pair therapy, 178, 181
Palestine, 334
Palestinian, 14, 96–98, 166
Pali, 39
Pan Valley Institute, 228–229
Papua New Guinea, 253
paradigms
    shifting, 133
Paragons Theater, 252
Parchman Prison, 244
participation mystique, 33
participatory action research, 208–269,
        271, 282
    principles of, 266
participatory
    arts, 208
    communication, 40–43, 263, 326

participatory (*Contd.*)
  definition of, 269
  hermeneutic research, 292
  knowing, 279
  practices, 27, 207
  research, 18, 192, 292
  spaces, 5
Partido dos Trabalhadores (Workers
    Party), 232
passive forgetting, 238
patriarchy, 280
peace circles, 322
peace psychology, 34
peacemaking, 8, 162
pedagogy
  participatory, 227
peña movement, 216
People's Health Assembly, 329
performance arts, 258
performances
  iconic, 120
periphery, 16, 167
permaculture, 45
perpetrators, 29, 51, 81–83, 86, 89, 91,
    95–96, 130, 231, 316, 331
  community reintegration of, 90
  construction of meaning, 98
  doubling, 84
  effects of violence on, 90
  families of, 83, 86, 95
  intrapsychic dynamics of, 81
  maimed subjectivity of, 96
  opting out of perpetration, 103
persona
  retrogressive restoration of, 138
perspectives
  coordination of, 178–184
  differentiation of, 178–184
Peru, 118, 254, 317
pesticides, 44
phenomenology, 283
Philadelphia, 221
Philippines, 99, 248, 275
phobia
  social context, 60
photovoice, 254–256, 293
pilgrimage, 5, 26, 36, 133–134, 147,
    160, 173
pilgrims, 23, 171
pilot conversations, 308
Pinochet, 116, 119–120, 324

place
  relation to, 77
Plato, 334
play, 138, 180–181, 188, 283, 286
  metaphors and, 22
playing possum, 110, 145
polarizations, 29, 118
polarized thinking, 83
political neutrality, 59
pollution, 43, 221
polyvocality, 287–293
postconventional identity, 23,
    171
postdevelopment, 11, 16, 40–43
post-empirical, 271, 281
postmemory, 124–126, 128
post-traumatic stress, 14, 91, 110
pragmatism, 27
precocious compliance, 66
pre-Columbian arts, 249
presymbolic, 33
prison
  creative writing program, 77
privilege
  masking, 65
  psychic costs of, 64–65
procedural knowing, 190
progress, 40
promotoras, 266–267
protean self, 23, 171
proximal zone of development, 179
proximity, 155
psuedo-objectivity, 306
psychic amputations, 49
psychic freezing, 109
psychic numbing, 73, 85
psychic splitting, 86–88
psychoanalysis, 49, 55–59, 62
  and economic privilege, 57
  cultural school in, 58
  disease models in, 57
  effects of poverty on children, 56
  ego psychology in, 57
  free clinics, 56
  Jewish émigré analysts to America,
    56
  kindergarten movement in, 56
  Lacanian, 12–13
  lay analysis, 57
  "night vision" in, 56–59
  Red Vienna, 56

settlement house psychology classes, 56
social context of early, 55
suppression of social theorists in, 58
whitening of, 56–59
psychoanalytic theory, 135
psychological research, 27, 305
 and social responsibility, 311–312
 as degradation ceremony, 307
 as identity-stripping process, 307
 communication of findings, 310
 competence to pursue, 303
 conflicts of interest, 311
 critical, 272
 data analysis, 308–310
 ethical considerations, 299–300, 302,
  309
 exclusion of African-Americans, 272
 exclusion of women, 272
 implementation of findings, 310–311
 informed consent, 305
 interpretation, 399
 issues of power, 300
 mainstream status quo values and, 272
 positivisitic approaches to, 271
 positivistic methodologies, 300
 psychological sequelae of, 90
 social location and, 305
psychological spaces, 138
 rebuilding, 2, 4, 8, 5
psychodynamic clinical theories, 5
psychological suffering
 historical and social contexts of, 49
psychological theories, 9, 24
 ahistoricity of, 24
 blind spots, 9
 reorientation of values, 10
 telos of, 10
 universalism in, 24
 values of, 9
psychological
 development, 20
 space, 19
psychologies of liberation, *See* liberation
  psychologies and depth psychology
psychology, 23–24
 academic, 4
 clinical programs, 2, 4
 Euro-American, 22
 goals and practices, 1
 hedonism and, 24
 indigenous, 15, 22

individual, 14
mainstream, 31
new epistemology, 26–27
new goals, 26
new praxis, 27
of regeneration, 2, 7
positivist orientation in, 4
reorientation of, 13
universalizing approach, 5
psychoneuroimmunology, 143
psychopathology, 26, 61, 63
 and individualism, 110
 cultural, 62
 epidemiology of, 63
psychopolitical literacy, 296
psychotheology, 128
psychotherapy, 14, 214, 274
 individual, 27
Public Conversations Project, 104, 202
public homeplaces, 190, 196, 207–209,
  215–220, 222, 226, 229–231, 243,
  268
 and appreciative inquiry, 200
 rebuilding of, 213–216
public memory, 238
pueblo, el, 29, 175
Puerto Rico, 99
Puntos de Encuentro, 256

Quaker process, 229
Quakers, 6, 72, 322
qualitative research, 302
quantitative studies, 271
questions, 203–204, 277
 art of crafting, 204

racism, 7
radio, 247–248
 Radio Animus, 248
 Radio Dijla, 330
 Radio Enriquillo, 248
 Radio Free Grenada, 248
 Radio La Voz de la Montana, 248
 Radio Qawinakel, 248
 Radio Sagarmatha, 248
 Radio Tubajon, 248
 Radio Wayna Tambo, 247
 Radio Xai-Xai, 248
radioactive fossils, 127
rapture, the, 145
received knowing, 189

Recife, 192
recollection, 238
Reconciliation Australia, 326
reconciliation propaganda, 319
reconciliation, 81, 208, 313–319,
    324–325, 331, 333
  and un-doing, 314
  defined, 314
  dialogue, 230
  postconflict society and, 316
  prerequisites for, 315
  supportive sites of, 209
Recovery of the Historical Memory
    Project, 324
reframings, 203
Refuseniks, 102
regenerative capacities, 48
reggae, 248
regression, 135
relatedness, 152–154
relationships
  authentic, 185, 290
  web of, 323
religious fanaticism, 115
REMHI, 324
remorse, 320, 331, 333
renormalization, 138–140, 141
repressive practices, 28
research
  and advocacy, 290
  and creative expression, 293
  colonizing, 275–278
  indigenous, 270, 275–278
  natural science tradition of, 291
  post-empirical, 280
research conversation, 285
  self-disclosure and, 307
research questions
  evolved through dialogue, 302
researcher
  as accompanier, 277
resignifying, 234, 247
resilience, 107, 185–186, 276, 286
resistance, 209, 217, 289
resistant interpretations, 233
restoration, 81, 109, 313–314, 317, 323,
    326–328, 330
  defined, 314
restorative approaches
  indigenous, 322

restorative justice, 82, 208, 320–323,
    331
  multiple roots of, 322
resymbolization, 132, 220, 234
retraumatization, 109, 263
retributive justice, 321–323
reversal, 85
revolt
  analytic, 218
  artistic, 218
  psychic, 218
revolution
  of the mind, 13
  ongoing, 25
rhetorics of normativity, 11, 164
Rio de Janeiro, 232
Roadside Theater, 252
Rockefeller Foundation, 42, 262
rupture, 128, 132 , 134–135,
    139–141, 145, 147, 151,
    194–195
  collective, 138
  endogenous, 134
  framing of, 147
  narrative approaches to, 131
Rwanda, 93, 229, 235, 317, 319,
    328

Sabbath, 219
sadism, 193
Safed, 334
salt march to Dandi, 20
Salvadoreans, 200
San Andreas Accords, 224
San Diego, 249
Sandinistas, 256
Santa Barbara, 21
Santiago, 121
Sardal Sarovar Dam, 262
Sarvodaya Movement, 37, 209, 229
scapegoating, 317
Scent of Green Papaya, 124
schizophrenia, 63
scientific methods, 271
secession, 149
secrecy clause, 311
seed saving movement, 221, 330
self
  acquisitive, 14
  bounded, 70

colonial, 69
competitive, 10, 163
empty, 70–71
individualistic, 9, 68, 163
mutilations of, 64, 68
severed, 66–68
self-liberation, 71
self-reliance, 40
self-sufficiency, 39
Selma, 235
Senzeni, 246
September Eleventh Families for
    Peaceful Tomorrows, 332
sexism, 7
Sexto Sentido, 258–259
shame, 125
Shiite, 330
Shoah, 50, 123
silence, 25, 106, 118, 234, 236–238
    cultures of, 192
silenced knowers, 187, 283
silencing, 234
sites of memory, 324
slave trade, 237
slavery, 14, 34, 36, 57, 67–68, 72,
    100, 128, 209, 242, 279,
    316
small-scale cultures, 137
snail shell, 207
SNCC, 244–245
social
    action projects, 22
    amnesia, 54–55, 57, 79
    catastrophe, 93–94
    divides, 2
    exclusion, 333
    glue, 137
    inequalities, 55
    justice, 55–56, 59
    location, 278–281
    networks, 314, 323
    reification, 55
    space
        creation of, 330
    ties, 314
sociogeny, 113
solidarity, 8, 163
    intercultural, 41
Solomon Islands, 253
Sorrow Songs, 313

South Africa, 82, 84, 89, 117–118, 235,
    246, 280, 317, 332
    death squads, 309
    townships, 301
South African Truth and Reconciliation
    Commission, 318, 321
South Carolina, 227
Southeast Asia, 145
spaces of recollection, 126–130
Spanish Harlem, 5
spectactors, 240
spectatorship, 137
Spice Island Radio, 248
spiritual
    conversion, 36
    crisis, 134
    practice, 322
Sri Lanka, 37, 209, 229
STASI, 101
state terror, 59, 242
stereotypes, 13, 165
    ethnic, 21
    gender, 21
    reversed, 21
sterilization, 86
Stoic philosophy, 334
Stolen Generations, The, 325, 326
studying up, 276
subjectification, 10
subjective knowing, 190
subjectivity, 6, 19, 25, 29, 52, 162, 168,
    171, 175, 233, 238, 239, 284
    diminished, 94–96
    ethics of, 1, 7, 158–162
    nomadic, 16, 167
    reworking of, 207
    reimagining, 6, 161
subjugated knowledges, 239
sub-Saharan cultures, 136
success
    compulsive drive for, 68
    personalistic understanding of, 67
Sudan, 4, 82, 328
Sufism, 334
suicide, 139, 140
Sunni, 330
support, 143
supportive sites of reconciliation, 209
sustainability, 39
Sutu, 247

sweat shops, 72
Sweet Honey in the Rock, 244
symbol formation, 73
symbolic
  interruptions, 20–22
  loss, 2
  meaning, 233
  resources, 263
symbolization, 10, 121, 149, 231
symptoms, 52, 54–55, 58, 61, 88–89, 91
  as memorials, 53–55
  cultural context of, 62
  gender and, 62
  ignoring, 59–63
  misattributed, 53
  misreading, 59–63
  neurasthenic, 73
  phobic, 60
  protest through, 61
  refusal to listen to, 59
  somatic, 53
  tracking, 61

Teatro Kerigma, 253
Teatro Tromo, 253
Tel Aviv, 123
telenovela, 257
Tennessee, 228
terror, 106
terrorism, 139, 332
testimonial practices, 293–295
testimonios, 276, 293–294
testimony, 16, 109, 251
Thailand, 37–39
The Great Wall of Los Angeles, 249
The Road of Poems and Borders, 261
The Stolen Generations, 325
*The World Wall: A Vision of a Future
    Without Fear*, 249
Theater of the Oppressed, 216, 232,
    253–254, 312
theory
  driven data, 291
  generating data, 291
  generating listening, 291
therapy, 207, 225
  depth, 54
  individual, 14, 21–22
third-person perspective, 177
Tijuana, 266
tikkun nefesh, 335

tikkun olam, 335
time maps, 105
torture, 90, 118
  Iraq, 331
torture victims, 119
torturers, 91–92, 259
  psychological distress in, 91
toxic waste, 220–221
toyi-toyi, 246–247
Toynbee Hall, 226, 229
transitional governments, 317
transitional justice, 324–325
transitional pathway, 218
transnational corporations, 1
transparency, 305
trauma, 4, 5, 10, 17, 25, 31, 38, 50, 95,
    105–108, 123, 127, 130, 159, 168,
    217, 238
  amputation of seeing, 52
  assault on seeing, 50
  collective, 4, 105, 106–108, 109, 124,
    128, 130
  defined, 108
  enclaves, 122
  environmental, 107
  individual, 105
  markers of, 108
  memory of, 111
  positionality in relation to, 51
  psychic crypts, 121–122, 124–125,
    128–129
  research, 107
  sequelae of, 326
  victim, 122, 125
trauma theory, 29, 236
traumatic events, 124
  defined, 108
traumatic past, 123
Truth and Reconciliation Commission of
    South Africa, 89, 118, 121, 153,
    208
truth commissions, 314, 317–318
Tunisia, 114
Tutsis, 328
Twas, 328

U.S./Mexico border, 80
ubuntu, 154–155, 321
Uganda, 82, 248
uncanny, 16, 167
unconscious, 5, 89

unconscious strategies, 53
undeadness, 129
underdevelopment, 33–35
underside of history, 99
unheimlichkeit, 152
unhomely, 16, 167, 230–231
United Auto Workers, 228
United States, 14, 19, 21, 29, 33–34,
    44, 80, 93, 128, 169, 211, 215,
    226–227, 252, 260, 266, 274,
    277, 285
universality
  claims of, 278–281
Universities of Alabama, 100
University of Central America, 23
Uprooted: The Katrina Project, 251
urban
  displacement, 220
  neighborhoods, 222
Uruguay, 118
USAID, 319
utopian dreams, 241
utopias, 36
  abstract, 28
utopic imagining, 36, 196–199, 219

validity, 295–298, 308
  and dialogue, 312
  catalytic, 296
  contextual, 295–296
  epistemic psychopolitical, 296
  interpretive, 296
  transformative psycholitical,
    296–298
Vermont, 218
Vertical Ray of the Sun, 124
Veterans for Peace, 21
victims, 15, 50, 68, 105, 315, 318
victims of injustice, 68
Vienna, 57
Vietnam, 99
Vietnam veterans, 98
Vietnam Veterans Against War, 98
Vietnam Veterans' Memorial, 239
Vietnam War, 316, 333
Vietnamese, 98
Villa Grimaldi, 121, 324
violence workers, 309
violence, 20, 73–74, 83–84, 114, 209,
    236–238, 313, 327, 336
  against women, 6, 161

and feelings of inferiority, 114
and secrecy, 84
awakening from, 96–99
normalization of, 93–94
perpetrators of, 81, 84
refusal of, 35
scapegoating and, 142
school, 140
Virgin of Guadalupe, 249
Virginia Tech, 323
Virginia, 101
voice work, 186
voice
  and class, 274
  and privilege, 186
  and race, 274
  development of voice in girls, 273
  outsider, 275
  polyphony of, 288
  sustaining one's, 184–187
voice-centered methods, 288–289
vulnerability, 28, 138, 174, 177,
    285–286
vulnerable coparticipant, 284–287
vulnerable transparency, 333

Wall of Names, 324
Washington, D.C, 221
Watch Out, Verwoerd!, 246
we-in-solidarity, 222
West, 275
Western assumptions, 4, 158
Westernization, 29
  resistance to, 114–115
White Americans, 20, 169, 295
White Citizens Councils, 146
Whiteness, 19, 20, 113, 169–170,
    173
Whites, 19, 20, 169, 170, 186, 228
  development of girls, 272
  in America, 67
  women, 279
witch burnings, 147
witness, 2, 105, 108, 116–119, 128, 207,
    240, 316
  active, 76
  bodily, 124
  creating spaces for, 20
  desire to, 78
  engaged, 64
Woman for Woman, 328–329

women's suffrage, 316
women's ways of knowing, 272
World Bank, 329
World Food Summit, 41
World Trade Center, 139
wounded cosmopolitanism, 15, 28,
    166, 174
Wounded Knee Massacre, 82

Xhosa, 247

Yale University, 251
Yesh Gevul, 103
Yohimbe, 336
Yoruba myth, 334

Zapatista communities, 224–225,
    229, 294
Zapatistas, 79, 207, 209, 213, 223, 228
Zimbabwe, 240, 246
Zulu, 247

Printed in the United States
134744LV00003BA/3/P

9 780230 537682